ROLE OF TUMOR MICROENVIRONMENT IN BREAST CANCER AND TARGETED THERAPIES

ROLE OF TUMOR MICROENVIRONMENT IN BREAST CANCER AND TARGETED THERAPIES

MANZOOR AHMAD MIR

Department of Bioresources, School of Biological Sciences, University of Kashmir, Srinagar, Jammu and Kashmir, India

ACADEMIC PRESS

An imprint of Elsevier

ELSEVIER

Academic Press is an imprint of Elsevier
125 London Wall, London EC2Y 5AS, United Kingdom
525 B Street, Suite 1650, San Diego, CA 92101, United States
50 Hampshire Street, 5th Floor, Cambridge, MA 02139, United States
The Boulevard, Langford Lane, Kidlington, Oxford OX5 1GB, United Kingdom

Notices
Knowledge and best practice in this field are constantly changing. As new research and experience broaden our understanding, changes in research methods, professional practices, or medical treatment may become necessary.

Practitioners and researchers must always rely on their own experience and knowledge in evaluating and using any information, methods, compounds, or experiments described herein. In using such information or methods they should be mindful of their own safety and the safety of others, including parties for whom they have a professional responsibility.

To the fullest extent of the law, neither the Publisher nor the authors, contributors, or editors, assume any liability for any injury and/or damage to persons or property as a matter of products liability, negligence or otherwise, or from any use or operation of any methods, products, instructions, or ideas contained in the material herein.

ISBN 978-0-443-18696-7

For information on all Academic Press publications
visit our website at https://www.elsevier.com/books-and-journals

Publisher: Stacy Masucci
Acquisitions Editor: Rafael E. Teixeira
Editorial Project Manager: Pat Gonzalez
Production Project Manager: Omer Mukthar
Cover Designer: Matthew Limbert

Typeset by STRAIVE, India

Working together
to grow libraries in
developing countries

www.elsevier.com • www.bookaid.org

Contents

Contributors

Shariqa Aisha
Department of Bioresources, School of Biological Sciences, University of Kashmir, Srinagar, Jammu and Kashmir, India

Mudasir A. Dar
Department of Plant Pathology, Sher-e-Kashmir University of Agricultural Sciences and Technology of Kashmir, Srinagar, India

Aabida Gul
Department of Bioresources, School of Biological Sciences, University of Kashmir, Srinagar, Jammu and Kashmir, India

Burhan ul Haq
Department of Biotechnology, Central University of Kashmir, Ganderbal, India

Ulfat Jan
Department of Bioresources, School of Biological Sciences, University of Kashmir, Srinagar, Jammu and Kashmir, India

Abrar Yousuf Mir
Department of Bioresources, School of Biological Sciences, University of Kashmir, Srinagar, Jammu and Kashmir, India

Manzoor Ahmad Mir
Department of Bioresources, School of Biological Sciences, University of Kashmir, Srinagar, Jammu and Kashmir, India

Tabasum Mushtaq
Department of Bioresources, School of Biological Sciences, University of Kashmir, Srinagar, Jammu and Kashmir, India

Ab Qayoom Naik
Laboratory of Endocrinology, Department of Biosciences, Barkatullah University, Bhopal, MP, India

Shreen Rasheid
Department of Bioresources, School of Biological Sciences, University of Kashmir, Srinagar, Jammu and Kashmir, India

Mohd Zahoor ul Haq Shah
Laboratory of Endocrinology, Department of Bioscience Barkatullah University, Bhopal, Madhya Pradesh, India

Shazia Sofi
Department of Bioresources, School of Biological Sciences, University of Kashmir, Srinagar, Jammu and Kashmir, India

Preface

Cancer is presently one of the main causes of death worldwide. Different stages of cancer have been identified, demonstrating that multiple gene alterations are implicated in cancer pathogenesis. The aberrant cell growth is caused by these gene alterations. The rise of cell proliferation is aided by genetic diseases induced by inheritance or hereditary factors. Lung, prostate, colon/rectal, and urinary tract cancers account for the greatest proportion of cancer deaths in men. Colon/rectal cancer, breast cancer, uterus cancer, lung cancer, and thyroid cancer are the most common cancers in women. Cigarette smoking; heavy alcohol intake; consumption of red meat, especially fried red meat, sugary beverages and snack foods, starchy meals, and processed carbohydrates such as sugars and refined grains; absence of physical exercise; and exposure to environmental pollutants are all risk factors associated with cancer. Breast cancer development is a complicated phenomenon governed by epigenetic and genetic mechanisms that regulate the interaction between cancer cells and tumor microenvironment (TME) factors. Immune cells, in particular, perform a dual function in cancer genesis and development because they can both defend against tumor development by eliminating immunogenic neoplasm cells; they also shape tumor immunogenicity, leading to tumor escape. Immunotherapy and several other anticancer treatments are influenced by the complicated interaction between cancer and immunological TME.

The TME has been identified as a target-rich setting for the production of new antitumor drugs throughout the past decade. Cancer-associated fibroblasts (CAFs), possessing a spindle shape that contributes to and alters the extracellular matrix (ECM) structure, is a prominent constituent of the TME. CAFs possess functional and phenotypic diversity and are significant constituents of the TME. Besides altering the ECM, the activation of CAFs plays a significant part in tumor growth, migration, and metastasis via various mechanisms. Various studies have already demonstrated the importance of tumor cell and CAF interaction during tumor growth and development. However, the combined interaction of CAFs and the tumor immune microenvironment (TIME) has recently been greatly identified as another critical element in tumor growth. The TIME is primarily composed of various immune cell types residing in the tumor and is strongly connected with the TME's antitumor immunological state. There occurs the interaction between various immune components and the CAFs through the secretion of various substances that lead to immune surveillance evasion. In-depth investigations of CAFs and their interactions with the TIME may yield innovative techniques for later targeted immunotherapies. In this book, we discuss recent developments in understanding the direct and indirect interplay between CAFs and TIME and highlight the probable immunosuppressive pathways caused by CAFs in the TME. In addition, we discuss existing CAF-targeting immunotherapies and shed light on possible future directions for CAF research at the conclusion.

Cross-talk between mesenchymal stem cells and tumor cells drastically alters the overall features of the TME. During tumor progression, changes within the microenvironment are seen, and mesenchymal stem cells play a crucial role in generating phenotypic plasticity along with tumors. The intracellular environment is critical for mesenchymal stem cell growth and diversity. The abundance of soluble substances generated from tumor cells, including the inflammatory environment and the ischemic situation inside the TME, are thought to play a role in the recruitment of MSCs to tumors as tumorigenesis progresses. Nonetheless, MSCs have been linked to the ability to modify the tumor microenvironment in favor of cancer cell suppression, with promising outcomes reported from both preclinical and clinical trials. The release of mediators (such as exosomes) and their innate migrative potential to tumor locations are two of MSCs' beneficial characteristics, enabling efficient medication administration and, as a result, efficient targeting of migrating tumor cells.

Regulatory T cells have achieved a key attribute in the immune system that itself immune regulation or prevention from auto reactions under normal conditions, therefore, is the main factor that participates in balancing the defense system of a body, but their disastrous and adverse effects on antitumor mechanism also exist. Regulatory T cells "CD4+, CD25+," and transcription factor FOXp3^{+} exert an antagonistic impact on the antitumor strategy developed by the body's immune system during malignancies. Different mechanisms have revealed that these cells act like well-trained enemies in hijacking a plethora of molecules that normally increase immune functioning efficiency; thus, modulation of T regulatory cells is considered a promising strategy in the management of different types of tumors. Although a few questions related to the role of regulated T cells in malignancy are under investigation, some of their aspects have been explained by different biomodels.

Out of all the TME cells, neutrophils are the key cells that possess dual roles: antitumor and protumor. We have to focus on this immune cell to improve the survival rates of cancer patients as well as other immune cells so that this dreadful disease can be controlled very soon. Neutrophils are the primary effective immune cells during inflammation as well as resistant against various infectious agents. Neutrophils interact with various cellular subtypes of the immune system and produce various types of effector molecules as well as cytokines. Therefore, neutrophils can be targeted in the case of various inflammatory diseases and numerous cancers/tumors including breast cancer because they have the regulating ability of both the inborn and specific immune system.

The ECM is an aggregation of an intricate collection of molecules that work together to give cells a structural and functional grasp. Collagenous and elastic fibers, proteoglycans, and proteins, such as fibronectin and laminin, all have a function in these qualities.

The composition of the ECM varies by tissue and matricellular proteins, whose primary function is to control cell-matrix interactions. In breast cancer, the ECM is becoming better identified as a key regulator. When collated to the mammary gland in homeostasis, the ECM in breast cancer advancement shows diverse alterations in constitution and organization, and some proteins of cell-matrix, such as collagen, certain laminin, fibronectin, and proteoglycans, show elevated levels in the breast cancer. Many of these increased ECM proteins appear to perform an important function in breast cancer growth and metastasis, according to mounting data. Induced ECM proteins have also been found to be the principal metastatic compounds boosting stem/progenitor signaling pathways and metastatic development. The amount of ECM remodeling enzymes is also significantly enhanced, resulting in significant alterations in biomechanical properties and the matrix structure. It provides structural support to cells and promotes cell growth and differentiation. Breast tumor growth and metastasis are greatly determined by changes in ECM architecture.

Breast cancer is said to have metastasized when it has spread to other regions of the body, and breast cancer stem cells (BCSCs) are critical in the spread of BC from its primary site to distant organs. BCSCs play a significant role in the breast tumor origin, development, metastasis, treatment resistance, and relapse, according to mounting data. BCSCs exhibit heterogeneity due to the expression of varied molecular markers and signaling mechanisms that regulate them. Besides, frequency and subtypes of breast tumor stem cells show variation between the BC subtypes. The aggressive behavior of BCSCs is attributed to their capacity for differentiation and self-renewal. Following the discovery of stem cells in both normal and cancerous breast tissue, BCS-like cells are thought to generate breast cancers and thereby influence the response of the tumor to therapy. The self-renewal potential of both normal and CSCs is the same; however, an imbalance between signaling pathways leads to tumorigenesis.

It has drawn a lot of attention for treating breast cancer. To address the low penetration and less accessibility which is witnessed in the case of chemotherapy, the property of the tumor microenvironment to show better penetration and accessibility for small-molecule inhibitors in comparison to the tumor cells is exploited, and special drug delivery systems have been introduced that release the cytotoxic drugs in the tumor microenvironment, specifically targeting its components. There has been tremendous improvement in the antitumor therapies, but the effective management of breast cancer faces significant hurdles because of drug resistance. Nanochemotherapeutics takes precedence over traditional cancer therapies due to the low drug toxicity with higher efficiency, meticulousness for the site of the tumor, upgraded stability and solubility of drugs, imaging methods, and higher half-life of drugs in circulation as well as a regulated release.

CHAPTER 1

Introduction to various types of cancers

Manzoor Ahmad Mir, Shariqa Aisha, and Shazia Sofi
Department of Bioresources, School of Biological Sciences, University of Kashmir, Srinagar, Jammu and Kashmir, India

1.1 Introduction

In the 21st century, cancer has been identified as a primary cause of death globally. Cancer was the primary or subsequent major reason for mortality below the age of 70 in many nations in 2015, according to the World Health Organization (WHO) (Bray et al., 2018; Mir et al., 2022a, b, c, d, e, f), with novel and more cancer occurrences and carcinoma-associated mortality predicted to exceed 21.4 million and 13.2 million yearly by 2030, respectively (Siegel et al., 2014a, b). On a global scale, cancer death rates are quickly rising. The causes of these rises are numerous, but they mostly reflect aging, population expansion, and alterations in the prime malignancy risk factors, among them few are linked to socioeconomic progress (Gersten and Wilmoth, 2002).

Cancer is characterized by unregulated cell division and multiplication. Through the bloodstream and lymphatic circulation, cancer cells can migrate and infiltrate other regions of the body (Hanahan and Weinberg, 2000). Cancer typically progresses via three phases at the cellular level: initiation, promotion, and then progression. The initial step, initiation, begins when the DNA molecule is damaged by metabolic, genetic, and cancerous factors (Qayoom et al., 2020; Cooper and Hausman, 2000). Both in humans and experimental animal models, cancerous agents such as chemicals, radiations, and viruses have proven to cause cancers (Cooper and Hausman, 2000; Blackadar, 2016). Carcinogens cause cancer by disrupting DNA and causing abnormalities through a process known as carcinogenesis, which entails the stimulation of oncogenes and/or the inactivation of tumor suppressors, resulting in cell-cycle disruption and inhibition of cell death (Sarkar et al., 2013). Promotion is the next step in the development of cancer. This is a lengthy step that begins with the growth of defective cells in the initial phase. The next and ultimate step is progression, described as the spreading of cancer cells that have grown throughout the proliferative stage (Fig. 1.1). Nevertheless, a single genetic alteration is insufficient to cause cancer; thus, the various hypothesis states that cancer is caused by a build-up of genetic abnormalities in a cell's DNA. Nordling was the first to report on this hypothesis, followed by Knudson (Alzahrani et al., 2021).

In various ways, cancerous cells vary from healthy cells. When compared to healthy cells, cancer cells are less tightly regulated (Cooper and Hausman, 2000). Cancerous cells

Role of Tumor Microenvironment in Breast Cancer and Targeted Therapies
https://doi.org/10.1016/B978-0-443-18696-7.00010-5

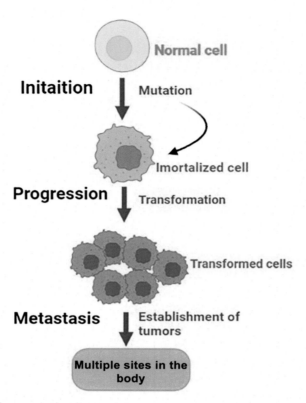

Fig. 1.1 Phases of the cancer development.

proliferate uncontrollably as an outcome of defects in an array of cell regulating processes, which indicate the behavior that differentiates cancerous cells from their healthy counterparts. In addition, cancer is characterized by a number of molecular and genetic changes (Hanahan and Weinberg, 2000; Fimognari et al., 2011). Six characteristics of cancerous cells behavior were identified by Hanahan and Weinberg: Lack of responsiveness to growth-suppressive signals, avoidance of cell death (apoptotic cell death) processes, boundless replicative capacity, prolonged angiogenesis, and tissue infiltration and metastases (Hanahan and Weinberg, 2000). Furthermore, the above-mentioned authors released the next generation of cancer characteristics, to which they included two additional key characteristics, including cellular metabolic reprogramming and immune systems evasion, bringing the total number of cancerous cells characteristics to eight. Genomic instability and inflammation are at the root of these symptoms (Hanahan and Weinberg, 2011). Tumor growth affects multiple signal transduction pathways at the same time, including apoptosis; cell cycle, DNA repair, and redox balance (Chaudhary et al., 2015; Mir et al., 2022a, b, c, d, e, f).

As previously stated, cancer can arise from the uncontrolled multiplication of any of the body's cell types; hence, there are over 100 different forms of cancer, each with its specific behavior and therapeutic responses (Cooper and Hausman, 2000).

The word "tumor" is used to denote aberrant cell proliferation, which can be malignant or benign. The most crucial issue in cancer biology is the differentiation between malignant and benign tumors (Cooper and Hausman, 2000). A quick growth rate, accelerated cell turnover, aggressive expansion, metastases, and lymphatic and/or vascular channel penetration are all markers that distinguish malignant from benign tumors (Van Raamsdonk et al., 2009). Benign tumors are restricted to their primary site, without invading adjacent healthy tissue or unfurl to further parts of the body. Malignant tumors, on the other hand, can simultaneously invade and move (metastasize) to different regions of the body through the lymphatic and circulatory systems (Sarkar et al., 2013). Only malignant tumors are called cancers, and cancer's potential to spread is what renders it deadly. Malignant tumors that metastasize to other parts of the body are typically resistant to treatments. Every year, almost one million new instances of cancers are reported in the United States, with more than half a million Americans succumbing to the disease.

The three forms of cancer that account for the majority of occurrences are sarcomas, carcinomas, and leukemia or lymphomas. Carcinomas are cancerous tumors that develop from epithelium tissues and account for 90% of all malignancies in humans. Sarcomas are infrequent solid tumors that develop from the bone and connective tissues (Hoang et al., 2018). Cancers that arise from bone marrow stem cells and cells of the immune systems, accordingly, are known as leukemia and lymphomas (Davis et al., 2014). Tumors are categorized depending on the kind of cells involved and the tissues from where they originated. Breast, bladder, colon/rectum, lung, liver, and uterine cancers, and also leukemia and lymphomas, account for more than 75% of all the cancers (Fig. 1.2). There are many different forms of cancer, but just a few are common. Breast, colorectal cancer (CRC), prostate, and lung are the four most frequent kinds of cancers, responsible for more than half of all cases of cancer (Cooper and Hausman, 2000) (Table 1.1).

1.2 Tissue homeostasis and the progression of cancer

The body's homeostasis is regulated via controlling cellular longevity. The choice of cells to expand, multiply, repair, or die is governed by interactive mechanisms that regulate the cell cycle, whereas a strong contact between proliferating, resting, and dying cells ensures that net cellular turnover is accurately managed and tissue mass is kept at a near-steady-state. This equilibrium between multiplication and death is disrupted in cancer. As a result, cancer can be defined as unrestrained tissue expansion caused by unregulated cell growth (Hart, 2004). From a medical aspect, this causes the body to lose nutrients and oxygen, culminating in physical exhaustion and death.

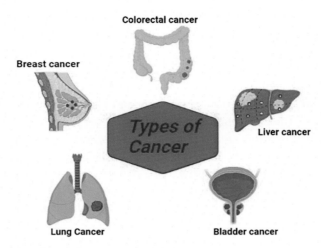

Fig. 1.2 Different types of cancers.

Table 1.1 The table estimates the number of new occurrences and fatalities for each prevalent form of cancer in 2021 (Howlader et al., 2021).

Type of cancer	Estimated new incidences	Estimated fatalities
Colorectal cancer	149,500	52,980
Bladder cancer	83,730	17,200
Lung cancer	235,760	131,880
Liver cancer	42,230	30,230
Prostate cancer	248,530	34,130
Breast cancer (female–male)	281,550–2650	43,600–530

Cells undergo daily genetic damages as a result of environmental exposures, typical "wear, and tear," faults during Novo DNA synthesis, and mitosis, which are regularly recognized and successfully corrected at cell-cycle checkpoints. When these damages are not fixed correctly during sequence patching or nucleotide excision, genetic alterations occur. Nucleotide insertions, deletions, duplications, and rearrangements all fall under the category of point mutations. Amplifications of segments that result in multiple gene copies, as well as chromosomal rearrangements (gene transfer to some other promoter that results in a misregulated expression) that occur during cell division are examples of bigger chromosomal abnormalities (Haber, 2006). The number, location, and severity of mutations influence whether or not a cell has the ability to overcome selection boundaries and, if so, whether or not it is passed on to daughter copies. This causes genomic instability at the nucleotide sequences and/or at the chromosomal level, resulting in the accumulation of numerous abnormalities (mutational set) and, finally, a changed genotype. When these abnormalities confer benefits for cellular development, differentiation, and lifespan,

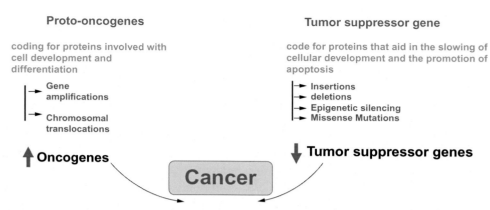

Fig. 1.3 Mechanism of carcinogenesis—alterations in either proto-oncogenes or tumor suppressor genes leads to carcinogenesis.

problems arise (Garay et al., 2007). This is referred to as carcinogenesis, and it is distinguished from other mutations by the two essential classes of impacted regulatory genes (Fig. 1.3).

(i) **Proto-oncogenes**: Growth factors, their receptors, signal transducers, or transcription factors are all expressed in a highly regulated manner to stimulate cell proliferation. Highly activated forms (i.e., oncogenes) cause carcinogenesis by overexpressing crucial regulatory pathways with a constant influx of proliferating signals. Oncogenes are especially prone to changes in expression rates because their allele pairs have genetic dominance, meaning that a mutation in one provides greater expression in the other (Garay et al., 2007).

(ii) **Tumor-suppressor genes (TSGs)**: coding for inhibitory molecules that stop cells from proliferating by halting the cell cycle for DNA repair or causing cell death. These are prevented during carcinogenesis by inherited abnormalities in the parent genes, epigenetic processes of histone modifications and DNA methylations, or protein disruption at the production level. Because the allele pairings are recessive, both genes must be altered before the function is lost (Doucas and Berry, 2006; Garay et al., 2007).

A cellular state changes from mortal to immortal (malignant) phenotype via these genes. This necessitates a massive shift in the systemic character of biological processes, which goes far beyond the circuits directly linked to the altered gene products. Multiple routes are branched and interwoven in such a complex fashion that alterations in one's rate have a varied impact on several others, leading to marginally similar effects. Such phenotypic traits, called "Hallmarks of Cancer," serve as a guide in identifying carcinogenesis (Palmieri et al., 2007; Hanahan and Weinberg, 2011; Ward and Thompson, 2012).

1.3 Major types of cancer

1.3.1 Colorectal cancer

In all areas of medical practices and study, colon carcinoma (CC) and rectal cancers (RC) are regarded as a single tumor form designated as CRC. The term CRC refers to three individual components. The first is that both CC and RC are believed to originate in a similar organ, namely the large intestine. The second feature is the colon and rectal walls' identical anatomical form, which includes the mucosal, muscular layer, and, in part, the serosa, and also their histology. The related actions of the colorectal tract, such as stool concentrations, stool transit, fluid resorption, and excretion, are the subsequent issue to address. Even though the prevalence of CRC commonly presents these figures together, CC accounted for 72%, and RC accounts for 28% of all the CRCs (Centelles, 2012). CRC is described as a transition of the regular colonic and rectal epithelial tissue into a precancerous lesion (adenomatous intermediate) and, ultimately, to invasive cancer (adenocarcinoma), which could also spread to other organs and cause metastatic abnormalities, with the liver being one of the most commonly impacted organs (Li et al., 2017; Recio-Boiles et al., 2018; Recio-Boiles and Cagir, 2021). This mechanism necessitates the buildup of somatic (acquired) and germline (hereditary) genetic alterations over a span of 10–15 years (Recio-Boiles and Cagir, 2021).

CRC is the third most frequent form of cancer (Siegel et al., 2014a, b) worldwide, but it is the second most lethal, posing a significant health and financial impact. The prevalence of CRC is expected to rise to 60% by 2030, despite the fact that it has declined to some degree (Guinney et al., 2015), probably due to greater cancer screenings and better available medicines (Recio-Boiles and Cagir, 2021). In 2018, around 1.8 million fresh CRC instances and 881,000 fatalities were predicted to occur globally for both sexes, accounting for one out of every 10 cancer diagnoses and deaths.

As cancer spreads and expands, it may begin to display signs and symptoms. Individuals with adenocarcinoma have a variety of medical presentations depending on the initial location of the tumor and the degree to which adjacent organs are affected (Mullangi and Lekkala, 2021). According to studies, the majority of CRC individuals who filled out surveys reported a variety of symptoms in varying degrees of frequency. Blood in the feces was the most common sign (32.8%), followed by a change in bowel movements (28.9%), additional symptoms include exhaustion, reduced appetite, nausea, fever (22.0%), and stomach discomfort (16.3%) (Jensen et al., 2015). The presence of blood in the stools was identified as a CRC-specific symptom, while nonspecific symptoms include tiredness, nausea, fever, reduced appetite (Jensen et al., 2015), loss of weight, abdominal discomfort, and bowel obstructions (Mullangi and Lekkala, 2021).

1.3.1.1 Risk factors

The occurrence of CRC, which is regarded as a diverse illness, is linked to a number of risk factors (Haggar and Boushey, 2009). Both hereditary and environmental variables play a significant role in the genesis of CRC and raise the chance of developing it (Kuipers et al., 2015; Mullangi and Lekkala, 2021), whereas additional risk factors are linked to a moderately elevated risk of developing CRC (Recio-Boiles and Cagir, 2021).

1. Risk factors based on genetic inheritance

One of the CRC risk variables that can't be managed is genetic factors. The risk of CRC is increased by a number of genetic CRC disorders (Mullangi and Lekkala, 2021). FAP (Familial Adenomatous Polyposis) and HNPCC (Hereditary Nonpolyposis Colorectal Cancer), often referred to as LS, are the two most frequent such disorders (Haggar and Boushey, 2009). These two hereditary disorders are responsible for about 5% of all CRC occurrences (Recio-Boiles and Cagir, 2021).

2. Family history

The existence of adenomatous polyps and familial or personal history of CRC are linked to a significant risk of synchronized and metachronous main CRC. Furthermore, having a personal background of IBD (Crohn's disease and ulcerative colitis) is linked to a higher risk of CRC (Recio-Boiles and Cagir, 2021).

3. Ethnicity and race

CRC survival varies widely, and it may be influenced by ethnicity and race. In the United States, Native Americans and African Americans, for instance, have a higher chance of getting CRC and have worse survival rates throughout all phases of the infection than Hispanic and white Americans (Zeichner et al., 2012).

4. Risk factors based on sex

When compared to women, men have a significantly increased risk of developing CRC (Mullangi and Lekkala, 2021). Men had a 1.5-fold higher chance of acquiring CRC than women across all ages and in all countries. Moreover, women are more prone to right-sided colorectal cancer, which has a much more severe phenotype than left-sided colorectal cancer, in comparison to males (Kim et al., 2015; Rawla et al., 2019).

5. Age

Another uncontrollable CRC risk factor is age (Kuipers et al., 2015; Mármol et al., 2017). CRC affects people over the age of 50 in approximately 90% of instances. CRC is more than 50 times more common in people aged 60 to 79 than in people under 40 (Ries et al., 2008).

6. Lifestyle and environmental factors

There are considerable links between lifestyle and environmental factors and the development of CRC, according to research (Haggar and Boushey, 2009). CRC risk is increased by inadequate socioeconomic level along with poor medical treatment. Excessive consumption of meat, red or processed consumption of meat (Recio-Boiles and Cagir, 2021), high-fat meals, and diets poor in fruits, vegetables, and fiber are all linked to an increased risk of CRC (Haggar and Boushey, 2009). Inadequate regular exercise, increased body mass, and obesity have all been linked to a higher risk of CRC (Kuipers et al., 2015). Smoking cigarettes and excessive alcohol intake have both been linked to an elevated risk of CRC (Haggar and Boushey, 2009; Recio-Boiles and Cagir, 2021).

1.3.2 Lung cancer

Pulmonary cancer or lung cancer is the chief cause of death in genders, men and women in the United States. It is a highly aggressive, quickly metastasizing, and common malignancy in the United States (Siegel et al., 2014a, b). In the United States, it eliminates more people each year than the next four most common cancers (colorectal, breast, pancreatic, and prostate). Its occurrence and mortality patterns are strongly associated with a smoking habitat of 20 years or more. Lung carcinoma is a greatly varied disease that can develop in a number of locations across the bronchial tree, leading to a wide range of symptoms and indications based on the anatomical site. Seventy percent of lung cancers have advanced-stage disease when they are detected (stage III or IV).

"Small-cell lung carcinoma" (SCLC) and "non–small-cell lung carcinoma" (NSCLC) are the two predominant subtypes of lung carcinoma, responsible for 15% and 85% of all pulmonary cancer cases, correspondingly (Sher et al., 2008). Squamous-cell carcinoma, adenocarcinoma, and large-cell carcinoma are the three dissimilar kinds of NSCLC.

Squamous-cell carcinoma accounts for 25%–30% of pulmonary cancer incidences. It develops from squamous cell precursors in the epithelium of the bronchial tubes in the lungs' core. This kind of NSCLC has a strong link to cigarette smoking (Kenfield et al., 2008).

Adenocarcinoma is the most recurrent type of pulmonary cancer, accounting for roughly 40% of all cases. It comes from type II alveoli cells, which are tiny airways epithelium cells that release mucous and other chemicals. Adenocarcinoma is the most frequent type of lung carcinoma in men and women of all ages, including smokers and nonsmokers (Couraud et al., 2012). It usually occurs in the lungs' periphery, which could be due to the insertion of a filter in cigarettes that prevents big particulates from reaching the lungs. As a consequence of the deeper intake of cigar smoking, peripheral ulcers develop (Stellman et al., 1997). Adenocarcinoma grows more slowly than other kinds of lung cancers and has a better probability of being discovered before it spreads out of the lungs.

Lung tumors that are large cell (undifferentiated) account for 5%–10% of all malignancies. Because there is no indication of squamous or glandular development in this kind of cancer, it is frequently identified by default to rule out alternative possibilities. Large cell carcinoma usually starts in the core of the lungs and spreads to adjacent lymph nodes, the breast wall, and distant tissues (Brambilla et al., 2001). Smoking is highly linked to large cell carcinoma tumors.

1.3.2.1 Risk factors

1. Smoking

Lung cancer is caused primarily by smoking. Lung cancers became increasingly widespread once cigarettes became the most popular tobacco product in the 1900s. The level of risk for lung carcinoma grows as the number of years or packets smoked each day rises. Lung carcinoma is caused by smoking in around 80% of cases. According to a systematic evaluation and thorough review, those who had never smoked yet resided with a smoker have a relative risk of acquiring lung carcinoma of 1.14–5.20 (Whitrow et al., 2003). Being with a smoker can raise a nonsmoker's risk of lung carcinoma by 20%–30%, based on the US Surgeon General.

2. Exposure to radon

Radon, a naturally existing carcinogen, is one of the risk factors for lung carcinoma, with radon exposures being connected to almost 21,000 lung carcinoma fatalities in the United States (the United States Environmental Protection Agency). Although radon was first connected to mine employees, indoor radon exposures from natural uranium reserves, which are abundant in the basement, have been a growing source of worry.

3. Workplace exposures

Lung carcinoma is among the most frequent cancers linked to work-related exposures. Asbestos usage in industries and manufacturing has been related to a rise in mesothelioma and lung carcinoma cases (Hodgson and Darnton, 2000; Berman and Crump, 2008). The size of asbestos fibers has been discovered to be a powerful indicator of lung cancer death (Stayner et al., 2008). As a result, the US government has undertaken measures to limit the use of asbestos in industrial and commercial projects. Other routes of exposure associated with lung cancer involve the utilization of arsenic and arsenic substances (antifungals, outdoor wood preservatives, pesticides and insecticides, etc.), exposure to beryllium and its oxides (X-ray and radiation techniques, etc.), inhaled substances such as cadmium, nickel compounds, silica, vinyl chloride, chromium compounds, mustard gas, coal products, and chloromethyl esters as well (Spyratos et al., 2013).

4. Familial history

A person's personal or familial background of lung carcinoma is a risk factor for developing lung cancer (Sellers and Yang, 2002). Several genes and chromosomes had been associated with a higher likelihood of lung cancer. Smokers with TP53 germline sequence alterations are three times more susceptible than nonsmokers to acquiring lung carcinoma (Hwang et al., 2003). There have also been reports of a chromosome 15 marker linked to lung cancer, which has been investigated in three separate genetic investigations (Amos et al., 2008; Thorgeirsson et al., 2008). Three genes for nicotine acetylcholine receptors subunits are found in the marker. When nicotine binds to this protein on the surface of the cell, it can cause cell transformation. According to the findings of these three independent studies, those with one copy of the markers had a 30% greater risk of lung cancer, whereas those with two copies have a 70%–80% higher risk.

1.3.3 Bladder cancer

Bladder cancer is responsible for approximately 500,000 new instances and 200,000 fatalities globally, with more than 80,000 fresh instances and 17,000 deaths in the United States alone every year (Siegel et al., 2018; Richters et al., 2020). It encompasses a broad series of disorders, from recurring noninvasive tumors that may be handled on a long-term basis to severe or advanced-stage cancer that need comprehensive and intrusive treatment. Understanding the fundamental biology of bladder carcinoma has revolutionized the way the illness is identified and managed dramatically.

Bladder carcinoma is a type of cancer that affects the urothelial (or "umbrella") cells lining the urinary bladder's lumens. Tumors of the bladder, upper urinary system (renal pelvis and ureters), or proximal urethra are all classified as urothelial cancer. Bladder cancer is made up of 75% pure urothelial cancer and 25% "diverse" histology, making treatment more difficult (Lobo et al., 2020). There are various classifications for bladder cancer. Based on standardized histomorphological features as defined by the WHO, it is divided into high-grade and low-grade diseases. The depth of bladder wall penetration is used to give a stage to the tumor (Table 1.2). Tumors confined to the urothelium (stage Ta) and lamina propria (stage T1) are referred to as non–muscle-invasive bladder carcinoma (NMIBC) and are treated differently than tumors that infiltrate the muscle (stage T2) or even beyond (stages T3 and T4), which are referred to as "muscle-invasive bladder carcinoma" (MIBC). Carcinoma in situ (CIS) is a unique phenotype described as a high-grade noninvasive tumor with significant progression and recurrence rates.

Genetic changes in DNA and consequent RNA expression underlie these symptoms, resulting in different molecular subtypes with prognostic, diagnostic, and therapeutic consequences. The discovery of a significant mutational burden in bladder carcinoma, similar to that found in melanoma and lung carcinoma provided a physiologic rationale for its immunotherapy responsiveness (Alexandrov et al., 2013). Numerous groups have independently found mutations that are frequent in low-grade NMIBC (Pik3CA, Fgfr3, Stag2, Rtk/Ras/Raf pathway genes) and high-grade MIBC/advanced

Table 1.2 Pathologic stages of bladder carcinoma.

Stage of tumor	Invasion depth
Ta	Papillary cancer that is not invasive
T1	Infiltrates the propria lamina
T2	Infiltrates the muscularis propria
T3	Infiltrates the perivesical tissues
T4	Extravesical expansion into neighboring organs

cancer (p53, ERbb2, RB1, CDKN2A, MDM2, KDM6A, ARID1A). Tumors are classified into molecular types (e.g., luminal, basal/squamous) that influence clinical outcomes like neoadjuvant chemotherapy efficacy, immunotherapy responsiveness, and recurrence risk (Matulay and Kamat, 2018).

1.3.3.1 Risk factors
1. Smoking
Tobacco usage is among the most well-known factor of threat for bladder cancer around the world, particularly in the United States, and it is also a worry in poorer nations (Letašiová et al., 2012). Pipe smoking and secondhand smoke are two more bladder cancer risk factors. According to the conclusions of a metaanalysis study, smokers have a 3 times greater threat of acquiring bladder cancer than nonsmokers. According to research, the number of cigarettes smoked, the duration of smoking, and the intensity of smoking are all linked to the risk of bladder cancer in both men and women (Freedman et al., 2011). According to a survey by Zeegers et al., cigarette intake is accountable for 23% of bladder cancer occurrences in women and 50% of instances in men (Zeegers et al., 2004). Tobacco flares, which include polycyclic aromatic hydrocarbons, nitrosamine, 2-naphthylamine, and other heterocyclic amines, all have a strong mutagenic role in the development of bladder cancer and the emission of at least 69 carcinogenic compounds (Kiriluk et al., 2012).

2. Workplace factors
Exposure to aromatic amines, such as 2-naphthylamine, benzidine, and 4-aminophenyl, is the major risk factor for getting bladder cancer following smoking. Chemical substances, dyes, polymers, hair color colorants, smoking cigarettes, plastics, automobile smoke, painting chemicals, and fungicides include these chemicals (Letašiová et al., 2012). According to the outcomes of a case study by Samniac et al., the incidence of bladder cancer among men working as a machine operators in the print sector (case group) was substantially greater than in the control cohort (Colt et al., 2009). Furthermore, the findings of cohort analysis of 784 Chinese employees revealed that their risk of bladder cancer raised 35-fold (Gago-Dominguez et al., 2001). Individuals who have been exposed to hair color and cosmetics, particularly barbers, are more likely to develop bladder cancer (Letašiová et al., 2012).

3. Familial history
Individuals with bladder cancer in their families are more likely to develop the disease, as the chance of developing the disease is two times higher in first-degree relations as in other individuals (Burger et al., 2013).

One cause for this link is that family members are subjected to similar risk variables (like those who come into contact with tobacco smoking). Inherited genetic alterations (including variations in glutathione S-transferase mu1 (GSTM1) and N-acetyltransferase

2 (NAT2) genotypes) make it hard to digest specific toxins in the body, resulting in bladder cancer (Kiemeney et al., 2010; Volanis et al., 2010).

4. Risk factors based on nutrition

The incidence of bladder cancer is increased when you don't drink enough fluids, particularly water. Bladder emptiness appears to promote chemical buildup due to a delay in bladder wastes clearance, potentially increasing the risk of bladder cancer. In other words, high fluid consumption (e.g., by diluting urine) and micturition will lower urothelial tissues' exposure to carcinogens (Burger et al., 2013). Vitamin D is one of the supplementary components that may help to lower the risk of cancer. Bladder cancer risk has a substantial connection with vitamin D insufficiency, according to the results of prospective research on male smokers. Numerous case investigations have also shown that the probability of BC was much less in people receiving vitamin D as well as those subjected to ultraviolet B (UVB) compared to the control groups (Brinkman et al., 2010; Chen et al., 2010; Mohr et al., 2010). The type of substances in drinkable water, like arsenic and disinfectants, can also influence bladder cancer risk. Water, cigarettes, air pollutants, glass items, and insecticides are all possible sources of arsenic (Kiriluk et al., 2012). In several regions of the world, arsenic in the water supply is a potential threat to bladder cancer (Naranmandura et al., 2011).

5. Age, gender, race, ethnicity, and socioeconomic level

The risk of bladder cancer rises with age, with 90% of reported cases in adults over the age of 55, with the mean age of diagnosis being 73 (Kiriluk et al., 2012). In terms of gender, men had a higher prevalence of bladder cancer than women; in certain studies, the prevalence in men is four times greater. Women, on the other hand, have a greater mortality incidence than men (Ranasinghe et al., 2012). The reduced frequency of smoking and reduced occupational risk in women appears to be one of the key reasons for the decreased prevalence of bladder cancer in women (Burger et al., 2013). However, the causes of women's greater mortality rates are unknown.

Whites have a two-fold larger threat of bladder cancer as compared to African Americans. In the United States, African Americans have a rate of 13 per 100,000, whereas Whites have a rate of 22 per 100,000 (Yee et al., 2011). Indian Americans, Asian Americans, and Spaniards have lower BC incidences than other races. The reasons for these disparities are not fully understood (Scosyrev et al., 2009).

1.3.4 Liver cancer

Cancer-related to the liver is emerging as the most prevalent malignancy globally (Torre et al., 2016). Every year, hundreds of thousands of individuals are identified with liver carcinoma. Sadly, hepatic cancer is the second-highest cause of cancer-related deaths, responsible for greater than 70% of all deaths. The most common form of hepatic carcinoma is "hepatocellular carcinoma" (HCC) (Mak et al., 2018). About two-thirds of new HCC cases are over 65 years old, and this percentage is predicted to rise as the global population ages. Moreover, the process of aging is heterogeneous, which adds to the difficulty of treatment options (Spolverato et al., 2015; Zhao et al., 2018). HCC develops from healthy hepatocytes. Hepatocytes are the cells that make up the liver's parenchymal tissues and account for most of the organ's mass. Hepatocytes are essential for liver functioning (Rui, 2014). They have a role in a variety of biological activities, such as glucose and lipid metabolism, protein biosynthesis, and, most importantly, body detoxification from toxic compounds. Hepatocytes produce essential proteins including prothrombin, serum albumin, transferrin, complement proteins, and fibrinogen. Hepatocytes synthesize fatty acids from carbohydrates, which leads to triglyceride production, in addition to its major involvement in glycogenesis. Hepatocytes play an important role in cholesterol production and lipid metabolism. Hepatocyte detoxification encompasses drug metabolism as well as the alteration of endogenous chemicals such as ammonia and steroids. Hepatocytes, on the other hand, may be overwhelmed by damaging chemicals and targeted by a variety of hepatic viruses, resulting in liver damage and, eventually, HCC (Wu et al., 2018). Hepatocytes are frequently employed in both academic and pharmaceutical research to examine the mechanisms of cancer, viral infections, and medication metabolisms. Presently, cutting-edge research in epigenetic changes and immunology is being conducted to learn more about liver illnesses and find new treatments for HCC.

1.3.4.1 Main risk factors for liver carcinoma
Hepatic viral infections with HBV and HCV are the most prevalent risk factors for HCC. The other main factor that increases the likelihood of getting HCC is fatty liver disease, which is connected or unconnected to alcohol consumption and often leads to cirrhosis of the liver (Fig. 1.4).

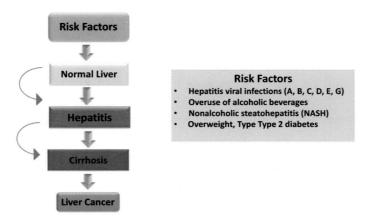

Fig. 1.4 Hepatocytes, the major liver cells, are exposed to unfavorable conditions like hepatitis viral infections, resulting in hepatitis, cirrhosis, and, eventually, HCC.

1. HBV–Hepatitis B virus infection

HBV is among the most prevalent causative factors in HCC around the globe. In individuals with chronic HBV infections, the chance of getting HCC is much more than 15-fold (Singh et al., 2018). In most developed nations, an HBV infection is related to approximately 10% of HCC, which arises either through parental contact with infectious blood or sexual transmissions. In other parts of the globe where HBV is prevalent, like Sub-Saharan Asia and Africa, HBV transmission can occur mostly through perinatal infection (Greten and Sangro, 2018; Yuen et al., 2018).

HBV patients are particularly susceptible to hepatitis D viral infection (HDV). To create its genome, HDV relies on HBV genetic products. HDV disease is more common in Sub-Saharan Africa, the Mediterranean, and South America (Lempp et al., 2016). At least 8 HDV genotypes had been identified, which are geographically spread over the globe. A total of 20 million persons are thought to be infected with one of the HDV genotypes. HDV causes liver failure and HCC when it is combined with HBV infection (Botelho-Souza et al., 2017). The right therapy for HDV infection is the HBV vaccination, which can be used to eradicate the virus. There are now 10 HBV genotypes known. HBV-infected individuals with the C and D genotypes appear to acquire cirrhosis of the liver and HCC more commonly than HBV individuals with other genotype variants. Moreover, conventional therapies relying on interferon's or other antiviral medications are ineffective in these patients (Greten and Sangro, 2018; Yuen et al., 2018).

2. HCV–Hepatitis C virus infection

HCV disease is likewise one of the most common risk factors for HCC over the world. In patients who have been infected with HCV for a long time, the risk of HCC is very significant (Axley et al., 2018). This risk was amplified by coinfection with HIV or HBV. A vast proportion of HIV or HBV coinfected individuals develop chronic hepatitis, which leads to HCC. IFN treatment appears to play a role in decreasing the development of HCC by suppressing the HCV burden (Ishikawa, 2008). Nevertheless, in the clinic, worries about the effect of HCV direct-acting drugs (DAAs) on the prevalence of HCC persist (Butt et al., 2018). HCC risk is higher in HCV individuals receiving DAAs treatment (Lee, 2018).

3. Overuse of alcoholic beverages

Long-term alcohol consumption has been linked to "alcoholic liver disease" (ALD) and a significant threat of acquiring HCC (Ramadori et al., 2017). Although ALD is widely understood, limited progress has been achieved in its management. Alcohol is generally known to be extremely harmful to hepatocytes. It stimulates the constant renewal of hepatocytes and sets the stage for carcinogenesis by generating continual cell death (McKillop and Schrum, 2009). Furthermore, alcohol damages the liver by increasing inflammation, which leads to cirrhosis and HCC (Ramadori et al., 2017). In persons with viral hepatitis, the impact of alcohol on liver illness is amplified (Dolganiuc, 2015).

4. Nonalcoholic steatohepatitis (NASH)

NASH is a type of fatty liver syndrome in which the liver accumulates excessive amounts of fat and is inflamed. Overweight, type 2 diabetes, and associated metabolic dysregulation are risk factors for NASH, while the actual cause is uncertain. Individuals with NASH who do not have cirrhosis had no elevated risk of HCC, showing that cirrhosis initiation is a significant cause of HCC. NASH, on the other hand, has a comparable prognosis to certain other severe hepatitis, like HCV infection (Said and Ghufran, 2017). While NASH individuals have a lower probability of getting HCC than HCV individuals, the degree of HCC and survival of patients are equal in both instances.

5. Cirrhosis of the liver and associated risk variables for HCC

Most of HCCs are caused by cirrhosis of the liver, a disease wherein scar tissue replaces liver tissues (Schuppan and Afdhal, 2008). Scar tissue impairs blood circulation to the liver and prevents it from working properly. Cirrhosis is caused mostly by prolonged hepatitis caused by viral diseases and fatty liver diseases caused by or independent of alcohol consumption. Aside from HCV, HBV, and HDV, 3 hepatitis viruses have been found and shown to cause hepatitis: HAV, HGV, and HEV. HBV and HCV, on the other hand, are the most frequent causes of hepatitis-related viral infections. Individuals who are persistently infected with both hepatitis B and C are more likely to get HCC.

Aflatoxin has been demonstrated to enhance the chance of getting HCC in addition to hepatitis viral disease and hyperlipidemia linked or independent of alcohol usage (Liu and Wu, 2010). An aflatoxin is a group of fungal toxins that can be found in large concentrations in commonly eaten foods including nuts, cereals, and spices that have not been properly picked or preserved. Aflatoxin is prevalent in either animal or human food, and it enters the food sources. Aflatoxin derivatives substances can be passed from animals to milk, eggs, and meat. Additional independent risk factors for HCC include being overweight or obese (Liu et al., 2012).

1.3.5 Prostrate cancer (PCa)

PCa is the second most common cancer in males in the world (Ferlay et al., 2010). Nevertheless, there are significant differences in prevalence rates among geographic regions, with a 25-fold gap among the countries with the greatest and smallest rates (Ferlay et al., 2010). In 2012, PCa claimed the lives of 307,000 men worldwide, making it the sixth highest cause of mortality in men. There is less variety in death rates around the globe (Ferlay et al., 2015). Because of better treatment, death rates have been dropping in many developed nations. PCa is still far less common in Asian countries than in Western nations (Ferlay et al., 2015). Northern America and Australia/New Zealand had the greatest estimated age-specific rates of PCa occurrence (111.6 and 97.2 per 100,000, correspondingly), while Southeast Asia, Eastern Asia, and South Central Asia have estimated rates of 10.5 and 11.2 per 100,000, respectively (Ferlay et al., 2015). Across several Asian countries, meanwhile, the frequency and death of PCa are increasing. Acinar adenocarcinoma is the most frequent kind of PCa, accounting for 90% of all cases.

The prostate is a small walnut-sized gland positioned between the bladder and the penis that gradually gets bigger in aged men to an estimated weight of 40 g. A prostate gland borders the urethras, which drains the bladder, and secretes prostate fluids, which preserve sperm. Several prostate illnesses, such as benign prostatic hyperplasia or hypertrophy, prostatitis, and cancer, might impair certain physiological activities. PCa develops when abnormal semen-secreting prostate glands cells multiply in an uncontrolled manner. PCa can spread to other regions of the body, especially the lymphatic nodes and bones when left untreated. Even though most individuals are asymptomatic in the initial stages, severe PCa can cause a range of urine symptoms such as painful nocturia, hematuria, dysuria, hematospermia, discomfort, and swelling in the legs or pelvic region, lack of urine control, and erection regulation. Hypertrophy or benign prostatic hyperplasia, on the other hand, can cause comparable symptoms but is seldom fatal. The utilization of total plasma prostate-specific antigen (tPSA) levels becomes critical in this circumstance. A tPSA level greater than the cut-off value of 4 ng/mL, as per ASC, may suggest the presence of PCa. Transrectal biopsies assisted by ultrasonography can be utilized to confirm the diagnosis to check out the potential of an increased tPSA level in a subgroup of nonmalignant illnesses (Catalona et al., 1995; Barry, 2009).

PCa can take up to 10 years to develop from precursor prostatic intraepithelial neoplasia (PIN) to invasive cancer because of its slow growth. The PIN can be categorized into higher and lower grades histologically, with each defined by a different molecular or cellular structure. PCa is a diverse disease, with a wide range of symptoms from one person to another, even within the similar tumor. Genomic instability and changes linked with different PCa risk factors may be to blame for the large variance in PCa architecture and occurrence rates.

1.3.5.1 Risk factors for prostate cancer
1. Food-related issues
Dietary variables in PCa may impact circulatory androgens and estrogens or act as a general mitogen-protective factor. A higher risk of PCa has been linked to high consumption of red meat, fats, milk products, and eggs (Kurahashi et al., 2008; Subahir et al., 2009; Munretnam et al., 2014; Bashir et al., 2015; Bashir and Malik, 2015). Saturated fats and cholesterol are abundant in meat, and milk products are similarly high in saturated fats. This would not mean, however, that animal fat is a risk factor for PCa. Other factors must be examined. Consumption of red meat, for example, may be associated with a lesser intake of plant foods. Calcium as well as other elements, like zinc, are found in dairy foods and have been linked to an elevated risk of PCa. Another key issue is how food is

cooked. In recent years, Asia's consumption of meat and dairy items has grown dramatically, but it remains lower than that of Western countries (Kearney, 2010; Leitzmann and Rohrmann, 2012).

2. Age

Prostate cancer risk rises with age, with around 60% of instances detected beyond the age of 65. It is unusual in younger males under the age of 40, and when it does occur, it is frequently linked to a familial background of the disease.

3. Ethnicity

Prostate cancers seem more common in black males than in other races, and they are more prone to get it at an early age. Prostate cancers are much more prone to be severe in Black males; however, the explanation for this is unknown. Prostate cancer is less common among Asian and Hispanic men than that in non-Hispanic white men. Because Asian-American males have a greater prevalence of prostate cancer than Asian men residing in Asia, the prevalence of prostate cancers in Asian men residing in the United States and Europe is now growing.

4. Familial history

Prostate cancer is more likely to occur in men who had a father, brother, or son who has cancer. If a male relative had got prostate cancer at an early age, or if several men in a family have been affected, the risk is higher. Prostate cancer is thought to be "familial" in about 20% of cases, which might be owing to a mix of related genes and lifestyles (American Society of Clinical Oncology).

1.3.6 Breast cancer

Breast malignancy (BC) is one of the most frequently diagnosed cancers in women globally, and it is also the common cause of tumor-related fatality in women (Freitas et al., 2017; Mehraj et al., 2022). Breast carcinoma is metastatic cancer that can metastasize to distant organs like the liver, bone, brain, and lung, making it almost difficult to cure. A good survival proportion and an excellent outcome can be attained if the disease is detected earlier. Women with breast carcinoma in North America have a 5-year comparative rate of survival of more than 80% because of early recognition of the disease (DeSantis et al., 2016; Mir et al., 2022a, b, c, d, e, f). A mammogram is a normally used screening procedure for identifying BC that has been demonstrated to significantly decrease mortality. Alternative screening procedures, including MRI, which is higher sensitive than mammograms, have also been introduced and investigated all over the previous decade (Drukteinis et al., 2013; Mir et al., 2020). Many risk factors, including sex, aging, estrogen, family background, gene abnormalities, and an unhealthy lifestyle, might raise the likelihood of getting breast carcinoma (Majeed et al., 2014). The majority of breast cancer instances occur in women, and the proportion of incidents in women is 100 times greater than in men (Siegel et al.,

2017; Qayoom et al., 2021). Despite the fact that the frequency of breast cancers in the United States rises every year, the mortality rate falls as a result of extensive early detection and better medical treatments. Biological therapies for breast carcinoma have been discovered in recent years and have shown to be effective.

1.3.6.1 Breast cancer pathogenesis

Breast cancer often begins as ductal hyperproliferation and progress to benign cancers or possibly spreading cancers as a result of constant activation of cancerous factors. Breast tumor growth and development are predisposed by cancer microenvironments including effects of stroma and macrophages. When just the stroma, neither the ECM nor the epithelium, of the rats breast glands was subjected to carcinogens, neoplasms could be generated (Maffini et al., 2004; Sonnenschein and Soto, 2016). Macrophages can produce a mutant inflammatory milieu, allowing cancerous cells to evade immunological rejections and increase angiogenesis (Qian and Pollard, 2010; Dumars et al., 2016; Mir and Mehraj, 2019). The regular and tumor-associated microenvironments exhibit distinct DNA methylation patterns, demonstrating that epigenetic changes in the tumor milieu can induce carcinogenesis (Polyak, 2007; Basse and Arock, 2015; Mir et al., 2022a, b, c, d, e, f). "Cancer stem cells" (CSCs), a new group of cancer cells seen in malignancies, have lately been revealed and associated with cancer progression, escape, and relapse. This tiny figure of cells, which can grow up from stem cells or precursor cells in healthy tissues, has the self-renewal ability and is resistant to radiotherapy and chemotherapy (Baumann et al., 2008; Smalley et al., 2013; Zhang et al., 2017). Ai Hajj was the first to discover "breast cancer stem cells" (bCSCs), and he discovered that as low as 100 bCSCs might create new tumors in immunocompromised mice (Al-Hajj et al., 2003; Mehraj et al., 2021). Luminal epithelium progenitors are more likely to give rise to bCSCs than basal stem cells (Molyneux et al., 2010). Notch, Wnt, Hedgehog, PI3K, p53, and HIF signaling cascades are implicated in the self-renewal, increase, and immigration of bCSCs (Kasper et al., 2009; El Helou et al., 2017; Shukla et al., 2017; Valenti et al., 2017; Mir et al., 2020). Nevertheless, more study is needed to better comprehend bCSCs and devise unique ways for eradicating them.

The malignant stem cell theory and also a stochastic theory (Polyak, 2007; Sgroi, 2010) are two possible hypotheses for how breast carcinoma begins and progresses. All tumor subgroups, as per the cancer stem cell theory, are descended from identical stem cells or transit-amplifying cells (progenitor cells). Various tumor morphologies are caused by inherited epigenetic and genetic alterations in stem and precursor cells. Each tumor subgroup begins with a single cell type, according to the stochastic theory (progenitor cell, stem cell, or differentiated cell). Random changes can collect over time in any mammary cell, ultimately transforming it into a tumor cell when enough alterations have accrued (Fig. 1.5). Despite the fact that both theories are supported by evidence, none can properly describe the genesis of human breast cancer.

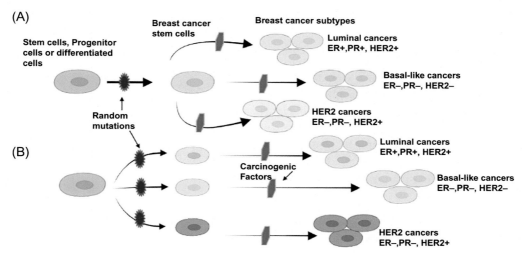

Fig. 1.5 There are two possible theories for the onset and progression of breast carcinoma. (A) All tumor subtypes are descended from the identical stem or progenitor cells. Subtype-specific transformation processes then generate distinct tumor morphologies. (B) Each tumor subtype develops from a unique type of cell (stem cell, progenitor cell, or differentiated cell). Random mutations can collect over time in any mammary cell, eventually transforming it into a tumor cell when enough mutations have accrued.

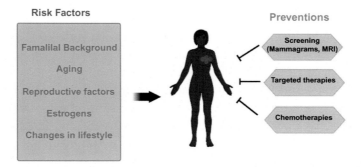

Fig. 1.6 Schematic representation of breast cancer risk factors and preventive strategies.

1.3.6.2 Risk factors for breast cancer
1. Familial background
A familial history of breast carcinoma is linked to almost half of all incidences (Brewer et al., 2017) (Fig. 1.6). BC is more likely in women whose mother or sibling has had the disease. Women who had one first-degree cousin with breast carcinoma had a 1.75-fold increased chance of having the disease compared to women who do not have

any relatives affected, based on a cohort analysis of approximately 113,000 women in the UK. Additionally, women with two or even more first-degree family members with breast malignancy face a 2.5-fold or greater risk. BC predisposition is inherited in part because of abnormalities in BC-associated genes like BRCA1 and BRCA2.

2. Aging

Apart from sex, one of the main significant risk factors for breast carcinoma is aging, since the prevalence of breast carcinoma increases with age. In 2016, women between the ages of 40 and 60 accounted for 99.3% and 71.2% of all breast cancer-related fatalities in the United States, correspondingly (Siegel et al., 2017). As a result, women over the age of 40 should have a mammogram done prior to time.

3. Reproductive factors

Reproductive factors like early menarche, delayed menopause, late ages at initial pregnancy, or poor parity can all raise the risk of BC. Every year that menopause is delayed, the risk of BC increases by 3%. For every 1-year delay in early puberty or successive delivery, the risk of BC is lowered by 5% or 10%, accordingly (Dall and Britt, 2017; Horn and Vatten, 2017). The hazard ratio (HR) between late (>35 years) and earlier (<20 years) ages at first birth are 1.54, according to recent Norwegian cohort research (Horn et al., 2013). Reproductive factors are substantially associated with ER status, with differences in the odds ratios (OR) for parity (0.7 vs. 0.9 for >3 births vs. nulliparae) or age at first delivery (1.6 vs. 1.2 for age >30 vs. <25 years) among ER + and ER − breast cancers (Rosato et al., 2014).

4. Estrogens

Estrogens, including exogenous and endogenous, have been associated with an increased risk of BC. In premenopausal women, the ovary synthesizes endogenous estrogens, and ovariectomy can decrease the BC risk (Hormones and Oncology, 2013). Oral contraceptive pills and hormone replacement therapy are the major sources of exogenous estrogens. Since the 1960s, oral contraceptive pills have been extensively used, with compositions that have been improved to lessen adverse effects. The OR for African American women and Iranian ethnicities, however, is still greater than 1.5 (Bethea et al., 2015; Soroush et al., 2016). Contraceptive pills, on the other hand, do not enhance the risk of BC in women who cease using them for greater than 10 years (Rojas and Stuckey, 2016; Mir et al., 2022a, b, c, d, e, f). For postmenopausal or menopausal women, HRT comprises the consumption of exogenous estrogens or other hormones. HRT use has been linked to an increased risk of BC in several studies. According to the Million Women Study in the United Kingdom, active HRT patients had a relative risk (RR) of 1.66 in comparison to those who have never taken it. While receiving HRT for 4 and 8 years, correspondingly, cohort analysis of 22,929 Asian women showed HRs of 1.48 and 1.95 (Liu et al., 2016). After 2 years of quitting HRT, however, the risk of BC has been observed to reduce considerably (Narod, 2011). Breast carcinoma patients who take HRT have a significant risk of recurrence, with an HR of 3.6 for a new breast tumor (Fahlén et al., 2013; Mir et al., 2022a, b, c, d, e, f).

5. Changes in lifestyle

Heavy alcohol intake and soaring dietary fats ingestion are two modern lifestyle reasons that can elevate the threat of BC. Intake of alcohol can be the reason behind the raise in estrogen-associated hormones in the bloodstream, as well as the inauguration of estrogen receptor mechanisms. As per a metaanalysis built on 53 epidemiologic research, intake of (35–44) grams of alcohol each day raises the threat of BC by 32%, with a 7.1% increase in the RR for every extra 10 g of alcohol consumed (Hamajima et al., 2002; Jung et al., 2016). Increased fat intake, especially saturated fats, is linked with mortality (RR = 1.3) and reduced outcomes in women with breast carcinoma (Makarem et al., 2013). Even though the link between smoking and the risk of breast carcinoma is still controversial, toxicants from cigarette smoking have been found in nonlactating female breast fluids. BC risk is similarly raised in women who drink and smoke (RR = 1.54) (Knight et al., 2017). Till now, increasing data have demonstrated that smoking, particularly when young, raises the breast tumor risk (Catsburg et al., 2015; Gaudet et al., 2017; Kispert and McHowat, 2017).

1.4 Summary

Cancer is a broader term that refers to a broad range of illnesses that can influence any part of the body. Malignant cancers and neoplasms are other words employed. The unique feature of malignant cells is the rapid expansion beyond their inclined boundaries, allowing them to contaminate adjoining parts of the body and wander to other regions; this is known as metastasis. The most common cause of cancer mortality is widespread metastasis. Scientists have reported a significant amount of knowledge about genes and proteins, as well as their functions in the development of cancerous cells, over the last three decades. Among the most crucial findings was the involvement of altered genes in cancerous cells. Environmental variables linked to genetic abnormalities have lately been discovered. We can measure the potency of gene expression and faulty proteins, and also discover novel potential biomarkers, using various molecular approaches. These discoveries could aid in the treatment of cancer and the reduction of cancer-related problems. Moreover, several studies to investigate epigenetic mechanisms and their connection to the incidence and development of numerous diseases, particularly cancer, are ongoing. Despite the fact that various genetic alterations have been linked to cancer, additional research is needed to fully understand the disease's origins. The most promising method for preventing cancer in many populations around the globe is to minimize cancer risk factors. Furthermore, studies focusing on the discovery and implementation of new treatments which are less severe and more successful than current treatments are required in the future to improve the overall longevity and comfort of life of cancer patients.

References

Alexandrov, L.B., Nik-Zainal, S., Wedge, D.C., Aparicio, S.A., Behjati, S., Biankin, A.V., Bignell, G.R., Bolli, N., Borg, A., Børresen-Dale, A.L., Boyault, S., Burkhardt, B., Butler, A.P., Caldas, C., Davies, H.-R., Desmedt, C., Eils, R., Eyfjörd, J.E., Foekens, J.A., Greaves, M., Hosoda, F., Hutter, B., Ilicic, T., Imbeaud, S., Imielinski, M., Jäger, N., Jones, D.T., Jones, D., Knappskog, S., Kool, M., Lakhani, S.R., López-Otín, C., Martin, S., Munshi, N.C., Nakamura, H., Northcott, P.A., Pajic, M., Papaemmanuil, E., Paradiso, A., Pearson, J.V., Puente, X.S., Raine, K., Ramakrishna, M., Richardson, A.L., Richter, J., Rosenstiel, P., Schlesner, M., Schumacher, T.N., Span, P.N., Teague, J.-W., Totoki, Y., Tutt, A.N., Valdés-Mas, R., van Buuren, M.M., Veer, L.v.'t., Vincent-Salomon, A., Waddell, N., Yates, L.R., Zucman-Rossi, J., Futreal, P.A., McDermott, U., Lichter, P., Meyerson, M., Grimmond, S.M., Siebert, R., Campo, E., Shibata, T., Pfister, S.M., Campbell, P.J., Stratton, M.R., 2013. Signatures of mutational processes in human cancer. Nature 500 (7463), 415–421.

Al-Hajj, M., Wicha, M.S., Benito-Hernandez, A., Morrison, S.J., Clarke, M.F., 2003. Prospective identification of tumorigenic breast cancer cells. Proc. Natl. Acad. Sci. U. S. A. 100 (7), 3983–3988.

Alzahrani, S.M., Al Doghaither, H.A., Al-Ghafari, A.B., 2021. General insight into cancer: an overview of colorectal cancer. Mol. Clin. Oncol. 15 (6), 1–8.

Amos, C.I., Wu, X., Broderick, P., Gorlov, I.P., Gu, J., Eisen, T., Dong, Q., Zhang, Q., Gu, X., Vijayakrishnan, J., 2008. Genome-wide association scan of tag SNPs identifies a susceptibility locus for lung cancer at 15q25. 1. Nat. Genet. 40 (5), 616–622.

Axley, P., Ahmed, Z., Ravi, S., Singal, A.K., 2018. Hepatitis C virus and hepatocellular carcinoma: a narrative review. J. Clin. Transl. Hepatol. 6 (1), 79.

Barry, M.J., 2009. Screening for prostate cancer—the controversy that refuses to die. N. Engl. J. Med. 360 (13), 1351.

Bashir, M.N., Malik, M.A., 2015. Case-control study of diet and prostate cancer in a rural population of Faisalabad, Pakistan. Asian Pac. J. Cancer Prev. 16 (6), 2375–2378.

Bashir, M.N., Ahmad, M.R., Malik, A., 2015. Risk factors of prostate cancer: a case-control study in Faisalabad, Pakistan. Asian Pac. J. Cancer Prev. 15 (23), 10237–10240.

Basse, C., Arock, M., 2015. The increasing roles of epigenetics in breast cancer: implications for pathogenicity, biomarkers, prevention and treatment. Int. J. Cancer 137 (12), 2785–2794.

Baumann, M., Krause, M., Hill, R., 2008. Exploring the role of cancer stem cells in radioresistance. Nat. Rev. Cancer 8 (7), 545–554.

Berman, D.W., Crump, K.S., 2008. A meta-analysis of asbestos-related cancer risk that addresses fiber size and mineral type. Crit. Rev. Toxicol. 38 (sup1), 49–73.

Bethea, T.N., Rosenberg, L., Hong, C.-C., Troester, M.A., Lunetta, K.L., Bandera, E.V., Schedin, P., Kolonel, L.N., Olshan, A.F., Ambrosone, C.B., 2015. A case–control analysis of oral contraceptive use and breast cancer subtypes in the African American Breast Cancer Epidemiology and Risk Consortium. Breast Cancer Res. 17 (1), 1–13.

Blackadar, C.B., 2016. Historical review of the causes of cancer. World J. Clin. Oncol. 7 (1), 54.

Botelho-Souza, L.F., Vasconcelos, M.P.A., Santos, A.D.O.D., Salcedo, J.M.V., Vieira, D.S., 2017. Hepatitis delta: virological and clinical aspects. Virol. J. 14 (1), 1–15.

Brambilla, E., Travis, W.D., Colby, T.V., Corrin, B., Shimosato, Y., 2001. The new World Health Organization classification of lung tumours. Eur. Respir. J. 18 (6), 1059–1068.

Bray, F., Ferlay, J., Soerjomataram, I., Siegel, R.L., Torre, L.A., Jemal, A., 2018. Global cancer statistics 2018: GLOBOCAN estimates of incidence and mortality worldwide for 36 cancers in 185 countries. CA Cancer J. Clin. 68 (6), 394–424.

Brewer, H.R., Jones, M.E., Schoemaker, M.J., Ashworth, A., Swerdlow, A.J., 2017. Family history and risk of breast cancer: an analysis accounting for family structure. Breast Cancer Res. Treat. 165 (1), 193–200.

Brinkman, M.T., Karagas, M.R., Zens, M.S., Schned, A., Reulen, R.C., Zeegers, M.P., 2010. Minerals and vitamins and the risk of bladder cancer: results from the New Hampshire Study. Cancer Causes Control 21 (4), 609–619.

Burger, M., Catto, J.W.F., Dalbagni, G., Grossman, H.B., Herr, H., Karakiewicz, P., Kassouf, W., Kiemeney, L.A., La Vecchia, C., Shariat, S., 2013. Epidemiology and risk factors of urothelial bladder cancer. Eur. Urol. 63 (2), 234–241.

Butt, A.S., Sharif, F., Abid, S., 2018. Impact of direct acting antivirals on occurrence and recurrence of hepatocellular carcinoma: biologically plausible or an epiphenomenon? World J. Hepatol. 10 (2), 267.

Catalona, W.J., Richie, J.P., deKernion, J.B., Ahmann, F.R., Ratliff, T.L., Dalkin, B.L., Kavoussi, L.R., MacFarlane, M.T., Southwick, P.C., Hudson, M.A., 1995. In reply: re comparison of prostate specific antigen concentration versus prostate specific antigen density in the early detection of prostate cancer receiver operating characteristic curves; re selection of optimal prostate specific antigen cutoffs for early detection of prostate cancer receiver operating characteristic curves. J. Urol. 154 (3), 1145–1146.

Catsburg, C., Miller, A.B., Rohan, T.E., 2015. Active cigarette smoking and risk of breast cancer. Int. J. Cancer 136 (9), 2204–2209.

Centelles, J.J., 2012. General aspects of colorectal cancer. ISRN Oncol. 2012, 139268.

Chaudhary, S., Devkar, R.A., Bhere, D., Setty, M.M., Pai, K.S.R., 2015. Selective cytotoxicity and pro-apoptotic activity of stem bark of Wrightia tinctoria (Roxb.) R. Br. in cancerous cells. Pharmacogn. Mag. 11 (Suppl 3), S481.

Chen, W., Clements, M., Rahman, B., Zhang, S., Qiao, Y., Armstrong, B.K., 2010. Relationship between cancer mortality/incidence and ambient ultraviolet B irradiance in China. Cancer Causes Control 21 (10), 1701–1709.

Colt, J., Karagas, M., Schwenn, M., Baris, D., Johnson, A., Stewart, P., Verrill, C., Moore, L., Lubin, J., Ward, M., 2009. Occupation and bladder cancer in a population-based case-control study in Northern New England. Epidemiology 20 (6), S128.

Cooper, G.M., Hausman, R., 2000. A molecular approach. In: The Cell, second ed. Sinauer Associates, Sunderland, MA.

Couraud, S., Zalcman, G., Milleron, B., Morin, F., Souquet, P.-J., 2012. Lung cancer in never smokers—a review. Eur. J. Cancer 48 (9), 1299–1311.

Dall, G.V., Britt, K.L., 2017. Estrogen effects on the mammary gland in early and late life and breast cancer risk. Front. Oncol. 7, 110.

Davis, A., Viera, A.J., Mead, M.D., 2014. Leukemia: an overview for primary care. Am. Fam. Physician 89 (9), 731–738.

DeSantis, C.E., Fedewa, S.A., Goding Sauer, A., Kramer, J.L., Smith, R.A., Jemal, A., 2016. Breast cancer statistics, 2015: convergence of incidence rates between black and white women. CA Cancer J. Clin. 66 (1), 31–42.

Dolganiuc, A., 2015. Alcohol and viral hepatitis: role of lipid rafts. Alcohol Res. 37 (2), 299.

Doucas, H., Berry, D.P., 2006. Basic principles of the molecular biology of cancer I. Surgery (Oxford) 24 (2), 43–47.

Drukteinis, J.S., Mooney, B.P., Flowers, C.I., Gatenby, R.A., 2013. Beyond mammography: new frontiers in breast cancer screening. Am. J. Med. 126 (6), 472–479.

Dumars, C., Ngyuen, J.-M., Gaultier, A., Lanel, R., Corradini, N., Gouin, F., Heymann, D., Heymann, M.-F., 2016. Dysregulation of macrophage polarization is associated with the metastatic process in osteosarcoma. Oncotarget 7 (48), 78343.

El Helou, R., Pinna, G., Cabaud, O., Wicinski, J., Bhajun, R., Guyon, L., Rioualen, C., Finetti, P., Gros, A., Mari, B., 2017. miR-600 acts as a bimodal switch that regulates breast cancer stem cell fate through WNT signaling. Cell Rep. 18 (9), 2256–2268.

Endogenous Hormones and Breast Cancer Collaborative Group, Key, T.J., 2013. Sex hormones and risk of breast cancer in premenopausal women: a collaborative reanalysis of individual participant data from seven prospective studies. Lancet Oncol. 14 (10), 1009–1019.

Fahlén, M., Fornander, T., Johansson, H., Johansson, U., Rutqvist, L.-E., Wilking, N., von Schoultz, E., 2013. Hormone replacement therapy after breast cancer: 10 year follow up of the Stockholm randomised trial. Eur. J. Cancer 49 (1), 52–59.

Ferlay, J., Shin, H.R., Bray, F., Forman, D., Mathers, C., Parkin, D.M., 2010. Estimates of worldwide burden of cancer in 2008: GLOBOCAN 2008. Int. J. Cancer 127 (12), 2893–2917.

Ferlay, J., Soerjomataram, I., Dikshit, R., Eser, S., Mathers, C., Rebelo, M., Parkin, D.M., Forman, D., Bray, F., 2015. Cancer incidence and mortality worldwide: sources, methods and major patterns in GLOBOCAN 2012. Int. J. Cancer 136 (5), E359–E386.

Fimognari, C., Lenzi, M., Ferruzzi, L., Turrini, E., Scartezzini, P., Poli, F., Gotti, R., Guerrini, A., Carulli, G., Ottaviano, V., 2011. Mitochondrial pathway mediates the antileukemic effects of Hemidesmus indicus, a promising botanical drug. PLoS One 6 (6), e21544.

Freedman, N.D., Silverman, D.T., Hollenbeck, A.R., Schatzkin, A., Abnet, C.C., 2011. Association between smoking and risk of bladder cancer among men and women. JAMA 306 (7), 737–745.

Freitas, S.A., MacKenzie, R., Wylde, D.N., Roudebush, B.T., Bergstrom, R.L., Holowaty, J.C., Hart, A., Rigatti, S.J., Gill, S., 2017. All-cause mortality for life insurance applicants with a history of breast cancer. J. Insur. Med. 47 (1), 6–22.

Gago-Dominguez, M., Castelao, J.E., Yuan, J.M., Yu, M.C., Ross, R.K., 2001. Use of permanent hair dyes and bladder-cancer risk. Int. J. Cancer 91 (4), 575–579.

Garay, R.P., Viens, P., Bauer, J., Normier, G., Bardou, M., Jeannin, J.-F., Chiavaroli, C., 2007. Cancer relapse under chemotherapy: why TLR2/4 receptor agonists can help. Eur. J. Pharmacol. 563 (1–3), 1–17.

Gaudet, M.M., Carter, B.D., Brinton, L.A., Falk, R.T., Gram, I.T., Luo, J., Milne, R.L., Nyante, S.J., Weiderpass, E., Beane Freeman, L.E., 2017. Pooled analysis of active cigarette smoking and invasive breast cancer risk in 14 cohort studies. Int. J. Epidemiol. 46 (3), 881–893.

Gersten, O., Wilmoth, J.R., 2002. The cancer transition in Japan since 1951. Demogr. Res. 7, 271–306.

Greten, T.F., Sangro, B., 2018. Targets for immunotherapy of liver cancer. J. Hepatol. 68 (1), 157–166.

Guinney, J., Dienstmann, R., Wang, X., De Reynies, A., Schlicker, A., Soneson, C., Marisa, L., Roepman, P., Nyamundanda, G., Angelino, P., 2015. The consensus molecular subtypes of colorectal cancer. Nat. Med. 21 (11), 1350–1356.

Haber, D.A., 2006. Molecular Genetics of Cancer: Oncogenes and Proto-Oncogenes. ACP Medicine Online Website.

Haggar, F.A., Boushey, R.P., 2009. Colorectal cancer epidemiology: incidence, mortality, survival, and risk factors. Clin. Colon Rectal Surg. 22 (04), 191–197.

Hamajima, N., Hirose, K., Tajima, K., Rohan, T., Calle, E.E., Heath Jr., C.W., Coates, R.J., Liff, J.M., Talamini, R., Chantarakul, N., Koetsawang, S., Rachawat, D., Morabia, A., Schuman, L., Stewart, W., Szklo, M., Bain, C., Schofield, F., Siskind, V., Band, P., Coldman, A.J., Gallagher, R.P., Hislop, T.G., Yang, P., Kolonel, L.M., Nomura, A.M., Hu, J., Johnson, K.C., Mao, Y., De Sanjosé, S., Lee, N., Marchbanks, P., Ory, H.W., Peterson, H.B., Wilson, H.G., Wingo, P.A., Ebeling, K., Kunde, D., Nishan, P., Hopper, J.L., Colditz, G., Gajalanski, V., Martin, N., Pardthaisong, T., Silpisornkosol, S., Theetranont, C., Boosiri, B., Chutivongse, S., Jimakorn, P., Virutamasen, P., Wongsrichanalai, C., Ewertz, M., Adami, H.O., Bergkvist, L., Magnusson, C., Persson, I., Chang-Claude, J., Paul, C., Skegg, D.C., Spears, G.F., Boyle, P., Evstifeeva, T., Daling, J.R., Hutchinson, W.B., Malone, K., Noonan, E.A., Stanford, J.L., Thomas, D.B., Weiss, N.S., White, E., Andrieu, N., Brêmond, A., Clavel, F., Gairard, B., Lansac, J., Piana, L., Renaud, R., Izquierdo, A., Viladiu, P., Cuevas, H.R., Ontiveros, P., Palet, A., Salazar, S.B., Aristizabel, N., Cuadros, A., Tryggvadottir, L., Tulinius, H., Bachelot, A., Lê, M.G., Peto, J., Franceschi, S., Lubin, F., Modan, B., Ron, E., Wax, Y., Friedman, G.D., Hiatt, R.A., Levi, F., Bishop, T., Kosmelj, K., Primic-Zakelj, M., Ravnihar, B., Stare, J., Beeson, W.L., Fraser, G., Bullbrook, R.D., Cuzick, J., Duffy, S.W., Fentiman, I.-S., Hayward, J.L., Wang, D.Y., McMichael, A.J., McPherson, K., Hanson, R.L., Leske, M.C., Mahoney, M.C., Nasca, P.C., Varma, A.O., Weinstein, A.L., Moller, T.R., Olsson, H., Ranstam, J., Goldbohm, R.A., van den Brandt, P.A., Apelo, R.A., Baens, J., de la Cruz, J.R., Javier, B., Lacaya, L.B., Ngelangel, C.A., La Vecchia, C., Negri, E., Marubini, E., Ferraroni, M., Gerber, M., Richardson, S., Segala, C., Gatei, D., Kenya, P., Kungu, A., Mati, J.G., Brinton, L.A., Hoover, R., Schairer, C., Spirtas, R., Lee, H.P., Rookus, M.A., van Leeuwen, F.E., Schoenberg, J.A., McCredie, M., Gammon, M.D., Clarke, E.A., Jones, L., Neil, A., Vessey, M., Yeates, D., Appleby, P., Banks, E., Beral, V., Bull, D., Crossley, B., Goodill, A., Green, J., Hermon, C., Key, T., Langston, N., Lewis, C., Reeves, G., Collins, R., Doll, R., Peto, R., Mabuchi, K., Preston, D., Hannaford, P., Kay, C., Rosero-Bixby, L., Gao, Y.T., Jin, F., Yuan, J.M., Wei, H.Y., Yun, T., Zhiheng, C., Berry, G., Cooper Booth, J., Jelihovsky, T., MacLennan, R., Shearman, R., Wang, Q.S., Baines, C.J., Miller, A.B., Wall, C., Lund, E., Stalsberg, H., Shu, X.O., Zheng, W., Katsouyanni, K., Trichopoulou, A., Trichopoulos, D., Dabancens, A., Martinez, L., Molina, R., Salas, O., Alexander, F.-E., Anderson, K., Folsom, A.R., Hulka, B.S., Bernstein, L., Enger, S., Haile, R.W., Paganini-Hill, A., Pike, M.C., Ross, R.K., Ursin, G., Yu, M.C., Longnecker, M.P., Newcomb, P., Bergkvist, L., Kalache, A., Farley, T.M., Holck, S., Meirik, O., 2002. Alcohol, tobacco and breast cancer—collaborative reanalysis of individual data from 53 epidemiological studies, including 58,515 women with breast cancer and 95,067 women without the disease. Br. J. Cancer 87 (11), 1234–1245.

Hanahan, D., Weinberg, R.A., 2000. The hallmarks of cancer. Cell 100 (1), 57–70.

Hanahan, D., Weinberg, R.A., 2011. Hallmarks of cancer: the next generation. Cell 144 (5), 646–674.

Hart, I.R., 2004. Biology of cancer. Medicine 32 (3), 1–5.

Hoang, N.T., Acevedo, L.A., Mann, M.J., Tolani, B., 2018. A review of soft-tissue sarcomas: translation of biological advances into treatment measures. Cancer Manag. Res. 10, 1089.

Hodgson, J.T., Darnton, A., 2000. The quantitative risks of mesothelioma and lung cancer in relation to asbestos exposure. Ann. Occup. Hyg. 44 (8), 565–601.

Horn, J., Vatten, L.J., 2017. Reproductive and hormonal risk factors of breast cancer: a historical perspective. Int. J. Womens Health 9, 265.

Horn, J., Åsvold, B.O., Opdahl, S., Tretli, S., Vatten, L.J., 2013. Reproductive factors and the risk of breast cancer in old age: a Norwegian cohort study. Breast Cancer Res. Treat. 139 (1), 237–243.

Howlader, N., A.M. Noone, M. Krapcho, D. Miller, A. Brest, M. Yu, J. Ruhl, Z. Tatalovich, A. Mariotto and D.R. Lewis (2021). "SEER Cancer Statistics Review, 1975–2018, National Cancer Institute." Bethesda, MD, April.

Hwang, S.-J., Cheng, L.S.-C., Lozano, G., Amos, C.I., Gu, X., Strong, L.C., 2003. Lung cancer risk in germline p53 mutation carriers: association between an inherited cancer predisposition, cigarette smoking, and cancer risk. Hum. Genet. 113 (3), 238–243.

Ishikawa, T., 2008. Secondary prevention of recurrence by interferon therapy after ablation therapy for hepatocellular carcinoma in chronic hepatitis C patients. World J Gastroenterol: WJG 14 (40), 6140.

Jensen, L.F., Hvidberg, L., Pedersen, A.F., Vedsted, P., 2015. Symptom attributions in patients with colorectal cancer. BMC Fam. Pract. 16 (1), 1–10.

Jung, S., Wang, M., Anderson, K., Baglietto, L., Bergkvist, L., Bernstein, L., van den Brandt, P.A., Brinton, L., Buring, J.E., Heather Eliassen, A., 2016. Alcohol consumption and breast cancer risk by estrogen receptor status: in a pooled analysis of 20 studies. Int. J. Epidemiol. 45 (3), 916–928.

Kasper, M., Jaks, V., Fiaschi, M., Toftgård, R., 2009. Hedgehog signalling in breast cancer. Carcinogenesis 30 (6), 903–911.

Kearney, J., 2010. Food consumption trends and drivers. Philos. Trans. R. Soc., B 365 (1554), 2793–2807.

Kenfield, S.A., Wei, E.K., Stampfer, M.J., Rosner, B.A., Colditz, G.A., 2008. Comparison of aspects of smoking among the four histological types of lung cancer. Tob. Control 17 (3), 198–204.

Kiemeney, L.A., Sulem, P., Besenbacher, S., Vermeulen, S.H., Sigurdsson, A., Thorleifsson, G., Gudbjartsson, D.F., Stacey, S.N., Gudmundsson, J., Zanon, C., 2010. A sequence variant at 4p16. 3 confers susceptibility to urinary bladder cancer. Nat. Genet. 42 (5), 415–419.

Kim, S.-E., Paik, H.Y., Yoon, H., Lee, J.E., Kim, N., Sung, M.-K., 2015. Sex-and gender-specific disparities in colorectal cancer risk. World J Gastroenterol: WJG 21 (17), 5167.

Kiriluk, K.J., Prasad, S.M., Patel, A.R., Steinberg, G.D., Smith, N.D., 2012. Bladder Cancer Risk from Occupational and Environmental Exposures. Elsevier.

Kispert, S., McHowat, J., 2017. Recent insights into cigarette smoking as a lifestyle risk factor for breast cancer. Breast Cancer 9, 127.

Knight, J.A., Fan, J., Malone, K.E., John, E.M., Lynch, C.F., Langballe, R., Bernstein, L., Shore, R.E., Brooks, J.D., Reiner, A.S., 2017. Alcohol consumption and cigarette smoking in combination: a predictor of contralateral breast cancer risk in the WECARE study. Int. J. Cancer 141 (5), 916–924.

Kuipers, E.J., Grady, W.M., Lieberman, D., Seufferlein, T., Sung, J.J., Boelens, P.G., van de Velde, C.J., Watanabe, T., 2015. Colorectal cancer. Nat. Rev. Dis. Primers. 1, 15065.

Kurahashi, N., Inoue, M., Iwasaki, M., Sasazuki, S., Tsugane, S., 2008. Dairy product, saturated fatty acid, and calcium intake and prostate cancer in a prospective cohort of Japanese men. Cancer Epidemiol. Biomark. Prev. 17 (4), 930–937.

Lee, M.-H., 2018. Risk of hepatocellular carcinoma for patients treated with direct-acting antivirals: steps after hepatitis C virus eradication to achieve elimination. Transl. Gastroenterol. Hepatol. 3, 96–107.

Leitzmann, M.F., Rohrmann, S., 2012. Risk factors for the onset of prostatic cancer: age, location, and behavioral correlates. Clin. Epidemiol. 4, 1.

Lempp, F.A., Ni, Y., Urban, S., 2016. Hepatitis delta virus: insights into a peculiar pathogen and novel treatment options. Nat. Rev. Gastroenterol. Hepatol. 13 (10), 580–589.

Letašiová, S., Medveďová, A., Šovčíková, A., Dušinská, M., Volkovová, K., Mosoiu, C., Bartonová, A., 2012. Bladder cancer, a review of the environmental risk factors. Environ. Health 11 (1), 1–5.

Li, M., Zhang, N., Li, M., 2017. Capecitabine treatment of HCT-15 colon cancer cells induces apoptosis via mitochondrial pathway. Trop. J. Pharm. Res. 16 (7), 1529–1536.

Liu, Y., Wu, F., 2010. Global burden of aflatoxin-induced hepatocellular carcinoma: a risk assessment. Environ. Health Perspect. 118 (6), 818–824.

Liu, Y., Chang, C.-C.H., Marsh, G.M., Wu, F., 2012. Population attributable risk of aflatoxin-related liver cancer: systematic review and meta-analysis. Eur. J. Cancer 48 (14), 2125–2136.

Liu, J.-Y., Chen, T.-J., Hwang, S.-J., 2016. The risk of breast cancer in women using menopausal hormone replacement therapy in Taiwan. Int. J. Environ. Res. Public Health 13 (5), 482.

Lobo, N., Shariat, S.F., Guo, C.C., Fernandez, M.I., Kassouf, W., Choudhury, A., Gao, J., Williams, S.B., Galsky, M.D., Taylor Iii, J.A., 2020. What is the significance of variant histology in urothelial carcinoma? Eur. Urol. Focus 6 (4), 653–663.

Maffini, M.V., Soto, A.M., Calabro, J.M., Ucci, A.A., Sonnenschein, C., 2004. The stroma as a crucial target in rat mammary gland carcinogenesis. J. Cell Sci. 117 (8), 1495–1502.

Majeed, W., Aslam, B., Javed, I., Khaliq, T., Muhammad, F., Ali, A., Raza, A., 2014. Breast cancer: major risk factors and recent developments in treatment. Asian Pac. J. Cancer Prev. 15 (8), 3353–3358.

Mak, L.Y., Cruz-Ramón, V., Chinchilla-López, P., Torres, H.A., LoConte, N.K., Rice, J.P., Foxhall, L.E., Sturgis, E.M., Merrill, J.K., Bailey, H.H., Méndez-Sánchez, N., Yuen, M.F., Hwang, J.P., 2018. Global epidemiology, prevention, and management of hepatocellular carcinoma. Am. Soc. Clin. Oncol. Educ. Book 38, 262–279.

Makarem, N., Chandran, U., Bandera, E.V., Parekh, N., 2013. Dietary fat in breast cancer survival. Annu. Rev. Nutr. 33, 319–348.

Mármol, I., Sánchez-de-Diego, C., Pradilla Dieste, A., Cerrada, E., Rodriguez Yoldi, M.J., 2017. Colorectal carcinoma: a general overview and future perspectives in colorectal cancer. Int. J. Mol. Sci. 18 (1), 197.

Matulay, J.T., Kamat, A.M., 2018. Advances in risk stratification of bladder cancer to guide personalized medicine. F1000Research 7, 1–13.

Mehraj, U., Dar, A.H., Wani, N.A., Mir, M.A., 2021. Tumor microenvironment promotes breast cancer chemoresistance. Cancer Chemother. Pharmacol. 87 (2), 147–158.

McKillop, I.H., Schrum, L.W., 2009. Role of alcohol in liver carcinogenesis. Semin. Liver Dis. 29 (2), 222–232.

Mehraj, U., Aisha, S., Sofi, S., Mir, M.A., 2022. Expression pattern and prognostic significance of baculoviral inhibitor of apoptosis repeat-containing 5 (BIRC5) in breast cancer: a comprehensive analysis. Adv. Cancer Biol. Metastasis 4, 100037.

Mir, M.A., Mehraj, U., 2019. Double-crosser of the immune system: macrophages in tumor progression and metastasis. Curr. Immunol. Rev. 15 (2), 172–184.

Mir, M.A., Qayoom, H., Mehraj, U., Nisar, S., Bhat, B., Wani, N.A., 2020. Targeting different pathways using novel combination therapy in triple negative breast cancer. Curr. Cancer Drug Targets 20 (8), 586–602.

Mir, M., Jan, S., Mehraj, U., 2022a. Current Therapeutics and Treatment Options in TNBC. Chapter-3, Elsevier, pp. 73–144.

Mir, M., Jan, S., Mehraj, U., 2022b. Triple-Negative Breast Cancer—An Aggressive Subtype of Breast Cancer. Elsevier, pp. 1–35.

Mir, M., Sofi, S., Qayoom, H., 2022c. The Interplay of Immunotherapy, Chemotherapy, and Targeted Therapy in Tripple Negative Breast Cancer (TNBC). Chapter-6, Elsevier, pp. 201–244.

Mir, M., Sofi, S., Qayoom, H., 2022d. Targeting Biologically Specific Molecules in Triple Negative Breast Cancer (TNBC). Chapter 7, Elsevier, pp. 245–277.

Mir, M., Jan, S., Mehraj, U., 2022e. Conventional Adjuvant Chemotherapy in Combination with Surgery, Radiotherapy and Other Specific Targets. Chapter 4, Elsevier, pp. 145–176.

Mir, M., Jan, S., Mehraj, U., 2022f. Novel Biomarkers In Triple-Negative Breast Cancer-Role and Perspective. Chapter-2, Elsevier, pp. 36–72.

Mohr, S.B., Garland, C.F., Gorham, E.D., Grant, W.B., Garland, F.C., 2010. Ultraviolet B irradiance and incidence rates of bladder cancer in 174 countries. Am. J. Prev. Med. 38 (3), 296–302.

Molyneux, G., Geyer, F.C., Magnay, F.-A., McCarthy, A., Kendrick, H., Natrajan, R., MacKay, A., Grigoriadis, A., Tutt, A., Ashworth, A., 2010. BRCA1 basal-like breast cancers originate from luminal epithelial progenitors and not from basal stem cells. Cell Stem Cell 7 (3), 403–417.

Mullangi, S., Lekkala, M.R., 2021. Adenocarcinoma. StatPearls [Internet].

Munretnam, K., Alex, L., Ramzi, N.H., Chahil, J.K., Kavitha, I.S., Hashim, N.A.N., Lye, S.H., Velapasamy, S., Ler, L.W., 2014. Association of genetic and non-genetic risk factors with the development of prostate cancer in Malaysian men. Mol. Biol. Rep. 41 (4), 2501–2508.

Naranmandura, H., Carew, M.W., Xu, S., Lee, J., Leslie, E.M., Weinfeld, M., Le, X.C., 2011. Comparative toxicity of arsenic metabolites in human bladder cancer EJ-1 cells. Chem. Res. Toxicol. 24 (9), 1586–1596.

Narod, S.A., 2011. Hormone replacement therapy and the risk of breast cancer. Nat. Rev. Clin. Oncol. 8 (11), 669–676.

Palmieri, D., Chambers, A.F., Felding-Habermann, B., Huang, S., Steeg, P.S., 2007. The biology of metastasis to a sanctuary site. Clin. Cancer Res. 13 (6), 1656–1662.

Polyak, K., 2007. Breast cancer: origins and evolution. J. Clin. Invest. 117 (11), 3155–3163.

Qayoom, H., Bhat, B.A., Mehraj, U., Mir, M.A., 2020. Rising trends of cancers in Kashmir valley: distribution pattern, incidence and causes. J Oncol Res Treat 5 (150), 2.

Qayoom, H., Mehraj, U., Aisha, S., Sofi, S., Mir, M.A., 2021. Integrating Immunotherapy with Chemotherapy: A New Approach to Drug Repurposing. Intech open.

Qian, B.-Z., Pollard, J.W., 2010. Macrophage diversity enhances tumor progression and metastasis. Cell 141 (1), 39–51.

Ramadori, P., Cubero, F.J., Liedtke, C., Trautwein, C., Nevzorova, Y.A., 2017. Alcohol and hepatocellular carcinoma: adding fuel to the flame. Cancer 9 (10), 130.

Ranasinghe, W.K.B., De Silva, D., De Silva, M.V.C., Ranasinghe, T.I.J., Lawrentschuk, N., Bolton, D., Persad, R., 2012. Incidence of bladder cancer in Sri Lanka: analysis of the cancer registry data and review of the incidence of bladder cancer in the South Asian population. Korean J. Urol. 53 (5), 304–309.

Rawla, P., Sunkara, T., Barsouk, A., 2019. Epidemiology of colorectal cancer: incidence, mortality, survival, and risk factors. Przegl. Gastroenterol. 14 (2), 89.

Recio-Boiles, A., Cagir, B., 2021. Colon cancer. In: StatPearls [Internet]. StatPearls Publishing.

Recio-Boiles, A., Kashyap, S., Tsoris, A., Babiker, H.M., 2018. Rectal Cancer. StatPearls.

Richters, A., Aben, K.K.H., Kiemeney, L.A.L.M., 2020. The global burden of urinary bladder cancer: an update. World J. Urol. 38 (8), 1895–1904.

Ries, L.A.G., Melbert, D., Krapcho, M., Stinchcomb, D.G., Howlader, N., Horner, M.J., Mariotto, A., Miller, B.A., Feuer, E.J., Altekruse, S.F., 2008. SEER Cancer Statistics Review, 1975–2005. National Cancer Institute, Bethesda, MD, p. 2999.

Rojas, K., Stuckey, A., 2016. Breast cancer epidemiology and risk factors. Clin. Obstet. Gynecol. 59 (4), 651–672.

Rosato, V., Bosetti, C., Negri, E., Talamini, R., Dal Maso, L., Malvezzi, M., Falcini, F., Montella, M., La Vecchia, C., 2014. Reproductive and hormonal factors, family history, and breast cancer according to the hormonal receptor status. Eur. J. Cancer Prev. 23 (5), 412–417.

Rui, L., 2014. Energy metabolism in the liver. Compr. Physiol. 4 (1), 177.

Said, A., Ghufran, A., 2017. Epidemic of non-alcoholic fatty liver disease and hepatocellular carcinoma. World J. Clin. Oncol. 8 (6), 429.

Sarkar, S., Horn, G., Moulton, K., Oza, A., Byler, S., Kokolus, S., Longacre, M., 2013. Cancer development, progression, and therapy: an epigenetic overview. Int. J. Mol. Sci. 14 (10), 21087–21113.

Schuppan, D., Afdhal, N.H., 2008. Liver cirrhosis. Lancet 371 (9615), 838–851.

Scosyrev, E., Noyes, K., Feng, C., Messing, E., 2009. Sex and racial differences in bladder cancer presentation and mortality in the US. Cancer 115 (1), 68–74.

Sellers, T.A., Yang, P., 2002. Familial and genetic influences on risk of lung cancer. Oxf. Monogr. Med. Genet. 44 (1), 700–712. Spandidos Publications.

Sgroi, D.C., 2010. Preinvasive breast cancer. Annu. Rev. Pathol. 5, 193–221.

Sher, T., Dy, G.K., Adjei, A.A., 2008. Small cell lung cancer. Mayo Clin. Proc. 83 (3), 355–367.

Shukla, G., Kour Khera, H., Kumar Srivastava, A., Khare, P., Patidar, R., Saxena, R., 2017. Therapeutic potential, challenges and future perspective of cancer stem cells in translational oncology: a critical review. Curr. Stem Cell Res. Ther. 12 (3), 207–224.

Siegel, R., DeSantis, C., Jemal, A., 2014a. Colorectal cancer statistics, 2014. CA Cancer J. Clin. 64 (2), 104–117.

Siegel, R., Ma, J., Zou, Z., Jemal, A., 2014b. Cancer statistics, 2014. CA Cancer J. Clin. 64 (1), 9–29.

Siegel, R.L., Miller, K.D., Jemal, A., 2017. Cancer statistics, 2017. CA Cancer J. Clin. 67 (1), 7–30.

Siegel, R.L., Miller, K.D., Jemal, A., 2018. Cancer statistics, 2018. CA Cancer J. Clin. 68 (1), 7–30.

Singh, A.K., Kumar, R., Pandey, A.K., 2018. Hepatocellular carcinoma: causes, mechanism of progression and biomarkers. Curr. Chem. Genom. Transl. Med. 12, 9.

Smalley, M., Piggott, L., Clarkson, R., 2013. Breast cancer stem cells: obstacles to therapy. Cancer Lett. 338 (1), 57–62.

Sonnenschein, C., Soto, A.M., 2016. Carcinogenesis explained within the context of a theory of organisms. Prog. Biophys. Mol. Biol. 122 (1), 70–76.

Soroush, A., Farshchian, N., Komasi, S., Izadi, N., Amirifard, N., Shahmohammadi, A., 2016. The role of oral contraceptive pills on increased risk of breast cancer in Iranian populations: a meta-analysis. J. Cancer Prev. 21 (4), 294.

Spolverato, G., Vitale, A., Ejaz, A., Kim, Y., Maithel, S.K., Cosgrove, D.P., Pawlik, T.M., 2015. The relative net health benefit of liver resection, ablation, and transplantation for early hepatocellular carcinoma. World J. Surg. 39 (6), 1474–1484.

Spyratos, D., Zarogoulidis, P., Porpodis, K., Tsakiridis, K., Machairiotis, N., Katsikogiannis, N., Kougioumtzi, I., Dryllis, G., Kallianos, A., Rapti, A., Li, C., Zarogoulidis, K., 2013. Occupational exposure and lung cancer. J. Thorac. Dis. 5 Suppl 4 (Suppl 4), S440–S445.

Stayner, L., Kuempel, E., Gilbert, S., Hein, M., Dement, J., 2008. An epidemiological study of the role of chrysotile asbestos fibre dimensions in determining respiratory disease risk in exposed workers. Occup. Environ. Med. 65 (9), 613–619.

Stellman, S.D., Muscat, J.E., Hoffmann, D., Wynder, E.L., 1997. Impact of filter cigarette smoking on lung cancer histology. Prev. Med. 26 (4), 451–456.

Subahir, M.N., Shah, S.A., Zainuddin, Z.M., 2009. Risk factors for prostate cancer in Universiti Kebangsaan Malaysia medical Centre: a case-control study. Asian Pac. J. Cancer Prev. 10 (10), 1015–1020.

Thorgeirsson, T.E., Geller, F., Sulem, P., Rafnar, T., Wiste, A., Magnusson, K.P., Manolescu, A., Thorleifsson, G., Stefansson, H., Ingason, A., 2008. A variant associated with nicotine dependence, lung cancer and peripheral arterial disease. Nature 452 (7187), 638–642.

Torre, L.A., Siegel, R.L., Ward, E.M., Jemal, A., 2016. Global cancer incidence and mortality rates and trends—an update. Cancer Epidemiol. Biomark. Prev. 25 (1), 16–27.

Valenti, G., Quinn, H.M., Heynen, G.J.J.E., Lan, L., Holland, J.D., Vogel, R., Wulf-Goldenberg, A., Birchmeier, W., 2017. Cancer stem cells regulate cancer-associated fibroblasts via activation of hedgehog signaling in mammary gland tumors. Cancer Res. 77 (8), 2134–2147.

Van Raamsdonk, C.D., Bezrookove, V., Green, G., Bauer, J., Gaugler, L., O'Brien, J.M., Simpson, E.M., Barsh, G.S., Bastian, B.C., 2009. Frequent somatic mutations of GNAQ in uveal melanoma and blue naevi. Nature 457 (7229), 599–602.

Volanis, D., Kadiyska, T., Galanis, A., Delakas, D., Logotheti, S., Zoumpourlis, V., 2010. Environmental factors and genetic susceptibility promote urinary bladder cancer. Toxicol. Lett. 193 (2), 131–137.

Ward, P.S., Thompson, C.B., 2012. Metabolic reprogramming: a cancer hallmark even Warburg did not anticipate. Cancer Cell 21 (3), 297–308.

Whitrow, M.J., Smith, B.J., Pilotto, L.S., Pisaniello, D., Nitschke, M., 2003. Environmental exposure to carcinogens causing lung cancer: epidemiological evidence from the medical literature. Respirology 8 (4), 513–521.

Wu, M.-Y., Yiang, G.-T., Cheng, P.-W., Chu, P.-Y., Li, C.-J., 2018. Molecular targets in hepatocarcinogenesis and implications for therapy. J. Clin. Med. 7 (8), 213.

Yee, D.S., Ishill, N.M., Lowrance, W.T., Herr, H.W., Elkin, E.B., 2011. Ethnic differences in bladder cancer survival. Urology 78 (3), 544–549.

Yuen, M.F., Chen, D.S., Dusheiko, G.M., Janssen, H.L.A., Lau, D.T.Y., Locarnini, S.A., Peters, M.G., Lai, C.L., 2018. Hepatitis B virus infection. Nat. Rev. Dis. Primers. 4, 18035.

Zeegers, M., Kellen, E., Buntinx, F., van den Brandt, P.A., 2004. The association between smoking, beverage consumption, diet and bladder cancer: a systematic literature review. World J. Urol. 21 (6), 392–401.

Zeichner, S.B., Raj, N., Cusnir, M., Francavilla, M., Hirzel, A., 2012. A De novo germline APC mutation (3927del5) in a patient with familial adenomatous polyposis: case report and literature review. Clin. Med. Insights Oncol. 6, 315–323.

Zhang, M., Lee, A.V., Rosen, J.M., 2017. The cellular origin and evolution of breast cancer. Cold Spring Harb. Perspect. Med. 7 (3), a027128.

Zhao, L.-Y., Huo, R.-R., Xiang, X., Torzilli, G., Zheng, M.-H., Yang, T., Liang, X.-M., Huang, X., Tang, P.-L., Xiang, B.-D., 2018. Hepatic resection for elderly patients with hepatocellular carcinoma: a systematic review of more than 17,000 patients. Expert Rev. Gastroenterol. Hepatol. 12 (10), 1059–1068.

CHAPTER 2

The tumor microenvironment

Manzoor Ahmad Mir, Shariqa Aisha, Shazia Sofi, and Shreen Rasheid
Department of Bioresources, School of Biological Sciences, University of Kashmir, Srinagar, Jammu and Kashmir, India

2.1 Introduction

Breast carcinoma is the most frequent cancer among women and the main incidence of cancer-related deaths (Jemal et al., 2010; Mehraj et al., 2022a). While local cancer is usually treatable, metastatic or recurring cancer has a poor prognosis. The tumor microenvironment is now acknowledged as a key player in tumor growth and therapy responsiveness. As a consequence, there is a growing focus on creating innovative medicines that target the microenvironment, especially in the context of aggressive and metastatic disease progression. The luminal epithelium cell layers of a healthy mammary duct are bordered by myoepithelial cells, which create and connect to the basement membranes. Extracellular matrix (ECM) and a variety of stromal cell populations, such as endothelial and immunological cells, fibroblasts, and adipocytes, make up the breast microenvironment. Mammary ducts formation has been demonstrated to be influenced by microenvironment factors such as macrophages, myoepithelial and endothelium cells, and numerous ECM components (Maller et al., 2010). The TME is also becoming more widely recognized as a key modulator of tumorigenesis (Hanahan and Weinberg, 2011) (Fig. 2.1). Breast cancers develop in phases, beginning with epithelium proliferation and differentiation and advancing to insitu, aggressive, and metastatic carcinomas (Polyak, 2007). DCIS appears to be a precursor to invasive ductal carcinoma (IDC), according to experimental and medical pieces of evidence. DCIS lesions are characterized by growing cancerous cells that are confined to the ducts. The change from in situ to invasive ductal carcinoma, which is defined by the breakdown of the myoepithelial cell layers and basement membranes, is a crucial yet poorly known phase in breast tumor development. Metastatic illness develops as a consequence of the migration of tumor cells to distant areas. Notably, each of these stages of cancer development has been linked to the TME (Mir et al., 2022a,b,c,d).

Breast tumor TME can be divided into three categories: soluble, cellular, and physical components (Soysal et al., 2015) (Table 2.1). Local (intratumoral), regional (breast), and metastatic components can be distinguished among the cellular components (Soysal et al., 2015; Stakheyeva et al., 2017). The biological properties of cancerous cells and tumor-infiltrating inflammatory cells such as DCs, lymphocytes, macrophages, plasma cells, and

Role of Tumor Microenvironment in Breast Cancer and Targeted Therapies
https://doi.org/10.1016/B978-0-443-18696-7.00007-5

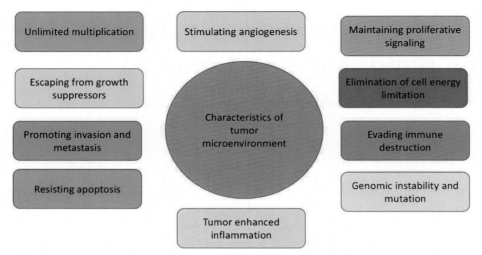

Fig. 2.1 Illustrates different characteristics of tumor microenvironment.

Table 2.1 Tumor microenvironment components.

Component	Local	Regional	Metastatic
Cellular	• Lymphocytes • Tumor cells • Cytotoxic T cells • Helper T cells • Follicular helper T cells • Regulatory T cells • Macrophages • Plasma cells • Dendritic cells • Neutrophils • Myeloid dendritic cells • Plasmacytoid dendritic cells	• Adipose cells • Fibroblasts • Myoepithelial cells • Capillaries • Endothelial cells • Lymphatics	• Immune cells • Lymph node • Lymphatics • Blood • Distant organs • Peripheral immune cells • Bone (osteoclasts) • Lung (alveolar macrophages)

neutrophils are referred to as the local compartments (Salgado et al., 2015; Mir and Mehraj, 2019; Wu et al., 2019). The interaction among tumor cells and neighboring cells in the stroma, especially at the infiltrating edge, includes stroma fibroblasts, myoepithelial cells, adipose cells, endothelium, and vascular or lymphatic endothelium cells (Soysal et al., 2015). The metastatic component pertains to host tissues that have spread to lymphatic nodes and distant regions, creating new TME (Pereira et al., 2022; Coleman et al., 2013). Cytokines, enzymes, and growth factors are among the soluble and physical components that play major part in tumor development in the breast as well as at distant regions.

2.1.1 The local microenvironment

While breast carcinoma is not considered an immunological hot tumor, but high-grade, hormone receptor-negative, or HER2-positive tumors have a significant number of tumor-infiltrating lymphocytes (TILs) (Tsang et al., 2017; Beguinot et al., 2018; Denkert et al., 2018). TILs in breast carcinoma are mostly T cells, with a small number of B cells (Ruffell et al., 2012; Garaud et al., 2019). T cells of various types have different impacts on the TME. CD8 cytotoxic T cells kill cancerous cells by producing granzyme and perforins, which are regulated via the production of interferons (IFN). IFN-γ and IL-12 signals activate type 1 helper (Th1) CD4 T cells, which permit antigen-presenting cells for efficient CD8 T-cell development and clonal proliferation (Karasar and Esendagli, 2014; Borst et al., 2018). T helper type 2 (Th2) and type 17 (Th17) cells play increasingly diverse functions in the advancement of breast carcinoma (Aspord et al., 2007). Follicular helper T cells (Tfh) perform a key part in antigen-specific B-cell maturity, memory cells differentiation, as well as the establishment of tertiary lymphatic organs, all of which contribute to an improved local antitumor immune responses (Gu-Trantien et al., 2013; Cao et al., 2021). Tregs are essential regulators of immunological system balance and tolerance, and their existence in TME enhances immunosuppression via immunosuppressive mediators (transforming growth factor-β (TGF-β), interleukin-10 (IL-10), or via direct cell contact inhibition) (Wachstein et al., 2012). Generally, positive Th1 responses are linked to good clinical results (Datta et al., 2015), but positive Treg responses can aid breast tumor development. The functions of tumor-infiltrating B cells are unknown. Based on the nature of the TME and its morphologies, they may both have protumor or antitumor actions. The detection of tumor-specific antigens and antibodies production or antigen presentation cell (APC) activity regulates their antitumor effects (Wittrup, 2017; Hollern et al., 2019; Mir et al., 2022e,f,g,h). B cells coexist with T cells in TME, notably in tertiary lymphoid structure (TLS) (Nelson, 2010); therefore, their existence is thought to be a good prognostic marker. B cells become plasma cells after being exposed to antigens. These also were identified in TLS, indicating that active antitumor humoral responses had developed (Seow et al., 2020). B cells also can play an important role in tumor progression. Regulatory B cells (Bregs) produce antiinflammatory cytokines including IL-10, IL-35, and TGF-β, as well as inhibiting compounds like programmed cell death-ligand 1 (PD-L1) and FAS ligands (FasL) that suppress immunological reactions (Mauri and Bosma, 2012). Their existence in breast tumor tissues has been observed, and they enhance breast tumor spread by transforming quiescent T cells into Treg (Olkhanud et al., 2011); however, their clinical significance is unknown at this time.

Dendritic cells (DCs) are the more powerful antigen presenters, presenting antigens to T cells, especially tumor-derived antigens. DC matures and becomes more powerful in immune activation when it interacts with T cells. Cancer cells prevent DC maturation, resulting in an immature morphology with poor tumor-derived antigens cross-presentation and reduced expression of costimulatory proteins in tumor-infiltrating DC (Harimoto et al., 2013). DCs are separated into two groups, plasmacytoid and myeloid, based on the expression of cell surface proteins. Myeloid DCs primarily work to activate immunological cells, but plasmacytoid DCs, which produce type I interferon (IFN), are higher tolerogenic and have poor prognostic consequences (Treilleux et al., 2004). TAMs (tumor-associated macrophages) are the most common innate immunity cells found in tumors. Based on cytokine exposure, they have two polarized morphologies (M1 and M2). Th1 cytokines (IFN-γ and tumor necrosis factor (TNF)) activate M1 macrophages, which then produce reactive oxygen and nitrogen species (ROS) and release proinflammatory cytokines, resulting in antitumor actions (Qiu et al., 2018). M2 macrophages, the alternately triggered phenotype, are protumor in origin and are triggered by Th2 factors (IL4, IL10, and IL-13) (Biswas and Mantovani, 2010). They decrease the antitumor immune responses; promote tumor development and metastasis (Qiu et al., 2018). Neutrophils are rapidly becoming identified as immune cells that infiltrate tumors. Tumor-associated neutrophils (TAN) have polarized characteristics identical to TAM. IFN-β and IFN-γ exposure produce N1 proinflammatory and antitumor TAN, while TGF-β exposure induces N2 antiinflammatory and protumor TAN (Fridlender et al., 2009; Ohms et al., 2020. In breast tumor mice models, TAN can inhibit CD8 growth and attract immunosuppressive cells in TME; however, the effects in humans are unknown (Burugu et al., 2017; Stakheyeva et al., 2017).

Due to the therapeutic effectiveness of immune checkpoint inhibition, immune checkpoint proteins, particularly programmed cell death protein 1 (PD1) as well as associated ligand PD-L1, are expressed by tumor cells and immunological cells (B cells, T cells, DC, and macrophages), have received a lot of interest (Agata et al., 1996; Dong et al., 1999). PD1 suppresses T-cell stimulation once it is activated by PD-L1; therefore, it is recognized to be a primary component of immunological resistance in the TME (Pardoll, 2012). Increased PD-L1 expression is detected in high TIL, high-grade, hormone receptor-negative, HER2 highly expressed, TNBCs (Bertucci and Gonçalves, 2017), and PD-1[+] TIL is linked with poor survival rates in women with breast carcinoma (Muenst et al., 2013). The major therapeutic significance of the PD-1/PD-L1 route, though, is in therapy utilizing PD-1/PD-L1 blockade, than in its predictive value. Another instance of a targetable immunological checkpoint in different human tumors is CTLA-4, a cell membrane receptor present on active T cells that produce anergy by competitive suppression of CD28 receptors (Mir and Agrewala, 2008; Rotte, 2019).

2.1.2 The regional microenvironment

The most important stromal constituents are cancer-associated fibroblasts (CAF). CAF has a greater proliferation index and abnormalities in tumor suppressor proteins than their healthy counterparts (Hawsawi et al., 2008). CAF promotes tumor development by boosting angiogenesis, tumor growth, and infiltration via the activities of soluble proteins and matrix modifying enzymes including vascular endothelial growth factor A and TGF-β, as well as matrix metalloproteases (MMP) (Aboussekhra, 2011). One of TGF-β's actions is to increase collagen I synthesis, resulting in a protumor fibrotic milieu (Cox and Erler, 2014). The current World Health Organization (WHO) categorization of breast cancers now includes fibrotic foci in breast carcinoma, which are now acknowledged as an unfavorable histologic predictive characteristic. CAF is a varied collection of tumor stromal cells with fibroblast-like morphology. They may come from a variety of tissues or progenitor cells, such as stellate cells, mesenchymal stem cells, bone marrow-derived fibrocytes, or even endothelium cells, adipose cells, smooth muscle cells, and pericytes, rather than normal fibroblasts in the TME (Giorello et al., 2021). CAF expresses FAP, α-SMA, S100A4, and PDGFR-β immunohistochemically. Such markers, though, are not cell type-specific, as they can be found in different cell types. Furthermore, each marker may be used to distinguish across various CAF populations. Four CAF types were identified in breast tumors based on differential marker expression employing multicolored flow cytometry research on FAP, FSP1, Integrinβ1, PDGFR, α-SMA, and caveolin1 as well as single-cell RNA sequencing (scRNA-seq). These various morphological populations reflected various functions and were linked to various breast carcinoma subtypes. The subtype CAF-S1 was shown to be more prevalent in TNBC and was linked to immunosuppression (Costa et al., 2018; Mir et al., 2020). The vascular CAF (vCAF) expressed genes associated with angiogenesis; the matrix CAF (mCAF) expressed ECM-related genes; while the developmental CAF (dCAF) expressed genes linked to stem cells; the latter two can arise from local fibroblasts and malignant epithelium cells, accordingly. Utilizing bulk RNA sequencing information from individual patients' samples, the mCAF and vCAF gene profiles can be discovered with biological and clinical significance (Bartoschek et al., 2018). Nevertheless, the link among various CAF subgroups is yet unknown, necessitating more research into biomarker expression and/or gene profiling findings.

Other biological components of the breast TME include endothelium cells and adipose cells. They likewise show mutual and variable interaction with tumor cells to promote tumor growth. TGF-β and vascular endothelial growth factor (VEGF) are reported to induce angiogenesis in breast tumor cells (Longatto Filho et al., 2010). When breast tumor cells were cocultured along with vascular endothelial cells, enhanced VEGF expression, migration, endothelial growth, and organization were observed (Buchanan et al., 2012). VEGF-C, which promotes lymphangiogenesis in lymphatic endothelium cells, has also been seen in breast tumors. Breast tumors that highly express VEGF-C have been linked to lymphatic vessel infiltration, lymph node metastases, and reduced disease-free survival (Kinoshita et al., 2001; Skobe et al., 2001). Breast tumor cells communicate with adipose tissues as well. Via IL-6 and IL-8, visceral adipose cells enhance tumor growth and cause epithelial-to-mesenchymal transition; however, subcutaneous adipose cells do not (Ritter et al., 2015). Because the breast is made up of a lot of fatty tissues, the impacts of visceral adipose tissues on the breast carcinoma TME are very strong (Pallegar and Christian, 2020). BC biology is influenced by localized TME oxygenation (Rundqvist and Johnson, 2013). The expression of an active phenotype (ER-negative), localized tumor growth, and nodal metastases are all accelerated in hypoxic conditions (Vaupel et al., 2002).

Standard chemotherapy and radiotherapy are harmed by reduced oxygen saturation and poor circulation (Vaupel et al., 2002). An acidic milieu promotes tumor growth by promoting tumor invasion and decreasing chemotherapeutic drug transcellular absorption (Webb et al., 2011). Altogether, hypoxia and acidosis give refractory tumor clones an adaptive survival benefit, leading to clonal selection; they further reduce the lethal impacts of neutrophils and lymphocytes by restricting ROS production, lowering cellular mobility, and generating an unfavorable extracellular milieu (Lardner, 2001).

2.1.3 The metastatic microenvironment

The invasion of tumor cells into lymphatics and blood arteries starts a critical phase in the metastatic cascade (Scully et al., 2012). In individuals with metastatic breast cancer, increased numbers of circulating tumor cells (CTCs) are linked to a poor prognosis (Cristofanilli et al., 2005; Trapp et al., 2019). Because CTCs can collect in the sinus and develop lymph node metastasis, the nearby lymph nodes are typically the initial site of metastases, a critical prognostic indication for relapse and poor survival. The tumor cells may then spread to other organs, resulting in distant metastasis (Scully et al., 2012) (Fig. 2.2). Bones and lungs are among the most common sites for BC metastases. Tumor cells' released cytokines/chemokines and growth factors are thought to cause responsive alterations that promote tumor seeding (Psaila et al., 2007; Mohme et al., 2017). When contrasted to native, benign sentinel lymphatic nodes, tumor-containing lymphatic nodes have a different immune cell makeup (greater Treg concentration) and shape (lymph node expansion and lymphangiogenesis) (Núñez et al., 2020). They additionally have a distinct cytokine profile and fewer CD83[+] DCs (Poindexter et al., 2004). Furthermore, as compared to primary tumors, BC metastasis had a significantly reduced TIL count and an elevation in immunosuppressive genetic profile (Szekely et al., 2018). The differences in immunological microenvironments between primary lesions and metastatic sites may play a role in advanced disease therapeutic failure. Tumor seeding may be aided by resident cells in metastatic areas. TGF-β (Sharma et al., 2015) is thought to suppress DC growth in lung metastasis when alveolar macrophages are preconditioned with BC cells. In a mouse breast metastasis model, alveolar macrophage

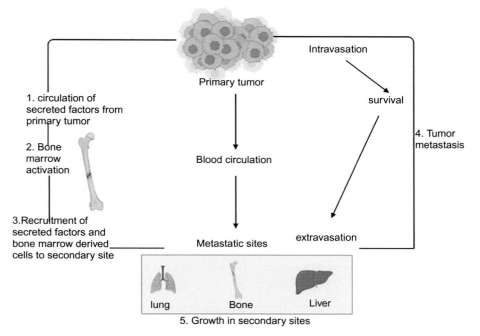

Fig. 2.2 The role of the microenvironment in the metastatic process.

reduction boosted the DC density and subsequently Th1 IFN-γ production (Sharma et al., 2015; Mehraj et al., 2021). Metastatic tumor cells in bone metastasis can trigger osteoclasts to resorb bone via direct and paracrine pathways, producing survival and growth hormones that aid tumor spread while also causing bone destruction. Metastatic tumor cells improved osteolysis with receptor activation of NF-κB ligand (RANKL) and parathyroid hormone-related peptide (PTHrP). TGF-β, which stimulates tumor cell growth and perpetuates the osteolytic vicious cycle, is released by osteoclastic bone resorption (Käkönen and Mundy, 2003; Hofbauer et al., 2021).

2.2 Important players in the breast cancer immune microenvironment

Many tumor characteristics, including persistent proliferative signaling, evasion of immune clearance, stimulation of angiogenesis, and stimulation of invasion and metastases, are shaped by a complicated and dynamic interaction between tumor cells and cells in the TME throughout the formation of a tumor (Hanahan and Weinberg, 2011). Furthermore, various kinds of immune cells have diverse functions in cancerous cells, forming a powerful crosstalk network. Tumor immunoediting by adaptive and innate

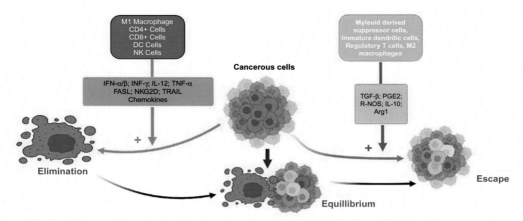

Fig. 2.3 Phases of cancer immunoediting: The elimination phase, in which mainly tumor cells are identified and killed by the immune system; the equilibrium phase, in which a balance among immune and cancer cells is established; and finally, the escape phase, in which immunosuppressive circuits are activated, allowing immunoescape and cancerous cells development.

immunological cell types, which make up the so-called BC Immune Microenvironment (BCIM), is a major predictor of tumor growth in this way. Immunoediting is a three-step dynamic mechanism that includes Elimination, Equilibrium, and Escape (Fig. 2.3). The initial step, also known as immunosurveillance, involves the destruction of altered cells by competent immune systems capable of activating a powerful immune reaction to cancer. Tumor cells that escaped the Elimination stage and immune cells shape each other in the Equilibrium stage. With a selective stress on cancer cells, that are genetically unstable and constantly changing, equilibrium is created between both the tumor as well as the immune systems. Tumor cell variations that have developed resistance to elimination, progress to the Escape stage, which is the final step, where the tumor develops and becomes clinically noticeable. The formation of an immunosuppressive TME is a hallmark of the Escape phase. Immune cells can be distinguished into two broad categories depending on the action of the adaptive and innate immune cellular groups participating in the immunoediting processes: immunostimulating and immunosuppressive cells (Fig. 2.4). The existence of these cells in the BCIM has been shown to have a major effect on BC development and therapeutic responsiveness, according to multiple lines of findings. Immunostimulating immune cells, like lymphocytes, macrophages, natural killer (NK) cells, DCs, eosinophils, and innate lymphoid cells (ILCs) infiltrate tumors and help to regulate malignancies (Gatti-Mays et al., 2019). Immunosuppressive cells, like mast cells (MCs), type 2-polarized tumor-associated macrophages (M2-like TAMs), myeloid-derived suppressor cells (MDSCs), and regulatory T cells (Tregs) that are integrally linked with the emerging TME; inhibit the anticancer immune reaction produced

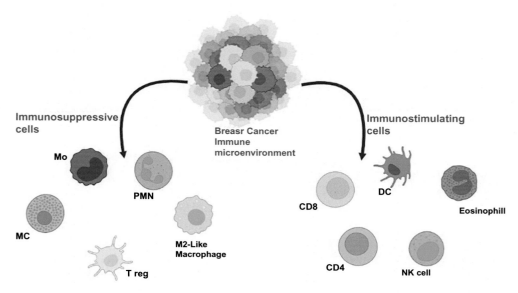

Fig. 2.4 Major players in immune breast TME.

by these cells. Therefore, we briefly outline the primary immunological subpopulations seen in BCIM, with a focus on their effect on the outcome of BC patients.

2.3 Immunosuppressive cells

2.3.1 Myeloid-derived suppressor cells

MDSCs are a diverse group of myeloid cell precursors and progenitors. The chemical processes underlying their emergence and genuine origins were still being debated, with various ideas being suggested. Immature myeloid cells (IMCs) may undergo urgent myelopoiesis, which involves them growing in the bone marrow and then moving to the periphery in response to an elevated need for myeloid cells. Otherwise, IMCs can proliferate by becoming functionally effective MDSCs outside of the medullary system (into organs like the spleen). Alternatively, in pathologic circumstances such as malignancy, on the other hand, numerous chemokines, cytokines, and factors released by the tumor, like granulocytic–colony stimulating factor (G-CSF), CC-chemokine ligand (CCL)2, C-X-C-chemokine ligand (CXCL)2, CCL5, CXCL12 and CXCL5. Two types of MDSCs had been discovered depending on the cell surface antigen presentation: polymorphonuclear or granulocytic MDSCs (PMN-MDSCs) and monocytic MDSCs (M-MDSCs). M-MDSCs and PMN-MDSCs are recognized in mice by phenotypes of $CD11b^+$-$Ly6G^+Ly6C^{low}$ and $CD11b^+Ly6G^+Ly6C^{high}$, correspondingly, but PMN-MDSCs are $CD11b^+CD14CD15^+CD33^+$ cells in humans, whereas M-MDSCs are $CD11b^+CD14^+$

CD15CD33$^+$HLADR/low cells. Some theories propose that M-MDSCs and PMN-MDSCs are monocytes and granulocytes that have been stimulated and reprogrammed (Mehraj et al., 2022b; Millrud et al., 2017). It is presently broadly acknowledged that all these IMCs can stimulate drastic anergy in effector immunologic cells, recruit Tregs, as well as promote M2-like TAM polarization, resulting in a powerful immunosuppressive TME, by secreting numerous soluble factors and also producing reactive nitrogen and oxygen species (RON and ROS). By the presence of the immunological CD40 stimulatory receptor on their membrane, MDSCs are capable to attract Tregs at the tumor sites. MDSCs use a similar receptor to limit the proliferation of T cells effectively by binding to the ligand CD40L present on the cell membrane of T cells (Pan et al., 2010; Law et al., 2020). MDSCs have lately been linked to the establishment of the premetastatic microenvironment, angiogenesis activation, as well as the cancer stem cells (CSCs) maintenance, a small group of cells involved in tumor initiation and metastasis (Bruno et al., 2019; Peng et al., 2019; Wang et al., 2019). MDSCs have been linked to a worse outcome in BC individuals in many investigations. Kumar et al. found that MDSCs are significantly abundant in triple-negative BC (TNBC) patient samples than in non-TNBC patient samples (Kumar et al., 2018; Mir et al., 2022a,b, c,d), adding that elevated levels of circulating MDSCs are associated with liver and bone metastasis as well as greater levels of circulatory tumor cells (Bergenfelz et al., 2020). In conclusion, numerous lines of research imply that MDSCs have a negative role in the course of BC.

2.3.2 Mast cells

MCs are innate immune cells that have inflammatory chemicals contained in cytoplasmic granules that are discharged when they come into contact with the right stimulus, like IgE, which plays a key function in allergic disorders (Frieri et al., 2015). In exposure to infections like bacteria, helminths, and viruses, MC degranulation has been shown to be helpful. They are found in a variety of locations inside the body and, alike other immunological cells, develop inside the bone marrow from hematopoietic stem cell progenitors that can mature into committed MC progenitors which move to peripheral regions via the blood circulation to finish maturation (Dahlin and Hallgren, 2015). Tissue microenvironmental substances influence their development, proliferation, and survival, with stem cell factor (SCF), a ligand for the c-Kit receptor, and interleukin (IL)-3 being the best-studied (Ito et al., 2012). Additional endogenous cytokines that assist in MC development and functioning include IL-6, IL-4, IL-9, IL-33, IL-10, NGF, and TGF-β (Dahlin and Hallgren, 2015). By establishing an adenosine-mediated immunosuppressive interaction with Tregs and MDSCs and restricting adaptive immunity via IL-13 production, MCs can dampen the antitumor immune reaction within the tumor (Varricchi et al., 2017, Gorzalczany and Sagi-Eisenberg, 2019). The role of MCs in BC prediction, on the other hand, is still highly debated. By the production of a wide range of bioactive substances found within cytoplasmic granules, MCs may have both anti- and pro-tumor actions. In vitro and in vivo experiments show that MCs promote tumor growth and metastases via promoting lymph and blood vessel production (Aponte-López et al., 2018). Samoszuk et al. found that depleting MCs with imatinib increased tumor growth in a mouse model of BC, indicating that MCs have an antitumor function (Samoszuk and Corwin, 2003). Another study links MCs to a higher rate of survival and a better outcome (Dabiri et al., 2004). Rajput et al. observed that stroma MCs were associated with a positive prognosis in a population of 4.444 aggressive BC individuals with such a long-term follow-up (Rajput et al., 2008).

2.3.3 M2-like tumor-associated macrophages

Macrophages are myeloid cells that have reached the end of their differentiation and are important for the removal of infectious pathogens as well as the control of the adaptive defense. Over many decades, bone marrow-derived precursors and blood monocyte precursors were thought to be the source of macrophages, which then differentiated into mature cells when implanted into organs (Kielbassa et al., 2019). Numerous genetic tracking findings, on the other hand, demonstrated that numerous macrophage communities arise from embryonic progenitors and can self-renew by localized multiplication of adult, differentiating cells. The functional and morphological properties of macrophages have been shown to be influenced by the tissue microenvironment (Mowat et al., 2017). Macrophages are divided into two categories depending on their essential functions: anti-tumoral M1-like polarized TAMs and protumoral M2-like polarized TAMs (Jayasingam et al., 2020). Both M1- and M2-like TAMs in the mouse model are identified by the expression of markers like F4/80, CD11b, and colony-stimulating factor-1 receptor (CSF-1R), as well as reduced expression levels of the myeloid distinction marker Gr1, while as MHC class II glycoproteins as well as CD206 have been used to differentiate M1- and M2-like TAMs, in both. The presence of CD312, CD68, CD115, and additional markers distinguishes macrophages in humans. TAM traits, on the other hand, are significantly more complicated, and classifying them into binary phases isn't entirely accurate (Cassetta et al., 2019). Many studies have found that the protumoral M2-like TAMs in the BCIM serve a key function in carcinogenesis and metastatic development through nonimmune and immunological processes. TAMs play a nonimmune role by secreting a variety of angiogenic variables, like VEGF, PDGF, as well as bFGF, which enhance angiogenesis inside of the tumor, as well as signaling factors like matrix metalloproteinases (MMPs), EGF, CCL18, CCL2, and macrophage (M)-CSF, which stimulates tumor cell epithelial–mesenchymal transition, metastasis, and invasion (Petty and Yang, 2017; Anfray et al., 2019). The invasion of protumoral M2-like TAM leads to the establishment of an immunosuppressive milieu. For instance, it has been shown that

M2-like TAMs decrease CD8[+] T-cell activities via immediate transcriptional suppression of genes that encode active mediators like perforins, cytotoxins, and granzymes via the release of TGF-β and IL-10 (Thomas and Massagué, 2005; Anfray et al., 2019). M2 TAMs also lessen the TME of the amino acids tryptophan and arginine, which are required for T and NK cell growth and maintenance, due to their elevated production levels of enzymes like indoleamine 2,3-dioxygenase 1 and arginase 1 (ARG1) (Petty and Yang, 2017). M2-TAMs have been shown in many investigations to be a poor predictive factor in BC (DeNardo et al., 2011; Choi et al., 2018). M2-TAMs, in particular, stimulate tumor development by enabling inflammation, immunosuppression, and angiogenesis, as well as tumor relapse following traditional therapy (Chanmee et al., 2014). In a study of 47 BC individuals, CSF1-expressing TAMs were significantly linked to more malignant tumors (Cassetta et al., 2019). Furthermore, in the luminal and TNBC subgroups of BC, signs of M2-like TAM invasion are associated with a poor outcome (Segovia-Mendoza and Morales-Montor, 2019).

2.3.4 FoxP3[+] regulatory T cells

Tregs are a specialized subset of T cells that suppresses the immune system. Fifty percent of the CD4[+] CD25[+] T-cell subset is Tregs. Moreover, in a large sample of BC individuals, a low proportion of CD8[+] FoxP3[+] Tregs has been discovered (Bates et al., 2006). Tregs are important in the control of T- and B-cell stimulation and the balance of cytotoxic cells in a physiologic sense (Gasteiger et al., 2013). FoxP3-expressing CD25[+] CD4[+] Tregs are produced in the healthy thymus. Certain naive CD25[-] CD4[+] T cells in the periphery also may develop into Tregs, in contrast to these normally existing Tregs (Sakaguchi, 2003). Tregs play a role in a variety of diseases, including autoimmunity, transplant rejections, and hypersensitivity. They may impair the host immunological system via a variety of pathways including cell–cell interactions and the generation of immunosuppressive cytokines and compounds, hence supporting tumor development and aggression. Tregs seem to play a key role in altering cancer's immunological regulation and are hence linked to poor patient outcomes (Paluskievicz et al., 2019).

Tregs had been found in higher quantities in the peripheral circulation of BC patients than in normal controls, and their propensity to invade tumors rises with tumor stage and is linked to a poor outcome in aggressive BCs (Martinez et al., 2019). Many cytokines and chemokines released by tumor cells, CAFs, or immunosuppressive cells attract Tregs toward the TME. CXCL12 is among the most important variables in Treg activation. Hypoxia increases the production of CXCL12 and its receptors CXCR4, which may help enhance Treg recruitment in breast cancers, particularly in the basal-like type (Yan et al., 2011). Treg invasion pattern has been linked to poor outcomes in luminal, TNBC, and HER2[+] BC, according to the distinct BC subgroups (Qayoom et al., 2021). Peng et al. also found that individuals with a lower FoxP3[+]/CD8[+] ratio had a greater disease-free survival (DFS) vs individuals with a greater FoxP3$^+$/CD8$^+$ ratio in a population of 122 individuals with initial invasive ductal BC (Peng et al., 2019). Furthermore, Treg reduction causes a robust CD4$^+$ T-cell or interferon (IFN)-dependent antitumor reaction in metastatic primary malignancies (Martinez et al., 2019). Interferon (IFN) produced from CD4$^+$ cells, but neither from CD8$^+$ nor NK cells is accountable for the tumoricidal actions in PyMT breast tumors following Treg reduction (Bos et al., 2013).

2.3.5 Antitumor immune cells

2.3.5.1 Tumor-infiltrating T cells

All lymphocytic cells invading tumor cells are classified as TILs. Cytotoxic (CD8$^+$) and helper (CD4$^+$) T-lymphocytes (Pruneri et al., 2018), which are important components of adaptive defense, are of specific importance. CD8$^+$ T-lymphocytes constitute the most important effector cells in the fight against cancer, as they recognize tumor-associated and neoantigens expressed on MHC class I molecules (Peng et al., 2019). Through the release of a variety of effector mediators, CD4$^+$ T cells may assist and aid the CD8$^+$ T cells throughout the antitumor reaction. TIL densities in tumors are critical for the formation of significant immune responses to cancer in general. Furthermore, a large body of evidence supports a link between TILs and a good outcome for BC sufferers. For instance, both in HER2-positive and TNBC BC individuals administered with neoadjuvant chemotherapy, a higher proportion of TILs are associated with improved DFS and overall survival (OS). Interestingly, in luminal A cancers, this association is completely lost (Denkert et al., 2018). More research is required to explain the fundamental mechanisms, which could be linked to the immune system impacts of hormonal therapy in Luminal A individuals.

2.3.6 Natural killer cells

NK cells develop in the bone marrow via a common lymphoid precursor, and then migrate to main and secondary lymphoid organs, and also nonlymphoid tissues such as the liver, lungs, and peripheral circulation (Spitzer et al., 2017; Hu et al., 2019). In mice, they are characterized as CD3NK1.1$^+$; however in humans, they are divided into two subgroups: cytokine-producing CD56^{bright}CD16 cells and cytotoxic CD56^{dim}CD16$^+$ cells. Depending on the presence of CD27 and CD11b membrane markers, NK cells in humans and mice may be classified into four subgroups, each correlating to a distinct maturation phase. These two markers are not expressed by immature NK cells. They gain CD27 expression and later CD11b during maturation, and completely developed NK in peripheral circulation are virtually all CD11b$^+$CD27$^-$. These various phenotypes correlate to various cell activities, with CD27$^+$ cells having the greatest capacity to release cytokines and CD11b$^+$ CD27 cells having the highest cytolytic activity (Chiossone et al., 2009; Fu et al., 2011). NK cells are critical in tumor immunosurveillance because they generate cytolytic granules comprising perforins and granzymes, which kill a number of altered cells. NK cells, unlike T lymphocytes, are involved in innate defense and may identify and kill changed cells without being sensitized. Furthermore, NK cells identify and kill cells that lack MHC class I, a process that most cancer cells, including BCSCs, use to avoid T-cell-mediated cytotoxic death (Tallerico et al., 2017; Melaiu et al., 2019). NK cells are the highly powerful immune cell subgroup for controlling and finally eliminating aberrant cells for such reasons. Tumor invading NK cells in BC and many other solid types of cancer, on the other hand, have a $CD56^{bright}CD16$ pattern, produce invasion-associated molecules, i.e., MMP9, and, like decidual NK cells, have proangiogenic capabilities via the production of angiogenin and VEGF (Levi et al., 2015; Bruno et al., 2018). VEGF promotes the multiplication of immunosuppressive cells, limits T-cell recruitment, and increases T-cell exhaustion through inducing tumor vascular development and immunosuppressive activities (Lapeyre-Prost et al., 2017). Surprisingly, the balance of pro- and antitumor action provided by NK cells varies with the BC subgroup. Moreover, in ER^+ and $HER2^+$ BC individuals, a high number of NK cells have been linked to a favorable outcome, but NK cell invasion has been linked to a bad prognosis in TNBC patient populations (Segovia-Mendoza and Morales-Montor, 2019).

2.3.7 Innate lymphoid cells

ILCs comprise immune system cells that are derived from the basic lymphoid progenitors and are T cells' innate equivalents. In effect, ILCs are thought to represent the evolutionary progenitors of T cells that lack antigen-specific receptors (Eberl et al., 2015a). These are tissue-specific cells that are relatively infrequent in the peripheral circulation (Mjösberg and Spits, 2016; Ebbo et al., 2017), capable of detecting changes in the localized milieu via cytokine receptors generated after tissue injury and triggering adaptive response (Bando and Colonna, 2016). ILCs are categorized into three main classes—ILC1s, ILC2s, and ILC3s—depending on their characteristics, like cytokine profile and morphology, even though two other immune cell categories, lymphoid tissue activator cells, and NK cells, are also classified in the ILC category (Vivier et al., 2018).

ILC1s release IFNγ in response to IL-15, IL-12, and IL-18, which are critical for inducing macrophages and DCs to remove pathogens and presenting antigens. ILC2s release type-2 cytokines including IL-9, IL-5, IL-13, and amphiregulin, that aid in the evacuation of helminth parasites and the healing of injured tissues, while also enhancing Treg activities and hence immunosuppression (Zaiss et al., 2015). ILC3s, on the other hand, produce IL-17 and IL-22, which increase epithelium and goblet cell secretions of antimicrobial peptides and mucus, respectively (Eberl et al., 2015b; Panda and Colonna, 2019).

ILC1s, like NK cells, are IL-15-dependent and have significant cytotoxic activity toward cancer cells, inhibiting tumor progression in a preclinical breast model (Dadi et al., 2016; Bruchard and Ghiringhelli, 2019). Irshad et al. in BC discovered an unusual method by which ILC3s and stroma cells can promote lymphatic metastases by modifying the localized chemokine environment. CCL21-dependent ILC3 entry into the main tumor enhances CXCL13 synthesis by stroma cells, which stimulates the synthesis of the cancerous cells' motile factor RANKL, which causes cell migration, in a preclinical murine model of TNBC (Irshad et al., 2017). Furthermore, in BC, ILC2s were found to be more abundant in tumors than in normal tissue, and IL-33 injection accelerated tumor growth and the progression of lung and liver metastasis in the 4T1 BC cell line, which was linked to enhanced intratumoral infiltration of ILCs, MDSCs, and Tregs (Jovanovic et al., 2014; Salimi et al., 2018). However, the true role of ILCs in cancer disease is still a point of discussion.

2.3.8 Dendritic cells

DCs are antigen-presenting cells with the ability to coordinate effective antitumor response while also participating in immunological tolerance. Standard DCs in mice and humans are derived from common DC progenitors in the bone marrow. DCs are divided into two types: monocytic DCs (mDCs), which are CD11c$^+$, and plasmacytoid DCs (pDCs), which are CD11c-negative (Robinson et al., 1999; Kini Bailur et al., 2016). DCs stimulate T lymphocyte stimulation and antitumor immune reactions by presenting antigens to T cells on class I and II MHC molecules, as well as by providing immunomodulatory messages via cell–cell interactions and soluble substances (Wculek et al., 2020).

Since the TME stimulates the synthesis of IL-10 and TGF-β, which lead to the growth of Tregs, DCs had been detected in various types of cancer, including BC, in which they are inadequately active and usually malfunctioning (Wculek et al., 2020). Furthermore, an elevation in DCs has been seen in the peripheral circulation of BC individuals, with larger numbers in HER2-positive BC individuals relative to HER2-negative BC patient populations, implying variations among the various BC subgroups (Paek et al., 2019). Nevertheless, the predictive value of DCs in patients is unknown, owing to their diverse composition, which includes cells at various stages of growth. Holsb and Olsen investigated gene expression patterns in patients' blood samples and looked for genes or gene sets linked to the likelihood of BC metastases in recent research about malignant BC. pDC-related genes and pathways were found among the major genes (Holsbø and Olsen, 2020). This was following some other investigation, which found that pDC infiltration in initial regional BC is associated with a poor prognosis, implying that they play a role in tumor growth (Treilleux et al., 2004). The findings of Bailur and coworkers, on the other hand, reveal a link between circulating pDCs with

BC survival (Treilleux et al., 2004). Likewise, in node-positive tumors, the existence of CD83$^+$ mature intratumor DCs were highly linked with improved patient survival (Iwamoto et al., 2003), while CD11c$^+$ mDCs were favorably associated with T-cell invasion and OS in TNBC individuals (Lee et al., 2018). Furthermore, various subgroups of DCs may have variable treatment response associations in BC individuals. Furthermore, in BC individuals whose tumors exhibited a favorable histological response after neoadjuvant docetaxel and capecitabine followed by cyclophosphamide and adriamycin, there was a considerable rise in DCs in the blood. Nevertheless, in both original breast cancers and advanced axillary lymph nodes, the appearance of fewer intratumoral CD1a$^+$ DCs had no meaningful connection with treatment response (Kaewkangsadan et al., 2017; Badr et al., 2020).

2.3.9 Eosinophils

Eosinophils are inherent immunity cells that play a role in the host's defensive immunological response to helminths, viruses (Samarasinghe et al., 2017), and microbial infections (Yousefi et al., 2008). Human eosinophils are made up of CD34$^+$CD117$^+$ pluripotent HSCs that mature in the bone marrow before being released into the blood circulation (Johnston and Bryce, 2017).

Eosinophils are defined as CD11b$^+$Gr-1loF4/80$^+$ cells morphologically. Eosinophils can be recognized from macrophages by their high granularity, absence of MHC-II expression, and appearance of the sialic acid-binding lectin Siglec-F (Carretero et al., 2015).

Eosinophils are drawn from the bloodstream to inflammatory sites, where, after stimulation, they can discharge a variety of inflammatory mediators, including cationic proteins (major basic proteins (MBP), eosinophil peroxide (EPX), eosinophil cationic proteins (ECP), and eosinophil-derived neurotoxin (EDN)), which are distinctive to eosinophil's and thus are essential in the defense toward parasitic infections (Woschnagg et al., 2009). Notably, IL-5, along with IL-3 and GM-CSF, is required for the development of human eosinophils inside the bone marrow (Varricchi et al., 2016) and regulates their survivability by NF-B-induced Bcl-xL, which prevents apoptosis.

Even though the processes behind eosinophil invasion into tumors are unknown, a piece of evidence suggests the existence of eosinophils in the TME of various human hematological and solid malignancies, including BC (Harbaum et al., 2015; Zhang et al., 2017; Onesti et al., 2020). Nevertheless, recent evidence suggests that the IL-1α, high mobility group box 1 protein (HMGB1), and IL-33 may all play a role in eosinophil infiltration (Bertheloot and Latz, 2017). Furthermore, macrophages and MCs can attract eosinophils by producing VEGFs (Detoraki et al., 2009; Granata et al., 2010) and/or releasing prostaglandin D2 (PGD2) and histamine via activating the chemoattractant-homologous receptors expressed on Th2 cells (CRTH2) (Schratl et al., 2007) and the H4 receptor (Capelo et al., 2016), correspondingly.

Eosinophils regulate various leukocytes within TME, including DCs, T cells, macrophages, and NK cells. They can attract and stimulate T cells using CCL5, CXCL9, and CXCL10, recruit NK cells using IL-12, IL-6, and CXCL10 and induce M1 polarization utilizing IL-12, IL-6, and CXCL10 (Simon et al., 2019). While data for a protumorigenic function for eosinophils has been revealed, the existence of eosinophils in the tumor or circulation is a good predictive factor for most malignancies (Varricchi et al., 2018). Eosinophils seem to be antitumorigenic in BC individuals, boosting their capacity to fight disease (Ownby et al., 1983). BC individuals with eosinophil levels lower than 55/mm^3 have a considerably increased risk of recurring disease than individuals with typical or higher eosinophil levels, according to Ownby et al. (Ownby et al., 1983). Furthermore, a trial of 930 BC patients found an advantage in BC-specific survival and duration to therapeutic failure when the relative eosinophil count (REC) was high vs low (Onesti et al., 2020).

2.4 Tumor microenvironment-targeting therapeutics

The PD-1/PD-L1 inhibitors constitute a significant advancement in medications that work effectively on the TME in breast carcinoma. PD-1/PD-L1 inhibitors are recommended for the management of advanced breast carcinoma and increase cytotoxic T-cell responses to cancerous cells (Vaddepally et al., 2020). Another immunological checkpoint being studied is cytotoxic T-lymphocyte antigen-4 (CTLA-4) (Gaynor et al., 2022; Mir et al., 2022e,f,g,h). CTLA-4 inhibitors mostly comprise ipilimumab and tremelimumab, both of which had been licensed for various cancers including non-small cell lung carcinoma, melanoma, and severe kidney cancer. CTLA-4 inhibitors are typically used in conjunction with various therapies in breast carcinoma, such as hormonal therapy and anti-PD-1/PD-L1 inhibitors. CTLA-4 inhibition was found to boost immunological activity in patients, although its therapeutic value has yet to be proven (Vonderheide et al., 2010). In breast cancer, several promising immune checkpoint approaches, such as T-cell immunoglobulin and mucin domain-containing protein 3 (TIM-3), lymphocyte activation gene-3 (LAG-3), B7-H3, and T-cell immunoglobulin and ITIM domain (TIGIT), are currently in clinical trials or in developing stage. Additional immunotherapeutic approaches are also being studied in clinical trials (Waldman et al., 2020). Adoptive T-cell immunotherapy utilizing chimeric antigen receptors is one technique (CAR-T). Hematological malignancies have been effectively treated using CAR-T-cell therapy. The restricted number of identified breast tumor neoantigens which could be targeted, as well as the immunosuppressive TME, has hampered their application in breast malignancy. Despite this, phase II investigations are being conducted on some possible neoantigen targets. To counteract the immunosuppressive TME,

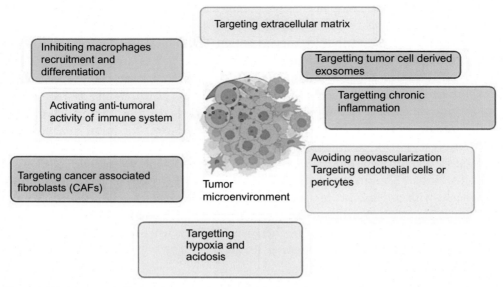

Fig. 2.5 Various cancer therapy strategies that target the tumor microenvironment.

chimeric CAR-T cells attacking both antigenic targets as well as other TME cells are being produced (Dees et al., 2020) (Fig. 2.5).

CAF, in addition to immune cells, could be used as targeted therapy. Attacking ECM elements, ECM remodeling proteins, and CAF through its membrane markers or signaling pathways were all used in CAF-related treatment. ECM molecules supplied tumor cells with structural cues and assistance. CAF produces hyaluronan (HA), a major glycosaminoglycan that plays an important role in stromal fibrosis and tumor growth (McCarthy et al., 2018). To dissolve intratumoral ECM, a pegylated synthetic human hyaluronidase has been created and is in treatment trials (Doherty et al., 2018; Mir et al., 2022a,b,c,d). Furthermore, substantial preclinical evidence supports the therapy's effectiveness in targeting ECM restructuring enzymes (MMP and LOX inhibitors) (Radisky et al., 2017; Saatci et al., 2020). Depleting CAF through its surface marker is an additional CAF-targeting strategy. Antibodies had been produced targeting FAP, a key CAF biomarker (Hofheinz et al., 2003; Mir et al., 2022a,b,c,d).

The use of hyperbaric oxygenation and oxygen therapies to overcome tumor hypoxia and restore radio and chemo-sensitivity is also a focus on targeting TME. The results have been disappointing so far, but improved new drugs are currently being tested in clinical trials (Graham and Unger, 2018; Mir et al., 2022a,b,c,d,e,f,g,h). In phase III randomized clinical investigation for bone metastases, denosumab, an Mab targeting RANKL that inhibits osteoclast activity, outperformed bisphosphonates in postponing skeletal associated events (Stopeck et al., 2010).

Table 2.2 Treatments that target the tumor microenvironment.

Targets	Therapeutic efficacies
Cytotoxic T-lymphocyte antigen-4 inhibitors	T-cell cytotoxicity against cancer cells is restored
PD-1/PD-L1 inhibitors	
T-cell immunoglobulin and ITIM domain	
T-cell immunoglobulin and mucin domain-containing protein-3	Possible checkpoint targets
B7-H3	
Lymphocyte activation gene-3	
Chimeric antigen receptor T-cell therapy	Antitumor T cells that have been genetically modified to recognize tumor antigens
Lysyl oxidase inhibitor	Extracellular matrix remodeling enzyme inhibitors
Matrix metalloproteinases inhibitors	
Pegylated recombinant human hyaluronidase	Degrades intratumoral ECM
VEGF inhibitors	Inhibits tumor angiogenesis
RANK ligand inhibitor	Osteoclast function is inhibited, causing skeletal events to be delayed

Hormone receptors play a role in the TME in the modulation of several immune cells (Mir et al., 2022e,f,g,h). Hormonal suppression reduced tumor-infiltrating Tregs (Generali et al., 2009) while increasing circulatory NK-cell function. Trastuzumab therapy reduces CCL2 synthesis in animals (Triulzi et al., 2018), while increasing PD-1 expression, overall immune cell, or follicular helper T-cell infiltration in HER2-positive breast carcinoma patients (Varadan et al., 2016) (Table 2.2).

2.5 Summary

Breast cancer continues to be a major clinical problem, with significant death and also treatment-related complications. Novel therapeutic methods are desperately needed, particularly in the context of metastatic illness, where results remain poor. The BC microenvironment is a diverse combination of cells, molecules secreted by them, and the Matrix wherein they live. Changes in the microenvironment are increasingly identified at important stages of tumor growth, making them appealing therapeutic targets. Stromal cells, infiltrating immune cells, and the metastatic milieu are all continually being identified as potential targets. Hundreds of clinical investigations are presently exploring various drug combinations, with some promising results. Nevertheless, we should keep in mind that BC as well as its TME is a highly diverse and dynamic complex that evolves as a consequence of complicated interplay among cancerous cells, immune cells, or cancer medications. This means that a better comprehending of the role of the inherent and adaptive immunologic reactions in individual BCs, as well as a better comprehension of the TME characteristics that most affect immunotherapeutic efficacy, are required to create more efficient treatment options that can concurrently stimulate antitumor immune function while also preventing tumor immune escape processes. Cancerous cells eradication and TME regulation are anticipated to be combined in the future strategy for breast cancer treatment, resulting in a greater synergistic impact.

References

Aboussekhra, A., 2011. Role of cancer-associated fibroblasts in breast cancer development and prognosis. Int. J. Dev. Biol. 55 (7-8-9), 841–849.

Agata, Y., Kawasaki, A., Nishimura, H., Ishida, Y., Tsubat, T., Yagita, H., Honjo, T., 1996. Expression of the PD-1 antigen on the surface of stimulated mouse T and B lymphocytes. Int. Immunol. 8 (5), 765–772.

Anfray, C., Ummarino, A., Torres Andon, F., Allavena, P., 2019. Current strategies to target tumor-associated-macrophages to improve anti-tumor immune responses. Cell 9 (1), 46.

Aponte-López, A., Fuentes-Pananá, E.M., Cortes-Muñoz, D., Muñoz-Cruz, S., 2018. Mast cell, the neglected member of the tumor microenvironment: role in breast cancer. J. Immunol. Res. 2018.

Aspord, C., Pedroza-Gonzalez, A., Gallegos, M., Tindle, S., Burton, E.C., Su, D., Marches, F., Banchereau, J., Palucka, A.K., 2007. Breast cancer instructs dendritic cells to prime interleukin 13–secreting CD4 + T cells that facilitate tumor development. J. Exp. Med. 204 (5), 1037–1047.

Badr, N.M., Berditchevski, F., Shaaban, A.M., 2020. The immune microenvironment in breast carcinoma: predictive and prognostic role in the neoadjuvant setting. Pathobiology 87 (2), 61–74.

Bando, J.K., Colonna, M., 2016. Innate lymphoid cell function in the context of adaptive immunity. Nat. Immunol. 17 (7), 783–789.

Bartoschek, M., Oskolkov, N., Bocci, M., Lövrot, J., Larsson, C., Sommarin, M., Madsen, C.D., Lindgren, D., Pekar, G., Karlsson, G., 2018. Spatially and functionally distinct subclasses of breast cancer-associated fibroblasts revealed by single cell RNA sequencing. Nat. Commun. 9 (1), 1–13.

Bates, G.J., Fox, S.B., Han, C., Leek, R.D., Garcia, J.F., Harris, A.L., Banham, A.H., 2006. Quantification of regulatory T cells enables the identification of high-risk breast cancer patients and those at risk of late relapse. J. Clin. Oncol. 24 (34), 5373–5380.

Beguinot, M., Dauplat, M.-M., Kwiatkowski, F., Lebouedec, G., Tixier, L., Pomel, C., Penault-Llorca, F., Radosevic-Robin, N., 2018. Analysis of tumour-infiltrating lymphocytes reveals two new biologically different subgroups of breast ductal carcinoma in situ. BMC Cancer 18 (1), 1–10.

Bergenfelz, C., Roxå, A., Mehmeti, M., Leandersson, K., Larsson, A.-M., 2020. Clinical relevance of systemic monocytic-MDSCs in patients with metastatic breast cancer. Cancer Immunol. Immunother. 69 (3), 435–448.

Bertheloot, D., Latz, E., 2017. HMGB1, IL-1α, IL-33 and S100 proteins: dual-function alarmins. Cell. Mol. Immunol. 14 (1), 43–64.

Bertucci, F., Gonçalves, A., 2017. Immunotherapy in breast cancer: the emerging role of PD-1 and PD-L1. Curr. Oncol. Rep. 19 (10), 1–11.

Biswas, S.K., Mantovani, A., 2010. Macrophage plasticity and interaction with lymphocyte subsets: cancer as a paradigm. Nat. Immunol. 11 (10), 889–896.

Borst, J., Ahrends, T., Bąbała, N., Melief, C.J.M., Kastenmüller, W., 2018. CD4 + T cell help in cancer immunology and immunotherapy. Nat. Rev. Immunol. 18 (10), 635–647.

Bos, P.D., Plitas, G., Rudra, D., Lee, S.Y., Rudensky, A.Y., 2013. Transient regulatory T cell ablation deters oncogene-driven breast cancer and enhances radiotherapy. J. Exp. Med. 210 (11), 2435–2466.

Bruchard, M., Ghiringhelli, F., 2019. Deciphering the roles of innate lymphoid cells in cancer. Front. Immunol. 10, 656.

Bruno, A., Bassani, B., D'Urso, D.G., Pitaku, I., Cassinotti, E., Pelosi, G., Boni, L., Dominioni, L., Noonan, D.M., Mortara, L., 2018. Angiogenin and the MMP9-TIMP2 axis are up-regulated in proangiogenic, decidual NK-like cells from patients with colorectal cancer. FASEB J. 32 (10), 5365–5377.

Bruno, A., Mortara, L., Baci, D., Noonan, D.M., Albini, A., 2019. Myeloid derived suppressor cells interactions with natural killer cells and pro-angiogenic activities: roles in tumor progression. Front. Immunol. 10, 771.

Buchanan, C.F., Szot, C.S., Wilson, T.D., Akman, S., Metheny-Barlow, L.J., Robertson, J.L., Freeman, J.-W., Rylander, M.N., 2012. Cross-talk between endothelial and breast cancer cells regulates reciprocal expression of angiogenic factors in vitro. J. Cell. Biochem. 113 (4), 1142–1151.

Burugu, S., Asleh-Aburaya, K., Nielsen, T.O., 2017. Immune infiltrates in the breast cancer microenvironment: detection, characterization and clinical implication. Breast Cancer 24 (1), 3–15.

Cao, Y., Dong, L., He, Y., Hu, X., Hou, Y., Dong, Y., Yang, Q., Bi, Y., Liu, G., 2021. The direct and indirect regulation of follicular T helper cell differentiation in inflammation and cancer. J. Cell. Physiol. 236 (8), 5466–5481.

Capelo, R., Lehmann, C., Ahmad, K., Snodgrass, R., Diehl, O., Ringleb, J., Flamand, N., Weigert, A., Stark, H., Steinhilber, D., 2016. Cellular analysis of the histamine H4 receptor in human myeloid cells. Biochem. Pharmacol. 103, 74–84.

Carretero, R., Sektioglu, I.M., Garbi, N., Salgado, O.C., Beckhove, P., Hämmerling, G.J., 2015. Eosinophils orchestrate cancer rejection by normalizing tumor vessels and enhancing infiltration of CD8+ T cells. Nat. Immunol. 16 (6), 609–617.

Cassetta, L., Fragkogianni, S., Sims, A.H., Swierczak, A., Forrester, L.M., Zhang, H., Soong, D.Y.H., Cotechini, T., Anur, P., Lin, E.Y., 2019. Human tumor-associated macrophage and monocyte transcriptional landscapes reveal cancer-specific reprogramming, biomarkers, and therapeutic targets. Cancer Cell 35 (4), 588–602.

Chanmee, T., Ontong, P., Konno, K., Itano, N., 2014. Tumor-associated macrophages as major players in the tumor microenvironment. Cancer 6 (3), 1670–1690.

Chiossone, L., Chaix, J., Fuseri, N., Roth, C., Vivier, E., Walzer, T., 2009. Maturation of mouse NK cells is a 4-stage developmental program. Blood 113 (22), 5488–5496.

Choi, J., Gyamfi, J., Jang, H., Koo, J.S., 2018. The role of tumor-associated macrophage in breast cancer biology. Histol. Histopathol. 33 (2), 133–145.

Coleman, R.E., Gregory, W., Marshall, H., Wilson, C., Holen, I., 2013. The metastatic microenvironment of breast cancer: clinical implications. Breast 22, S50–S56.

Costa, A., Kieffer, Y., Scholer-Dahirel, A., Pelon, F., Bourachot, B., Cardon, M., Sirven, P., Magagna, I., Fuhrmann, L., Bernard, C., 2018. Fibroblast heterogeneity and immunosuppressive environment in human breast cancer. Cancer Cell 33 (3), 463–479.

Cox, T.R., Erler, J.T., 2014. Molecular pathways: connecting fibrosis and solid tumor metastasis. Clin. Cancer Res. 20 (14), 3637–3643.

Cristofanilli, M., Hayes, D.F., Budd, G.T., Ellis, M.J., Stopeck, A., Reuben, J.M., Doyle, G.V., Matera, J., Allard, W.J., Miller, M.C., 2005. Circulating tumor cells: a novel prognostic factor for newly diagnosed metastatic breast cancer. J. Clin. Oncol. 23 (7), 1420–1430.

Dabiri, S., Huntsman, D., Makretsov, N., Cheang, M., Gilks, B., Badjik, C., Gelmon, K., Chia, S., Hayes, M., 2004. The presence of stromal mast cells identifies a subset of invasive breast cancers with a favorable prognosis. Mod. Pathol. 17 (6), 690–695.

Dadi, S., Chhangawala, S., Whitlock, B.M., Franklin, R.A., Luo, C.T., Oh, S.A., Toure, A., Pritykin, Y., Huse, M., Leslie, C.S., 2016. Cancer immunosurveillance by tissue-resident innate lymphoid cells and innate-like T cells. Cell 164 (3), 365–377.

Dahlin, J.S., Hallgren, J., 2015. Mast cell progenitors: origin, development and migration to tissues. Mol. Immunol. 63 (1), 9–17.

Datta, J., Rosemblit, C., Berk, E., Showalter, L., Namjoshi, P., Mick, R., Lee, K.P., Brod, A.M., Yang, R.-L., Kelz, R.R., 2015. Progressive loss of anti-HER2 CD4+ T-helper type 1 response in breast tumorigenesis and the potential for immune restoration. Oncoimmunology 4 (10), e1022301.

Dees, S., Ganesan, R., Singh, S., Grewal, I.S., 2020. Emerging CAR-T cell therapy for the treatment of triple-negative breast cancer. Mol. Cancer Ther. 19 (12), 2409–2421.

DeNardo, D.G., Brennan, D.J., Rexhepaj, E., Ruffell, B., Shiao, S.L., Madden, S.F., Gallagher, W.M., Wadhwani, N., Keil, S.D., Junaid, S.A., 2011. Leukocyte complexity predicts breast cancer survival and functionally regulates response to chemotherapy. Cancer Discov. 1 (1), 54–67.

Denkert, C., von Minckwitz, G., Darb-Esfahani, S., Lederer, B., Heppner, B.I., Weber, K.E., Budczies, J., Huober, J., Klauschen, F., Furlanetto, J., 2018. Tumour-infiltrating lymphocytes and prognosis in different subtypes of breast cancer: a pooled analysis of 3771 patients treated with neoadjuvant therapy. Lancet Oncol. 19 (1), 40–50.

Detoraki, A., Staiano, R.I., Granata, F., Giannattasio, G., Prevete, N., de Paulis, A., Ribatti, D., Genovese, A., Triggiani, M., Marone, G., 2009. Vascular endothelial growth factors synthesized by human lung mast cells exert angiogenic effects. J. Allergy Clin. Immunol. 123 (5), 1142–1149.

Doherty, G.J., Tempero, M., Corrie, P.G., 2018. HALO-109-301: a phase III trial of PEGPH20 (with gemcitabine and nab-paclitaxel) in hyaluronic acid-high stage IV pancreatic cancer. Future Oncol. 14 (1), 13–22.

Dong, H., Zhu, G., Tamada, K., Chen, L., 1999. B7-H1, a third member of the B7 family, co-stimulates T-cell proliferation and interleukin-10 secretion. Nat. Med. 5 (12), 1365–1369.

Ebbo, M., Crinier, A., Vély, F., Vivier, E., 2017. Innate lymphoid cells: major players in inflammatory diseases. Nat. Rev. Immunol. 17 (11), 665–678.

Eberl, G., Colonna, M., Di Santo, J.P., McKenzie, A.N.J., 2015a. Innate lymphoid cells: a new paradigm in immunology. Science 348 (6237), aaa6566.

Eberl, G., Di Santo, J.P., Vivier, E., 2015b. The brave new world of innate lymphoid cells. Nat. Immunol. 16 (1), 1–5.

Fridlender, Z.G., Sun, J., Kim, S., Kapoor, V., Cheng, G., Ling, L., Worthen, G.S., Albelda, S.M., 2009. Polarization of tumor-associated neutrophil phenotype by TGF-β:"N1" versus "N2" TAN. Cancer Cell 16 (3), 183–194.

Frieri, M., Kumar, K., Boutin, A., 2015. Role of mast cells in trauma and neuroinflammation in allergy immunology. Ann. Allergy Asthma Immunol. 115 (3), 172–177.

Fu, B., Wang, F., Sun, R., Ling, B., Tian, Z., Wei, H., 2011. CD11b and CD27 reflect distinct population and functional specialization in human natural killer cells. Immunology 133 (3), 350–359.

Garaud, S., Buisseret, L., Solinas, C., Gu-Trantien, C., de Wind, A., Van den Eynden, G., Naveaux, C., Lodewyckx, J.-N., Boisson, A., Duvillier, H., 2019. Tumor-infiltrating B cells signal functional humoral immune responses in breast cancer. JCI Insight 4 (18).

Gasteiger, G., Hemmers, S., Firth, M.A., Le Floc'h, A., Huse, M., Sun, J.C., Rudensky, A.Y., 2013. IL-2–dependent tuning of NK cell sensitivity for target cells is controlled by regulatory T cells. J. Exp. Med. 210 (6), 1167–1178.

Gatti-Mays, M.E., Balko, J.M., Gameiro, S.R., Bear, H.D., Prabhakaran, S., Fukui, J., Disis, M.L., Nanda, R., Gulley, J.L., Kalinsky, K., 2019. If we build it they will come: targeting the immune response to breast cancer. NPJ Breast Cancer 5 (1), 1–13.

Gaynor, N., Crown, J., Collins, D.M., 2022. Immune checkpoint inhibitors: key trials and an emerging role in breast cancer. Semin. Cancer Biol. 79, 44–57. Elsevier.

Generali, D., Bates, G., Berruti, A., Brizzi, M.P., Campo, L., Bonardi, S., Bersiga, A., Allevi, G., Milani, M., Aguggini, S., 2009. Immunomodulation of FOXP3 + regulatory T cells by the aromatase inhibitor letrozole in breast cancer patients. Clin. Cancer Res. 15 (3), 1046–1051.

Giorello, M.B., Borzone, F.R., Labovsky, V., Piccioni, F.V., Chasseing, N.A., 2021. Cancer-associated fibroblasts in the breast tumor microenvironment. J. Mammary Gland Biol. Neoplasia 26 (2), 135–155.

Gorzalczany, Y., Sagi-Eisenberg, R., 2019. Role of mast cell-derived adenosine in cancer. Int. J. Mol. Sci. 20 (10), 2603.

Graham, K., Unger, E., 2018. Overcoming tumor hypoxia as a barrier to radiotherapy, chemotherapy and immunotherapy in cancer treatment. Int. J. Nanomedicine 13, 6049.

Granata, F., Frattini, A., Loffredo, S., Staiano, R.I., Petraroli, A., Ribatti, D., Oslund, R., Gelb, M.H., Lambeau, G., Marone, G., 2010. Production of vascular endothelial growth factors from human lung macrophages induced by group IIA and group X secreted phospholipases A2. J. Immunol. 184 (9), 5232–5241.

Gu-Trantien, C., Loi, S., Garaud, S., Equeter, C., Libin, M., De Wind, A., Ravoet, M., Le Buanec, H., Sibille, C., Manfouo-Foutsop, G., 2013. CD4 + follicular helper T cell infiltration predicts breast cancer survival. J. Clin. Invest. 123 (7), 2873–2892.

Hanahan, D., Weinberg, R., 2011. Hallmarks of cancer: the next generation. Cell 144, 646–674.

Harbaum, L., Pollheimer, M.J., Kornprat, P., Lindtner, R.A., Bokemeyer, C., Langner, C., 2015. Peritumoral eosinophils predict recurrence in colorectal cancer. Mod. Pathol. 28 (3), 403–413.

Harimoto, H., Shimizu, M., Nakagawa, Y., Nakatsuka, K., Wakabayashi, A., Sakamoto, C., Takahashi, H., 2013. Inactivation of tumor-specific CD8 + CTLs by tumor-infiltrating tolerogenic dendritic cells. Immunol. Cell Biol. 91 (9), 545–555.

Hawsawi, N.M., Ghebeh, H., Hendrayani, S.-F., Tulbah, A., Al-Eid, M., Al-Tweigeri, T., Ajarim, D., Alaiya, A., Dermime, S., Aboussekhra, A., 2008. Breast carcinoma–associated fibroblasts and their counterparts display neoplastic-specific changes. Cancer Res. 68 (8), 2717–2725.

Hofbauer, L.C., Bozec, A., Rauner, M., Jakob, F., Perner, S., Pantel, K., 2021. Novel approaches to target the microenvironment of bone metastasis. Nat. Rev. Clin. Oncol. 18 (8), 488–505.

Hofheinz, R.D., Al-Batran, S.E., Hartmann, F., Hartung, G., Jäger, D., Renner, C., Tanswell, P., Kunz, U., Amelsberg, A., Kuthan, H., Stehle, G., 2003. Stromal antigen targeting by a humanised monoclonal antibody: an early phase II trial of sibrotuzumab in patients with metastatic colorectal cancer. Onkologie 26 (1), 44–48.

Hollern, D.P., Xu, N., Thennavan, A., Glodowski, C., Garcia-Recio, S., Mott, K.R., He, X., Garay, J.P., Carey-Ewend, K., Marron, D., 2019. B cells and T follicular helper cells mediate response to checkpoint inhibitors in high mutation burden mouse models of breast cancer. Cell 179 (5), 1191–1206.

Holsbø, E., Olsen, K.S., 2020. Metastatic breast cancer and pre-diagnostic blood gene expression profiles—the Norwegian women and cancer (NOWAC) post-genome cohort. Front. Oncol. 10, 2277.

Hu, W.L., Wang, G.S., Huang, D.S., Sui, M.H., Xu, Y.B., 2019. Cancer immunotherapy based on natural killer cells: current progress and new opportunities. Front. Immunol. 10, 1205.

Irshad, S., Flores-Borja, F., Lawler, K., Monypenny, J., Evans, R., Male, V., Gordon, P., Cheung, A., Gazinska, P., Noor, F., 2017. RORγt+ innate lymphoid cells promote lymph node metastasis of breast cancers. Cancer Res. 77 (5), 1083–1096.

Ito, T., Smrž, D., Jung, M.-Y., Bandara, G., Desai, A., Smržová, Š., Kuehn, H.S., Beaven, M.A., Metcalfe, D.D., Gilfillan, A.M., 2012. Stem cell factor programs the mast cell activation phenotype. J. Immunol. 188 (11), 5428–5437.

Iwamoto, M., Shinohara, H., Miyamoto, A., Okuzawa, M., Mabuchi, H., Nohara, T., Gon, G., Toyoda, M., Tanigawa, N., 2003. Prognostic value of tumor-infiltrating dendritic cells expressing CD83 in human breast carcinomas. Int. J. Cancer 104 (1), 92–97.

Jayasingam, S.D., Citartan, M., Thang, T.H., Mat Zin, A.A., Ang, K.C., Ch'ng, E.S., 2020. Evaluating the polarization of tumor-associated macrophages into M1 and M2 phenotypes in human cancer tissue: technicalities and challenges in routine clinical practice. Front. Oncol. 9, 1512.

Jemal, A., Siegel, R., Xu, J., Ward, E., 2010. Cancer statistics, 2010. CA Cancer J. Clin. 60 (5), 277–300.

Johnston, L.K., Bryce, P.J., 2017. Understanding interleukin 33 and its roles in eosinophil development. Front. Med. 4, 51.

Jovanovic, I.P., Pejnovic, N.N., Radosavljevic, G.D., Pantic, J.M., Milovanovic, M.Z., Arsenijevic, N.N., Lukic, M.L., 2014. Interleukin-33/ST2 axis promotes breast cancer growth and metastases by facilitating intratumoral accumulation of immunosuppressive and innate lymphoid cells. Int. J. Cancer 134 (7), 1669–1682.

Kaewkangsadan, V., Verma, C., Eremin, J.M., Cowley, G., Ilyas, M., Satthaporn, S., Eremin, O., 2017. The differential contribution of the innate immune system to a good pathological response in the breast and axillary lymph nodes induced by neoadjuvant chemotherapy in women with large and locally advanced breast cancers. J. Immunol. Res. 2017.

Käkönen, S.M., Mundy, G.R., 2003. Mechanisms of osteolytic bone metastases in breast carcinoma. Cancer 97 (S3), 834–839.

Karasar, P., Esendagli, G., 2014. T helper responses are maintained by basal-like breast cancer cells and confer to immune modulation via upregulation of PD-1 ligands. Breast Cancer Res. Treat. 145 (3), 605–614.

Kielbassa, K., Vegna, S., Ramirez, C., Akkari, L., 2019. Understanding the origin and diversity of macrophages to tailor their targeting in solid cancers. Front. Immunol., 2215.

Kini Bailur, J., Gueckel, B., Pawelec, G., 2016. Prognostic impact of high levels of circulating plasmacytoid dendritic cells in breast cancer. J. Transl. Med. 14 (1), 1–10.

Kinoshita, J., Kitamura, K., Kabashima, A., Saeki, H., Tanaka, S., Sugimachi, K., 2001. Clinical significance of vascular endothelial growth factor-C (VEGF-C) in breast cancer. Breast Cancer Res. Treat. 66 (2), 159–164.

Kumar, S., Wilkes, D.W., Samuel, N., Blanco, M.A., Nayak, A., Alicea-Torres, K., Gluck, C., Sinha, S., Gabrilovich, D., Chakrabarti, R., 2018. ΔNp63-driven recruitment of myeloid-derived suppressor cells promotes metastasis in triple-negative breast cancer. J. Clin. Invest. 128 (11), 5095–5109.

Lapeyre-Prost, A., Terme, M., Pernot, S., Pointet, A.L., Voron, T., Tartour, E., Taieb, J., 2017. International review of cell and molecular biology. Int. Rev. Cell Mol. Biol. 330, 295–342.

Lardner, A., 2001. The effects of extracellular pH on immune function. J. Leukoc. Biol. 69 (4), 522–530.

Law, A.M.K., Valdes-Mora, F., Gallego-Ortega, D., 2020. Myeloid-derived suppressor cells as a therapeutic target for cancer. Cell 9 (3), 561.

Lee, H., Lee, H.J., Song, I.H., Bang, W.S., Heo, S.H., Gong, G., Park, I.A., 2018. CD11c-positive dendritic cells in triple-negative breast Cancer. In Vivo 32 (6), 1561–1569.

Levi, I., Amsalem, H., Nissan, A., Darash-Yahana, M., Peretz, T., Mandelboim, O., Rachmilewitz, J., 2015. Characterization of tumor infiltrating natural killer cell subset. Oncotarget 6 (15), 13835.

Longatto Filho, A., Lopes, J.M., Schmitt, F.C., 2010. Angiogenesis and breast cancer. J. Oncol. 2010.

Maller, O., Martinson, H., Schedin, P., 2010. Extracellular matrix composition reveals complex and dynamic stromal-epithelial interactions in the mammary gland. J. Mammary Gland Biol. Neoplasia 15 (3), 301–318.

Martinez, L.M., Robila, V., Clark, N.M., Du, W., Idowu, M.O., Rutkowski, M.R., Bos, P.D., 2019. Regulatory T cells control the switch from in situ to invasive breast cancer. Front. Immunol., 1942.

Mauri, C., Bosma, A., 2012. Immune regulatory function of B cells. Annu. Rev. Immunol. 30, 221–241.

McCarthy, J.B., El-Ashry, D., Turley, E.A., 2018. Hyaluronan, cancer-associated fibroblasts and the tumor microenvironment in malignant progression. Front. Cell Dev. Biol. 6, 48.

Mehraj, U., Qayoom, H., Mir, M.A., 2021. Prognostic significance and targeting tumor-associated macrophages in cancer: new insights and future perspectives. Breast Cancer 28 (3), 539–555.

Mehraj, U., Aisha, S., Sofi, S., Mir, M.A., 2022a. Expression pattern and prognostic significance of baculoviral inhibitor of apoptosis repeat-containing 5 (BIRC5) in breast cancer: a comprehensive analysis. Adv. Cancer Biol. Metastasis, 100037.

Mehraj, U., Mushtaq, U., Mir, M.A., Saleem, A., Macha, M.A., Lone, M.N., Hamid, A., Zargar, M.A., Ahmad, S.M., Wani, N.A., 2022b. Chemokines in triple-negative breast cancer heterogeneity: new challenges for clinical implications. Semin. Cancer Biol. Elsevier.

Melaiu, O., Lucarini, V., Cifaldi, L., Fruci, D., 2019. Influence of the tumor microenvironment on NK cell function in solid tumors. Front. Immunol. 10, 3038.

Millrud, C.R., Bergenfelz, C., Leandersson, K., 2017. On the origin of myeloid-derived suppressor cells. Oncotarget 8 (2), 3649.

Mir, M.A., Agrewala, J.N., 2008. Signaling through CD80: an approach for treating lymphomas. Expert Opin. Ther. Targets 12 (8), 969–979.

Mir, M.A., Mehraj, U., 2019. Double-crosser of the immune system: macrophages in tumor progression and metastasis. Curr. Immunol. Rev. 15 (2), 172–184.

Mir, M.A., Qayoom, H., Mehraj, U., Nisar, S., Bhat, B., Wani, N.A., 2020. Targeting different pathways using novel combination therapy in triple negative breast cancer. Curr. Cancer Drug Targets 20 (8), 586–602.

Mir, M., Jan, S., Mehraj, U., 2022a. Conventional Adjuvant Chemotherapy in Combination With Surgery, Radiotherapy and Other Specific Targets. Chapter-4, Elsevier, pp. 145–176.

Mir, M., Jan, S., Mehraj, U., 2022b. Current therapeutics and treatment options in TNBC. Chapter-3, Elsevier, pp. 73–144.

Mir, M., Jan, S., Mehraj, U., 2022c. Novel biomarkers in triple-negative breast cancer-role and perspective (Chapter-2). Elsevier, pp. 36–72.

Mir, M., Jan, S., Mehraj, U., 2022d. Triple-Negative breast Cancer – An Aggressive Subtype of Breast Cancer. Elsevier, pp. 1–35.

Mir, M., Sofi, S., Qayoom, H., 2022e. Different drug delivery approaches in combinational therapy in TNBC. Chapter-8, Elsevier, pp. 278–311.

Mir, M., Sofi, S., Qayoom, H., 2022f. The interplay of immunotherapy, chemotherapy, and targeted therapy in tripple negative breast cancer (TNBC). Chapter-6, Elsevier, pp. 201–244.

Mir, M., Sofi, S., Qayoom, H., 2022g. Role of immune system in triple negative breast cancer (TNBC). Chapter-5, Elsevier, pp. 177–201.

Mir, M., Sofi, S., Qayoom, H., 2022h. Targeting biologically specific molecules in triple negative breast cancer (TNBC). Chapter-7, Elsevier, pp. 245–277.

Mjösberg, J., Spits, H., 2016. Human innate lymphoid cells. J. Allergy Clin. Immunol. 138 (5), 1265–1276.

Mohme, M., Riethdorf, S., Pantel, K., 2017. Circulating and disseminated tumour cells—mechanisms of immune surveillance and escape. Nat. Rev. Clin. Oncol. 14 (3), 155–167.

Mowat, A.M., Scott, C.L., Bain, C.C., 2017. Barrier-tissue macrophages: functional adaptation to environmental challenges. Nat. Med. 23 (11), 1258–1270.

Muenst, S., Soysal, S.D., Gao, F., Obermann, E.C., Oertli, D., Gillanders, W.E., 2013. The presence of programmed death 1 (PD-1)-positive tumor-infiltrating lymphocytes is associated with poor prognosis in human breast cancer. Breast Cancer Res. Treat. 139 (3), 667–676.

Nelson, B.H., 2010. CD20+ B cells: the other tumor-infiltrating lymphocytes. J. Immunol. 185 (9), 4977–4982.

Núñez, N.G., Tosello Boari, J., Ramos, R.N., Richer, W., Cagnard, N., Anderfuhren, C.D., Niborski, L.-L., Bigot, J., Meseure, D., De La Rochere, P., 2020. Tumor invasion in draining lymph nodes is associated with Treg accumulation in breast cancer patients. Nat. Commun. 11 (1), 1–15.

Ohms, M., Möller, S., Laskay, T., 2020. An attempt to polarize human neutrophils toward N1 and N2 phenotypes in vitro. Front. Immunol., 532.

Olkhanud, P.B., Damdinsuren, B., Bodogai, M., Gress, R.E., Sen, R., Wejksza, K., Malchinkhuu, E., Wersto, R.P., Biragyn, A., 2011. Tumor-evoked regulatory B cells promote breast cancer metastasis by converting resting CD4+ T cells to T-regulatory cells. Cancer Res. 71 (10), 3505–3515.

Onesti, C.E., Josse, C., Boulet, D., Thiry, J., Beaumecker, B., Bours, V., Jerusalem, G., 2020. Blood eosinophilic relative count is prognostic for breast cancer and associated with the presence of tumor at diagnosis and at time of relapse. Onco. Targets. Ther. 9 (1), 1761176.

Ownby, H.E., Roi, L.D., Isenberg, R.R., Brennan, M.J., 1983. Peripheral lymphocyte and eosinophil counts as indicators of prognosis in primary breast cancer. Cancer 52 (1), 126–130.

Paek, S.H., Kim, H.G., Lee, J.W., Woo, J., Kwon, H., Kim, J.B., Lim, W., Kim, J.R., Moon, B.-I., Paik, N.-S., 2019. Circulating plasmacytoid and myeloid dendritic cells in breast cancer patients: a pilot study. J. Breast Cancer 22 (1), 29–37.

Pallegar, N.K., Christian, S.L., 2020. Adipocytes in the tumour microenvironment. In: Tumor Microenvironment. Springer, pp. 1–13.

Paluskievicz, C.M., Cao, X., Abdi, R., Zheng, P., Liu, Y., Bromberg, J.S., 2019. T regulatory cells and priming the suppressive tumor microenvironment. Front. Immunol., 2453.

Pan, P.-Y., Ma, G., Weber, K.J., Ozao-Choy, J., Wang, G., Yin, B., Divino, C.M., Chen, S.-H., 2010. Immune stimulatory receptor CD40 is required for T-cell suppression and T regulatory cell activation mediated by myeloid-derived suppressor cells in cancer. Cancer Res. 70 (1), 99–108.

Panda, S.K., Colonna, M., 2019. Innate lymphoid cells in mucosal immunity. Front. Immunol. 10, 861.

Pardoll, D.M., 2012. The blockade of immune checkpoints in cancer immunotherapy. Nat. Rev. Cancer 12 (4), 252–264.

Peng, G.-L., Li, L., Guo, Y.-W., Yu, P., Yin, X.-J., Wang, S., Liu, C.-P., 2019. CD8+ cytotoxic and FoxP3+ regulatory T lymphocytes serve as prognostic factors in breast cancer. Am. J. Transl. Res. 11 (8), 5039.

Pereira, E.R., Jones, D., Jung, K., Padera, T.P., 2022. The lymph node microenvironment and its role in the progression of metastatic cancer. Semin. Cell Dev. Biol. 38, 98–105. Elsevier.

Petty, A.J., Yang, Y., 2017. Tumor-associated macrophages: implications in cancer immunotherapy. Immunotherapy 9 (3), 289–302.

Poindexter, N.J., Sahin, A., Hunt, K.K., Grimm, E.A., 2004. Analysis of dendritic cells in tumor-free and tumor-containing sentinel lymph nodes from patients with breast cancer. Breast Cancer Res. 6 (4), 1–8.

Polyak, K., 2007. Breast cancer: origins and evolution. J. Clin. Invest. 117 (11), 3155–3163.

Pruneri, G., Vingiani, A., Denkert, C., 2018. Tumor infiltrating lymphocytes in early breast cancer. Breast 37, 207–214.

Psaila, B., Kaplan, R.N., Port, E.R., Lyden, D., 2007. Priming the 'soil' for breast cancer metastasis: the pre-metastatic niche. Breast Dis. 26 (1), 65–74.

Qayoom, H., Mehraj, U., Aisha, S., Sofi, S., Mir, M.A., 2021. Integrating Immunotherapy with Chemotherapy: A New Approach to Drug Repurposing. Intech Open.

Qiu, S.-Q., Waaijer, S.J.H., Zwager, M.C., de Vries, E.G.E., van der Vegt, B., Schröder, C.P., 2018. Tumor-associated macrophages in breast cancer: innocent bystander or important player? Cancer Treat. Rev. 70, 178–189.

Radisky, E.S., Raeeszadeh-Sarmazdeh, M., Radisky, D.C., 2017. Therapeutic potential of matrix metalloproteinase inhibition in breast cancer. J. Cell. Biochem. 118 (11), 3531–3548.

Rajput, A.B., Turbin, D.A., Cheang, M.C.U., Voduc, D.K., Leung, S., Gelmon, K.A., Gilks, C.B., Huntsman, D.G., 2008. Stromal mast cells in invasive breast cancer are a marker of favourable prognosis: a study of 4,444 cases. Breast Cancer Res. Treat. 107 (2), 249–257.

Ritter, A., Friemel, A., Fornoff, F., Adjan, M., Solbach, C., Yuan, J., Louwen, F., 2015. Characterization of adipose-derived stem cells from subcutaneous and visceral adipose tissues and their function in breast cancer cells. Oncotarget 6 (33), 34475.

Robinson, S.P., Patterson, S., English, N., Davies, D., Knight, S.C., Reid, C.D.L., 1999. Human peripheral blood contains two distinct lineages of dendritic cells. Eur. J. Immunol. 29 (9), 2769–2778.

Rotte, A., 2019. Combination of CTLA-4 and PD-1 blockers for treatment of cancer. J. Exp. Clin. Cancer Res. 38 (1), 1–12.

Ruffell, B., Au, A., Rugo, H.S., Esserman, L.J., Hwang, E.S., Coussens, L.M., 2012. Leukocyte composition of human breast cancer. Proc. Natl. Acad. Sci. U. S. A. 109 (8), 2796–2801.

Rundqvist, H., Johnson, R.S., 2013. Tumour oxygenation: implications for breast cancer prognosis. J. Intern. Med. 274 (2), 105–112.

Saatci, O., Kaymak, A., Raza, U., Ersan, P.G., Akbulut, O., Banister, C.E., Sikirzhytski, V., Tokat, U.M., Aykut, G., Ansari, S.A., 2020. Targeting lysyl oxidase (LOX) overcomes chemotherapy resistance in triple negative breast cancer. Nat. Commun. 11 (1), 1–17.

Sakaguchi, S., 2003. The origin of FOXP3-expressing CD4+ regulatory T cells: thymus or periphery. J. Clin. Invest. 112 (9), 1310–1312.

Salgado, R., Denkert, C., Demaria, S., Sirtaine, N., Klauschen, F., Pruneri, G., Wienert, S., Van den Eynden, G., Baehner, F.L., Pénault-Llorca, F., 2015. The evaluation of tumor-infiltrating lymphocytes (TILs) in breast cancer: recommendations by an International TILs Working Group 2014. Ann. Oncol. 26 (2), 259–271.

Salimi, M., Wang, R., Yao, X., Li, X., Wang, X., Hu, Y., Chang, X., Fan, P., Dong, T., Ogg, G., 2018. Activated innate lymphoid cell populations accumulate in human tumour tissues. BMC Cancer 18 (1), 1–10.

Samarasinghe, A.E., Melo, R.C.N., Duan, S., LeMessurier, K.S., Liedmann, S., Surman, S.L., Lee, J.J., Hurwitz, J.L., Thomas, P.G., McCullers, J.A., 2017. Eosinophils promote antiviral immunity in mice infected with influenza A virus. J. Immunol. 198 (8), 3214–3226.

Samoszuk, M., Corwin, M.A., 2003. Acceleration of tumor growth and peri-tumoral blood clotting by imatinib mesylate (Gleevec™). Int. J. Cancer 106 (5), 647–652.

Schratl, P., Royer, J.F., Kostenis, E., Ulven, T., Sturm, E.M., Waldhoer, M., Hoefler, G., Schuligoi, R., Lippe, I.T., Peskar, B.A., 2007. The role of the prostaglandin D2 receptor, DP, in eosinophil trafficking. J. Immunol. 179 (7), 4792–4799.

Scully, O.J., Bay, B.H., Yip, G., Yu, Y., 2012. Breast cancer metastasis. Cancer Genomics Proteomics 9 (5), 311–320.

Segovia-Mendoza, M., Morales-Montor, J., 2019. Immune tumor microenvironment in breast cancer and the participation of estrogen and its receptors in cancer physiopathology. Front. Immunol. 10, 348.

Seow, D.Y.B., Yeong, J.P.S., Lim, J.X., Chia, N., Lim, J.C.T., Ong, C.C.H., Tan, P.H., Iqbal, J., 2020. Tertiary lymphoid structures and associated plasma cells play an important role in the biology of triple-negative breast cancers. Breast Cancer Res. Treat. 180 (2), 369–377.

Sharma, S.K., Chintala, N.K., Vadrevu, S.K., Patel, J., Karbowniczek, M., Markiewski, M.M., 2015. Pulmonary alveolar macrophages contribute to the premetastatic niche by suppressing antitumor T cell responses in the lungs. J. Immunol. 194 (11), 5529–5538.

Simon, S., Utikal, J., Umansky, V., 2019. Opposing roles of eosinophils in cancer. Cancer Immunol. Immunother. 68 (5), 823–833.

Skobe, M., Hawighorst, T., Jackson, D.G., Prevo, R., Janes, L., Velasco, P., Riccardi, L., Alitalo, K., Claffey, K., Detmar, M., 2001. Induction of tumor lymphangiogenesis by VEGF-C promotes breast cancer metastasis. Nat. Med. 7 (2), 192–198.

Soysal, S.D., Tzankov, A., Muenst, S.E., 2015. Role of the tumor microenvironment in breast cancer. Pathobiology 82 (3–4), 142–152.

Spitzer, M.H., Carmi, Y., Reticker-Flynn, N.E., Kwek, S.S., Madhireddy, D., Martins, M.M., Gherardini, P.F., Prestwood, T.R., Chabon, J., Bendall, S.C., 2017. Systemic immunity is required for effective cancer immunotherapy. Cell 168 (3), 487–502.

Stakheyeva, M., Riabov, V., Mitrofanova, I., Litviakov, N., Choynzonov, E., Cherdyntseva, N., Kzhyshkowska, J., 2017. Role of the immune component of tumor microenvironment in the efficiency of cancer treatment: perspectives for the personalized therapy. Curr. Pharm. Des. 23 (32), 4807–4826.

Stopeck, A.T., Lipton, A., Body, J.-J., Steger, G.G., Tonkin, K., De Boer, R.H., Lichinitser, M., Fujiwara, Y., Yardley, D.A., Viniegra, M., 2010. Denosumab compared with zoledronic acid for the treatment of bone metastases in patients with advanced breast cancer: a randomized, double-blind study. J. Clin. Oncol. 28 (35), 5132–5139.

Szekely, B., Bossuyt, V., Li, X., Wali, V.B., Patwardhan, G.A., Frederick, C., Silber, A., Park, T., Harigopal, M., Pelekanou, V., 2018. Immunological differences between primary and metastatic breast cancer. Ann. Oncol. 29 (11), 2232–2239.

Tallerico, R., Conti, L., Lanzardo, S., Sottile, R., Garofalo, C., Wagner, A.K., Johansson, M.H., Cristiani, C.M., Kärre, K., Carbone, E., 2017. NK cells control breast cancer and related cancer stem cell hematological spread. Onco. Targets. Ther. 6 (3), e1284718.

Thomas, D.A., Massagué, J., 2005. TGF-β directly targets cytotoxic T cell functions during tumor evasion of immune surveillance. Cancer Cell 8 (5), 369–380.

Trapp, E., Janni, W., Schindlbeck, C., Jückstock, J., Andergassen, U., de Gregorio, A., Alunni-Fabbroni, M., Tzschaschel, M., Polasik, A., Koch, J.G., Friedl, T.W.P., Fasching, P.A., Haeberle, L., Fehm, T., Schneeweiss, A., Beckmann, M.W., Pantel, K., Mueller, V., Rack, B., Scholz, C., 2019. Presence of circulating tumor cells in high-risk early breast cancer during follow-up and prognosis. J. Natl. Cancer Inst. 111 (4), 380–387.

Treilleux, I., Blay, J.-Y., Bendriss-Vemare, N., Ray-Coquard, I., Bachelot, T., Guastalla, J.-P., Bremond, A., Goddard, S., Pin, J.-J., Barthelemy-Dubois, C., 2004. Dendritic cell infiltration and prognosis of early stage breast cancer. Clin. Cancer Res. 10 (22), 7466–7474.

Triulzi, T., Forte, L., Regondi, V., Di Modica, M., Ghirelli, C., Carcangiu, M.L., 2018. HER2 signaling regulates the tumor immune microenvironment and trastuzumab efficacy. Onco. Targets. Ther. 8 (1), e1512942. 2019.

Tsang, J., Au, W.-L., Lo, K.-Y., Ni, Y.-B., Hlaing, T., Hu, J., Chan, S.-K., Chan, K.-F., Cheung, S.-Y., Tse, G.M., 2017. PD-L1 expression and tumor infiltrating PD-1 + lymphocytes associated with outcome in HER2 + breast cancer patients. Breast Cancer Res. Treat. 162 (1), 19–30.

Vaddepally, R.K., Kharel, P., Pandey, R., Garje, R., Chandra, A.B., 2020. Review of indications of FDA-approved immune checkpoint inhibitors per NCCN guidelines with the level of evidence. Cancer 12 (3), 738.

Varadan, V., Gilmore, H., Miskimen, K.L.S., Tuck, D., Parsai, S., Awadallah, A., Krop, I.E., Winer, E.P., Bossuyt, V., Somlo, G., 2016. Immune signatures following single dose trastuzumab predict pathologic response to preoperativetrastuzumab and chemotherapy in HER2-positive early breast cancer. Clin. Cancer Res. 22 (13), 3249–3259.

Varricchi, G., Bagnasco, D., Borriello, F., Heffler, E., Canonica, G.W., 2016. Interleukin-5 pathway inhibition in the treatment of eosinophilic respiratory disorders: evidence and unmet needs. Curr. Opin. Allergy Clin. Immunol. 16 (2), 186.

Varricchi, G., Galdiero, M.R., Loffredo, S., Marone, G., Iannone, R., Marone, G., Granata, F., 2017. Are mast cells MASTers in cancer? Front. Immunol. 8, 424.

Varricchi, G., Galdiero, M.R., Loffredo, S., Lucarini, V., Marone, G., Mattei, F., Marone, G., Schiavoni, G., 2018. Eosinophils: the unsung heroes in cancer? Onco. Targets. Ther. 7 (2), e1393134.

Vaupel, P., Briest, S., Höckel, M., 2002. Hypoxia in breast cancer: pathogenesis, characterization and biological/therapeutic implications. Wien. Med. Wochenschr. 152 (13–14), 334–342.

Vivier, E., Artis, D., Colonna, M., Diefenbach, A., Di Santo, J.P., Eberl, G., Koyasu, S., Locksley, R.M., McKenzie, A.N.J., Mebius, R.E., 2018. Innate lymphoid cells: 10 years on. Cell 174 (5), 1054–1066.

Vonderheide, R.H., LoRusso, P.M., Khalil, M., Gartner, E.M., Khaira, D., Soulieres, D., Dorazio, P., Trosko, J.A., Rüter, J., Mariani, G.L., 2010. Tremelimumab in combination with exemestane in patients with advanced breast cancer and treatment-associated modulation of inducible costimulator expression on patient T cells. Clin. Cancer Res. 16 (13), 3485–3494.

Wachstein, J., Tischer, S., Figueiredo, C., Limbourg, A., Falk, C., Immenschuh, S., Blasczyk, R., Eiz-Vesper, B., 2012. HSP70 enhances immunosuppressive function of CD4+ CD25+ FoxP3+ T regulatory cells and cytotoxicity in CD4+ CD25− T cells. PLoS One 7 (12), e51747.

Waldman, A.D., Fritz, J.M., Lenardo, M.J., 2020. A guide to cancer immunotherapy: from T cell basic science to clinical practice. Nat. Rev. Immunol. 20 (11), 651–668.

Wang, Y., Ding, Y., Guo, N., Wang, S., 2019. MDSCs: key criminals of tumor pre-metastatic niche formation. Front. Immunol. 172.

Wculek, S.K., Cueto, F.J., Mujal, A.M., Melero, I., Krummel, M.F., Sancho, D., 2020. Dendritic cells in cancer immunology and immunotherapy. Nat. Rev. Immunol. 20 (1), 7–24.

Webb, B.A., Chimenti, M., Jacobson, M.P., Barber, D.L., 2011. Dysregulated pH: a perfect storm for cancer progression. Nat. Rev. Cancer 11 (9), 671–677.

Wittrup, K.D., 2017. Antitumor antibodies can drive therapeutic T cell responses. Trends Cancer 3 (9), 615–620.

Woschnagg, C., Rubin, J., Venge, P., 2009. Eosinophil cationic protein (ECP) is processed during secretion. J. Immunol. 183 (6), 3949–3954.

Wu, L., Saxena, S., Awaji, M., Singh, R.K., 2019. Tumor-associated neutrophils in cancer: going pro. Cancer 11 (4), 564.

Yan, M., Jene, N., Byrne, D., Millar, E.K.A., O'Toole, S.A., McNeil, C.M., Bates, G.J., Harris, A.L., Banham, A.H., Sutherland, R.L., 2011. Recruitment of regulatory T cells is correlated with hypoxia-induced CXCR4 expression, and is associated with poor prognosis in basal-like breast cancers. Breast Cancer Res. 13 (2), 1–10.

Yousefi, S., Gold, J.A., Andina, N., Lee, J.J., Kelly, A.M., Kozlowski, E., Schmid, I., Straumann, A., Reichenbach, J., Gleich, G.J., 2008. Catapult-like release of mitochondrial DNA by eosinophils contributes to antibacterial defense. Nat. Med. 14 (9), 949–953.

Zaiss, D.M.W., Gause, W.C., Osborne, L.C., Artis, D., 2015. Emerging functions of amphiregulin in orchestrating immunity, inflammation, and tissue repair. Immunity 42 (2), 216–226.

Zhang, B., Wei, C.Y., Chang, K.K., Yu, J.J., Zhou, W.J., Yang, H.L., Shao, J., Yu, J.J., Li, M.Q., Xie, F., 2017. TSLP promotes angiogenesis of human umbilical vein endothelial cells by strengthening the cross-talk between cervical cancer cells and eosinophils. Oncol. Lett. 14 (6), 7483–7488.

CHAPTER 3

Role of cancer-associated fibroblasts in tumor microenvironment

Manzoor Ahmad Mir, Shazia Sofi, and Shariqa Aisha
Department of Bioresources, School of Biological Sciences, University of Kashmir, Srinagar, Jammu and Kashmir, India

3.1 Introduction

Over the last decades, the role of the tumor TME in the genesis and progression of a variety of cancers has been identified (Quail and Joyce, 2013; Altorki et al., 2019; Mehraj et al., 2021a). The TME consists of a wide variety of cells including endothelial, mesenchymal, and hematopoietic origins that are organized in the ECM and interact intimately with tumor cells, hence accelerating carcinogenesis. The tumor–TME interaction can influence the growth of cancer both positively as well as negatively (Fig. 3.1). While the TME of early-stage cancers can come up with antimalignant activity, certain cancer cells may resist repression and reprogram the TME to bestow promalignancy functions (Maman and Witz, 2018; Mir et al., 2020). The presence of various secretory substances, such as chemokine's and cytokines within the TME; as well as other parameters, including hypoxia, metabolites, angiogenesis, and pH changes, contribute to the development of immunosuppressive, chronic inflammatory, and proangiogenic intratumoral environment (Zhuang et al., 2019; Jan et al., 2021; Mir et al., 2022b,c,d). The TME has been identified as a target for the production of new anticancer drugs throughout the last decade (Turley et al., 2015; Mir et al., 2022b,c,d). Cancer-associated fibroblasts (CAFs), possessing a spindle shape that contributes to and alter the ECM structure, are a major component of the TME (Kalluri and Zeisberg, 2006; Jan and Mir, 2021). CAFs have been widely researched in vitro without a doubt due to their ease of isolation and innate flexibility (Chen and Song, 2019). CAFs were first found as detrimental factors in tumor formation with little influence on tumor cells; nevertheless, they have now been recognized as a critical component of tumor progression (Cirri and Chiarugi, 2012; Mir et al., 2020). CAFs exhibit a variety of morphological and metabolic changes in response to tumor growth due to the reciprocal interaction between tumor cells and fibroblasts (Cirri and Chiarugi, 2012; Mir et al., 2022a,e,f,g). Additionally, CAFs contribute significantly to the maintenance of an optimum microenvironment for tumor cell growth and proliferation (Cirri and Chiarugi, 2012; Marsh et al., 2013; Mehraj et a., 2021b). Numerous studies published in the last few years have shown CAFs as critical regulators of the anticancer immune response (Lambrechts et al., 2018; Ziani et al., 2018). Fibroblasts, also

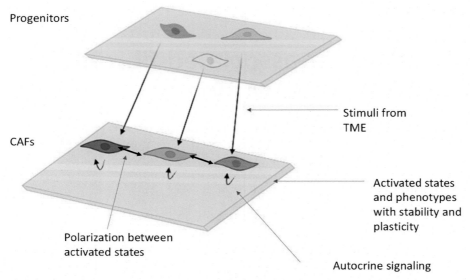

Fig. 3.1 Polarization between the different phenotypes of CAF can lead either to the progression or retardation of the tumorigenesis.

known as myofibroblasts, are normally dormant but can be triggered during a wound healing response (Kalluri and Zeisberg, 2006). The long-held belief that tumors are "never-healing wounds" (Kobayashi et al., 2019) suggests that CAFs might be targeted for cancer treatment. Certain studies have clearly indicated that CAFs may be selected as a novel target for antitumor immunotherapy (Kobayashi et al., 2019; Mir et al., 2022b,c,d).

The current chapter summarizes recent advancements in CAF research to increase our understanding of the molecular processes underpinning CAF participation in tumor growth. Additionally, the advancements in terms of phenotypic plasticity of CAFs with more emphasis on the functional role of different phenotypes of CAFs in specific immune cells have also been discussed. The chapter will also throw light on the therapeutic options targeting CAFs in the realm of cancer immunotherapy.

3.2 An overview of cancer-associated fibroblasts

3.2.1 Fibroblasts

Fibroblasts are the primary makers of connective tissue ECM during normal development and physiology, with growing findings showing that this role is altered with age (Kaur et al., 2016; Ecker et al., 2019). Additionally, they serve a critical function in tissue healing and are triggered in response to tissue injury (Gabbiani, 2003). They may create a transforming growth factor (TGF) and express a great constrictive phenotype linked with α SMA expression during wound healing (Rockey et al., 2013; Mir et al., 2020). The term "myofibroblasts" refers to fibroblasts in this stage. They possess the ability to interact with nearby epithelia during the process of normal homeostasis as well as during tissue damage, with multiple studies demonstrating their potential to impact the behavior of nearby epithelial stem cells (Brizzi et al., 2012; Le Guen et al., 2015). They can also enhance angiogenesis by producing vascular endothelial growth factor A (VEGFA) (Fukumura et al., 1998) and maintain the immune system's activity by producing cytokines and chemokine's, but the cytokines generated by various fibroblasts are heterogeneous (Buechler and Turley, 2018; Wang et al., 2019; Kraman et al., 2010; Philippeos et al., 2018; Biffi et al., 2019). Fibroblasts also have a structural function in the immune system; within lymph nodes, fibroblastic reticular cells (FRCs) produce ECM conduits for the passage of potential antigens and act as leukocytes migratory "highways" (Brown and Turley, 2015). This enables efficient immune surveillance. Additionally, they enhance immunological tolerance by expressing and presenting antigens that are ordinarily tissue-specific (Fletcher et al., 2011). Recent research demonstrates a complicated interaction between epithelial cells and fibroblastic in exocrine organs. For instance, stellate cells are a kind of fibroblast present within the pancreas and liver and contain lipid droplets and certain retinoic acid derivatives. The vitamin D receptor regulates the balance between the dormant and active state of stellate cells, and its loss results in spontaneous fibrosis of the pancreas and liver (Sherman et al., 2014), with further research revealing that stellate cells exhibit a larger function in metabolic homeostasis (Blaner et al., 2009; Apte et al., 2015). Thus, fibroblasts are more than just makers of ECM; they also play a potential role in interacting with a variety of other cell types in the process of normal homeostasis and tissue repair.

3.2.2 Cancer-associated fibroblasts (CAFs)

CAFs are a subset of activated fibroblasts that have a mesenchymal cell lineages and exhibit TME heterogeneity. They release several active molecules that contribute to the creation and balancing of cancer cell stemness, metabolic response, immunological control, angiogenesis, ECM remodeling, treatment resistance, stability, and other activities (Fig. 3.2) (Álvarez-Teijeiro et al., 2018; Chen and Song, 2019). CAFs are a highly diverse stromal cell population that plays a significant function in the TME. CAFs represent the most remarkable stromal cells in some cancers, including pancreatic and breast carcinomas. The number and function of activated CAFs in the TME have been associated to a poor outcome in a variety of cancers (Fiori et al., 2019). Additionally, tumors with a high level of stromal markers have been linked to therapeutic resistance and disease recurrence (Calon et al., 2015). CAFs are composed of numerous subgroups that have been demonstrated to originate from a variety of origins, like bone marrow–derived mesenchymal cells (MSCs) (Kalluri, 2016), reprogrammed resident tissue fibroblasts (Raz et al., 2018), adipocytes (Kidd et al., 2012), and endothelial cells (Zeisberg et al., 2007). CAFs have been shown to enhance tumor development in many ways, such as

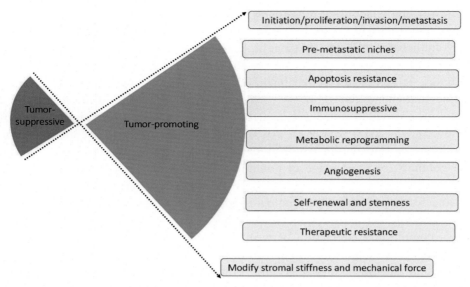

Fig. 3.2 CAFs show tumor-suppressive functions in the early stages of tumors. But with the progression of the tumor, CAFs evolve into a tumor-promoting phenotype and possess tumor-promoting function from different aspects.

directly promoting cancer cell multiplication through the production of growth factors, causing angiogenesis, and change in the ECM, which promotes tumor cell invasion (LeBleu and Kalluri, 2018). Notably, CAFs have shown their importance in tumor-promoting inflammation in a variety of tumors by their release of chemokines and cytokines that promote in the recruitment of immune cell and their activation, as well as through their reciprocal association with TME immune cells (Cohen et al., 2017). Recent research has established that various tumor assisting functions of CAFs are associated with functionally different fibroblast subgroups (Öhlund et al., 2017; Costa et al., 2018). The studies have highlighted that CAFs do play their role in the opposition of tumor cell proliferation, thereby highlighting the two opposite roles shown by the CAFs. The dual opposite roles shown by the CAFs are mainly due to the functional phenotypic plasticity of CAFs that in the different phenotypic states perform a specific function, thereby leading to the progression or regression in tumor growth (Monteran and Erez, 2019).

3.2.3 Origin of cancer-associated fibroblasts

The absence of precise biomarkers in CAFs had made it difficult to determine their origin. The majority of viewpoints agree that fibroblasts have mesenchymal cells as their source of origin, whereas CAFs originate from those fibroblasts that are in their active state in local tissues (Du and Che, 2017; Bu et al., 2019). The studies have revealed that

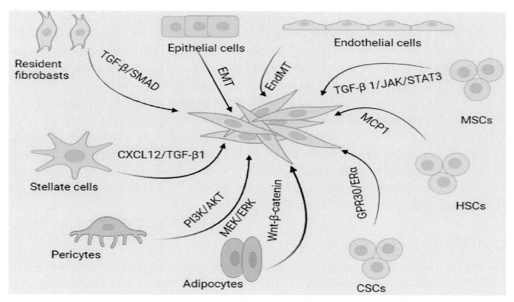

Fig. 3.3 CAFs have heterogeneous origins and can originate from resident fibroblasts, epithelial cells, endothelial cells, bone marrow-derived MSCs, HSCs, CSCs, adipocytes, pericytes, and stellate cells.

by endocytosing exosomes generated by bladder cancerous cells, healthy fibroblasts can multiply, activate, and display CAFs biomarkers. Additionally, bladder cancerous cells have been found to stimulate healthy fibroblasts into CAFs via exosomal-mediated TGF-β transmission and SMAD signaling pathways (Fig. 3.3) (Goulet et al., 2018). Additionally, the researchers developed a novel microfluidic model capable of controlling the 3-D TME in vitro. They discovered that exosomes produced from melanoma can stimulate the transformation of endothelium cells into CAFs via the endothelium–mesenchymal transition (EndMT). Additionally, exosomes produced from mesenchymal stem cells (MSCs) can suppress the EndMT and stimulate CAFs to revert back into endothelium cells (Ning et al., 2018). The capacity of exosomes to trigger invert differentiation of CAFs may make them effective carriers of anticancer medicines. Additionally, epithelial cells inside the TME are capable of undergoing EMT and transforming into CAFs. CAFs then produce cytokines to enhance tumor cell EMT, which results in invasion and tumor spread (Fiori et al., 2019). Other studies have demonstrated that the activation of the JAK/STAT3 signaling pathway will lead to the differentiation of bone marrow-derived MSCs into CAFs with the help of TGF-1, as well as accelerate colorectal cancer cell invasion and motility (Tan et al., 2019). Simultaneously, several studies suggest the derivation of PDGF–CAFs cells from MSCs (Raz et al., 2018). Finally, data indicate that CAFs can be derived from a variety of different sources, like hematopoietic stem cells (HSCs), adipocytes, CSCs, stellate cells, and pericytes (Abangan et al., 2010;

Nair et al., 2017). Nonetheless, evidence for these origins is few, and their relevance to other kinds of malignancies is restricted (Liao et al., 2019). To conclude, CAFs are formed from the following cell types: fibroblasts, endothelial cells, epithelial cells, hematopoietic stem cells, bone marrow-derived MSCs, adipocytes, stellate cells, CSCs, and pericytes. To a certain extent, the diversity in the source of CAFs explains the variability of CAFs. CAFs formed from distinct sources are controlled by distinct signals or active factors, resulting in divergent differentiation paths. Further study into the source of CAFs may provide insight into the identification and exploration of CAF biomarkers or targets, their activation pathways, and signaling process, all of which may have significant therapeutic implications. Regardless of the source of their phenotypes, origin, function and their states alter dynamically throughout tumor growth, which varies according to the pathological stage.

3.2.4 Biomarkers of CAFs

Identifying precise CAF biomarkers is one of the most significant ongoing issues. Although several CAF biomarkers have been identified, not even a single biomarker is CAF specific. The most frequently utilized biomarkers are displayed in the majority of CAF subgroups (Nurmik et al., 2020). According to the studies, CAF biomarkers fall into the following categories: cytokines, ECM components, receptors, growth factors (GFs), and other membrane-bound proteins (MBPs), cytoplasmic proteins, cytoskeleton, and extracellular vesicles (Table 3.1). At the current level of study, the majority of CAF biomarkers are recognized qualitatively, and the application of certain common positive biomarkers serves as a guide for research on the function and CAF phenotype (Table 3.2). Numerous research studies have analyzed the link between immunotherapy impact on metastatic melanoma and CAFs using different quantitative methodologies depending upon cell count and immunofluorescence quantification. They discovered that

Table 3.1 Potential biomarkers associated with CAFs in Breast Cancer.

Type	Biomarker
Cytokines	IL–32
	CXC14
	CXCL16
Growth factors	TGF-β
	CTGF
ECM components	Fibronectin
	Stromal stiffness
Receptors and MBPs	Rock
	Integrin α11/PDGFRβ
	ITGB4
	DDR2

Table 3.2 Function of different Potential biomarkers of CAFs in Breast Cancer.

Biomarker	Function
IL-32	Invasion, metastasis
CXC14	EMT, Invasion, metastasis
CXCL16	Progression, poor outcomes
TGF-β	EMT, metastasis
CTGF	Migration, invasion
Fibronectin	Cancer cell invasion
Stromal stiffness	Stromal desmoplasia, tumor progression
Rock	Progression
Integrin α11/PDGFRβ	Tumor invasiveness
ITGB4	Metabolic reprogramming
DDR2	Tumor stiffness and metastasis

Thy1+CAFs and FAP+CAFs were strongly associated with PF and OS, but SMA +CAFs were linked with a worse prognosis in patients undergoing programmed death 1 (PD-1) treatment (Singh et al., 2017; Naito et al., 2019). These findings indicate that qualitative positive biomarker combination with various quantitative analyses of CAF approaches has a lot of clinical promise as an objective and auxiliary tool for tumor detection (Wong et al., 2019). CAFs have a variable phenotype and quantity in different types of malignancies. To be specific, different tumors are associated with the expression of specific biomarkers mentioned above, and many different tumor types can be associated with the same CAFs biomarkers (Table 3.1). Additionally, sometimes tumor cells, as well as normal cells, may be characterized by certain biomarkers. Further investigation of CAFs may involve the use of various biomarkers in combination (Cremasco et al., 2018). Given the fact that the quantity of the same CAFs biomarkers differs between tumor types, quantitative variations in CAFs subgroups may be exploited as tumor-specific indicators.

3.3 Heterogeneity of CAFs

Studies have revealed that CAFs show heterogeneous behavior in terms of their functions, phenotypes, location, and biomarkers (Fig. 3.4). This heterogeneity arises due to the heterogeneity in their origin, thus leading to the formation of various subsets of CAFs.

3.3.1 Original heterogeneity

Several studies depicted that CAFs are a diverse group of cells (Kalluri and Zeisberg, 2006). This variability may be because CAFs have various cellular progenitors. CAFs can be localized and activated from local fibroblasts in the tissue (Kojima et al., 2010).

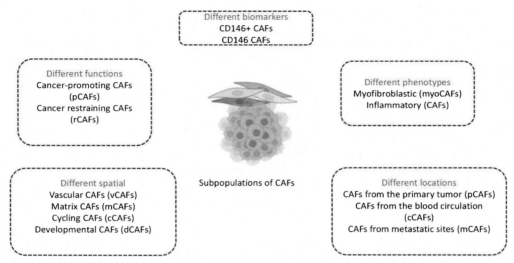

Fig. 3.4 According to different classification conventions, CAFs can be divided into different subpopulations and exhibit diverse phenotypes and functions.

As with fibroblasts involved in wound healing (Kojima et al., 2010), this activation usually dependent on TME stimuli, including oxidative stress, regional hypoxia, and growth chemicals secreted by adjacent tumor cells and penetrating immune cells. Fundamentally, the most significant regulators for the recruitment and activation of fibroblasts include PDGF, TGF-β, and FGF-2 (Löhr et al., 2001; Aoyagi et al., 2004). Additionally, IL-1 produced from immune cells activates NF-β in fibroblasts, which is implicated in their education and proinflammatory secretome (Erez et al., 2010). For instance, quiescent hepatic stellate fibroblasts and pancreatic stellate cells can take a myofibroblast-like phenotype, in response to the activation of PDGF and TGF-β. Apart from local origins, certain CAFs can develop from nonfibroblastic cells like blood vessels (Potenta et al., 2008), epithelial cells (Fischer et al., 2015), adipocytes, smooth muscle cells (Jotzu et al., 2011), and pericytes. Generally, the EMT shown by epithelial cells and EndMT shown by endothelial cells along with an expression of FSP-1 protein is associated with the development of fibroblastic phenotype (Zeisberg et al., 2007).

Additionally, a pool of CAFs inside the TME can also be differentiated from the circulating mesenchymal cell groups known as fibrocytes, as has been seen in breast cancer (Barth et al., 2002). Simultaneously, several studies suggest the derivation of PDGF–CAFs cells from MSCs (Barth et al., 2002). To conclude, CAFs are formed from the following cell types: fibroblasts, endothelial cells, epithelial cells, hematopoietic stem cells, bone marrow-derived MSCs, adipocytes, stellate cells, CSCs, and pericytes (Fig. 3.3). To a certain extent, the diversity in the origin of CAFs explains the variability of CAFs.

3.3.2 Phenotypic heterogeneity

Due to the varied origins of activated fibroblasts, CAFs exhibit diversity in their pheno-types, which can be represented by a variety of biological markers inside the TME. Previous studies have depicted that CAFs may be recognized utilizing markers that get expressed at lower levels or are absent entirely in their normal counterparts, including S100A4, tenascin-C, SMA, neuron glial antigen (NG2), FAP, CD90/THY, PDGFRα/β, desmin, and podoplanin (PDPN) (Turley et al., 2015; Chen and Song, 2019). None of these indicators, however, are solely expressed by CAFs, highlighting the variety of CAFs. α-SMA is one of them, and it is employed not just to recognize CAFs having a myofi-broblast character, but also as a generic marker for pericytes and vascular muscular cells (Öhlund et al., 2017). Another identified marker, S100A4, is present nearly exclusively on fibroblasts (Zhang et al., 2018). Additionally, FAP is expressed in a subpopulation of CD45 + immune cells (Arnold et al., 2014). Furthermore, PDPN can be used to iden-tify lymphatic endothelial cells (Augsten, 2014). Recent research discovered a novel CAF subgroup (CD10 + GRP77 +) that is related to cancer stemness and resistance to chemotherapy (Su et al., 2018). Mechta-Grigoriou and coworkers describe four dif-ferent CAF subsets in ovarian and breast malignancies by analyzing six fibroblast markers concurrently (αSMA, FAP, β1CD29, PDGFR, S100A4, and caveolin1) (Costa et al., 2018; Givel et al., 2018). Further investigations employing single-cell RNA sequencing (scRNA-seq) have identified two specific CAF subgroups in human colorectal cancers, with the expression of DCN, MMP2, and COLIA2 by CAF-A cells and the expression of TAGLN, CAF-B cells displaying ACTA2, and PDGFA (Li et al., 2017). A scRNA-seq analysis of lung tumors from individuals with NSCLC reveals the presence of five different fibroblast classes. Interestingly, each of these fibroblast classes expresses a different kind of collagen or other ECM protein, with class 1 expressing COL10A1 while class 2 expressing COL4A1 (Lambrechts et al., 2018). Furthermore, scRNA-seq analysis of 768 CAFs produced from genetically modified MMTYPyMT mice carrying breast cancer indicated the existence of four distinct CAF subtypes. Notably, PDGFR is expressed exclusively by subtype 2, whereas PDGFR is expressed by all cells except for subtype 4. ACTA2, FAP, and S100A4 are expressed in the major-ity of four populations (Bartoschek et al., 2018). Despite the multiplicity of CAF markers, it remains difficult to define functioning subsets of CAFs using cell surface markers. ScRNA-seq and in vivo models might be used in the future to understand the heterogeneity of CAFs in terms of cellular origins, RNA profiles, surface markers, activation phases, and spatial distribution.

3.3.3 Functional heterogeneity

CAFs consist of functionally distinct subsets that either enhance or retard cancer progres-sion (Chen and Song, 2019). CAFs' protumorigenic properties have been widely explored in vitro and in vivo (Labernadie et al., 2017; Yamamura et al., 2020). For instance, α-SMA+ CAFs enhance the proliferation of cancer stem cells via the CXCL12–CXCR4 connection (Kobayashi et al., 2019). Numerous additional CAF-derived factors, like TGF-β, matrix metallopeptidase 2, IL-6, and CXCL12 have been shown to stimulate the proliferation of tumor cells and their invasion of a variety of malignancies (Kojima et al., 2010). CAFs, on the other hand, have lately been recognized for their antitumor properties. For example, in pancreatic cancer, deleting α-SMA+ myofibroblasts impairs immune surveillance by boosting CD4+ Foxp3+ Tregs in tumors (Özdemir et al., 2014). Similarly, ablation of fibroblast-rich desmoplastic stroma using a sonic hedgehog inhibitor promotes tumor aggressiveness in pancreatic ductal cancer (Rhim et al., 2014). Interestingly, breast TME is found to have at least 2 CAF subtypes based on the expression of CD146. CD146 CAFs, in particular, inhibit the production of estrogen receptors and the susceptibility of tumor cells to estrogen. CD146+ CAF, on the other hand, can increase tamoxifen sensitivity in luminal BC cells (Brechbuhl et al., 2017). CAFs have been implicated in, immunosuppression, carcinogenesis, metastasis, drug resistance, ECM remodeling, angiogenesis, cancer stemness maintenance, and metabolic reprogramming (Bartoschek et al., 2018).

3.4 CAFs' activation mechanism

The coordinating advantageous and reciprocal association between cancer cells and CAFs is mediated by a tight association mechanism (identical to that between "seed" and "soil" tumor cells) and is capable of initiating the formation of CAFs and maintaining their active state. Activated CAFs, on the other hand, can enhance tumor cell invasion, movement, and proliferation by reprogramming and altering the TME, eventually resulting in tumor growth, metastasis, and resistance to treatment (Fig. 3.5, Table 3.2) (Kuzet and Gaggioli, 2016). The presence of different growth factors, transcription factors, signaling pathways, and metalloproteinases lead to the activation and differentiation of fibroblasts into specific CAF phenotypes (Fig. 3.5). The cascade of CAF activation is regulated by a signaling pathway known as leukemia inhibitory factor/glycoprotein 130/interleukin 6R (LIF/GP130/IL-6R) signaling pathway (Kuzet and Gaggioli, 2016). Numerous metalloproteinases controlled by the TIMP gene family have been shown to affect the human TME. In normal fibroblasts, silencing the TIMP gene dramatically activates metalloproteinases in the TME and promotes the conversion of regular fibroblasts into CAFs. CAFs lacking TIMP1 promotes cell stemness of tumors and migration capability through exosome generation, hence increasing tumor growth (Shimoda et al., 2014). Furthermore, exosomal miR-1247-3p generated from metastatic liver cancerous cells activates the integrin 1-NF-B signaling cascade in regular fibroblasts and facilitates their differentiation into CAFs (Fig. 3.5). Following activation, active CAFs produce protumor cytokines IL-8 and IL-6, which enhance tumor growth and promote lung metastases

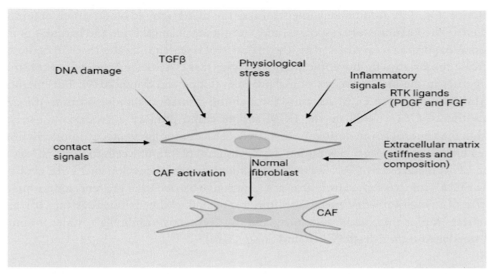

Fig. 3.5 Diverse mechanisms of CAF activation. Multiple mechanisms that can activate CAF include FGF, fibroblast growth factor; PDGF, platelet-derived growth factor; ROS, reactive oxygen species; RTK, receptor tyrosine kinase; TGFβ, transforming growth factor-β; TNF, tumor necrosis factor.

(Fang et al., 2018). Additionally, exosomes derived from primary and metastatic tumor cells from human colorectal cancer can transform normal fibroblasts into the CAF phenotype. Additionally, altering the CAF proteome results in functional heterogeneity (Rai et al., 2019). Similar to their origins, CAFs have a varied and complicated activation mechanism. Through the JAK–STAT signaling pathway, the inflammatory cytokine IL1 increases the interconversion of CAFs via NF-B and IL6. Increased stromal firmness and mechanical stress also lead to activation of CAFs in terms of physical alterations to the TME (Sahai et al., 2020). From a therapeutic standpoint, clinical interventions (e.g., radiation, chemotherapy, and targeted therapy) might stimulate the formation and activity of CAFs, resulting in therapeutic resistance and adverse consequences (Tommelein et al., 2018; Sahai et al., 2020). Nonetheless, while the maximum allowed dosage of chemotherapy can stimulate CAFs, frequent chemotherapy can diminish the stimulation of CAFs generated by CT (Chan et al., 2016). More crucially, activated CAFs may self-maintenance and activate tumor cells to sustain their activation, producing a positive feedback loop.

3.5 Role of CAFs

CAFs' heterogeneity in terms of their origin and activation methods dictates their functional variety. CAFs are a significant source of chemokines, ECM, cytokines, numerous proteins, growth factors, and several enzymes. They can influence the initiation of a tumor, its growth, and resistance to therapy via a variety of processes and effects, including maintenance of tumor immune surveillance, metabolism of local, and tumor cell behavior (Fig. 3.2). Additionally, they can alter the ECM, rebuild blood vessels of tumor, modulate the inflammatory responses, and alter the mechanical force and hardness of the stroma. According to available data, the majority of research indicates that CAFs mostly increase tumor growth, but some studies indicate that CAFs may have some antitumor properties in the primary stages of malignancies (Chen and Song, 2019). For instance, CAFs can modify the ECM structure through the formation and degradation of ECM constituents. CAFs modulate the ECM structure and produce a "restrictive barrier" within the regional lesion during the first stages of the tumor, preventing tumor cells from spreading. Nonetheless, it may inhibit the localization of immune cells to the local lesion. The ECM mediated by CAFs is constantly altered as tumors develop and TME evolves. The ECM's role has shifted from that of a "restrictive barrier" that prevents tumor spread to that of a "highway" that encourages tumor spread; the "therapeutic resistance barrier" promotes tumor therapeutic resistance, and the "protective umbrella" evades immune cell-mediated tumor death (Chen and Song, 2019).

3.5.1 Tumor-promoting CAFs

Numerous signaling pathways and substances assist in the regulating of the protumori-genic activity of CAFs. CAFs and the RT4 (bladder cancer cell line) were cocultured in a conditioned media in studies. The data revealed that CAFs overexpressed IL6 and attach to the IL6 receptor displayed by RT4 cells, inducing EMT and enhancing bladder cancer cell growth and migration. By inhibiting CAFs' IL6 production with particular Abs, the EMT process generated by IL6 may be greatly reversed, demonstrating that CAFs initiate EMT to enhance bladder cancer via IL6 secretion (Goulet et al., 2018). Other research has demonstrated that CAFs in ovarian cancer are involved in EMT via the IL6/JAK2/STAT3 pathway, hence increasing tumor growth, migration, and resistance to chemotherapy (Wang et al., 2018). TGF β is the primary constituent of the ECM in humans and plays role in both wound healing and tumor growth (Mir et al., 2022b,c,d). TGF1 is one of the most abundant CAF secretomes and is a critical mediator of stromal cell-cancer cell communication. CAFs increase the HOX antisense RNA transcription (HOTAIR) via paracrine TGF1, hence inducing EMT and promoting breast cancer spread. As a result, blocking TGF1 expression have been demonstrated to greatly reduce tumor development and lung metastasis produced by CAF (Ren et al., 2018). The TGF1/HOTAIR pathway has been considered as a potential focus for BC therapy. Other studies have demonstrated that autocrine CAFs are critical regulators of their role and phenotype via the TGF1/miR-200s/miR-221/DNA methyltransferase 3 beta (DNMT3B) pathway, a critical mechanism implicated in the advancement of BC by CAFs (Tang et al., 2019). Researchers demonstrated that through modulating the mechanical force mediated by integrins, the collagen receptor generated by CAFs modulates the matrix firmness and metastasis of BC to lungs. DDR2 can restructure the fibers of collagen in the TME, hence altering its characteristics. This enhances the TME's suitability for initiating and maintaining tumor cell invasion and migration (Bayer et al., 2019; Mir et al., 2022a,e,f,g). For the above reasons, tissue fibrosis may trigger tumor cell growth and survival signals, resulting in a cascade of events, including an enhancement in mechanical stress, the disruption of circulation of the blood, and the development of hypoxia in nearby tissues. These actions enhance the emergence of tumor phenotypes but impair therapeutic efficacy. As a result, while examining the differentiation and role of CAFs, it is vital to take into account the mechanical stress and stromal hardness of the in vitro culture systems.

3.5.2 Tumor-suppressive CAFs

Numerous in vitro and in vivo researches confirm the role of CAFs in tumor initiation and progression (Von Ahrens et al., 2017). However, it has been demonstrated that matrix-specific Hedgehog-activated subpopulations of CAFs prevent tumor development and growth in animal models of several kinds of malignancies, including pancreatic, bladder, and colon cancer (Yoshida, 2020). Based on this process, studies have proposed a novel therapeutic technique for CAFs known as "matrix conversion." This method attempts to transform protumor CAFs into antitumor phenotypes and to decrease matrix firmness (Yoshida, 2020). In animal models having prostate cancer, it was shown that the Hedgehog signaling is significantly shown in CAFs and smooth muscle cells. Increased Hedgehog signaling results in a more complete smooth muscle cell layer and reduces the formation of micro-lesions (Yang et al., 2017; Mir et al., 2022a,e,f,g). This suggests that the Hedgehog signaling can prevent tumor growth by preserving the smooth muscle's integrity. Certain researchers employed genetic engineering to remove αSMA + myofibroblasts in mice and discovered large increases in EMT, hypoxia, and CSCs. Additionally, there was inhibition in the mice's immune surveillance, and the animals did not react to gemcitabine treatment. Additionally, their survival time was decreased. Another study discovered that individuals with pancreatic tumors had a lower amount of αSMA + myofibroblasts, which was related to a poor survival rate. These findings show that these cells possess some antitumor properties and that their full eradication may result in acceleration in tumor malignancy. This should be considered when attempting to target myofibroblasts with αSMA + (Özdemir et al., 2014). It is worth noting, however, that αSMA + cells in vivo are not restricted to CAFs and myofibroblasts. The tumor-enhancing impact of eliminating all αSMA + cells may not be due to αSMA + CAF loss alone but may be due to the elimination of additional cells or signals. According to researchers, fibroblasts or CAFs can act as tumor suppressors or tumor promoters in the early and late phases of malignancies, respectively (Miyai et al., 2020). However, because tumor samples from the same illness at various stages are difficult to collect, it is hard to directly observe the alterations in cell status that occur between primary and metastatic tumor stages. As a result, verifying this idea using human biopsy tissue is challenging. Further study has revealed an antitumor biomarker for CAFs (i.e., Meflin) that is displayed in cells like pancreatic stellate cells, fibroblasts, and undifferentiated MSCs, and adjacent ductal or acinar tissue. Antitumor CAFs have been shown in animal models to manifest in the primary stages of pancreatic carcinoma. They can develop into protumorigenic CAFs when stimulated by TGF, stiffness of stroma, mechanical stress, and other TME factors (Mizutani et al., 2019).

3.6 CAF–immune microenvironment interaction in tumors

CAFs are critical in balancing the anticancer activities of tumor–infiltrating immune cells, including adaptive and innate immune cells in the TIME (Table 3.3) (Harper and Sainson, 2014; Mir et al., 2022a,e,f,g). Additionally, they increase the development of immunological checkpoint chemicals and the remodeling of the ECM, which has an indirect influence on the recruitment and activation of immune cells (Kim et al.,

Table 3.3 Modulation of Immune cell differentiation by CAFs.

Effect on immune cells	Type of immune cells	Cancer type	Molecule produced by CAFs
M2-like differentiation	Circulating monocytes	Prostate	SDF-1
	TAMs	Breast	Chi3L1
Inhibition of Th1 immunity	Th1/Th2 cells	Breast	Not specified
Th17 Differentiation	T cells (Th17 polarization)	Lung	IL-6
Shaping the activity of dendritic cells	Th2 polarization via DC conditioning	Pancreatic	TSLP
	DC	Hepatocellular carcinoma	IL-6
	DC	Lung	Kyn
MDSCs differentiation & Activation Monocytes	Monocytes	Hepatocellular carcinoma	SDF-1
	MDSCs	Melanoma and lung adenocarcinoma	Dkk1
	Peripheral blood mononuclear cells	Pancreatic	IL-6, VEGF, M-CSF, SDF-1, MCP-1
Treg cell Differentiation	CD4 + CD25 + FOXP3 +	Treg Breast and HGSOC	B7H3, CD73, DPP4

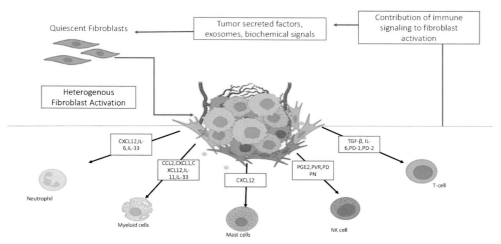

Fig. 3.6 CAFs in the TME maintain the anticancer activities of tumor-infiltrating immune cells, including adaptive and innate immune cells in the TIME. They stimulate the production of immunological checkpoint substances and ECM remodeling, which has an indirect effect on immune cell recruitment and their activity.

2019). CAFs can stimulate immune cells to engage in the initiation and formation of tumors by secreting various substances like chemokines, cytokines, and other effector substances, including CXCL2, TGF-β, MMPs, collagens, and laminin (Ueshima et al., 2019, Mehraj et al., 2022). They can also facilitate the breakdown and modification of the ECM. Naturally, some immune cells have been identified as having notable effects on CAFs (Shiga et al., 2015; Mir et al., 2019). Numerous studies have demonstrated that the association between immune cells and CAFs, as well as other immunological components, can modulate the TIME, hence limiting the anticancer immune response (Fig. 3.6) (Mantovani et al., 2004).

3.6.1 Interaction between CAFs and tumor-associated macrophages (TAMs)

TAMs are divided into two separate subsets that are triggered by unique polarizing cytokines, referred to as M1 and M2 (Allavena et al., 2008). M1-type primarily act as antitumor agents in the TIME leading to Ab-dependent cellular cytotoxicity and producing TNF and reactive oxygen species (ROS) (Mantovani et al., 2008), whereas M2-type act as tumor promoters by activating immune suppression, tumor angiogenesis, cancer cell invasion, and migration, and ECM remodeling (Hu et al., 2020).

TAMs, being a crucial constituent of the TME, are involved in its regulation, most notably in tumor immune suppression (Herrera et al., 2013). TAMs are the major immune cells in regions inhabited by CAFs, implying a direct link between these two types of cells (Tan et al., 2018). It has been demonstrated that increased levels of TAM and CAF biomarkers, such as FAP, α-SMA, and S100A4, as well as CD209 and CD163, are associated with a poor clinical outcome in individuals with certain malignancies (Ksiazkiewicz et al., 2010). Numerous studies have demonstrated that CAFs enhance monocyte recruitment (macrophage progenitors) and development into tumor-promoting macrophage subsets (M2-type TAMs) through various regulatory substances, resulting in weakening effector T-cell responses and eliciting immunological suppression in the TME (Comito et al., 2014). For instance, CAFs can accelerate monocyte migration and increase their ability to change into the M2 phenotype in breast cancer by secreting chitinase 3-like 1 (Chi3L1), SDF-1, and monocyte chemotactic protein-1 (MCP-1) (Wang et al., 2018). Additionally, CAFs have been shown to have a similar effect on TAMs in prostate cancer (Tang et al., 2019). Furthermore, Mace and coworkers (Mace et al., 2013) established a critical function for CAF-derived M-CSF1, CCL2, and IL-6 in monocyte recruitment and an elevated M2/M1 macrophage ratio in pancreatic tumor. Other cytokines released by CAFs, like IL-10, IL-8, TGF-β, and CCL2 (in skin cancers), have also been shown to increase monocyte recruitment and transformation into M2 macrophages (Nagarsheth et al., 2017). Besides assisting the recruitment of macrophages and their development, CAFs can trigger the immunoinhibitory features of TAMs. Gordon and coworkers analyzed the flow cytometry data and revealed that M2 macrophages induced by CAFs are associated with increased PD-1 expression (Gordon et al., 2017). Following investigations established that an increased level of PD-1 expression in TAMs is implicated in the regulation of both innate and acquired anticancer immune responses, including lowering their phagocytic capacity against tumor cells and limiting the infiltration of T cells and their proliferation (Gok Yavuz et al., 2019). CAFs, in addition to stimulating TAMs, may also inhibit several aspects of TAM activity. For example, ERα expression in its entirety on CAFs inhibits infiltration of macrophage prostate tumor invasion, which is mediated by reduced levels of IL-6 and CCL5. Mazur and coworkers (Mazur et al., 2016) demonstrated the role of FAP (a CAF marker) in the association between TAMs and CAFs mechanistically. The scientists discovered that FAP was involved in the interaction between SR-A (class A scavenger receptors) + TAMs and CAFs primarily through type I collagen cleavage and macrophage adherence. M2 type TAMs also influence CAF activation and development in a reciprocal manner (Takahashi et al., 2017). Furthermore, TAM-like macrophages were shown to increase both growth and migration of CAF-like BM-MSCs in an in vitro coculture research, ultimately contributing to the development of neuroblastoma (Wu et al., 2019). Following that, CAF activation created by macrophages further boosts the functions of TAM, forming a positive feedback loop that enhances cancer progression and immune suppression in the TME.

3.6.2 CAFs and tumor-associated neutrophils (TANs)

The studies have demonstrated that TANs are important constituents of TIME, and show heterogenicity in terms of their phenotypes and functions (Fridlender et al., 2009). Similar to TAMs, TANs may also acquire either tumor-promoting (N2) or tumor-inhibiting (N1) character depending upon their activation by TGF-β (Jablonska et al., 2010). However, unlike TAMs, N1 and N2 phenotypes can be characterized based on the extent to which they are activated rather than on the presence of unique polarizing chemicals (Song et al., 2021). Notably, CAFs may be capable of modulating TANs' polarization. According to recent research on hepatic tumors, CAF-derived CLCF1 stimulates the polarization of N2 TANs in tumor cells by increasing the expression of TGFβ and CXCL6 (Cheng et al., 2018). More critically, CAFs are likely to be involved in all phases of TAN malignancy, eventually suppressing the anticancer immune response in the TME. CAFs can attract peripheral neutrophils to tumors via the production of SDF-1α (Raman et al., 2007). Additionally, CAFs produce a cytokine receptor, namely C-X-C chemokine receptor 2 (CXCR2) that is the main factor in recruiting peripheral neutrophils to the tumor site, implying that CAFs may increase TAN recruitment in a CXCR2-dependent way. Following that, IL-6 produced by CAF activates the STAT3 signaling pathway in TANs, limiting T-cell function and promoting immunological tolerance via PD-L1 expression (Raman et al., 2007). Additionally, Zhu and coworkers (Zhu et al., 2014) demonstrated that neutrophils and gastric cancer mesenchymal stem cells (GC-MSCs) interact bidirectionally. On the one hand, the chemotaxis, activation, survival of neutrophils is regulated by GC-MSCs via the STAT3-extracellular regulated protein kinases 1/2 (ERK1/2) axis promoted by IL-6. On the other hand, activation of TANs stimulates the differentiation of MSCs into CAFs. Due to the scarcity of data, the specific processes behind the reciprocal effects of CAFs and TANs on one another remain unknown.

3.6.3 CAFs and mast cells (MCs)

Research on MCs have shifted attention in recent decades away from their functions in cancer and toward their roles in allergy illnesses (Dalton and Noelle, 2012). Interestingly, as a constituent of the TIME, MCs have a dual effect on tumor development, inhibiting and promoting tumor growth, depending on the specific MC location, type of cancer, and stage of tumor progression (Hölzel et al., 2016; Gentles et al., 2020). On the one hand, MCs enhance cancer progression by the secretion of proangiogenic substances (FGF-2, histamine, heparin, VEGF-A, VEGF-B, and stem cell factor (SCF)) (Medina et al., 2006; Beer et al., 2008), MMP-9, lymphangiogenic molecules (VEGF-C and VEGF-D) (Baram et al., 2001), proteases (tryptase and chymase) (Baram et al., 2001). On the other hand, MCs release mediators (e.g., IL-1, IL-6, tryptase, chondroitin sulfate, TNF) that enhance antitumor immune responses by inducing tumor apoptosis and lowering tumor cell invasiveness (Ribatti and Crivellato, 2011). The overexpression of MCs and CAF in tumor islets is highly related to cancer aggressiveness, and their association contributes directly to tumor growth (Pereira et al., 2019). The overexpression of estrogen in prostate cancer leads to the proliferation, invasiveness, and inflammatory cytokine production by CAFs, thereby showing the tumor-enhancing effects (Ellem et al., 2014). Meanwhile, estrogen-induced CAF-derived CXCL12 was found to be important in the migration of MCs when combined with CXCR4. Additionally, Ma and coworkers (Ma et al., 2013) demonstrated that PSCs can promote the stimulation and division of MCs. Furthermore, this study established the provoking action of MCs on CAFs. In contrast, MC-released tryptase and IL-13 increase the proliferation of CAFs in a TGF-β 2/STAT6-independent way (Pereira et al., 2019). The rise in CAF levels led to the creation of a fibrotic TME, which inhibited anticancer immunity and treatment responses. Additionally, it has been revealed that MCs in neurofibroma can promote CAF activity by boosting the growth and secretion of CAFs via the TGF-β signaling pathway, hence strengthening the antitumor effects of CAFs (Yang et al., 2006). Furthermore, recent research in prostate tumors using a microtissue model has shown that CAFs and MCs collaborated to trigger the early malignant morphological transformation of benign epithelial cells (Pereira et al., 2019).

3.6.4 Targeting CAFs for clinical benefit

Numerous patient investigations have established a relationship between CAF quantity or their role and outcome (Calon et al., 2015; Franco-Barraza et al., 2017; Mariathasan et al., 2018), and hence targeting CAFs would constitute an intriguing enhancement to the current arsenal of anticancer medicines. Additional targeting processes, such as TGF β signaling, that activate CAFs or originate from CAFs to modify the tumor group types are being investigated intensively (Tauriello et al., 2018). There has already been much action in the field of CAF targeting and in-depth studies (Valkenburg et al., 2018). However, the variety of CAF activities and the possibility of subtype interconversion represent a problem for the research, with preclinical data indicating that nonspecific targeting or elimination of stromal fibroblasts may not improve tumor inhibition (Rhim et al., 2014). Thus, the patient benefit may necessitate targeting the CAF subgroup or reprogramming CAFs to either a regular fibroblast or an antitumorigenic fibroblast subtype. This demonstrates the critical nature of distinguishing CAF subgroups and their interactions. One intriguing technique is to normalize CAFs. The targeting of the vitamin D receptor in pancreatic cancer is an illustration of this strategy. The introduction of vitamin D receptor ligand-induced the reversion of active stellate cells to a more dormant state, hence decreasing disease aggressiveness (Hah et al., 2015). Thus, it is critical to distinguish if separate fibroblast populations represent states and are thus interchangeable or whether discrete "lineage-restricted" effects occur, since this may mandate a different treatment strategy. Although the functional contributions of CAFs to tumor biology is often considered to be conserved among tumor types, this has yet to be established, and caution will be required when extrapolating among various tumor types. In actuality, therapeutic benefit may not need the deletion or reprogramming of CAFs, but may be obtained by inhibiting signals emanating from the CAFs. For instance, inhibiting CXCL12 signaling may be seen as targeting CAFs, as they are the primary source of the chemokine in a number of tumors (Feig et al., 2013). Similarly, inhibiting tumor–CAF interaction by targeting ECM constituents and downstream signaling is a method of interfering with CAF–tumor cell interaction. Indeed, several already available medicines affect CAF–tumor cell interaction and have already changed the way CAFs impact the tumor cells. As previously stated, BRAF inhibitors can stimulate stromal fibroblasts, promoting a compensatory process for ERK–MAPK activation in tumor cells (Hirata et al., 2015). Numerous inhibitors of receptor tyrosine kinase show some effect on PDGF and FGF receptors, which are involved in fibroblast function (Anderberg et al., 2009; Bai et al., 2015). This is demonstrated by the repurposing of nintedanib for the treatment of idiopathic pulmonary fibrosis1 (Richeldi et al., 2014), which was initially designed for cancer. Finally, both traditional DNA-damaging chemotherapy and radiation have the potential to alter the biology of the CAF, with fibrosis being a frequent late consequence of radiotherapy (Hirata et al., 2015). These findings suggest that more research is necessary to determine the extent to which changed CAF biology may impact therapeutic responses.

3.7 Challenges and directions

Given that a significant number of CAF features may vary as the culture environment is changed (from in vivo to in vitro), several issues have emerged and needs to be resolved. To begin, researchers tested various culture parameters to preserve the CAF subtypes as much as possible in vitro conditions and discovered that for maintaining the original state of CAFs, there needs to have less concentration of serum and matrices with good physiological mechanical characteristics (Sahai et al., 2020). Recent research has demonstrated that the inhibition of molecules that inhibit CAF activation like TGF-β can potentially retard the conversion of CAF subtypes in in vitro conditions (Franco-Barraza et al., 2017), implying that incorporating CAF activator inhibitors in vivo conditions can turn into an effective new strategy for accurately preserving the in vivo phenotype of CAFs. Certainly, further research is necessary to determine more optimal in vitro growing conditions for CAFs. Second, single-cell transcriptome investigations have recently been shown to be an effective tool for deciphering the features and CAF heterogeneity. Apart from single-cell transcriptome investigation, scientists often detect CAFs in tissue using immunoassay techniques, like good-quality Abs against CAF marker proteins. However, because CAFs are heterogeneous, Abs against specific CAF subtype markers require extensive tuning, limiting their usage in labs. Multiplexed mRNA probe technology has advanced quickly in recent years, and hence reliable quantitative approaches for the identification of CAFs are looking increasingly promising in the long future (Sahai et al., 2020). Further research should be conducted in the future to investigate and create more general, reliable, standardized, and accurate quantitative approaches for CAF identification. Additionally, while numerous methods for detecting CAF subtype expression have been started recently, as mentioned previously, such as mRNA probes, specific Abs, and transcriptome investigations, there is still a need for a strategy for detecting CAF subtype changes with their dependence on time in a very accurate way during the cultivation phase. Finally, it is crucial to advance our knowledge of the sources and subpopulations of CAFs, particularly their temporal and stage heterogeneity (Ping et al., 2021), by researching CAFs at various experimental and clinical phases.

3.8 Conclusion

Despite their abundance in the tumor stroma, CAFs have been overlooked for decades. The critical significance of CAFs in cancer biology has recently gained widespread attention. Targeting CAFs or their secretomes enables us to conquer malignancies by lowering immunosuppressive conditions and altering the TME, but not by directly destroying tumor cells. Thus, immunotherapies targeting checkpoints, in combination with the development of CAF-targeted treatments, have potential for treating a common tumor that flourishes in a fibroblast-rich TME. Several obstacles, nevertheless, must be addressed to hasten the transition from bench to bedside. To begin, the origins of CAFs in various types of cancer remain unknown. Second, given CAFs' inherent and functional variability, which CAF subtypes fill the immunosuppressive TME? Thirdly, are separate CAF subclasses with varied phenotypes and immunological roles the result of distinct cellular origins? Finally, the notion that the CAF-specific secretome modulates the antitumor immune response is based mostly on in vitro investigations. To aid in the integration of CAF research into clinical treatment, future genetic destiny mapping and single-cell transcriptional analysis are encouraged, since these techniques may provide new ideas about the diversity, hierarchy, and adaptability of CAFs. Finally, and perhaps most importantly, we should investigate in vivo models to clearly describe the action of CAF-released molecules that influence tumor immunity.

References

Abangan Jr., R.S., Williams, C.R., Mehrotra, M., Duncan, J.D., LaRue, A.C., 2010. MCP1 directs trafficking of hematopoietic stem cell-derived fibroblast precursors in solid tumor. Am. J. Pathol. 176 (4), 1914–1926.

Allavena, P., Sica, A., Garlanda, C., Mantovani, A., 2008. The Yin-Yang of tumor-associated macrophages in neoplastic progression and immune surveillance. Immunol. Rev. 222 (1), 155–161.

Altorki, N.K., Markowitz, G.J., Gao, D., Port, J.L., Saxena, A., Stiles, B., McGraw, T., Mittal, V., 2019. The lung microenvironment: an important regulator of tumour growth and metastasis. Nat. Rev. Cancer 19 (1), 9–31.

Álvarez-Teijeiro, S., García-Inclán, C., Villaronga, M.Á., Casado, P., Hermida-Prado, F., Granda-Díaz, R., Rodrigo, J.P., Calvo, F., del-Río-Ibisate, N., Gandarillas, A., 2018. Factors secreted by cancer-associated fibroblasts that sustain cancer stem properties in head and neck squamous carcinoma cells as potential therapeutic targets. Cancer 10 (9), 334.

Anderberg, C., Li, H., Fredriksson, L., Andrae, J., Betsholtz, C., Li, X., Eriksson, U., Pietras, K., 2009. Paracrine signaling by platelet-derived growth factor-CC promotes tumor growth by recruitment of cancer-associated fibroblasts. Cancer Res. 69 (1), 369–378.

Aoyagi, Y., Oda, T., Kinoshita, T., Nakahashi, C., Hasebe, T., Ohkohchi, N., Ochiai, A., 2004. Overexpression of TGF-β by infiltrated granulocytes correlates with the expression of collagen mRNA in pancreatic cancer. Br. J. Cancer 91 (7), 1316–1326.

Apte, M., Pirola, R.C., Wilson, J.S., 2015. Pancreatic stellate cell: physiologic role, role in fibrosis and cancer. Curr. Opin. Gastroenterol. 31 (5), 416–423.

Arnold, J.N., Magiera, L., Kraman, M., Fearon, D.T., 2014. Tumoral immune suppression by macrophages expressing fibroblast activation protein-α and heme oxygenase-1. Cancer Immunol. Res. 2 (2), 121–126.

Augsten, M., 2014. Cancer-associated fibroblasts as another polarized cell type of the tumor microenvironment. Front. Oncol. 4, 62.

Bai, Y.P., Shang, K., Chen, H., Ding, F., Wang, Z., Liang, C., Xu, Y., Sun, M.H., Li, Y.Y., 2015. FGF-1/−3/FGFR 4 signaling in cancer-associated fibroblasts promotes tumor progression in colon cancer through Erk and MMP-7. Cancer Sci. 106 (10), 1278–1287.

Baram, D., Vaday, G.G., Salamon, P., Drucker, I., Hershkoviz, R., Mekori, Y.A., 2001. Human mast cells release metalloproteinase-9 on contact with activated T cells: juxtacrine regulation by TNF-α. J. Immunol. 167 (7), 4008–4016.

Barth, P.J., Ebrahimsade, S., Ramaswamy, A., Moll, R., 2002. CD34 + fibrocytes in invasive ductal carcinoma, ductal carcinoma in situ, and benign breast lesions. Virchows Arch. 440 (3), 298–303.

Bartoschek, M., Oskolkov, N., Bocci, M., Lövrot, J., Larsson, C., Sommarin, M., Madsen, C.D., Lindgren, D., Pekar, G., Karlsson, G., 2018. Spatially and functionally distinct subclasses of breast cancer-associated fibroblasts revealed by single cell RNA sequencing. Nat. Commun. 9 (1), 1–13.

Bayer, S.V.H., Grither, W.R., Brenot, A., Hwang, P.Y., Barcus, C.E., Ernst, M., Pence, P., Walter, C., Pathak, A., Longmore, G.D., 2019. DDR2 controls breast tumor stiffness and metastasis by regulating integrin mediated mechanotransduction in CAFs. Elife 8, e45508.

Beer, T.W., Ng, L.B., Murray, K., 2008. Mast cells have prognostic value in Merkel cell carcinoma. Am. J. Dermatopathol. 30 (1), 27–30.

Biffi, G., Oni, T.E., Spielman, B., Hao, Y., Elyada, E., Park, Y., Preall, J., Tuveson, D.A., 2019. IL1-induced JAK/STAT signaling is antagonized by TGFβ to shape CAF heterogeneity in pancreatic ductal adenocarcinoma. Cancer Discov. 9 (2), 282–301.

Blaner, W.S., O'Byrne, S.M., Wongsiriroj, N., Kluwe, J., D'Ambrosio, D.M., Jiang, H., Schwabe, R.F., Hillman, E.M.C., Piantedosi, R., Libien, J., 2009. Hepatic stellate cell lipid droplets: a specialized lipid droplet for retinoid storage. Biochim. Biophys. Acta Mol. Cell. Biol. Lipids 1791 (6), 467–473.

Brechbuhl, H.M., Finlay-Schultz, J., Yamamoto, T.M., Gillen, A.E., Cittelly, D.M., Tan, A.-C., Sams, S.B., Pillai, M.M., Elias, A.D., Robinson, W.A., 2017. Fibroblast subtypes regulate responsiveness of luminal breast cancer to estrogen. Clin. Cancer Res. 23 (7), 1710–1721.

Brizzi, M.F., Tarone, G., Defilippi, P., 2012. Extracellular matrix, integrins, and growth factors as tailors of the stem cell niche. Curr. Opin. Cell Biol. 24 (5), 645–651.

Brown, F.D., Turley, S.J., 2015. Fibroblastic reticular cells: organization and regulation of the T lymphocyte life cycle. J. Immunol. 194 (4), 1389–1394.

Bu, L., Baba, H., Yoshida, N., Miyake, K., Yasuda, T., Uchihara, T., Tan, P., Ishimoto, T., 2019. Biological heterogeneity and versatility of cancer-associated fibroblasts in the tumor microenvironment. Oncogene 38 (25), 4887–4901.

Buechler, M.B., Turley, S.J., 2018. A Short Field Guide to Fibroblast Function in Immunity. Semin. Immunol. 35, 48–58. Elsevier.

Calon, A., Lonardo, E., Berenguer-Llergo, A., Espinet, E., Hernando-Momblona, X., Iglesias, M., Sevillano, M., Palomo-Ponce, S., Tauriello, D.V.F., Byrom, D., 2015. Stromal gene expression defines poor-prognosis subtypes in colorectal cancer. Nat. Genet. 47 (4), 320–329.

Chan, T.-S., Hsu, C.-C., Pai, V.C., Liao, W.-Y., Huang, S.-S., Tan, K.-T., Yen, C.-J., Hsu, S.-C., Chen, W.-Y., Shan, Y.-S., 2016. Metronomic chemotherapy prevents therapy-induced stromal activation and induction of tumor-initiating cells. J. Exp. Med. 213 (13), 2967–2988.

Chen, X., Song, E., 2019. Turning foes to friends: targeting cancer-associated fibroblasts. Nat. Rev. Drug Discov. 18 (2), 99–115.

Cheng, Y., Li, H., Deng, Y., Tai, Y., Zeng, K., Zhang, Y., Liu, W., Zhang, Q., Yang, Y., 2018. Cancer-associated fibroblasts induce PDL1 + neutrophils through the IL6-STAT3 pathway that foster immune suppression in hepatocellular carcinoma. Cell Death Dis. 9 (4), 1–11.

Cirri, P., Chiarugi, P., 2012. Cancer-associated-fibroblasts and tumour cells: a diabolic liaison driving cancer progression. Cancer Metastasis Rev. 31 (1), 195–208.

Cohen, N., Shani, O., Raz, Y., Sharon, Y., Hoffman, D., Abramovitz, L., Erez, N., 2017. Fibroblasts drive an immunosuppressive and growth-promoting microenvironment in breast cancer via secretion of Chitinase 3-like 1. Oncogene 36 (31), 4457–4468.

Comito, G., Giannoni, E., Segura, C.P., Barcellos-de-Souza, P., Raspollini, M.R., Baroni, G., Lanciotti, M., Serni, S., Chiarugi, P., 2014. Cancer-associated fibroblasts and M2-polarized macrophages synergize during prostate carcinoma progression. Oncogene 33 (19), 2423–2431.

Costa, A., Kieffer, Y., Scholer-Dahirel, A., Pelon, F., Bourachot, B., Cardon, M., Sirven, P., Magagna, I., Fuhrmann, L., Bernard, C., 2018. Fibroblast heterogeneity and immunosuppressive environment in human breast cancer. Cancer Cell 33 (3), 463–479.

Cremasco, V., Astarita, J.L., Grauel, A.L., Keerthivasan, S., MacIsaac, K., Woodruff, M.C., Wu, M., Spel, L., Santoro, S., Amoozgar, Z., 2018. FAP delineates heterogeneous and functionally divergent stromal cells in immune-excluded breast tumors. Cancer Immunol. Res. 6 (12), 1472–1485.

Dalton, D.K., Noelle, R.J., 2012. The roles of mast cells in anticancer immunity. Cancer Immunol. Immunother. 61 (9), 1511–1520.

Du, H., Che, G., 2017. Genetic alterations and epigenetic alterations of cancer-associated fibroblasts. Oncol. Lett. 13 (1), 3–12.

Ecker, B.L., Kaur, A., Douglass, S.M., Webster, M.R., Almeida, F.V., Marino, G.E., Sinnamon, A.J., Neuwirth, M.G., Alicea, G.M., Ndoye, A., 2019. Age-related changes in HAPLN1 increase lymphatic permeability and affect routes of melanoma metastasis. Cancer Discov. 9 (1), 82–95.

Ellem, S.J., Taylor, R.A., Furic, L., Larsson, O., Frydenberg, M., Pook, D., Pedersen, J., Cawsey, B., Trotta, A., Need, E., 2014. A pro-tumourigenic loop at the human prostate tumour interface orchestrated by oestrogen, CXCL12 and mast cell recruitment. J. Pathol. 234 (1), 86–98.

Erez, N., Truitt, M., Olson, P., Hanahan, D., 2010. Cancer-associated fibroblasts are activated in incipient neoplasia to orchestrate tumor-promoting inflammation in an NF-κB-dependent manner. Cancer Cell 17 (2), 135–147.

Fang, T., Lv, H., Lv, G., Li, T., Wang, C., Han, Q., Yu, L., Su, B., Guo, L., Huang, S., 2018. Tumor-derived exosomal miR-1247-3p induces cancer-associated fibroblast activation to foster lung metastasis of liver cancer. Nat. Commun. 9 (1), 1–13.

Feig, C., Jones, J.O., Kraman, M., Wells, R.J.B., Deonarine, A., Chan, D.S., Connell, C.M., Roberts, E.W., Zhao, Q., Caballero, O.L., 2013. Targeting CXCL12 from FAP-expressing carcinoma-associated fibroblasts synergizes with anti–PD-L1 immunotherapy in pancreatic cancer. Proc. Natl. Acad. Sci. U. S. A. 110 (50), 20212–20217.

Fiori, M.E., Di Franco, S., Villanova, L., Bianca, P., Stassi, G., De Maria, R., 2019. Cancer-associated fibroblasts as abettors of tumor progression at the crossroads of EMT and therapy resistance. Mol. Cancer 18 (1), 1–16.

Fischer, K.R., Durrans, A., Lee, S., Sheng, J., Li, F., Wong, S.T.C., Choi, H., El Rayes, T., Ryu, S., Troeger, J., 2015. Epithelial-to-mesenchymal transition is not required for lung metastasis but contributes to chemoresistance. Nature 527 (7579), 472–476.

Fletcher, A.L., Malhotra, D., Turley, S.J., 2011. Lymph node stroma broaden the peripheral tolerance paradigm. Trends Immunol. 32 (1), 12–18.

Franco-Barraza, J., Francescone, R., Luong, T., Shah, N., Madhani, R., Cukierman, G., Dulaimi, E., Devarajan, K., Egleston, B.L., Nicolas, E., 2017. Matrix-regulated integrin αvβ5 maintains α5β1-dependent desmoplastic traits prognostic of neoplastic recurrence. Elife 6, e20600.

Fridlender, Z.G., Sun, J., Kim, S., Kapoor, V., Cheng, G., Ling, L., Worthen, G.S., Albelda, S.M., 2009. Polarization of tumor-associated neutrophil phenotype by TGF-β:"N1" versus "N2" TAN. Cancer Cell 16 (3), 183–194.

Fukumura, D., Xavier, R., Sugiura, T., Chen, Y., Park, E.-C., Lu, N., Selig, M., Nielsen, G., Taksir, T., Jain, R.K., 1998. Tumor induction of VEGF promoter activity in stromal cells. Cell 94 (6), 715–725.

Gabbiani, G., 2003. The myofibroblast in wound healing and fibrocontractive diseases. J. Pathol. 200 (4), 500–503.

Gentles, A.J., Hui, A.B.-Y., Feng, W., Azizi, A., Nair, R.V., Bouchard, G., Knowles, D.A., Yu, A., Jeong, Y., Bejnood, A., 2020. A human lung tumor microenvironment interactome identifies clinically relevant cell-type cross-talk. Genome Biol. 21 (1), 1–22.

Givel, A.-M., Kieffer, Y., Scholer-Dahirel, A., Sirven, P., Cardon, M., Pelon, F., Magagna, I., Gentric, G., Costa, A., Bonneau, C., 2018. miR200-regulated CXCL12β promotes fibroblast heterogeneity and immunosuppression in ovarian cancers. Nat. Commun. 9 (1), 1–20.

Gok Yavuz, B., Gunaydin, G., Gedik, M.E., Kosemehmetoglu, K., Karakoc, D., Ozgur, F., Guc, D., 2019. Cancer associated fibroblasts sculpt tumour microenvironment by recruiting monocytes and inducing immunosuppressive PD-1 + TAMs. Sci. Rep. 9 (1), 1–15.

Gordon, S.R., Maute, R.L., Dulken, B.W., Hutter, G., George, B.M., McCracken, M.N., Gupta, R., Tsai, J.M., Sinha, R., Corey, D., 2017. PD-1 expression by tumour-associated macrophages inhibits phagocytosis and tumour immunity. Nature 545 (7655), 495–499.

Goulet, C.R., Bernard, G., Tremblay, S., Chabaud, S., Bolduc, S., Pouliot, F., 2018. Exosomes induce fibroblast differentiation into cancer-associated fibroblasts through TGFβ signaling. Mol. Cancer Res. 16 (7), 1196–1204.

Hah, N., Sherman, M.H., Ruth, T.Y., Downes, M., Evans, R.M., 2015. Targeting Transcriptional and Epigenetic Reprogramming in Stromal Cells in Fibrosis and Cancer. Cold Spring Harb. Symp. Quant. Biol. 80, 249–255. Cold Spring Harbor Laboratory Press.

Harper, J., Sainson, R.C.A., 2014. Regulation of the Anti-Tumour Immune Response by Cancer-Associated Fibroblasts. Semin. Cancer Biol. 25, 69–77. Elsevier.

Herrera, M., Herrera, A., Domínguez, G., Silva, J., García, V., García, J.M., Gómez, I., Soldevilla, B., Muñoz, C., Provencio, M., 2013. Cancer-associated fibroblast and M 2 macrophage markers together predict outcome in colorectal cancer patients. Cancer Sci. 104 (4), 437–444.

Hirata, E., Girotti, M.R., Viros, A., Hooper, S., Spencer-Dene, B., Matsuda, M., Larkin, J., Marais, R., Sahai, E., 2015. Intravital imaging reveals how BRAF inhibition generates drug-tolerant microenvironments with high integrin β1/FAK signaling. Cancer Cell 27 (4), 574–588.

Hölzel, M., Landsberg, J., Glodde, N., Bald, T., Rogava, M., Riesenberg, S., Becker, A., Jönsson, G., Tüting, T., 2016. A preclinical model of malignant peripheral nerve sheath tumor-like melanoma is characterized by infiltrating mast cells. Cancer Res. 76 (2), 251–263.

Hu, B., Wang, Z., Zeng, H., Qi, Y., Chen, Y., Wang, T., Wang, J., Chang, Y., Bai, Q., Xia, Y., 2020. Blockade of DC-SIGN + tumor-associated macrophages reactivates antitumor immunity and improves immunotherapy in muscle-invasive bladder cancer. Cancer Res. 80 (8), 1707–1719.

Jablonska, J., Leschner, S., Westphal, K., Lienenklaus, S., Weiss, S., 2010. Neutrophils responsive to endogenous IFN-β regulate tumor angiogenesis and growth in a mouse tumor model. J. Clin. Invest. 120 (4), 1151–1164.

Jan, S., Mir, M., 2021. Therapeutic landscape of metaplastic breast cancer. Combination Therapies and their Effectiveness in Breast Cancer Treatment. Nova Biomedical Science, New York, USA.

Jan, S., Qayoom, H., Mehraj, U., Mir, M A, 2021. Therapeutic Options for Breast Cancer, first ed. vol. 1 Nova Biomedical Science, New York, USA, pp. 357–396.

Jotzu, C., Alt, E., Welte, G., Li, J., Hennessy, B.T., Devarajan, E., Krishnappa, S., Pinilla, S., Droll, L., Song, Y.-H., 2011. Adipose tissue derived stem cells differentiate into carcinoma-associated fibroblast-like cells under the influence of tumor derived factors. Cell. Oncol. 34 (1), 55–67.

Kalluri, R., 2016. The biology and function of fibroblasts in cancer. Nat. Rev. Cancer 16 (9), 582–598.

Kalluri, R., Zeisberg, M., 2006. Fibroblasts in cancer. Nat. Rev. Cancer 6 (5), 392–401.

Kaur, A., Webster, M.R., Marchbank, K., Behera, R., Ndoye, A., Kugel, C.H., Dang, V.M., Appleton, J., O'Connell, M.P., Cheng, P., 2016. sFRP2 in the aged microenvironment drives melanoma metastasis and therapy resistance. Nature 532 (7598), 250–254.

Kidd, S., Spaeth, E., Watson, K., Burks, J., Lu, H., Klopp, A., Andreeff, M., Marini, F.C., 2012. Origins of the tumor microenvironment: quantitative assessment of adipose-derived and bone marrow–derived stroma. PLoS One 7 (2), e30563.

Kim, S., Chen, J., Cheng, T., Gindulyte, A., He, J., He, S., Li, Q., Shoemaker, B.A., Thiessen, P.A., Yu, B., 2019. PubChem 2019 update: improved access to chemical data. Nucleic Acids Res. 47 (D1), D1102–D1109.

Kobayashi, H., Enomoto, A., Woods, S.L., Burt, A.D., Takahashi, M., Worthley, D.L., 2019. Cancer-associated fibroblasts in gastrointestinal cancer. Nat. Rev. Gastroenterol. Hepatol. 16 (5), 282–295.

Kojima, Y., Acar, A., Eaton, E.N., Mellody, K.T., Scheel, C., Ben-Porath, I., Onder, T.T., Wang, Z.C., Richardson, A.L., Weinberg, R.A., 2010. Autocrine TGF-β and stromal cell-derived factor-1 (SDF-1) signaling drives the evolution of tumor-promoting mammary stromal myofibroblasts. Proc. Natl. Acad. Sci. U. S. A. 107 (46), 20009–20014.

Kraman, M., Bambrough, P.J., Arnold, J.N., Roberts, E.W., Magiera, L., Jones, J.O., Gopinathan, A., Tuveson, D.A., Fearon, D.T., 2010. Suppression of antitumor immunity by stromal cells expressing fibroblast activation protein–α. Science 330 (6005), 827–830.

Ksiazkiewicz, M., Gottfried, E., Kreutz, M., Mack, M., Hofstaedter, F., Kunz-Schughart, L.A., 2010. Importance of CCL2-CCR2A/2B signaling for monocyte migration into spheroids of breast cancer-derived fibroblasts. Immunobiology 215 (9–10), 737–747.

Kuzet, S.-E., Gaggioli, C., 2016. Fibroblast activation in cancer: when seed fertilizes soil. Cell Tissue Res. 365 (3), 607–619.

Labernadie, A., Kato, T., Brugués, A., Serra-Picamal, X., Derzsi, S., Arwert, E., Weston, A., González-Tarragó, V., Elosegui-Artola, A., Albertazzi, L., 2017. A mechanically active heterotypic E-cadherin/N-cadherin adhesion enables fibroblasts to drive cancer cell invasion. Nat. Cell Biol. 19 (3), 224–237.

Lambrechts, D., Wauters, E., Boeckx, B., Aibar, S., Nittner, D., Burton, O., Bassez, A., Decaluwé, H., Pircher, A., Van den Eynde, K., 2018. Phenotype molding of stromal cells in the lung tumor microenvironment. Nat. Med. 24 (8), 1277–1289.

Le Guen, L., Marchal, S., Faure, S., de Santa Barbara, P., 2015. Mesenchymal–epithelial interactions during digestive tract development and epithelial stem cell regeneration. Cell. Mol. Life Sci. 72 (20), 3883–3896.

LeBleu, V.S., Kalluri, R., 2018. A peek into cancer-associated fibroblasts: origins, functions and translational impact. Dis. Model. Mech. 11 (4), dmm029447.

Li, H., Courtois, E.T., Sengupta, D., Tan, Y., Chen, K.H., Goh, J.J.L., Kong, S.L., Chua, C., Hon, L.K., Tan, W.S., 2017. Reference component analysis of single-cell transcriptomes elucidates cellular heterogeneity in human colorectal tumors. Nat. Genet. 49 (5), 708–718.

Liao, Z., Tan, Z.W., Zhu, P., Tan, N.S., 2019. Cancer-associated fibroblasts in tumor microenvironment-accomplices in tumor malignancy. Cell. Immunol. 343, 103729.

Löhr, M., Schmidt, C., Ringel, J., Kluth, M., Müller, P., Nizze, H., Jesnowski, R., 2001. Transforming growth factor-β1 induces desmoplasia in an experimental model of human pancreatic carcinoma. Cancer Res. 61 (2), 550–555.

Ma, Y., Hwang, R.F., Logsdon, C.D., Ullrich, S.E., 2013. Dynamic mast cell–stromal cell interactions promote growth of pancreatic cancer. Cancer Res. 73 (13), 3927–3937.

Mace, T.A., Ameen, Z., Collins, A., Wojcik, S., Mair, M., Young, G.S., Fuchs, J.R., Eubank, T.D., Frankel, W.L., Bekaii-Saab, T., 2013. Pancreatic cancer-associated stellate cells promote differentiation of myeloid-derived suppressor cells in a STAT3-dependent manner. Cancer Res. 73 (10), 3007–3018.

Maman, S., Witz, I.P., 2018. A history of exploring cancer in context. Nat. Rev. Cancer 18 (6), 359–376.

Mantovani, A., Sica, A., Sozzani, S., Allavena, P., Vecchi, A., Locati, M., 2004. The chemokine system in diverse forms of macrophage activation and polarization. Trends Immunol. 25 (12), 677–686.

Mantovani, A., Allavena, P., Sica, A., Balkwill, F., 2008. Cancer-related inflammation. Nature 454 (7203), 436–444.

Mariathasan, S., Turley, S.J., Nickles, D., Castiglioni, A., Yuen, K., Wang, Y., Kadel Iii, E.E., Koeppen, H., Astarita, J.L., Cubas, R., 2018. TGFβ attenuates tumour response to PD-L1 blockade by contributing to exclusion of T cells. Nature 554 (7693), 544–548.

Marsh, T., Pietras, K., McAllister, S.S., 2013. Fibroblasts as architects of cancer pathogenesis. Biochim. Biophys. Acta Mol. Basis Dis. 1832 (7), 1070–1078.

Mazur, A., Holthoff, E., Vadali, S., Kelly, T., Post, S.R., 2016. Cleavage of type I collagen by fibroblast activation protein-α enhances class A scavenger receptor mediated macrophage adhesion. PLoS One 11 (3), e0150287.

Medina, V., Cricco, G., Nuñez, M., Martín, G., Mohamad, N., Correa-Fiz, F., Sanchez-Jimenez, F., Bergoc, R., Rivera, E.S., 2006. Histamine-mediated signaling processes in human malignant mammary cells. Cancer Biol. Ther. 5 (11), 1462–1471.

Mehraj, U., Dar, A.H., Wani, N.A., Mir, M.A., 2021a. Tumor microenvironment promotes breast cancer chemoresistance. Cancer Chemother. Pharmacol., 1–12.

Mehraj, U., Ganai, R.A., Macha, M.A., Hamid, A., Zargar, M.A., Bhat, A.A., Nasser, M.W., Haris, M., Batra, S.K., Alshehri, B., 2021b. The tumor microenvironment as driver of stemness and therapeutic resistance in breast cancer: new challenges and therapeutic opportunities. Cell. Oncol., 1–21.

Mehraj, U., Aisha, S., Sofi, S., Mir, M.A., 2022. Expression pattern and prognostic significance of baculoviral inhibitor of apoptosis repeat-containing 5 (BIRC5) in breast cancer: a comprehensive analysis. Adv. Cancer Biol. Metastasis, 100037.

Mir, M.A., Hamdani, S.S., Sheikh, B.A., Mehraj, U., 2019. Recent advances in metabolites from medicinal plants in cancer prevention and treatment. Curr. Immunol. Rev. 15 (2), 185–201.

Mir, M.A., Qayoom, H., Mehraj, U., Nisar, S., Bhat, B., Wani, N.A., 2020. Targeting different pathways using novel combination therapy in triple negative breast cancer. Curr. Cancer Drug Targets 20 (8), 586–602.

Mir, M., Jan, S., Mehraj, U., 2022a. Current Therapeutics and Treatment Options in TNBC. Chapter-3, Elsevier, pp. 73–144.

Mir, M., Sofi, S., Qayoom, H., 2022b. Different Drug Delivery Approaches in Combinational Therapy in TNBC. Chapter-8, Elsevier, pp. 278–311.

Mir, M., Sofi, S., Qayoom, H., 2022c. The Interplay of Immunotherapy, Chemotherapy, and Targeted Therapy in Tripple Negative Breast Cancer (TNBC). Chapter-6, Elsevier, pp. 201–244.

Mir, M., Sofi, S., Qayoom, H., 2022d. Targeting Biologically Specific Molecules in Triple Negative Breast Cancer (TNBC). Chapter-7, Elsevier, pp. 245–277.

Mir, M., Jan, S., Mehraj, U., 2022e. Conventional Adjuvant Chemotherapy in Combination With Surgery, Radiotherapy and Other Specific Targets. Chapter-4, Elsevier, pp. 145–176.

Mir, M., Jan, S., Mehraj, U., 2022f. Novel Biomarkers in Triple-Negative Breast Cancer-Role and Perspective (Chapter-2). Elsevier, pp. 36–72.

Mir, M., Jan, S., Mehraj, U., Qayoom, H., Nisar, S., 2022g. Immuno-Onco-Metabolism and Therapeutic Resistance. Springer, pp. 1–32.

Miyai, Y., Esaki, N., Takahashi, M., Enomoto, A., 2020. Cancer-associated fibroblasts that restrain cancer progression: Hypotheses and perspectives. Cancer Sci. 111 (4), 1047–1057.

Mizutani, Y., Kobayashi, H., Iida, T., Asai, N., Masamune, A., Hara, A., Esaki, N., Ushida, K., Mii, S., Shiraki, Y., 2019. Meflin-positive cancer-associated fibroblasts inhibit pancreatic carcinogenesis. Cancer Res. 79 (20), 5367–5381.

Monteran, L., Erez, N., 2019. The dark side of fibroblasts: cancer-associated fibroblasts as mediators of immunosuppression in the tumor microenvironment. Front. Immunol., 1835.

Nagarsheth, N., Wicha, M.S., Zou, W., 2017. Chemokines in the cancer microenvironment and their relevance in cancer immunotherapy. Nat. Rev. Immunol. 17 (9), 559–572.

Nair, N., Calle, A.S., Zahra, M.H., Prieto-Vila, M., Oo, A.K.K., Hurley, L., Vaidyanath, A., Seno, A., Masuda, J., Iwasaki, Y., 2017. A cancer stem cell model as the point of origin of cancer-associated fibroblasts in tumor microenvironment. Sci. Rep. 7 (1), 1–13.

Naito, Y., Yamamoto, Y., Sakamoto, N., Shimomura, I., Kogure, A., Kumazaki, M., Yokoi, A., Yashiro, M., Kiyono, T., Yanagihara, K., 2019. Cancer extracellular vesicles contribute to stromal heterogeneity by inducing chemokines in cancer-associated fibroblasts. Oncogene 38 (28), 5566–5579.

Ning, X., Zhang, H., Wang, C., Song, X., 2018. Exosomes released by gastric cancer cells induce transition of pericytes into cancer-associated fibroblasts. Med. Sci. Monit. 24, 2350.

Nurmik, M., Ullmann, P., Rodriguez, F., Haan, S., Letellier, E., 2020. In search of definitions: cancer-associated fibroblasts and their markers. Int. J. Cancer 146 (4), 895–905.

Öhlund, D., Handly-Santana, A., Biffi, G., Elyada, E., Almeida, A.S., Ponz-Sarvise, M., Corbo, V., Oni, T.-E., Hearn, S.A., Lee, E.J., 2017. Distinct populations of inflammatory fibroblasts and myofibroblasts in pancreatic cancer. J. Exp. Med. 214 (3), 579–596.

Özdemir, B.C., Pentcheva-Hoang, T., Carstens, J.L., Zheng, X., Wu, C.-C., Simpson, T.R., Laklai, H., Sugimoto, H., Kahlert, C., Novitskiy, S.V., 2014. Depletion of carcinoma-associated fibroblasts and fibrosis induces immunosuppression and accelerates pancreas cancer with reduced survival. Cancer Cell 25 (6), 719–734.

Pereira, B.A., Lister, N.L., Hashimoto, K., Teng, L., Flandes-Iparraguirre, M., Eder, A., Sanchez-Herrero, A., Niranjan, B., Frydenberg, M., Papargiris, M.M., 2019. Tissue engineered human prostate microtissues reveal key role of mast cell-derived tryptase in potentiating cancer-associated fibroblast (CAF)-induced morphometric transition in vitro. Biomaterials 197, 72–85.

Philippeos, C., Telerman, S.B., Oulès, B., Pisco, A.O., Shaw, T.J., Elgueta, R., Lombardi, G., Driskell, R.-R., Soldin, M., Lynch, M.D., 2018. Spatial and single-cell transcriptional profiling identifies functionally distinct human dermal fibroblast subpopulations. J. Investig. Dermatol. 138 (4), 811–825.

Ping, Q., Yan, R., Cheng, X., Wang, W., Zhong, Y., Hou, Z., Shi, Y., Wang, C., Li, R., 2021. Cancer-associated fibroblasts: overview, progress, challenges, and directions. Cancer Gene Ther. 28 (9), 984–999.

Potenta, S., Zeisberg, E., Kalluri, R., 2008. The role of endothelial-to-mesenchymal transition in cancer progression. Br. J. Cancer 99 (9), 1375–1379.

Quail, D.F., Joyce, J.A., 2013. Microenvironmental regulation of tumor progression and metastasis. Nat. Med. 19 (11), 1423–1437.

Rai, A., Greening, D.W., Chen, M., Xu, R., Ji, H., Simpson, R.J., 2019. Exosomes derived from human primary and metastatic colorectal cancer cells contribute to functional heterogeneity of activated fibroblasts by reprogramming their proteome. Proteomics 19 (8), 1800148.

Raman, D., Baugher, P.J., Thu, Y.M., Richmond, A., 2007. Role of chemokines in tumor growth. Cancer Lett. 256 (2), 137–165.

Raz, Y., Cohen, N., Shani, O., Bell, R.E., Novitskiy, S.V., Abramovitz, L., Levy, C., Milyavsky, M., Leider-Trejo, L., Moses, H.L., 2018. Bone marrow–derived fibroblasts are a functionally distinct stromal cell population in breast cancer. J. Exp. Med. 215 (12), 3075–3093.

Ren, Y., Jia, H.-H., Xu, Y.-Q., Zhou, X., Zhao, X.-H., Wang, Y.-F., Song, X., Zhu, Z.-Y., Sun, T., Dou, Y., 2018. Paracrine and epigenetic control of CAF-induced metastasis: the role of HOTAIR stimulated by TGF-ss1 secretion. Mol. Cancer 17 (1), 1–14.

Rhim, A.D., Oberstein, P.E., Thomas, D.H., Mirek, E.T., Palermo, C.F., Sastra, S.A., Dekleva, E.N., Saunders, T., Becerra, C.P., Tattersall, I.W., 2014. Stromal elements act to restrain, rather than support, pancreatic ductal adenocarcinoma. Cancer Cell 25 (6), 735–747.

Ribatti, D., Crivellato, E., 2011. Mast cells, angiogenesis and cancer. In: Mast Cell Biology. Elsevier, pp. 270–288.

Richeldi, L., Du Bois, R.M., Raghu, G., Azuma, A., Brown, K.K., Costabel, U., Cottin, V., Flaherty, K.R., Hansell, D.M., Inoue, Y., 2014. Efficacy and safety of nintedanib in idiopathic pulmonary fibrosis. N. Engl. J. Med. 370 (22), 2071–2082.

Rockey, D.C., Weymouth, N., Shi, Z., 2013. Smooth muscle α actin (Acta2) and myofibroblast function during hepatic wound healing. PLoS One 8 (10), e77166.

Sahai, E., Astsaturov, I., Cukierman, E., DeNardo, D.G., Egeblad, M., Evans, R.M., Fearon, D., Greten, F.-R., Hingorani, S.R., Hunter, T., 2020. A framework for advancing our understanding of cancer-associated fibroblasts. Nat. Rev. Cancer 20 (3), 174–186.

Sherman, M.H., Ruth, T.Y., Engle, D.D., Ding, N., Atkins, A.R., Tiriac, H., Collisson, E.A., Connor, F., Van Dyke, T., Kozlov, S., 2014. Vitamin D receptor-mediated stromal reprogramming suppresses pancreatitis and enhances pancreatic cancer therapy. Cell 159 (1), 80–93.

Shiga, K., Hara, M., Nagasaki, T., Sato, T., Takahashi, H., Takeyama, H., 2015. Cancer-associated fibroblasts: their characteristics and their roles in tumor growth. Cancer 7 (4), 2443–2458.

Shimoda, M., Principe, S., Jackson, H.W., Luga, V., Fang, H., Molyneux, S.D., Shao, Y.W., Aiken, A., Waterhouse, P.D., Karamboulas, C., 2014. Loss of the Timp gene family is sufficient for the acquisition of the CAF-like cell state. Nat. Cell Biol. 16 (9), 889–901.

Singh, U., Chashoo, G., Khan, S.U., Mahajan, P., Nargotra, A., Mahajan, G., Singh, A., Sharma, A., Mintoo, M.J., Guru, S.K., 2017. Design of novel 3-pyrimidinylazaindole CDK2/9 inhibitors with potent in vitro and in vivo antitumor efficacy in a triple-negative breast cancer model. J. Med. Chem. 60 (23), 9470–9489.

Song, M., He, J., Pan, Q.Z., Yang, J., Zhao, J., Zhang, Y.J., Huang, Y., Tang, Y., Wang, Q., He, J., 2021. Cancer-associated fibroblast-mediated cellular crosstalk supports hepatocellular carcinoma progression. Hepatology 73 (5), 1717–1735.

Su, S., Chen, J., Yao, H., Liu, J., Yu, S., Lao, L., Wang, M., Luo, M., Xing, Y., Chen, F., 2018. CD10 + GPR77 + cancer-associated fibroblasts promote cancer formation and chemoresistance by sustaining cancer stemness. Cell 172 (4), 841–856.

Takahashi, H., Sakakura, K., Kudo, T., Toyoda, M., Kaira, K., Oyama, T., Chikamatsu, K., 2017. Cancer-associated fibroblasts promote an immunosuppressive microenvironment through the induction and accumulation of protumoral macrophages. Oncotarget 8 (5), 8633.

Tan, B., Shi, X., Zhang, J., Qin, J., Zhang, N., Ren, H., Qian, M., Siwko, S., Carmon, K., Liu, Q., 2018. Inhibition of Rspo-Lgr4 facilitates checkpoint blockade therapy by switching macrophage polarization. Cancer Res. 78 (17), 4929–4942.

Tan, H.-X., Cao, Z.-B., He, T.-T., Huang, T., Xiang, C.-L., Liu, Y., 2019. TGFβ1 is essential for MSCs-CAFs differentiation and promotes HCT116 cells migration and invasion via JAK/STAT3 signaling. OncoTargets Ther. 12, 5323.

Tang, X., Tu, G., Yang, G., Wang, X., Kang, L., Yang, L., Zeng, H., Wan, X., Qiao, Y., Cui, X., 2019. Autocrine TGF-β1/miR-200s/miR-221/DNMT3B regulatory loop maintains CAF status to fuel breast cancer cell proliferation. Cancer Lett. 452, 79–89.

Tauriello, D.V.F., Palomo-Ponce, S., Stork, D., Berenguer-Llergo, A., Badia-Ramentol, J., Iglesias, M., Sevillano, M., Ibiza, S., Cañellas, A., Hernando-Momblona, X., 2018. TGFβ drives immune evasion in genetically reconstituted colon cancer metastasis. Nature 554 (7693), 538–543.

Tommelein, J., De Vlieghere, E., Verset, L., Melsens, E., Leenders, J., Descamps, B., Debucquoy, A., Vanhove, C., Pauwels, P., Gespach, C.P., 2018. Radiotherapy-activated cancer-associated fibroblasts promote tumor progression through paracrine IGF1R activation. Cancer Res. 78 (3), 659–670.

Turley, S.J., Cremasco, V., Astarita, J.L., 2015. Immunological hallmarks of stromal cells in the tumour microenvironment. Nat. Rev. Immunol. 15 (11), 669–682.

Ueshima, E., Fujimori, M., Kodama, H., Felsen, D., Chen, J., Durack, J.C., Solomon, S.B., Coleman, J.A., Srimathveeravalli, G., 2019. Macrophage-secreted TGF-β1 contributes to fibroblast activation and ureteral stricture after ablation injury. Am. J. Physiol. Renal Physiol. 317 (7), F52–F64.

Valkenburg, K.C., De Groot, A.E., Pienta, K.J., 2018. Targeting the tumour stroma to improve cancer therapy. Nat. Rev. Clin. Oncol. 15 (6), 366–381.

Von Ahrens, D., Bhagat, T.D., Nagrath, D., Maitra, A., Verma, A., 2017. The role of stromal cancer-associated fibroblasts in pancreatic cancer. J. Hematol. Oncol. 10 (1), 1–8.

Wang, L., Zhang, F., Cui, J.Y., Chen, L., Chen, Y.T., Liu, B.W., 2018. CAFs enhance paclitaxel resistance by inducing EMT through the IL-6/JAK2/STAT3 pathway. Oncol. Rep. 39 (5), 2081–2090.

Wang, J.L., Ibrahim, A.K., Zhuang, H., Ali, A.M., Li, A.Y., Wu, A., 2019. A Study on Automatic Detection of IDC Breast Cancer with Convolutional Neural Networks. IEEE.

Wong, P.F., Wei, W., Gupta, S., Smithy, J.W., Zelterman, D., Kluger, H.M., Rimm, D.L., 2019. Multiplex quantitative analysis of cancer-associated fibroblasts and immunotherapy outcome in metastatic melanoma. J. Immunother. Cancer 7 (1), 1–10.

Wu, L., Saxena, S., Awaji, M., Singh, R.K., 2019. Tumor-associated neutrophils in cancer: going pro. Cancer 11 (4), 564.

Yamamura, M., Sato, Y., Takahashi, K., Sasaki, M., Harada, K., 2020. The cyclin-dependent kinase pathway involving CDK1 is a potential therapeutic target for cholangiocarcinoma. Oncol. Rep. 43 (1), 306–317.

Yang, F.-C., Chen, S., Clegg, T., Li, X., Morgan, T., Estwick, S.A., Yuan, J., Khalaf, W., Burgin, S., Travers, J., 2006. Nf1 +/− mast cells induce neurofibroma like phenotypes through secreted TGF-β signaling. Hum. Mol. Genet. 15 (16), 2421–2437.

Yang, Z., Peng, Y.-C., Gopalan, A., Gao, D., Chen, Y., Joyner, A.L., 2017. Stromal hedgehog signaling maintains smooth muscle and hampers micro-invasive prostate cancer. Dis. Model. Mech. 10 (1), 39–52.

Yoshida, G.J., 2020. Regulation of heterogeneous cancer-associated fibroblasts: the molecular pathology of activated signaling pathways. J. Exp. Clin. Cancer Res. 39 (1), 1–15.

Zeisberg, E.M., Potenta, S., Xie, L., Zeisberg, M., Kalluri, R., 2007. Discovery of endothelial to mesenchymal transition as a source for carcinoma-associated fibroblasts. Cancer Res. 67 (21), 10123–10128.

Zhang, D., Li, L., Jiang, H., Li, Q., Wang-Gillam, A., Yu, J., Head, R., Liu, J., Ruzinova, M.B., Lim, K.-H., 2018. Tumor–stroma IL1β-IRAK4 feedforward circuitry drives tumor fibrosis, chemoresistance, and poor prognosis in pancreatic cancer. Cancer Res. 78 (7), 1700–1712.

Zhu, Q., Zhang, X., Zhang, L., Li, W., Wu, H., Yuan, X., Mao, F., Wang, M., Zhu, W., Qian, H., 2014. The IL-6–STAT3 axis mediates a reciprocal crosstalk between cancer-derived mesenchymal stem cells and neutrophils to synergistically prompt gastric cancer progression. Cell Death Dis. 5 (6), e1295.

Zhuang, X., Zhang, H., Hu, G., 2019. Cancer and microenvironment plasticity: double-edged swords in metastasis. Trends Pharmacol. Sci. 40 (6), 419–429.

Ziani, L., Chouaib, S., Thiery, J., 2018. Alteration of the antitumor immune response by cancer-associated fibroblasts. Front. Immunol., 414.

CHAPTER 4

Role of mesenchymal stem cells in tumor microenvironment

Manzoor Ahmad Mir[a], Abrar Yousuf Mir[a], Ulfat Jan[a], Mudasir A. Dar[b], and Mohd Zahoor ul Haq Shah[c]

[a]Department of Bioresources, School of Biological Sciences, University of Kashmir, Srinagar, Jammu and Kashmir, India
[b]Department of Plant Pathology, Sher-e-Kashmir University of Agricultural Sciences and Technology of Kashmir, Srinagar, India
[c]Laboratory of Endocrinology, Department of Bioscience Barkatullah University, Bhopal, Madhya Pradesh, India

4.1 Introduction

MSCs are diverse groups of human mesenchymal stroma/stem-like cells that could be developed from the tunica adventitia in perivascular regions of numerous mature tissues and organs, including bone marrow, adipocytes, and blood plasma, tooth pulp, and many more (Viswanathan et al., 2019; Corselli et al., 2012; Bergfeld and DeClerck, 2010; Papaccio et al., 2017). Numerous biological roles are connected to MSCs, like multipotent MSCs or therapeutic signaling cell lines; according to additional terminology, several of these are often contentiously addressed (Caplan, 2017). Including different restorative activities of injured tissues (Sasaki et al., 2008), participation in renewal procedures (Chapel et al., 2003), immunosuppressive properties (Poggi and Zocchi, 2019), formation of new blood vessels (Ghajar et al., 2010), antibacterial properties, paracrine activity (Caplan and Correa, 2011), as well as antitumor (Fong et al., 2012) and protumor attributes (Mandel et al., 2013; Yang et al., 2015; Melzer et al., 2016) are also shown by MSCs. Fetal human mesenchymal stem cells, derived through birth-associated organs including the placenta, fetal membranes, as well as embryonic outer layer had greater in situ expansion potential and increased regeneration ability when contrasted to adult-human tissues (Viswanathan et al., 2019; Caplan, 1991; Bianco, 2014; Hass et al., 2011). In vitro dynamic adhesion, concurrent activation of the adhesion molecules such as CD73, CD90, as well as CD105l, and in vitro maturation ability, at least across osteogenic, adipogenic, and chondrogenic lines, are all characteristics of mesenchymal stem cells (Viswanathan et al., 2019; Bianco, 2014; Pittenger et al., 1999). Along with all the above properties, some of the mesenchymal stem cells possess supplementary properties, not shown by the abiding cell types. These properties include mesenchymal stem cells that are obtained from the umbilical cord generated as well as deliver higher quantities of transforming growth factor-β and decreased amounts of VEGF-α along with elongation growth factor in comparison to MSCs that are derived from adipose tissue and amnion. This suggests that there are immunoediting properties in between tissue-

Role of Tumor Microenvironment in Breast Cancer and Targeted Therapies
https://doi.org/10.1016/B978-0-443-18696-7.00004-X

specific mesenchymal stem cells (Dabrowski et al., 2017). Furthermore, CD146 + ve cells having mesenchymal stem cell–like characteristics were identified inside bone marrow as hematopoiesis supporting angiopoietin-1 expressing osteoprogenitors having in vitro self-renewal capabilities as well as stem cell–like characters (Sacchetti et al., 2007). Not all cells but a small subtype of cells demonstrate similar properties likewise stem cells, mesenchymal stem cells are diverse, composed of numerous interconnected subtypes. Furthermore, certain organs/tissues manifest tissue-specific conditions that put on the irregular mesenchymal stem cell characteristics. The intracellular environment is critical for mesenchymal stem cell growth as well as diversity. Numerous variations can sometimes be purposefully produced in advance, such as at the time of MSC separation using both anomalous enzymatic degradation or tissue culture, in addition to MSC proliferation in xeno-free medium, culture over-restrictive or sensitive interfaces, passaging, as well as in situ differentiation (Sacchetti et al., 2016). Moreover, specific alterations in the microhabitat like decreasing/increasing pH, anoxia/hypoxia/hyperoxia, by increasing or decreasing ion gradients as well as abiding culturing method assists irregular circumstances that can be adventitious for developing new and divergent subtypes of MSCs, this can lead to clonogenic collapse or greater variability (Selich et al., 2016). It has been seen in in vitro studies that the basic growth properties of mesenchymal stem cells could be sustained for just a specified duration (Otte et al., 2013), and mesenchymal stem cell–like cells that proliferate indefinitely provide a cell pool having repeatable features (Melzer et al., 2020). Thus, during the culturing few attributes of these stem cells might differentiate from the normal in vivo conditions. During tumor progression, changes within the microenvironment are seen, and mesenchymal stem cells play a crucial role in generating phenotypic plasticity along with tumors. The TME of solid tumors seems to be an organ–like structure formed by an arrangement of ECM and diverse cell populations. As a result, sturdy tumors could be viewed as a composite structure composed of cancerous cells in various stages of expansion (differentiated, parent, or cancer progenitor cell cells) in conjunction with such a wide range of preferentially organized cell lines, constructing reconfigurable immunogenicity, helping to tumor progression as well as vasculature, and forming an ECM, that allows the affiliated isoforms to interact inside the Tumor micro environment and interdependently rely upon each other. Abrasion and localized tissue damage are caused by tumor cells' aggressive amplification and expansion. Such tissue damage causes chronic inflammation, that recruits a variety of leukocytes (Fridman et al., 2012). Certain immune cells functions, including the transformation of monocytes/macrophages with so-called TAMs, could adjust toward the TME. Mesenchymal stem cells are further drawn to tumor cell-induced abrasions to facilitate the healing process because of their regenerative power. Several proinflammatory cytokines, growth regulators, and intermediates are generated inside the tumor microenvironment after MSC peripheral immune functions are activated. The immune cell response can be modulated by these active substances. Mesenchymal stem cells can directly interact between immune cells, tumor cells, and other Tumor microenvironment subsets including

Table 4.1 Interaction between MSc and TME.

MSC source	Mediators
Bone marrow, cord blood	CXCR4, MMP2
Bone marrow	Lysyl oxidase
Human fetal bones	Urokinase plasminogen activator and its receptor, IL-8, IL-6, MCP-1
Bone marrow	Race-1, Rho A, Cdc-42, p125FAK focal adhesion kinase
Bone marrow	TGF-β1
Human epithelial ovarian cancers	BMP2, BMP4, BMP6

endothelial cells to enhance tumor angiogenesis in addition to such an independent mechanism (Suzuki et al., 2011). Finally, it is understandable that either directly or indirectly there is an established communication of mesenchymal stem cells within the TME, showing both pros as well as antitumorigenic properties. Cross-talk between mesenchymal stem cells and tumor cells drastically alters the overall features of such distinct cellular subsets (Table 4.1). Such biological interconnections may cause cancerous cells to initiate a maturation program/clonal selection of specific mesenchymal stem cell subpopulations, allowing the stroma/stem-like cells to adjust to the oncogenic milieu by developing specialized roles (Fig. 4.1). As a result, earlier research revealed that mesenchymal stem cells

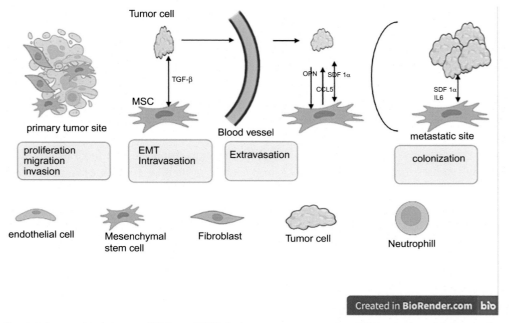

Fig. 4.1 Interaction between MSCs and TME during cancer progression. MSCs regulate this interaction and thus promote tumor progression from primary site to metastatic site.

were a mash-up of diverse closely interrelated subgroups, which together shared the same basic morphology (Melzer et al., 2020). As a result, certain MSCs switch overall differentiation and proliferation and develop a cassette shape, and also transform into cancer-associated fibroblasts (CAFs) (Mishra et al., 2008; Spaeth et al., 2009). Moreover, the abnormal proliferation of nearby cell lines, such as the expansion of cancer-associated fibroblasts or the generation of tumor associate macrophages, that construct a vascularized structure as a component of such cancer extracellular matrix, attracts mesenchymal stem cells to tumor locations.

4.2 MSC phenotype and origin

Friedenstein et al. (1968) were the first who reported the mesenchymal stem cells in the bone marrow, and these cells are the primordial multipotent fibroblast-like cells. These cells possess the capability of regenerating the stroma of the bone marrow in different places (Sacchetti et al., 2007). Nowadays, it is said that these cell types occupy almost all embryonic as well as postneonatal tissues and organs (Marrazzo et al., 2016) having the ability to carry tissue-specific regulatory patterns as well as inheritance patterns (Sacchetti et al., 2016). Because there are no unambiguous biomarkers for indigenous mesenchymal stem cells, the current understanding of their characteristics is based on in vitro investigations. The complications observed while distinguishing naive mesenchymal stem cells from other cell populations including fibroblasts, and pericytes in vitro, persist in cancer too. In reality, CAFs cohabit as a diverse cell population with overlapping characteristics, whose percentage varies depending on the tumor, and of which MSCs make up just a small amount, resulting in contradiction as well as a misunderstanding in this domain. Several investigations used the unique morphological profiles to separate MSCs from other origins, especially tumors because bone hematopoietic stem cells are the oldest and best-defined mesenchymal stem cells (BM-MSC). In 2006, the International Society for Cellular Therapy published a policy statement (ISCT) (Dominici et al., 2006; Ren et al., 2012; Galland et al., 2017) that outlined a list of minimum parameters for detecting adult BM-MSC in vitro, including (a) flexible adhesion; (b) high expressions of CD105, CD73, and CD90, as well as the lack of such myeloid markers CD45, CD34, CD14 or CD11b, CD79 or CD19, plus human leukocyte antigen-DR; as well as (c) multilineage proliferation. The BM-MSC morphology is frequently utilized as a reference for the TA-MSC type. MSCs were identified out of a range of human cancers, particularly head and neck cancers (Kansy et al., 2014), glioma (Behnan et al., 2014), metastatic breast cancer (Gonzalez et al., 2017), cervical (Ávila-Ibarra et al., 2019), ovarian cancer (McLean et al., 2011), lung carcinoma (Galland et al., 2017), prostate cancer (Hughes et al., 2019), neuroblastoma (Pelizzo et al., 2018), as well as colorectal cancer (Zhang et al., 2018b). However, if the mesenchymal stem cells in such trials were ISCT phenotypes (Dominici et al., 2006), it's vital to remember that tumor cells might have a mesenchymal-like appearance, enabling differentiation versus MSCs very difficult, sometimes even unattainable. Several areas of MSC science had caused controversy within the research world. There is a lingering problem in cancer research - whether TA-MSCs come out of the localized microenvironment or are solicited out from distant organs. CAFs can be derived from localized fibroblasts, and according to several investigations, MSCs can be derived from (Kojima et al., 2010) the adipocytes and adipocyte-associated stromal cells (Bochet et al., 2013), via recruitment of BM-MSCs into the tumor tissue (Bhagat et al., 2019), through endothelial-to-mesenchymal transition (EndMT) of tumor-associated endothelial cells (Zeisberg et al., 2007), and from epithelial-to-mesenchymal transition (EMT) of nonmalignant or malignant epithelial cells (Radisky et al., 2007) (Fig. 4.2). There are diverse pathways that have been described to understand the phenomenon of the conversion of mesenchymal stem cells into the cancer-associated fibroblasts including phenotypic reprogramming through lactate, particularly in pancreatic cancer (Bhagat et al., 2019), breast cancer via subjection to oxidative stress (Toullec et al., 2010), CXCR6 (Jung et al., 2013), as well as TGFβ1 (Barcellos-de-Souza et al., 2016). A favorable impact of CD44 for retaining a robust morphology of Cancer-associated fibroblast has been revealed in prostate cancer signaling (Spaeth et al., 2013). While inside the tumor, BM-MSCs stimulate and display myofibroblast-specific biomarkers like alpha-smooth muscle actin (α-SMA), vimentin, and fibroblast-specific protein (FSP) (Quante et al., 2011) as well as they help to rebuild

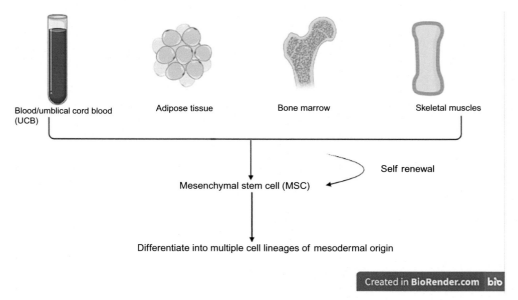

Fig. 4.2 Origin of MSCs. MSCs can be originated from bone marrow, umbilical cord, and adipose tissue. They possess the ability to renew themselves and differentiate into multiple cell lineages.

the extracellular matrix (Dumont et al., 2013), Ultimately, they'll fine-tune their operational state-based mostly on cues they observe (Augsten, 2014). As a result of TGF1, stimulated fibroblast cells have increased regenerative as well as invasive potential (Löhr et al., 2001), and PDGF (Vignaud et al., 1994) activation among others as well. Cancer-associated fibroblasts undergo physiological remodeling, reliant on oxidative metabolism, to maintain the current high-energy, high-cost "habit." This can be done in collaboration with tumor cells (Lyssiotis and Kimmelman, 2017). Stroma cells, which can enhance or inhibit tumorigenesis, do this via modulating individual elements of the tumor micro-environment, particularly immune cells.

4.3 Homing to the tumor microenvironment

The abundance of soluble substances generated from tumor cells, including the inflammatory environment as well as the ischemic situation inside the TME, are thought to play a role in the recruitment of MSCs to tumors as tumorigenesis progresses. Cytokines, chemokine's, and growth factors including Interleukin-6 (Rattigan et al., 2010), Interleukin-1 (Tu et al., 2008), TGF-β1, and SDF-1 are secreted by tumor cells (Table 4.2) (Gao et al., 2009). Mesenchymal stem cell abidance, as well as escape, is mainly promoted through various types of signaling cascades. Asphyxiation, a state of low oxygen that commonly coincides with inflammation, is also present in various cancers. Oxygen starvation is implicated in the systemic inflammation in tumors, leading to the production of proinflammatory cytokines which are engaged in immune cells, as well as MSC recruitment to tumors. Breast cancer cells generate large quantities

Table 4.2 MSCs secretion during cross-talk with cancer cells responsible for homing, growth, and stemness in tumor cells (7).

Homing of MSCs in tumor	Cytokine	TNF-α, IFN-γ, IL-1β, IL-6, IL-8
	Chemokine	SDF-1/CXCR4, MCP-1, GRO-a
	Growth factors	TGF-β, PGF, PDGF, HGF
MSC-mediated cancer growth	Cytokine	IL-6, IL-10, TNF-α
	Chemokine	CCL5, CXCL1, CXCL3, CXCL5, CXCL6, CXCL8, CCL2, CCL8, CCL20
	Growth factors	IGF-1, TGF β1, HGF
MSC-mediated cancer cell stemness	Cytokine	IL-1α, IL-1β, IL-6
	Chemokine	CXCL1, CXCL8, CXCL5, CXCL6, CXCL7, CCL5
	Growth factors	BMP4, PGE2

of Interleukin-6 in ischemic circumstances (1.5% O2), which serves both to stimulate as well as recruit MSCs (Rattigan et al., 2010).

4.4 Functions in the tumor microenvironment

Mesenchymal stem cells enhance tumor cell growth as well as progression within TME (Fig. 4.3). The interaction of MSCs and tumors is intricate. MSCs vary their gene expression once they are activated via tumor cells. According to findings of previous research, tumor cells revealed modified bioactivity of some nucleotide sequences after coculture using MSCs and investigation by transcriptome approaches, particularly ones associated with increased invasive potential, propagation, as well as resistance to drugs (Lis et al., 2012). Malignant cells activities are therefore endorsed in several stages when they communicate with mesenchymal stem cells. MSCs possess the multipotent capability, as well as providing a favorable environment for tumor cells and enhancing tumor cell pluripotency via numerous processes. MSCs plus tumor cells cocultured in breast cancer, for instance, encouraged mammosphere development, a three-dimensional culture architecture comprising tumor-initiating cell populations (Yan et al., 2012; Klopp et al., 2010). Breast cancer stem cell self-restoration is regulated by mesenchymal stem cells via cytokine looping including interleukin-6 and CXCL7 (Liu et al., 2011a). Mesenchymal stem cells from cancer patients (CA-MSCs), aided tumor progression through bone

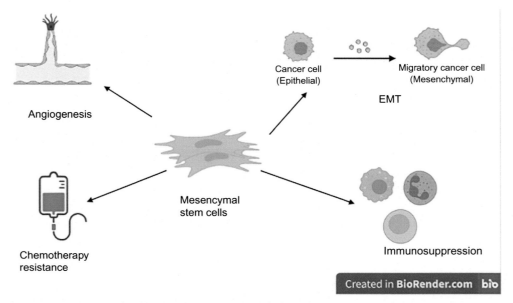

Fig. 4.3 MSCs are involved in various processes including EMT, angiogenesis, immunosuppression, and chemotherapy resistance.

morphogenetic protein signaling by enhancing the number of cancer stem cells (McLean et al., 2011). The WNT, TGF- (Nishimura et al., 2012) and IL-6–JAK2–STAT3 signal transduction pathways are among the others that also aid in tumor progression (Hsu et al., 2012; Tsai et al., 2011). Along with these above pathways, there is another signaling pathway activated via cancerous cells that specifically ensures tumor/cancer cell stemness. Malignant cells might cause mesenchymal stem cells to produce a lot of PGE2; this, when combined also with cytokine mediators that are also generated in mesenchymal stem cells, contributes to the ALDH-positive percentage of cancerous cells increase (Li et al., 2012a).

Epithelial–mesenchymal transition (EMT): It is the very first step in the invasion of tumor cells. EMT causes podocytes to become transposable elements, allowing them to separate from the basal lamina. There is an upregulated activation of different zinc finger proteins including fibronectin, fibroblast specific protein-1 (FSP1/S100A4), snail and slug, and vimentin. These all are associated with protumor behavior and mesenchymal phenotype (Thiery, 2003; Kalluri and Weinberg, 2009). Mesenchymal stem cells that are recruited toward TME might prompt epithelial-mesenchymal transition in multiple tumors as well as can constructively expand the metastasis of the tumor cells or can expand tumorigenesis. It has been observed that when there is coculturing of MSCs and breast carcinoma cells, there is an increased expression of snail and slug, vimentin and in turn lowers expressions of E-cadherin and Beta-catenin (Klopp et al., 2010). Mesenchymal stem cells boosted the Twist transcription factor, which regulates the MSC-induced EMT of cancer cells, by promoting the synthesis of lysyl oxidase in breast carcinoma cells. As a result, mesenchymal stem cells aid cancer cells to spread toward the bones as well as lungs (El-Haibi et al., 2012). Also, it was discovered that MSC-secreted TGF-β1 and TGF-β1 governed EMT in MCF7 cells by inhibiting the ZEBmiR 200 feedback loop (Xu et al., 2012). Also, the same event might be perceived in the case of hepatic cell carcinomas. Along with it, when MSCs are cocultured with cancerous cells, these mesenchymal stem cells obtain SDF-1 and tenascin-c markers (Bhattacharya et al., 2012; Jing et al., 2012). Mesenchymal stem cells were discovered to modulate epithelial-mesenchymal transition and sphere formation in carcinoma cells throughout a Notch-dependent strategy in a pancreatic cancer investigation (Kabashima-Niibe et al., 2013). Along with epithelial-mesenchymal transition, there are various procedures by which mesenchymal stem cells influence the recruitment of tumor cells toward TME including the CXCL/CXCL5–CXCR2 mechanism (Halpern et al., 2011), CXCR4 and ER pathways (Rhodes et al., 2010) or the synchronization of RANTES and Interleukin-6 (Gallo et al., 2012) in breast tumors. CCL5 activity in MSCs could be induced by breast tumor cells, which increases cancerous cells' mobility as well as aggressive power (Karnoub et al., 2007). Mesenchymal stem cells increase prostate cancer proliferation and metastasis via overexpressing Matrix metalloproteinase 2/9 levels, according to prior research (Ye et al., 2012).

Angiogenesis is one of mesenchymal stem cells' consequences on tumor cells, MSC-conditioned medium can promote overall branching of human fetal umbilical vein endothelium cells related to VEGF synthesis from mesenchymal stem cells, according to prior studies (Beckermann et al., 2008). Coinjected MSCs supported the angiogenesis in vivo via localizing along vascular endothelium and expressed CD31 (Suzuki et al., 2011). Mesenchymal stem cells showed a particular propensity to aggregate and develop a capillary-like structure when cocultured along with tumor cells (Comşa et al., 2012). There are numerous soluble mediators produced by mesenchymal stem cells to increase vasculature. These factors are TNF-α, IFN-γ, VEGF, MIP-2, LIF, M-CSF, etc. (Suzuki et al., 2011; Liu et al., 2011b). Exosomes, that are 40–100 nm in diameter produced from MSCs, have previously been shown to increase neovascularization via VEGF and CXCR4 production in tumor cells via the ERK12 and p38 MAPK cascades (Zhu et al., 2012).

Immunosuppression: Mesenchymal stem cells suppress the functions of T-lymphocytes (Krampera et al., 2003), B-lymphocytes (Tabera et al., 2008), DCs (Jiang et al., 2005; Nauta et al., 2006) as well as NK cells (Sotiropoulou et al., 2006; Maria Spaggiari and Moretta, 2013). Mesenchymal stem cell–based immunological treatment in allogeneic cell and organ transplants has been the subject of recent research (Batten et al., 2006; Casiraghi et al., 2013; Reinders et al., 2015). Mesenchymal stem cells secrete various types of cytokines including Interleukin-10 (Batten et al., 2006), Transforming growth factor-β (Groh et al., 2005), NO (Sato et al., 2007), indoleamine 2,3-dioxygenase (Meisel et al., 2004), and also prostaglandin E2 (Aggarwal and Pittenger, 2005). These all cytokines are engaged as immunosuppressive against various immune cells and immune reactions. Moreover, MSC-mediated immunodeficiency has been implicated in tumor formation as well as advancement in a variety of ways. Besides boosting Treg cells and decreasing the activity of natural killer cells and cytotoxic T cells, MSCs might preserve breast cancer cells (Patel et al., 2010). Interferon-γ and tumor necrosis factor-α (TNF-α) induced the immunosuppressive effect of MSCs in melanoma cells. MSCs expressed inducible nitric oxide synthase as a result of certain cytokine interactions (Han et al., 2011). Tumor necrosis growth factor-β was upregulated in mesenchymal stem cells in response to the inflammatory background in prostate cancer, allowing prostate cancer cells to evade immune recognition (Cheng et al., 2012).

Chemotherapy resistance: It is a term used to describe a person's ability to elevate the functioning of strong promoters of tumorigenesis, including transforming genes, lack of tumor-suppressor gene function, deactivation of apoptotic pathways or increased life span of cancerous cells, and stimulation of telomerase are among the processes implicated in classical chemoresistance. Environment mediated drug-resistance (EMDR) results from such a dynamic, bidirectional signaling conversation among tumor cells and the TME, along with previously known reasons for chemotherapeutic resistance. EMDR can be categorized into two kinds: dissolved component therapeutic resistance, which is caused by chemokines, cytokines, and growth regulators naturally produced by fibroblast cells like tumor stroma, and cell adhesion-mediated chemotherapy resistance, which is caused by tumor cell adhesion molecules adhering to an extracellular matrix including fibronectin, laminin, and collagen (Meads et al., 2009). Mesenchymal stem cells are linked to EMDR because they secrete soluble biological mediators like SDF-1, IL-6, NO, IL-3, G-CSF, M-CSF, and GM-CSF, as well as activate tumor cell propagation mechanisms as well as produce ECM that shield tumor cells from chemotherapy treatments. To help adjacent tumor cells survive and flourish, MSCs use self-digestion to recover proteins and manufacture antiapoptotic substances (Sanchez et al., 2011). MSCs enhanced tumor cell survivability in colorectal cancer by releasing dissolved NRG1, which activated the HER2/HER3-dependent PI3K/AKT signaling pathways (De Boeck et al., 2013). In breast cancer, platinum-based immunotherapy might cause MSCs to release two distinct triglycerides that impart chemotherapy resistance (Roodhart et al., 2011).

4.5 MSCs exosomes therapy in tumors

Exosomes are extracellular vesicles (EVs) that might be produced inside the endosomal section of membrane-bound cells (Raposo and Stoorvogel, 2013). Exosomes and other extracellular vesicles could be identified in tissues and organic liquids, like pee, blood, and cerebrospinal liquid. Exosomes overwhelmingly hold micro-RNAs [miRs] and proteins encompassed through the membrane of the lipid bilayer (Braicu et al., 2015; Zhang et al., 2018a). Further, ribonucleic acid types like nucleolar ribonucleic acid, elongated noncoding RNA, and rRNA conjointly parts of DNA might be located within the exosomes (Guescini et al., 2010). Exosomes released by cells can be guided to other cells by proteins called tetraspanins, which are found on the cell surface (Neviani and Fabbri, 2015). Mesenchymal stem cells create exosomes that could direct cancer cell angiogenesis, metastasis, and expansion by regulating a group of pathways associated with cellular signaling (Ratajczak et al., 2006). Exosomes generated from MSCs can also have a paracrine role by transmitting signaling molecules. Exosomes generated from MSCs have a supportive or suppressive effect on tumor growth. Different types of prodrug suicide gene therapy MSCs can transfer chemotherapeutic drugs and activate prodrugs directly into tumors, resulting in hazardous compounds for cancer cells (Table 4.3) (Kucerova et al., 2007; Cihova et al., 2011). MSCs generated from fat-laden adipose tissue express the Herpes simplex virus's thymidine kinase and use *ganciclovir* as a prodrug transforming cellular carrier for the selected treatment (Matuskova et al., 2010). The approach revealed the efficiency of MSCs generated from fat-laden tissue as prodrug converting gene delivery vehicles. Researchers generated mesenchymal stem cells from several tissues and transduced them with the Ycd:UPR-transferase gene in another investigation. Ycd:Uprt-MSC's secreted prodrug messenger-RNA and exosomes, which were absorbed by cancer cells, followed by the internal cellular translation of the mRNA to a protein

Table 4.3 Clinical trials involving MScs for treating cancer.

Cancer	NCT trial no.	Phase
Hematological cancers	NCT01045382	II
	NCT01092026	I, II
Myelodysplastic syndromes	NCT01129739	II
	NCT03184935	I, II
Solid tumor metastases	NCT01844661	I, II
Prostate tumors	NCT01983709	I
Ovarian cancer	NCT02068794	I, II
	NCT02530047	I
Lung adenocarcinoma	NCT03298763	I, II
Pancreatic cancer	NCT03608631	I

that caused cancer cell necrosis (Altanerova et al., 2019). *Paclitaxel* is an efficient anticancer mediator in opposition to malignant cells (Rowinsky and Donehower, 1995; Kalimuthu et al., 2018). Packed *Paclitaxel* in mesenchymal stem cell exosome imitates established cellular toxicity of MDA-MB-231 cancers of the breast and mobile traces while managed with Ptx-mesenchymal cells. In the latest observation, small dimensional vesicles produced by using Msc had been used to enclose *doxorubicin* and decided for capability therapeutic in rectal malignancy, ensuring incorporation of [MUC-1 aptamer] embellished mesenchymal stem cell extracted exosomes as a potential stage for tumor cure (Bagheri et al., 2020). Generally, these steps augment the competence of chemotherapy via recruiting cancer attacking features of mesenchymal stem cells, which can luckily amplify the possibility of malignant remedy in diverse concrete cancers. The constitution and biotic pursuit and remedial efficiency of mesenchymal stem cells extracted vesicles in malignancy have been broadly assessed by Xunian and Kalluri (2020). The virtual impact of mesenchymal stem cells obtained exosomes on the cancer cells continues to be discussed and maybe cancer supporting or suppressing outcomes, build on various questions, just like the foundation of the exosomes, additives of the exosomes, and kind of Tumors.

4.6 MSC crosstalk with immune components of the inflammatory niche in solid cancer

Numerous investigations have highlighted the importance of MSC in promoting carcinogenesis by targeting various TME components and pathways. Voluminous facts back MSCs' paracrine activities on cancer immunological cells, as well as their capacity to change the micro-environment and, as a result, the action of new cells (Wang et al., 2014). MSCs could be prompted by cytokines like interferon [IFN], TNF, and interleukins-1 to discharge particles that regulate the immune system's innate and adaptive responses, including prostaglandin e-2 [Pge-2] and indoleamine 2,three-dioxygenase [ido], as well as chemokines like CXCL, (Ren et al., 2008). Hepatocyte growth factor (HGF), its component, IGF-1, and various components of the family FGF can straightly excite tumor cell production and liberate chemokines like "stromal cell-derived factor-1" (SDF-1/Cxcl-12), which can activate the employment of primogenitor cells or stem cell multiplication (Franco et al., 2010). In fact, it has been proposed that the stromal compartment has a role in chemoresistance (Castells et al., 2012). In 3D-based experiments, mixed culture patterns increased invasiveness that has been documented when TA-mesenchymal stem cells regulate ECM hardness through the production of matrix and renovation, enabling cancer cell movement and its assault (Åkerfelt et al., 2015). Cxcl-12, which has been demonstrated to encourage EMT in prostate-associated tumor abnormality (Jung et al., 2013) and in combination with IGF-1 to choose for clones with spreading potential in tumors linked with breast, has been connected to a seasoned-metastatic phenotype in TA-MSC'S (Zhang et al., 2013). Exosomes, the minute extracellular vesicle members of the family, operate as a shipper for mRNA and other paracrine stimuli or substances that might modulate cancer cell and immunological responses in the TME (Figueroa et al., 2017).

4.6.1 MSCs and cells of the innate immune system

MSCs within the TM plays an applicable function in advocating the employment and division of various subgroups of inborn immunological cells (Fig. 4.4). Investigations based on experiments have proven that mesenchymal stem cells remoted from various origins are capable of influencing monocyte division in the direction of antigen-providing cells, inclined them from the canonical stirring external makeup to collect capabilities ordinary of tolerogenic cells (Spaggiari et al., 2009). Additionally, mesenchymal stem cells tilt the division of monocyte obtained dendrites closer to MDC's by the movement of the growth-controlled oncogene chemokines (Chen et al., 2013). Furthermore, mesenchymal cells could activate the development of mesenchymal cells via the discharge of excessive volume of Hgfs, representing the system of a feature of the mesenchymal cells became not sternly related to the discharge of immunoregulator cytokines. Few have pointed up the applicable role of cancers cells in instructing the stromal component linked with cancer, therefore effect their features. The equal outcome changed into not observed while the experiments had been accomplished through the usage of nontumor bone marrow mesenchymal stem cells (Ren et al., 2012). The high appearance of the CCR-2 ligand on mesenchymal stem cells was suggested to be firmly connected with the publicity of the provocative cytokine TNF-α (Ren et al., 2012). Consistent with those notes, "tumor-knowledgeable" MSCs and more exclusively mesenchymal cells separated from pulmonary carcinoma, which appears highly immunologically repressive in comparison to mesenchymal stem cells remoted from a

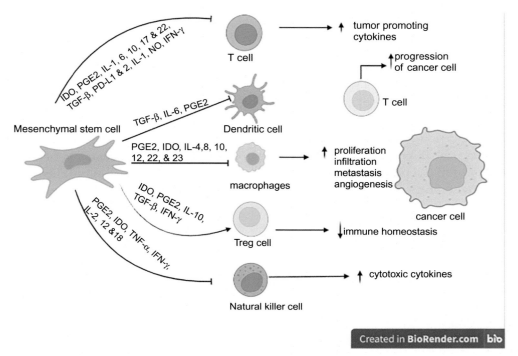

Fig. 4.4 Interaction between the immune cells and MSCs.

healthful group of cells. Certainly, trained mesenchymal stem cells had been capable of not affecting the external appearance although they lower the cytotoxic capacity of killer cells and diminished their immunological capacity (Galland et al., 2017). The immunorepressive pathways, as elucidated with the aid of the category and amount of immunorepressive cytokines generated and the magnitude of NK cellular ligands indicated, might vary among strong and tumor-linked mesenchymal stem cells. Moreover, human and rat tumor-linked MS-cell exosomes had been shown to speed up breast cancer development by promoting the growth of repression cells having myeloid origin into notably immunological repressive M2-diversified macrophages (Biswas et al., 2019). In latent tissues and lack of inflammatory signals, MSCs drop off or even in a short period drop their immunorepressive properties. Alternatively, in a T-micro-environment that imitates tissue treatment and possesses a diverse order of cytokines obtained from malignant cells–stem cells can be activated to produce immunologically repressive molecules.

4.6.2 MSCs and cells of the adaptive immune system

Immunity acquired in nature plays an elementary part in the control of cancer development. Inside the tumor, lymphocytes like T and B cells are the second most common kind of cells associated with the defense system of the body after macrophages are linked with malignancy (Speiser et al., 2016). Actually, with the advancement of cancer, its associated cells lose the efficiency to provoke the immune system along with initiation of tolerance, causing cancer to elude the act of the cytotoxic part of the network (Karolina and Coussens Lisa, 2016). The working induction of the second branch of tolerance is contemplated to be a component of the usual control network of the inflammatory reaction; Tumor stroma and the MSCs have a key function in this system. Tregs initiation has been depicted to happen via the discharge of Tgf-β-one, finally shielding cells linked with breast malignancy from the body's defense attack. In fact, laboratory studies committed the capability of mesenchymal stem cells to affect the TM-environment, an immune repressive microenvironment, wherein bone marrow-MSCs have been capable of shielding T-4/7-D breast malignant cells from the cytotoxic act of CD-8 and killer cells via means of instigating Tregs diversification (Patel et al., 2010). Moreover, marrow mesenchymal stem cells were proven to lessen the chemokine CXCL12 appearance via way of means of lowering the appointment of PBMC to cancer, with the aid of diversification of lymphocytes in the direction of a Th-2 subgroup with the growth of T (regs) (Patel et al., 2010). The repressive impact of mesenchymal-SC was illustrated in a mouse cancer model in which under skin injection of B-16 cancer cells with mesenchymal-SC caused a cancer boom in allogeneic mice. This impact changed into associated with the potential of mesenchymal stem cells to reduce cancer nonacceptance, comparatively via the stimulation of RTC type cd8+. Contrastingly, the mesenchymal part is depicted to obstruct the cytotoxic activity of cd-8 cells in culture with marrow mesenchymal-SC through less expression of HLA-I via CASKI cancer cells and less expression of Il-10 (Montesinos et al., 2013). Intriguingly, the removal of cancer-associated fibroblasts and the usage of a FAP focused on deoxyribose nucleic acid vaccine within the 4-T1 mouse model of breast cancers turns the immune-ME of cancer from a Th-2 to a Th-1 (proinflammatory) phenotype, representing the main function for cancer-associated fibroblasts in diversifying the immunological reactions to a procancer kind (Liao et al., 2009). Comparably, consequences have been additionally acquired in a rat version of breast cancers wherein implanted human mesenchymal stem cells notably decreased cd3+,Nk-p46,Killer-T like cells, accelerated Cd-4+, Foxp-3 cells, and Il-10–producing cd-4+ cells, accelerated fluid Th-2 cytokines, and reduced serum Th-1 cytokines (Ljujic et al., 2013). Such effects reveal that mesenchymal stem cells and immunorepressive surroundings that in the long run facilitate the spread of breast cancer in rats. Such type of research offer proof that mesenchymal stem cells and CAF-mediated repression of acquired immune cells speed up the increase of cancer. Mesenchymal stem cell cross-talk with immunological cells based on TIE despite what has been high pointed out to date approximately the function performed via way of means of MSCs within the Tumor–ME, M-stem cells also can apply an immunostimulatory impact generating the immune reaction while the inflammatory situations are inadequate. An in vitro takes a look at validated the capability of antigen-pulsed mesenchymal cells primed with small stages of IFN-gamma to cause the cytotoxic interest of cd-8T cells (Chan et al., 2006). correspondingly, Maurine Bone marrow mesenchymal-SCs with decreased or genetically eroded iNOS generation, handled with a small volume of IFN-γ and TNF-α, have been observed to beautify the division of active T cells (Li et al., 2012b). Same data were also revealed by other investigations that the growth of B-16 mouse tumors was increased when the carcinoma was coinjected with mesenchymal cells pregrown with IFN-γ and TNF-α compared with controls.

4.7 Perinatal MSC as therapeutic strategy in cancer

At this very spot, we will look at "perinatal mesenchymal stromal cells as external MSCs" used in cancer treatment. From distinct placental areas, we can separate perinatal MSCs like "maternal decidua" [DMSC], a membrane of amnion, umbilical cord, villi of the chorion (Silini et al., 2017a). In comparison to alternative materials, perinatal tissue is found to be valuable in both biological as well as technical methods. With aid to bone marrow and adipose tissue, technically perinatal tissue has a benefit over these two in tissue accessibility and MSC quality. Through noninvasive techniques, which are generally thought medical waste; we retrieved perinatal tissue for instance placenta after following a normal delivery. The cancer tropism of perinatal MSCs is one of the biological characteristics that make them profitable in anticancer treatment methods. For instance, "Human amniotic fluid MSCs" have been shown to move into the ovarian tumor as well as bladder carcinoma (Chinnadurai et al., 2015), similarly, mouse UC-mesenchymal stem cells have been revealed to migrate toward mammary adenocarcinoma (Ganta et al., 2009) as well as Lewis lung cancer (Maurya et al., 2010), and human UC-mesenchymal cells were identified in the immediate vicinity to mice breast cancer (Ayuzawa et al., 2009). Furthermore, perinatal mesenchymal stem cells extensively acquire "intrinsic immune-regulatory" characteristics and have been shown to reduce the proliferation of both T as well as B lymphocytes by inhabiting the production of inflammatory cytokine as well as show activity in APCs such as dendrites, macrophages, and killer cells as well these magnify the production of cells with aid to regulatory property like T-regs as well as M2 type macrophage (Fig. 4.5). Perinatal MScs turned out to be successfully used in already available clinical therapy of "inflammatory and immune-based-illnesses," examined in various clinical-pathway comparatively in "peripheral arterial disease and Crohn's disease" owing to immunomodulatory capabilities. Contrarily, for BM-MSCs several immunogenic, as well as immune-activating functions, have been examined (Magatti et al., 2015), reduced quantity of "fetal (hAMSC, UC-MSC) and maternal (decidual) placental MSCs" has depicted a longer effect on the multiplication of PB-mesenchymal calls (Wolbank et al., 2007). As a result, in a disease like cancer, in which defense system activation had been recommended as an

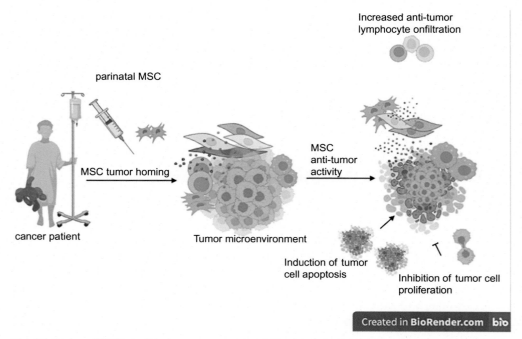

Fig. 4.5 Perinatal MSCs and their anticancer actions. They are involved in the apoptosis of tumor cells, inhibition of tumor cell proliferation, and the recruitment of CD4, CD8, and NK cells near tumor site.

effective treatment approach (Ichim, 2005), as per the processes which underpin the perinatal MSCs immune activation is critical for exploiting these features for anticancer treatment. Another crucial element that needs to be looked into the safety, worry about MSC's possible carcinogenesis, various studies demonstrated that placental mesenchymal stem cells never develop cancer when delivered "subcutaneously or intravenously" inside rat (Rachakatla et al., 2007). Furthermore, the amniotic membrane and rest tissues that are formed from the MSCs (Pessina et al., 2011) cannot grow, when filled by the chemotherapeutic agent *paclitaxel,* termed as crucial for carcinogenesis as well as considered for safe use. Furthermore, bio-active components aid to anti as well as protumor effects (created by MSC and mediate as bystander actions in the tumor micro-environment) is yet to be identified before clinical usage of perinatal MSCs in the oncology area can be predicted.

Perinatal MSCs used as anticancer depends on SPME characteristics which include (a) their capacity to migrate toward the tumor area, (b) in vitro antiproliferative functions on several cancer cell lines, and (c) their capacity to figure the inflammatory place via their "intrinsic immune-stimulatory as well as regulatory potential." It has been demonstrated that perinatal MSCs carry out both the actions such as support as well as tumor- prevention, although its differential consequences delineate the diverse immune regulatory system remain to be unseen. So various in vitro as well as in vivo research has examined the anticancer cations of perinatal MSCs and their subordinate by-products which include conditioned medium (CM) obtained from extracellular vesicles generated from conditional medium (Silini et al., 2017b). Most oppressed perinatal-mesenchymal stem cells in a tumor are represented by UC-MSC/WJ-MSCs. Various studies revealed the actions of UC-MSCs, and also their exudates in the case of breast tumors which includes MDA-MB-231 and Mcf-7, apart from disparity outcomes. For instance, in vitro multiplication of breast tumor cells like MDamb-231 and Mcf-7, is inhibited by both UC-mesenchymal stem cells (Ma et al., 2012) and their CM (Ayuzawa et al., 2009), although another study revealed that "conditional medium (Li et al., 2015) and EV from UC-MSCs" (Zhou et al., 2019) enhance the rapid increase and relocation of similar cells.

4.8 Conclusion

MSCs have been linked to tumor growth at various stages. In summary, soluble substances released by tumor cells during carcinogenesis attract them to a tumor. MSCs can develop into more mature mesenchymal cells and encourage tumor progression when they surround the tumor. MSCs drive cancer cell EMT in the tumor stroma. Similarly, MSCs promote cancer cell motility and can lead to cancer cells colonizing distant metastatic locations. MSCs undergo phenotypic alterations and have their gene expression altered by several tumor-promoting substances released by tumor cells. MSCs also enhance tumor cell stemness and angiogenesis, and their immunosuppressive or immunomodulatory capabilities in the tumor microenvironment can modulate immune responses. As a result, MSCs help tumors progress by controlling the tumor microenvironment. As a result, MSCs can be used as a marker for tumor progression. MSCs have been linked to tumor cell proliferation and metastasis in several studies. MSCs are also involved in the development of cancer at various stages. This shows that MSCs could be used as a therapeutic target in the treatment of cancer patients.

References

Aggarwal, S., Pittenger, M.F., 2005. Human mesenchymal stem cells modulate allogeneic immune cell responses. Blood 105, 1815–1822.

Åkerfelt, M., Bayramoglu, N., Robinson, S., Toriseva, M., Schukov, H.-P., Härmä, V., Virtanen, J., Sormunen, R., Kaakinen, M., Kannala, J., 2015. Automated tracking of tumor-stroma morphology in microtissues identifies functional targets within the tumor microenvironment for therapeutic intervention. Oncotarget 6, 30035.

Altanerova, U., Jakubechova, J., Benejova, K., Priscakova, P., Pesta, M., Pitule, P., Topolcan, O., Kausitz, J., Zduriencikova, M., Repiska, V., 2019. Prodrug suicide gene therapy for cancer targeted intracellular by mesenchymal stem cell exosomes. Int. J. Cancer 144, 897–908.

Augsten, M., 2014. Cancer-associated fibroblasts as another polarized cell type of the tumor microenvironment. Front. Oncol. 4, 62.

Ávila-Ibarra, L.R., Mora-Garcia, M.D.L., García-Rocha, R., Hernández-Montes, J., Weiss-Steider, B., Montesinos, J.J., Lizano Soberon, M., García-López, P., López, C.A.D., Torres-Pineda, D.B., 2019. Mesenchymal stromal cells derived from normal cervix and cervical cancer tumors increase CD73 expression in cervical cancer cells through TGF-β1 production. Stem Cells Dev. 28, 477–488.

Ayuzawa, R., Doi, C., Rachakatla, R.S., Pyle, M.M., Maurya, D.K., Troyer, D., Tamura, M., 2009. Naive human umbilical cord matrix derived stem cells significantly attenuate growth of human breast cancer cells in vitro and in vivo. Cancer Lett. 280, 31–37.

Bagheri, E., Abnous, K., Farzad, S.A., Taghdisi, S.M., Ramezani, M., Alibolandi, M., 2020. Targeted doxorubicin-loaded mesenchymal stem cells-derived exosomes as a versatile platform for fighting against colorectal cancer. Life Sci. 261, 118369.

Barcellos-De-Souza, P., Comito, G., Pons-Segura, C., Taddei, M.L., Gori, V., Becherucci, V., Bambi, F., Margheri, F., Laurenzana, A., Del Rosso, M., 2016. Mesenchymal stem cells are recruited and activated into carcinoma-associated fibroblasts by prostate cancer microenvironment-derived TGF-β1. Stem Cells 34, 2536–2547.

Batten, P., Sarathchandra, P., Antoniw, J.W., Tay, S.S., Lowdell, M.W., Taylor, P.M., Yacoub, M.H., 2006. Human mesenchymal stem cells induce T cell anergy and downregulate T cell allo-responses via the TH2 pathway: relevance to tissue engineering human heart valves. Tissue Eng. 12, 2263–2273.

Beckermann, B., Kallifatidis, G., Groth, A., Frommhold, D., Apel, A., Mattern, J., Salnikov, A., Moldenhauer, G., Wagner, W., Diehlmann, A., 2008. VEGF expression by mesenchymal stem cells contributes to angiogenesis in pancreatic carcinoma. Br. J. Cancer 99, 622–631.

Behnan, J., Isakson, P., Joel, M., Cilio, C., Langmoen, I.A., Vik-Mo, E.O., Badn, W., 2014. Recruited brain tumor-derived mesenchymal stem cells contribute to brain tumor progression. Stem Cells 32, 1110–1123.

Bergfeld, S.A., Declerck, Y.A., 2010. Bone marrow-derived mesenchymal stem cells and the tumor microenvironment. Cancer Metastasis Rev. 29, 249–261.

Bhagat, T.D., Von Ahrens, D., Dawlaty, M., Zou, Y., Baddour, J., Achreja, A., Zhao, H., Yang, L., Patel, B., Kwak, C., 2019. Lactate-mediated epigenetic reprogramming regulates formation of human pancreatic cancer-associated fibroblasts. Elife 8, e50663.

Bhattacharya, S.D., Mi, Z., Talbot, L.J., Guo, H., Kuo, P.C., 2012. Human mesenchymal stem cell and epithelial hepatic carcinoma cell lines in admixture: concurrent stimulation of cancer-associated fibroblasts and epithelial-to-mesenchymal transition markers. Surgery 152, 449–454.

Bianco, P., 2014. "Mesenchymal" stem cells. Annu. Rev. Cell Dev. Biol. 30, 677–704.

Biswas, S., Mandal, G., Chowdhury, S.R., Purohit, S., Payne, K.K., Anadon, C., Gupta, A., Swanson, P., Yu, X., Conejo-Garcia, J.R., 2019. Exosomes produced by mesenchymal stem cells drive differentiation of myeloid cells into immunosuppressive M2-polarized macrophages in breast cancer. J. Immunol. 203, 3447–3460.

Bochet, L., Lehuédé, C., Dauvillier, S., Wang, Y.Y., Dirat, B., Laurent, V., Dray, C., Guiet, R., Maridonneau-Parini, I., Le Gonidec, S., 2013. Adipocyte-derived fibroblasts promote tumor progression and contribute to the desmoplastic reaction in breast cancer. Cancer Res. 73, 5657–5668.

Braicu, C., Tomuleasa, C., Monroig, P., Cucuianu, A., Berindan-Neagoe, I., Calin, G., 2015. Exosomes as divine messengers: are they the Hermes of modern molecular oncology? Cell Death Differ. 22, 34–45.

Caplan, A.I., 1991. Mesenchymal stem cells. J. Orthop. Res. 9, 641–650.

Caplan, A.I., 2017. Mesenchymal stem cells: time to change the name! Stem Cells Transl. Med. 6, 1445–1451.

Caplan, A.I., Correa, D., 2011. The MSC: an injury drugstore. Cell Stem Cell 9, 11–15.

Casiraghi, F., Perico, N., Remuzzi, G., 2013. Mesenchymal stromal cells to promote solid organ transplantation tolerance. Curr. Opin. Organ Transplant. 18, 51–58.

Castells, M., Thibault, B., Delord, J.-P., Couderc, B., 2012. Implication of tumor microenvironment in chemoresistance: tumor-associated stromal cells protect tumor cells from cell death. Int. J. Mol. Sci. 13, 9545–9571.

Chan, J.L., Tang, K.C., Patel, A.P., Bonilla, L.M., Pierobon, N., Ponzio, N.M., Rameshwar, P., 2006. Antigen-presenting property of mesenchymal stem cells occurs during a narrow window at low levels of interferon-γ. Blood 107, 4817–4824.

Chapel, A., Bertho, J.M., Bensidhoum, M., Fouillard, L., Young, R.G., Frick, J., Demarquay, C., Cuvelier, F., Mathieu, E., Trompier, F., 2003. Mesenchymal stem cells home to injured tissues when co-infused with hematopoietic cells to treat a radiation-induced multi-organ failure syndrome. J. Gene Med. 5, 1028–1038.

Chen, H.-W., Chen, H.-Y., Wang, L.-T., Wang, F.-H., Fang, L.-W., Lai, H.-Y., Chen, H.-H., Lu, J., Hung, M.-S., Cheng, Y., 2013. Mesenchymal stem cells tune the development of monocyte-derived dendritic cells toward a myeloid-derived suppressive phenotype through growth-regulated oncogene chemokines. J. Immunol. 190, 5065–5077.

Cheng, J., Li, L., Liu, Y., Wang, Z., Zhu, X., Bai, X., 2012. Interleukin-1α induces immunosuppression by mesenchymal stem cells promoting the growth of prostate cancer cells. Mol. Med. Rep. 6, 955–960.

Chinnadurai, R., Copland, I.B., Ng, S., Garcia, M., Prasad, M., Arafat, D., Gibson, G., Kugathasan, S., Galipeau, J., 2015. Mesenchymal stromal cells derived from Crohn's patients deploy indoleamine 2, 3-dioxygenase-mediated immune suppression, independent of autophagy. Mol. Ther. 23, 1248–1261.

Cihova, M., Altanerova, V., Altaner, C., 2011. Stem cell based cancer gene therapy. Mol. Pharm. 8, 1480–1487.

Comşa, Ş., Ciuculescu, F., Raica, M., 2012. Mesenchymal stem cell-tumor cell cooperation in breast cancer vasculogenesis. Mol. Med. Rep. 5, 1175–1180.

Corselli, M., Chen, C.-W., Sun, B., Yap, S., Rubin, J.P., Péault, B., 2012. The tunica adventitia of human arteries and veins as a source of mesenchymal stem cells. Stem Cells Dev. 21, 1299–1308.

Dabrowski, F.A., Burdzinska, A., Kulesza, A., Sladowska, A., Zolocinska, A., Gala, K., Paczek, L., Wielgos, M., 2017. Comparison of the paracrine activity of mesenchymal stem cells derived from human umbilical cord, amniotic membrane and adipose tissue. J. Obstet. Gynaecol. Res. 43, 1758–1768.

De Boeck, A., Pauwels, P., Hensen, K., Rummens, J.-L., Westbroek, W., Hendrix, A., Maynard, D., Denys, H., Lambein, K., Braems, G., 2013. Bone marrow-derived mesenchymal stem cells promote colorectal cancer progression through paracrine neuregulin 1/HER3 signalling. Gut 62, 550–560.

Dominici, M., Le Blanc, K., Mueller, I., Slaper-Cortenbach, I., Marini, F., Krause, D., Deans, R., Keating, A., Prockop, D., Horwitz, E., 2006. Minimal criteria for defining multipotent mesenchymal stromal cells. The International Society for Cellular Therapy position statement. Cytotherapy 8, 315–317.

Dumont, N., Liu, B., Defilippis, R.A., Chang, H., Rabban, J.T., Karnezis, A.N., Tjoe, J.A., Marx, J., Parvin, B., Tlsty, T.D., 2013. Breast fibroblasts modulate early dissemination, tumorigenesis, and metastasis through alteration of extracellular matrix characteristics. Neoplasia 15, 249-IN7.

El-Haibi, C.P., Bell, G.W., Zhang, J., Collmann, A.Y., Wood, D., Scherber, C.M., Csizmadia, E., Mariani, O., Zhu, C., Campagne, A., 2012. Critical role for lysyl oxidase in mesenchymal stem cell-driven breast cancer malignancy. Proc. Natl. Acad. Sci. U. S. A. 109, 17460–17465.

Figueroa, J., Phillips, L.M., Shahar, T., Hossain, A., Gumin, J., Kim, H., Bean, A.J., Calin, G.A., Fueyo, J., Walters, E.T., 2017. Exosomes from glioma-associated mesenchymal stem cells increase the tumorigenicity of glioma stem-like cells via transfer of miR-1587. Cancer Res. 77, 5808–5819.

Fong, C.-Y., Subramanian, A., Gauthaman, K., Venugopal, J., Biswas, A., Ramakrishna, S., Bongso, A., 2012. Human umbilical cord Wharton's jelly stem cells undergo enhanced chondrogenic differentiation when grown on nanofibrous scaffolds and in a sequential two-stage culture medium environment. Stem Cell Rev. Rep. 8, 195–209.

Franco, O.E., Shaw, A.K., Strand, D.W., Hayward, S.W., 2010. Cancer associated fibroblasts in cancer pathogenesis. Semin. Cell Dev. Biol., 33–39. Elsevier.

Fridman, W.H., Sautès-Fridman, C., Galon, J., 2012. The immune contexture in human tumours: impact on clinical outcome. Nat. Rev. Cancer 12, 298–306.

Friedenstein, A.J., Petrakova, K.V., Kurolesova, A.I., Frolova, G.P., 1968. Heterotopic transplants of bone marrow. Transplantation 6, 230–247.

Galland, S., Vuille, J., Martin, P., Letovanec, I., Caignard, A., Fregni, G., Stamenkovic, I., 2017. Tumor-derived mesenchymal stem cells use distinct mechanisms to block the activity of natural killer cell subsets. Cell Rep. 20, 2891–2905.

Gallo, M., De Luca, A., Lamura, L., Normanno, N., 2012. Zoledronic acid blocks the interaction between mesenchymal stem cells and breast cancer cells: implications for adjuvant therapy of breast cancer. Ann. Oncol. 23, 597–604.

Ganta, C., Ayuzawa, R., Rachakatla, R., Pyle, M., Andrews, G., Weiss, M., Tamura, M., Troyer, D., 2009. Rat umbilical cord stem cells completely abolish rat mammary carcinomas with no evidence of metastasis or recurrence 100 days post–tumor cell inoculation. Cancer Res. 69, 1815–1820.

Gao, H., Priebe, W., Glod, J., Banerjee, D., 2009. Activation of signal transducers and activators of transcription 3 and focal adhesion kinase by stromal cell-derived factor 1 is required for migration of human mesenchymal stem cells in response to tumor cell-conditioned medium. Stem Cells 27, 857–865.

Ghajar, C.M., Kachgal, S., Kniazeva, E., Mori, H., Costes, S.V., George, S.C., Putnam, A.J., 2010. Mesenchymal cells stimulate capillary morphogenesis via distinct proteolytic mechanisms. Exp. Cell Res. 316, 813–825.

Gonzalez, M.E., Martin, E.E., Anwar, T., Arellano-Garcia, C., Medhora, N., Lama, A., Chen, Y.-C., Tanager, K.S., Yoon, E., Kidwell, K.M., 2017. Mesenchymal stem cell–induced DDR2 mediates stromal-breast cancer interactions and metastasis growth. Cell Rep. 18, 1215–1228.

Groh, M.E., Maitra, B., Szekely, E., Koç, O.N., 2005. Human mesenchymal stem cells require monocyte-mediated activation to suppress alloreactive T cells. Exp. Hematol. 33, 928–934.

Guescini, M., Genedani, S., Stocchi, V., Agnati, L.F., 2010. Astrocytes and glioblastoma cells release exosomes carrying mtDNA. J. Neural Transm. 117, 1–4.

Halpern, J.L., Kilbarger, A., Lynch, C.C., 2011. Mesenchymal stem cells promote mammary cancer cell migration in vitro via the CXCR2 receptor. Cancer Lett. 308, 91–99.

Han, Z., Tian, Z., Lv, G., Zhang, L., Jiang, G., Sun, K., Wang, C., Bu, X., Li, R., Shi, Y., 2011. Immunosuppressive effect of bone marrow-derived mesenchymal stem cells in inflammatory microenvironment favours the growth of B16 melanoma cells. J. Cell. Mol. Med. 15, 2343–2352.

Hass, R., Kasper, C., Böhm, S., Jacobs, R., 2011. Different populations and sources of human mesenchymal stem cells (MSC): a comparison of adult and neonatal tissue-derived MSC. Cell Commun. Signal 9, 1–14.

Hsu, H.-S., Lin, J.-H., Hsu, T.-W., Su, K., Wang, C.-W., Yang, K.-Y., Chiou, S.-H., Hung, S.-C., 2012. Mesenchymal stem cells enhance lung cancer initiation through activation of IL-6/JAK2/STAT3 pathway. Lung Cancer 75, 167–177.

Hughes, R.M., Simons, B.W., Khan, H., Miller, R., Kugler, V., Torquato, S., Theodros, D., Haffner, M.C., Lotan, T., Huang, J., 2019. Asporin restricts mesenchymal stromal cell differentiation, alters the tumor microenvironment, and drives metastatic progression. Cancer Res. 79, 3636–3650.

Ichim, C.V., 2005. Revisiting immunosurveillance and immunostimulation: implications for cancer immunotherapy. J. Transl. Med. 3, 1–13.

Jiang, X.-X., Zhang, Y., Liu, B., Zhang, S.-X., Wu, Y., Yu, X.-D., Mao, N., 2005. Human mesenchymal stem cells inhibit differentiation and function of monocyte-derived dendritic cells. Blood 105, 4120–4126.

Jing, Y., Han, Z., Liu, Y., Sun, K., Zhang, S., Jiang, G., Li, R., Gao, L., Zhao, X., Wu, D., Cai, X., Wu, M., Wei, L., 2012. Mesenchymal stem cells in inflammation microenvironment accelerates hepatocellular carcinoma metastasis by inducing epithelial-mesenchymal transition. PLoS One 7 (8), e43272.

Jung, Y., Kim, J.K., Shiozawa, Y., Wang, J., Mishra, A., Joseph, J., Berry, J.E., McGee, S., Lee, E., Sun, H., 2013. Recruitment of mesenchymal stem cells into prostate tumours promotes metastasis. Nat. Commun. 4, 1–11.

Kabashima-Niibe, A., Higuchi, H., Takaishi, H., Masugi, Y., Matsuzaki, Y., Mabuchi, Y., Funakoshi, S., Adachi, M., Hamamoto, Y., Kawachi, S., 2013. Mesenchymal stem cells regulate epithelial–mesenchymal transition and tumor progression of pancreatic cancer cells. Cancer Sci. 104, 157–164.

Kalimuthu, S., Gangadaran, P., Rajendran, R.L., Zhu, L., Oh, J.M., Lee, H.W., Gopal, A., Baek, S.H., Jeong, S.Y., Lee, S.-W., 2018. A new approach for loading anticancer drugs into mesenchymal stem cell-derived exosome mimetics for cancer therapy. Front. Pharmacol. 9, 1116.

Kalluri, R., Weinberg, R.A., 2009. The basics of epithelial-mesenchymal transition. J. Clin. Invest. 119, 1420–1428.

Kansy, B.A., Dißmann, P.A., Hemeda, H., Bruderek, K., Westerkamp, A.M., Jagalski, V., Schuler, P., Kansy, K., Lang, S., Dumitru, C.A., 2014. The bidirectional tumor-mesenchymal stromal cell interaction promotes the progression of head and neck cancer. Stem Cell Res. Ther. 5, 1–10.

Karnoub, A.E., Dash, A.B., Vo, A.P., Sullivan, A., Brooks, M.W., Bell, G.W., Richardson, A.L., Polyak, K., Tubo, R., Weinberg, R.A., 2007. Mesenchymal stem cells within tumour stroma promote breast cancer metastasis. Nature 449, 557–563.

Karolina, P.A., Coussens Lisa, M., 2016. The basis of oncoimmunology. Cell 164, 1233–1247.

Klopp, A.H., Lacerda, L., Gupta, A., Debeb, B.G., Solley, T., Li, L., Spaeth, E., Xu, W., Zhang, X., Lewis, M.T., 2010. Mesenchymal stem cells promote mammosphere formation and decrease E-cadherin in normal and malignant breast cells. PLoS One 5, e12180.

Kojima, Y., Acar, A., Eaton, E.N., Mellody, K.T., Scheel, C., Ben-Porath, I., Onder, T.T., Wang, Z.C., Richardson, A.L., Weinberg, R.A., 2010. Autocrine TGF-β and stromal cell-derived factor-1 (SDF-1) signaling drives the evolution of tumor-promoting mammary stromal myofibroblasts. Proc. Natl. Acad. Sci. U. S. A. 107, 20009–20014.

Krampera, M., Glennie, S., Dyson, J., Scott, D., Laylor, R., Simpson, E., Dazzi, F., 2003. Bone marrow mesenchymal stem cells inhibit the response of naive and memory antigen-specific T cells to their cognate peptide. Blood 101, 3722–3729.

Kucerova, L., Altanerova, V., Matuskova, M., Tyciakova, S., Altaner, C., 2007. Adipose tissue–derived human mesenchymal stem cells mediated prodrug cancer gene therapy. Cancer Res. 67, 6304–6313.

Li, H.-J., Reinhardt, F., Herschman, H.R., Weinberg, R.A., 2012a. Cancer-stimulated mesenchymal stem cells create a carcinoma stem cell niche via prostaglandin E2 signaling. Cancer Discov. 2, 840–855.

Li, W., Ren, G., Huang, Y., Su, J., Han, Y., Li, J., Chen, X., Cao, K., Chen, Q., Shou, P., 2012b. Mesenchymal stem cells: a double-edged sword in regulating immune responses. Cell Death Differ. 19, 1505–1513.

Li, T., Zhang, C., Ding, Y., Zhai, W., Liu, K., Bu, F., Tu, T., Sun, L., Zhu, W., Zhou, F., 2015. Umbilical cord-derived mesenchymal stem cells promote proliferation and migration in MCF-7 and MDA-MB-231 breast cancer cells through activation of the ERK pathway. Oncol. Rep. 34, 1469–1477.

Liao, D., Luo, Y., Markowitz, D., Xiang, R., Reisfeld, R.A., 2009. Cancer associated fibroblasts promote tumor growth and metastasis by modulating the tumor immune microenvironment in a 4T1 murine breast cancer model. PLoS One 4, e7965.

Lis, R., Touboul, C., Raynaud, C.M., Malek, J.A., Suhre, K., Mirshahi, M., Rafii, A., 2012. Mesenchymal cell interaction with ovarian cancer cells triggers pro-metastatic properties. PLoS One 7, e38340.

Liu, S., Ginestier, C., Ou, S.J., Clouthier, S.G., Patel, S.H., Monville, F., Korkaya, H., Heath, A., Dutcher, J., Kleer, C.G., 2011a. Breast cancer stem cells are regulated by mesenchymal stem cells through cytokine networks. Cancer Res. 71, 614–624.

Liu, Y., Han, Z.-P., Zhang, S.-S., Jing, Y.-Y., Bu, X.-X., Wang, C.-Y., Sun, K., Jiang, G.-C., Zhao, X., Li, R., 2011b. Effects of inflammatory factors on mesenchymal stem cells and their role in the promotion of tumor angiogenesis in colon cancer. J. Biol. Chem. 286, 25007–25015.

Ljujic, B., Milovanovic, M., Volarevic, V., Murray, B., Bugarski, D., Przyborski, S., Arsenijevic, N., Lukic, M.L., Stojkovic, M., 2013. Human mesenchymal stem cells creating an immunosuppressive environment and promote breast cancer in mice. Sci. Rep. 3, 1–9.

Löhr, M., Schmidt, C., Ringel, J., Kluth, M., Müller, P., Nizze, H., Jesnowski, R., 2001. Transforming growth factor-β1 induces desmoplasia in an experimental model of human pancreatic carcinoma. Cancer Res. 61, 550–555.

Lyssiotis, C.A., Kimmelman, A.C., 2017. Metabolic interactions in the tumor microenvironment. Trends Cell Biol. 27, 863–875.

Ma, Y., Hao, X., Zhang, S., Zhang, J., 2012. The in vitro and in vivo effects of human umbilical cord mesenchymal stem cells on the growth of breast cancer cells. Breast Cancer Res. Treat. 133, 473–485.

Magatti, M., Caruso, M., De Munari, S., Vertua, E., De, D., Manuelpillai, U., Parolini, O., 2015. Human amniotic membrane-derived mesenchymal and epithelial cells exert different effects on monocyte-derived dendritic cell differentiation and function. Cell Transplant. 24, 1733–1752.

Mandel, K., Yang, Y., Schambach, A., Glage, S., Otte, A., Hass, R., 2013. Mesenchymal stem cells directly interact with breast cancer cells and promote tumor cell growth in vitro and in vivo. Stem Cells Dev. 22, 3114–3127.

Maria Spaggiari, G., Moretta, L., 2013. Cellular and molecular interactions of mesenchymal stem cells in innate immunity. Immunol. Cell Biol. 91, 27–31.

Marrazzo, P., Paduano, F., Palmieri, F., Marrelli, M., Tatullo, M., 2016. Highly efficient in vitro reparative behaviour of dental pulp stem cells cultured with standardised platelet lysate supplementation. Stem Cells Int. 2016.

Matuskova, M., Hlubinova, K., Pastorakova, A., Hunakova, L., Altanerova, V., Altaner, C., Kucerova, L., 2010. HSV-tk expressing mesenchymal stem cells exert bystander effect on human glioblastoma cells. Cancer Lett. 290, 58–67.

Maurya, D.K., Kawabata, A., Pyle, M.M., King, C., Wu, Z., Troyer, D., Tamura, M., 2010. Therapy with un-engineered naive rat umbilical cord matrix stem cells markedly inhibits growth of murine lung adenocarcinoma. BMC Cancer 10, 1–10.

Mclean, K., Gong, Y., Choi, Y., Deng, N., Yang, K., Bai, S., Cabrera, L., Keller, E., McCauley, L., Cho, K.-R., 2011. Human ovarian carcinoma–associated mesenchymal stem cells regulate cancer stem cells and tumorigenesis via altered BMP production. J. Clin. Invest. 121, 3206–3219.

Meads, M.B., Gatenby, R.A., Dalton, W.S., 2009. Environment-mediated drug resistance: a major contributor to minimal residual disease. Nat. Rev. Cancer 9, 665–674.

Meisel, R., Zibert, A., Laryea, M., Göbel, U., Däubener, W., Dilloo, D., 2004. Human bone marrow stromal cells inhibit allogeneic T-cell responses by indoleamine 2, 3-dioxygenase–mediated tryptophan degradation. Blood 103, 4619–4621.

Melzer, C., Yang, Y., Hass, R., 2016. Interaction of MSC with tumor cells. Cell Commun. Signal 14, 1–12.

Melzer, C., Jacobs, R., Dittmar, T., Pich, A., Von Der Ohe, J., Yang, Y., Hass, R., 2020. Reversible growth-arrest of a spontaneously-derived human MSC-like cell line. Int. J. Mol. Sci. 21, 4752.

Mishra, P.J., Mishra, P.J., Humeniuk, R., Medina, D.J., Alexe, G., Mesirov, J.P., Ganesan, S., Glod, J.W., Banerjee, D., 2008. Carcinoma-associated fibroblast–like differentiation of human mesenchymal stem cells. Cancer Res. 68, 4331–4339.

Montesinos, J.J., Mora-García, M.D.L., Mayani, H., Flores-Figueroa, E., García-Rocha, R., Fajardo-Orduna, G.R., Castro-Manrreza, M.E., Weiss-Steider, B., Monroy-García, A., 2013. In vitro evidence of the presence of mesenchymal stromal cells in cervical cancer and their role in protecting cancer cells from cytotoxic T cell activity. Stem Cells Dev. 22, 2508–2519.

Nauta, A.J., Kruisselbrink, A.B., Lurvink, E., Willemze, R., Fibbe, W.E., 2006. Mesenchymal stem cells inhibit generation and function of both CD34 +-derived and monocyte-derived dendritic cells. J. Immunol. 177, 2080–2087.

Neviani, P., Fabbri, M., 2015. Exosomic microRNAs in the tumor microenvironment. Front. Med. 2, 47.

Nishimura, K., Semba, S., Aoyagi, K., Sasaki, H., Yokozaki, H., 2012. Mesenchymal stem cells provide an advantageous tumor microenvironment for the restoration of cancer stem cells. Pathobiology 79, 290–306.

Otte, A., Bucan, V., Reimers, K., Hass, R., 2013. Mesenchymal stem cells maintain long-term in vitro stemness during explant culture. Tissue Eng. Part C Methods 19, 937–948.

Papaccio, F., Paino, F., Regad, T., Papaccio, G., Desiderio, V., Tirino, V., 2017. Concise review: cancer cells, cancer stem cells, and mesenchymal stem cells: influence in cancer development. Stem Cells Transl. Med. 6, 2115–2125.

Patel, S.A., Meyer, J.R., Greco, S.J., Corcoran, K.E., Bryan, M., Rameshwar, P., 2010. Mesenchymal stem cells protect breast cancer cells through regulatory T cells: role of mesenchymal stem cell-derived TGF-β. J. Immunol. 184, 5885–5894.

Pelizzo, G., Veschi, V., Mantelli, M., Croce, S., Di Benedetto, V., D'angelo, P., Maltese, A., Catenacci, L., Apuzzo, T., Scavo, E., 2018. Microenvironment in neuroblastoma: isolation and characterization of tumor-derived mesenchymal stromal cells. BMC Cancer 18, 1–12.

Pessina, A., Bonomi, A., Coccè, V., Invernici, G., Navone, S., Cavicchini, L., Sisto, F., Ferrari, M., Viganò, L., Locatelli, A., 2011. Mesenchymal stromal cells primed with paclitaxel provide a new approach for cancer therapy. PLoS One 6, e28321.

Pittenger, M.F., Mackay, A.M., Beck, S.C., Jaiswal, R.K., Douglas, R., Mosca, J.D., Moorman, M.A., Simonetti, D.W., Craig, S., Marshak, D.R., 1999. Multilineage potential of adult human mesenchymal stem cells. Science 284, 143–147.

Poggi, A., Zocchi, M.R., 2019. Immunomodulatory properties of mesenchymal stromal cells: still unresolved "Yin and Yang". Curr. Stem Cell Res. Ther. 14, 344–350.

Quante, M., Tu, S.P., Tomita, H., Gonda, T., Wang, S.S., Takashi, S., Baik, G.H., Shibata, W., Diprete, B., Betz, K.S., 2011. Bone marrow-derived myofibroblasts contribute to the mesenchymal stem cell niche and promote tumor growth. Cancer Cell 19, 257–272.

Rachakatla, R.S., Marini, F., Weiss, M.L., Tamura, M., Troyer, D., 2007. Development of human umbilical cord matrix stem cell-based gene therapy for experimental lung tumors. Cancer Gene Ther. 14, 828–835.

Radisky, D.C., Kenny, P.A., Bissell, M.J., 2007. Fibrosis and cancer: do myofibroblasts come also from epithelial cells via EMT? J. Cell. Biochem. 101, 830–839.

Raposo, G., Stoorvogel, W., 2013. Extracellular vesicles: exosomes, microvesicles, and friends. J. Cell Biol. 200, 373–383.

Ratajczak, J., Miekus, K., Kucia, M., Zhang, J., Reca, R., Dvorak, P., Ratajczak, M., 2006. Embryonic stem cell-derived microvesicles reprogram hematopoietic progenitors: evidence for horizontal transfer of mRNA and protein delivery. Leukemia 20, 847–856.

Rattigan, Y., Hsu, J.-M., Mishra, P.J., Glod, J., Banerjee, D., 2010. Interleukin 6 mediated recruitment of mesenchymal stem cells to the hypoxic tumor milieu. Exp. Cell Res. 316, 3417–3424.

Reinders, M.E., Dreyer, G.J., Bank, J.R., Roelofs, H., Heidt, S., Roelen, D.L., Zandvliet, M.L., Huurman, V.A., Fibbe, W.E., Van Kooten, C., 2015. Safety of allogeneic bone marrow derived mesenchymal stromal cell therapy in renal transplant recipients: the Neptune study. J. Transl. Med. 13, 1–8.

Ren, G., Zhang, L., Zhao, X., Xu, G., Zhang, Y., Roberts, A.I., Zhao, R.C., Shi, Y., 2008. Mesenchymal stem cell-mediated immunosuppression occurs via concerted action of chemokines and nitric oxide. Cell Stem Cell 2, 141–150.

Ren, G., Zhao, X., Wang, Y., Zhang, X., Chen, X., Xu, C., Yuan, Z.-R., Roberts, A.I., Zhang, L., Zheng, B., 2012. CCR2-dependent recruitment of macrophages by tumor-educated mesenchymal stromal cells promotes tumor development and is mimicked by TNFα. Cell Stem Cell 11, 812–824.

Rhodes, L.V., Antoon, J.W., Muir, S.E., Elliott, S., Beckman, B.S., Burow, M.E., 2010. Effects of human mesenchymal stem cells on ER-positive human breast carcinoma cells mediated through ER-SDF-1/CXCR4 crosstalk. Mol. Cancer 9, 1–15.

Roodhart, J.M., Daenen, L.G., Stigter, E.C., Prins, H.-J., Gerrits, J., Houthuijzen, J.M., Gerritsen, M.G., Schipper, H.S., Backer, M.J., Van Amersfoort, M., 2011. Mesenchymal stem cells induce resistance to chemotherapy through the release of platinum-induced fatty acids. Cancer Cell 20, 370–383.

Rowinsky, E.K., Donehower, R.C., 1995. Paclitaxel (taxol). N. Engl. J. Med. 332, 1004–1014.

Sacchetti, B., Funari, A., Michienzi, S., Di Cesare, S., Piersanti, S., Saggio, I., Tagliafico, E., Ferrari, S., Robey, P.G., Riminucci, M., 2007. Self-renewing osteoprogenitors in bone marrow sinusoids can organize a hematopoietic microenvironment. Cell 131, 324–336.

Sacchetti, B., Funari, A., Remoli, C., Giannicola, G., Kogler, G., Liedtke, S., Cossu, G., Serafini, M., Sampaolesi, M., Tagliafico, E., 2016. No identical "mesenchymal stem cells" at different times and sites: human committed progenitors of distinct origin and differentiation potential are incorporated as adventitial cells in microvessels. Stem Cell Rep. 6, 897–913.

Sanchez, C.G., Penfornis, P., Oskowitz, A.Z., Boonjindasup, A.G., Cai, D.Z., Dhule, S.S., Rowan, B.G., Kelekar, A., Krause, D.S., Pochampally, R.R., 2011. Activation of autophagy in mesenchymal stem cells provides tumor stromal support. Carcinogenesis 32, 964–972.

Sasaki, M., Abe, R., Fujita, Y., Ando, S., Inokuma, D., Shimizu, H., 2008. Mesenchymal stem cells are recruited into wounded skin and contribute to wound repair by transdifferentiation into multiple skin cell type. J. Immunol. 180, 2581–2587.

Sato, K., Ozaki, K., Oh, I., Meguro, A., Hatanaka, K., Nagai, T., Muroi, K., Ozawa, K., 2007. Nitric oxide plays a critical role in suppression of T-cell proliferation by mesenchymal stem cells. Blood 109, 228–234.

Selich, A., Daudert, J., Hass, R., Philipp, F., Von Kaisenberg, C., Paul, G., Cornils, K., Fehse, B., Rittinghausen, S., Schambach, A., 2016. Massive clonal selection and transiently contributing clones during expansion of mesenchymal stem cell cultures revealed by lentiviral RGB-barcode technology. Stem Cells Transl. Med. 5, 591–601.

Silini, A.R., Cancelli, S., Signoroni, P.B., Cargnoni, A., Magatti, M., Parolini, O., 2017a. The dichotomy of placenta-derived cells in cancer growth. Placenta 59, 154–162.

Silini, A.R., Magatti, M., Cargnoni, A., Parolini, O., 2017b. Is immune modulation the mechanism underlying the beneficial effects of amniotic cells and their derivatives in regenerative medicine? Cell Transplant. 26, 531–539.

Sotiropoulou, P.A., Perez, S.A., Gritzapis, A.D., Baxevanis, C.N., Papamichail, M., 2006. Interactions between human mesenchymal stem cells and natural killer cells. Stem Cells 24, 74–85.

Spaeth, E.L., Dembinski, J.L., Sasser, A.K., Watson, K., Klopp, A., Hall, B., Andreeff, M., Marini, F., 2009. Mesenchymal stem cell transition to tumor-associated fibroblasts contributes to fibrovascular network expansion and tumor progression. PLoS One 4, e4992.

Spaeth, E.L., Labaff, A.M., Toole, B.P., Klopp, A., Andreeff, M., Marini, F.C., 2013. Mesenchymal CD44 expression contributes to the acquisition of an activated fibroblast phenotype via TWIST activation in the tumor microenvironment. Cancer Res. 73, 5347–5359.

Spaggiari, G.M., Abdelrazik, H., Becchetti, F., Moretta, L., 2009. MSCs inhibit monocyte-derived DC maturation and function by selectively interfering with the generation of immature DCs: central role of MSC-derived prostaglandin E2. Blood 113, 6576–6583.

Speiser, D.E., Ho, P.-C., Verdeil, G., 2016. Regulatory circuits of T cell function in cancer. Nat. Rev. Immunol. 16, 599–611.

Suzuki, K., Sun, R., Origuchi, M., Kanehira, M., Takahata, T., Itoh, J., Umezawa, A., Kijima, H., Fukuda, S., Saijo, Y., 2011. Mesenchymal stromal cells promote tumor growth through the enhancement of neovascularization. Mol. Med. 17, 579–587.

Tabera, S., Pérez-Simón, J.A., Díez-Campelo, M., Sánchez-Abarca, L.I., Blanco, B., López, A., Benito, A., Ocio, E., Sánchez-Guijo, F.M., Cañizo, C., 2008. The effect of mesenchymal stem cells on the viability, proliferation and differentiation of B-lymphocytes. Haematologica 93, 1301–1309.

Thiery, J.P., 2003. Epithelial–mesenchymal transitions in development and pathologies. Curr. Opin. Cell Biol. 15, 740–746.

Toullec, A., Gerald, D., Despouy, G., Bourachot, B., Cardon, M., Lefort, S., Richardson, M., Rigaill, G., Parrini, M.C., Lucchesi, C., 2010. Oxidative stress promotes myofibroblast differentiation and tumour spreading. EMBO Mol. Med. 2, 211–230.

Tsai, K.S., Yang, S.H., Lei, Y.P., Tsai, C.C., Chen, H.W., Hsu, C.Y., Chen, L.L., Wang, H.W., Miller, S.-A., Chiou, S.H., 2011. Mesenchymal stem cells promote formation of colorectal tumors in mice. Gastroenterology 141, 1046–1056.

Tu, S., Bhagat, G., Cui, G., Takaishi, S., Kurt-Jones, E.A., Rickman, B., Betz, K.S., Penz-Oesterreicher, M., Bjorkdahl, O., Fox, J.G., 2008. Overexpression of interleukin-1β induces gastric inflammation and cancer and mobilizes myeloid-derived suppressor cells in mice. Cancer Cell 14, 408–419.

Vignaud, J.-M., Marie, B., Klein, N., Plénat, F., Pech, M., Borrelly, J., Martinet, N., Duprez, A., Martinet, Y., 1994. The role of platelet-derived growth factor production by tumor-associated macrophages in tumor stroma formation in lung cancer. Cancer Res. 54, 5455–5463.

Viswanathan, S., Shi, Y., Galipeau, J., Krampera, M., Leblanc, K., Martin, I., Nolta, J., Phinney, D., Sensebe, L., 2019. Mesenchymal stem versus stromal cells: International Society for Cell & Gene Therapy (ISCT®) Mesenchymal Stromal Cell committee position statement on nomenclature. Cytotherapy 21, 1019–1024.

Wang, Y., Chen, X., Cao, W., Shi, Y., 2014. Plasticity of mesenchymal stem cells in immunomodulation: pathological and therapeutic implications. Nat. Immunol. 15, 1009–1016.

Wolbank, S., Peterbauer, A., Fahrner, M., Hennerbichler, S., Van Griensven, M., Stadler, G., Redl, H., Gabriel, C., 2007. Dose-dependent immunomodulatory effect of human stem cells from amniotic membrane: a comparison with human mesenchymal stem cells from adipose tissue. Tissue Eng. 13, 1173–1183.

Xu, Q., Wang, L., Li, H., Han, Q., Li, J., Qu, X., Huang, S., Zhao, R.C., 2012. Mesenchymal stem cells play a potential role in regulating the establishment and maintenance of epithelial-mesenchymal transition in MCF7 human breast cancer cells by paracrine and induced autocrine TGF-β. Int. J. Oncol. 41, 959–968.

Xunian, Z., Kalluri, R., 2020. Biology and therapeutic potential of mesenchymal stem cell-derived exosomes. Cancer Sci. 111, 3100–3110.

Yan, X.-L., Fu, C.-J., Chen, L., Qin, J.-H., Zeng, Q., Yuan, H.-F., Nan, X., Chen, H.-X., Zhou, J.-N., Lin, Y.-L., 2012. Mesenchymal stem cells from primary breast cancer tissue promote cancer proliferation and enhance mammosphere formation partially via EGF/EGFR/Akt pathway. Breast Cancer Res. Treat. 132, 153–164.

Yang, Y., Bucan, V., Baehre, H., Von Der Ohe, J., Otte, A., Hass, R., 2015. Acquisition of new tumor cell properties by MSC-derived exosomes. Int. J. Oncol. 47, 244–252.

Ye, H., Cheng, J., Tang, Y., Liu, Z., Xu, C., Liu, Y., Sun, Y., 2012. Human bone marrow-derived mesenchymal stem cells produced TGFbeta contributes to progression and metastasis of prostate cancer. Cancer Invest. 30, 513–518.

Zeisberg, E.M., Potenta, S., Xie, L., Zeisberg, M., Kalluri, R., 2007. Discovery of endothelial to mesenchymal transition as a source for carcinoma-associated fibroblasts. Cancer Res. 67, 10123–10128.

Zhang, X.H.-F., Jin, X., Malladi, S., Zou, Y., Wen, Y.H., Brogi, E., Smid, M., Foekens, J.A., Massagué, J., 2013. Selection of bone metastasis seeds by mesenchymal signals in the primary tumor stroma. Cell 154, 1060–1073.

Zhang, L., Hao, C., Yao, S., Tang, R., Guo, W., Cong, H., Li, J., Bao, L., Wang, D., Li, Y., 2018a. Exosomal miRNA profiling to identify nanoparticle phagocytic mechanisms. Small 14, 1704008.

Zhang, X., Hu, F., Li, G., Li, G., Yang, X., Liu, L., Zhang, R., Zhang, B., Feng, Y., 2018b. Human colorectal cancer-derived mesenchymal stem cells promote colorectal cancer progression through IL-6/ JAK2/STAT3 signaling. Cell Death Dis. 9, 1–13.

Zhou, X., Li, T., Chen, Y., Zhang, N., Wang, P., Liang, Y., Long, M., Liu, H., Mao, J., Liu, Q., 2019. Mesenchymal stem cell-derived extracellular vesicles promote the in vitro proliferation and migration of breast cancer cells through the activation of the ERK pathway. Int. J. Oncol. 54, 1843–1852.

Zhu, W., Huang, L., Li, Y., Zhang, X., Gu, J., Yan, Y., Xu, X., Wang, M., Qian, H., Xu, W., 2012. Exosomes derived from human bone marrow mesenchymal stem cells promote tumor growth in vivo. Cancer Lett. 315, 28–37.

CHAPTER 5

Role of regulatory T cells in cancer

Manzoor Ahmad Mir and Abrar Yousuf Mir
Department of Bioresources, School of Biological Sciences, University of Kashmir, Srinagar, Jammu and Kashmir, India

5.1 Introduction

It is widely set up and established that abundant inborn and acquired immunological effector cells and molecules take part in the identification and devastation of carcinoma cells. This exercise is termed immunosurveillance. Throughout tumor development, immune components interact, and this interaction has significant implications with significant negative outcomes for cancer therapy. T regulatory cells are naturally occurring T cells that moderate immune repression to prevent autoimmune disorders. They account for about 5%–6% of total $CD4^+$ T cells. Autoimmune defects arise due to the reduction of a subset of T regulatory cells in normal hosts when the individual defense system remains unnoticed, thus aggression on self-tissues is noticed (Wang and Wang, 2007). Although Tregs play a vital role in auto-immune defect progression, their presence during malignancies lowers the antitumor potential of the body against cancer growth. Thus, modulation of the function of regulatory T cells has become an essential topic of research currently in the field of cancer biology (Wang and Wang, 2007). T regulatory cells of the innate and adaptive systems form an important part of the T-cell immune system. This component of T-cell immunity defends the body from auto reactions and from immune responses that are either not required or unsuitable. The regulatory T-cell system manages immune tolerance by deteriorating the immune responses that may lead to autoimmunity. In these situations, the cell has to be controlled by immunogen-specific $CD8^+$ or $CD4^+$ T cells. However, more defense cells like phagocytes, dendrites, and NK cells are also targets of the T-cell regulatory system. Tregs themselves have thymic origins (innate) and grow as a stable subset of T cells. Moreover, T regulatory cells can either be adapted from new T cells from the peripheral circulation or antigen-specific T cells at the site of a vigorous immunological response (Sakaguchi et al., 2008). Type $CD4^+$ cells are highly immunosuppressive subsets of T (regs) defined by the production of the master dogmatic $FOXP3^+$ molecule. Regulatory T cells were originally identified by Sakaguchi and his associates as "$CD4^+$ $CD25^+$." T cells have been observed to play a central role in upholding auto-tolerance in fit and healthy folks. T regulatory cells are subsequently involved in regulating immune equilibrium. They safeguard the host from the growth of self-immune disorders and

Role of Tumor Microenvironment in Breast Cancer and Targeted Therapies
https://doi.org/10.1016/B978-0-443-18696-7.00001-4

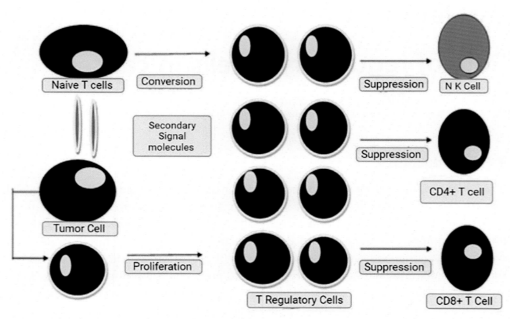

Fig. 5.1 Diagrammatic representation of cancer-regulated production of Tregs in tumor surrounding.

hypersensitivity, while in carcinoma growth; they encourage cancer development by repressing anticancer defense. Tumors can divide, spread and activate T regulatory cells in different ways and potently break antitumor immunity (Liu et al., 2009) (Fig. 5.1).

5.2 Different subgroups of T regulatory cells

T (regs) were first identified by Sakaguchi and his team of researchers (Sakaguchi et al., 1995). Mainly, two main subgroups of regulatory T cells are there; n Tregs, which grow during T–cell development in the thymus, have a very suitable expression of Foxp3 molecule (Komatsu et al., 2009), while as another type, inducible T regulatory cells have the flexibility and growth in the periphery when new cd4$^+$ T cells interact with tolerogenic antigen–presenting cells (Quezada et al., 2011). Moreover, there are several other subsets

Table 5.1 Various subsets of T regulatory cells.

Cell type	Origin	Phenotype
nCD4$^+$ T cells	Thymus	Cd4$^+$, cd25$^+$, FoxP3$^+$, cd127$^+$//low Ctla-4$^+$, lag-3$^+$, Gitr$^+$
Ncd8$^+$ T cells	Thymus	Cd8$^+$, Cd25$^+$, FoxP3$^+$, Ctla-4$^+$, Cd122$^+$
i CD4$^+$ T cells	Periphery	Cd4$^+$, Cd25$^+$, FoxP3$^+$, Ctla-4$^+$, Gitr$^+$
i CD8$^+$ T cells	Periphery	Cd8$^+$, Cd25$^+$, FoxP3$^+$

Sakaguchi (2004), Terabe et al. (2005), and Chaput et al. (2009).

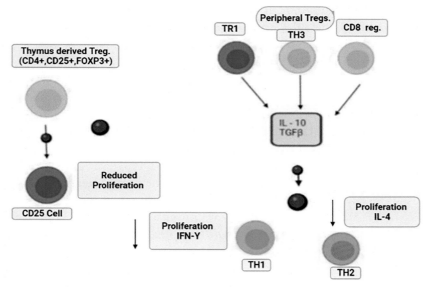

Fig. 5.2 Subsets of T regulatory cells.

of T cells like CD4$^+$, CD8$^+$, NKT (Table 5.1 and Fig. 5.2) but the most studied T regulatory cell is CD4$^+$ and is efficient in producing the Foxp3$^+$ factor which in turn is a potential molecule in developing antitumor strategy during different types of malignancies. Similarly, studies support that NKTs play a key role in the repression of the immune system (Terabe et al., 2005). Tregs are considered potent and well-investigated repressive phenotypes seen within cancer surroundings. Growing facts indicate T regulatory cell takes part in a significant way in immune escape pathways employed by tumors (Ke et al., 2008).

5.2.1 Naturally occurring CD4$^+$ Tregs

Tregs mainly CD4$^+$ cells having thymic origin fundamentally express cells like CD25$^+$ which signify a fully grown functional cell colony. Progress, as well as the role of natural T regulatory cells, is based on the factor FOXP3 expression. This factor contains Activator Protein one, which in short is termed AP-one, and another binding site called six- NF-AT (Mantel et al., 2006). Earlier investigations suggest that a factor named FOXP3 is a suppressor of IL-2, 4, and Ifng gene transcription by NF-b, NF-At direct contact. For repression activities, FOXP3 and PF-At complex formation plays a vital role (Bettelli et al., 2005).

One sign of naturally occurring T regulatory cells is anergy evident by their incapability to divide and create cytokine-like IL-2 upon activation of TCR. Interleukin-2 is a highly essential cytokine for its smooth functioning, and production in vivo state (Malek et al., 2002; Suzuki et al., 1997; Wolf et al., 2001). Other types of cytokines like interleukin-4,7, and 15 also play a key role in the growth and repressive activity of natural regulatory T cells, in addition to IL-2(Cupedo et al., 2005). The natural T regulatory cells' function is to suppress the inauguration and development of cells from acquired as well as inborn immunity, hindering cell-based and humoral immunological response. Type like Cd4$^+$ Cd25$^+$ FoxP3$^+$ natural T regulatory cells effectively restrict effector and memory T cells in both the cd4$^+$ and cd8$^+$ compartments in terms of activation, division, and function (Levings et al., 2001). Natural T regulatory cells have the capability to suppress B cell expansion, Ig synthesis, and Ig class switch, which is arbitrated in part by TGF-beta production (Lim et al., 2005; Nakamura et al., 2004). Moreover, the action and growth of dendrites, as well as N killer cells also get inhibited by the natural T regulatory cells (Azuma et al., 2003; Misra et al., 2004). However, naive dendrites contribute unusually in activating T cells which would be new and potentially convert them into induced T regulatory cells, thus forming a positive loop. Macrophages can flip between M1 and M2 phenotypes, which are proinflammatory and antiinflammatory, respectively. A tolerogenic environment, which is common in malignancies, causes macrophages to adopt the M2 phenotype (Tiemessen et al., 2007).

5.2.2 Induced CD4$^+$ T regulatory cells

Regulatory T cells of the induced type are accountable for controlling the immunological reaction to an ample range of microbial assaults by pathogens. Their development takes place in the peripheral lymphoid tissues of new T cells, often at a lower frequency at a steady position, which provides the defense system with the ability to adapt to a specific environment. The physiological pathways and surrounding environment propel their growth, but they are not fully established. The tumor-promoted T regulatory cells are physically distinguishable from other T regulatory cells and also from nTregs. Furthermore, it remains to be considered whether tumor-associated induced T regulatory cells attain particular distinctiveness donated by the tumor. A precondition for induced T regulatory cell progress is TCR activation of new T cells by antigenic activation. The situation below is not favorable for the production of effector T cells. They exist amid conditions that are not the most favorable for the generation of effector T cells. The circumstances under which i-T regulatory cells are induced and spread may involve the presence of a few cytokines, typically high levels of interleukin-2, 10t, or TGF-β, and a small number of APCs displaying changes in growth and role (Lohr et al., 2006). Cells invaded by the tumor can increase the stimulation of T regulatory cells via numerous factors like CD-70, cyclo-oxygenase-2, indoleamine-2,3-dioxygenase, IL-10, Galectin-1, and TGF-β (Bergmann et al., 2007; Li et al., 2007; Liu et al., 2007).

5.2.3 CD8$^+$ T regulatory cells, naturally occurring and induced

T regulatory cells of type CD8$^+$ develops both in the thymus and in the side-line tissue. CD-8$^+$, CD-25$^+$, FOXP3$^+$, and CTLA-4$^+$ cell types are natural T regulatory cells that were studied in several studies of species, e.g., rodents and humans. In reality, they mostly act through the cell to cell contact (Cosmi et al., 2003). Peripherally induced CD8$^+$ T regulatory cells arise from new cells like cd8$^+$, cd25$^+$, upon the stimulus of antigenic molecules (Mills, 2004). The presence and role of CD28$^+$ Tregs have been shown in many reports. In prostate cancer patients, these were classified as cd25$^+$, cd122$^+$, Foxp3$^+$, and partly GITR$^+$. Cells like CD8$^+$ CD25$^+$ FOXP3$^+$ class were observed in colon tumors which were positive and active for factor TGF-βeta (Chaput et al., 2009) while as cancer plasma–cytoid dendritic cells from ovarian carcinoma patients, CD8$^+$ induced Tregs under in vitro which in contrast with the external data indicates an accretion of cd8$^+$. T regulatory cells (Wei et al., 2005), CD8$^+$ T regulatory cells show division within tumor tissues (Kiniwa et al., 2003; Chaput et al., 2009) Can be peptide-specifically activated (Andersen et al., 2009).

Another kind of cell-like cd8$^+$, cd28$^-$ also called induced T regulatory cell types, was first explained in the allogeneic and was induced through class I MHC peptide stimulation; however, it has been seen in cancer patients (Cortesini et al., 2001). CD8$^+$, CD28$^-$ induced T regulatory cells are repressive by contact-dependent pathways, secretions of IL-10 molecules, and up-regulation of blocking immunity protein-like transcription receptors IT-3 and IT-4 on antigen-presenting cells (Filaci et al., 2007; Suciu-Foca and Cortesini, 2007).

5.3 Immunosuppressive potential of T regulatory cells and cancer

Tregs play a significant part in upholding self-tolerance, immune balance, autoimmunity prevention, and the rise of inflammatory responses (Piccirillo and Shevach, 2001). The suppressive potential of Tregs is based on multiple complex mechanisms which differ according to their position in normal and abnormal illness conditions. Previous facts indicate that T regulatory cells are a part of the cd4$^+$ and cd25$^+$ T-cell population (Suzuki et al., 1997). At beginning of the 2000s, it was shown that T regulatory cells work via primarily transcription factor, FoxP3 (Li et al., 2015). Epigenetic processes also take part in a significant role in inciting Tregs (Lal and Bromberg, 2009). The important role of Tregs in tumor immunity has also been studied extensively (Paluskievicz et al., 2019). Regardless of the reality that their immunosuppressive capacity helps to avert self-immunity and graft-vs.-host rejection in transplantation therapies (Whiteside, 2015), the same property produces a major risk via its various new mechanisms mediating immunosuppression and cancer development (Romano et al., 2017). The key characteristic of the stroke of Tregs is through the "transforming growth factor (TGF) beta pathway." T regulatory cells are well-known to generate "TGF beta," which can prop up the division of new cd4$^+$ T cells into Tregs through the expression of FOXP3$^+$ (Tone et al., 2008). Furthermore, TGF-beta is famous for the reduction of effector T cells and antigen-presenting cells (Sanjabi et al., 2017).

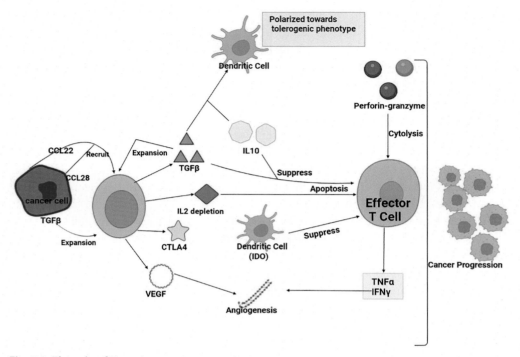

Fig. 5.3 The role of Tregs in cancer progression.

Generally, Tregs can restrain antitumor immune response via TGF-beta. Cancer cells run away from this pathway, which leads to immunosuppressive tumor microenvironment "TME," consequently resulting in tumor development (Chen et al., 2019). In the same way, T regulatory cells by the discharge of interleukin-10 illustrate a major role in regulating immune responses. Granzyme B being part of this mechanism helps natural killer cells and cytotoxic T cells to eradicate carcinoma cells (Cullen et al., 2010). One more significant aspect of T regulatory cells causing tumor progression is through promoting vessel formation (Facciabene et al., 2012). The entry of Tregs in TME activates, angiogenic markers like (vascular endothelial factor), so promoting cancer angiogenesis through some direct and indirect mechanisms. For a case, the T regulatory cells encourage cancer angiogenesis by blocking cancer-reactive T cells (Casares et al., 2003) (Fig. 5.3).

5.4 T regulatory cell infiltration in tumor microenvironment

Heavy T regulatory cell movement and presence in the tumor microenvironment have been observed and studied widely (Fig. 5.4) and it is largely associated with an

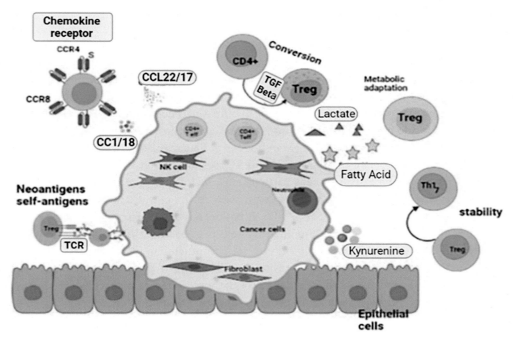

Fig. 5.4 T regulatory cell movement and presence in tumor microenvironment.

unfavorable prognosis in many malignancy types (Fu et al., 2007). In colon cancer, T regulatory cells may suppress tumor favoring inflammatory signals that are evoked by the gut microbial pool. The occurrence of T regulatory cells may also have difficulties in estimating advanced responses to immunotherapy. Advanced pretreatment levels of circulating T regulatory cells were linked with better survival in skin carcinoma patients treated with "*ipilimumab*" (Martens et al., 2016). Correspondingly, in non–small-cell lung carcinoma patients, an optimistic relationship has been seen between response to PD-1 blockade and occurrence of PD-L1^{+} T regulatory cells in the TME (Wu et al., 2018). Several mechanisms could be used through the Tregs to suppress antitumor immune responses. Molecules like the IL-2/Rα chain could divest local surroundings through the expression of high levels of IL-2 and effector T-cell role and contraction (Pandiyan et al., 2007). The change in IL-2 concentration by T regulatory cells affects natural killer cell (NK) function and homeostatic state (Gasteiger et al., 2013). Antigen-presenting cells are also controlled by T regulatory cells, by specific extension of dendritic cells, and activation of T regulatory cell depletion (Kim et al., 2007). This subduing is due to CTLA-4–dependent downward regulation of factor CD-80 and CD-86 appearance by a course known as trans Endocytosis (Qureshi et al., 2011).

5.5 Regulatory T-cell antigen specificity in cancer

Regulatory T cells play a central role in different malignancies related to humans through the reduction of definite TAA T-cell defense that adds to tumor growth. The first mark antigen of human regulatory T cells was (Lage) one, a relative part of NY-ESO-one. Targets of T regulatory cells are auto-antigenic proteins that are necessary to be visible within the thymic gland. Cancer proteins are generally coded by auto-oncofetal antigens that usually appear in epithelium made of epithelial cells. Auto-immunogenic proteins, such as Lage-one and Artc-one, are found in cancer-crossing lymphocytes. These regulatory T cells are phenotypically analogous to those of thymic-originated T (regs) (Wang et al., 2004; Wang et al., 2005a). Currently, T regulatory cells particular for malignancy antigenic proteins, e.g., gp100, Trp-one, and Ny-Eso-one were given away in the peripheral blood of folks suffering from skin cancer (Vence et al., 2007). It has been analyzed that Tregs are skilled by providing thymic education; the T regulatory cells produced in the periphery cannot be expelled. Tsa-associated T regulatory cells must be stimulated in the periphery due to the nature of tumor-associated antigenic proteins (TSA). All of these examples show that cancer-creating T regulatory cells can identify both their own and cancer cells' foreign proteins. In addition, both of these kinds provide tumor-associated tolerance.

5.6 Role of regulatory T cells in cancer

The contribution of the defense system to tumor development and its role in the development of cancer has been a topic of discussion since the 19th century when the concept of immune surveillance came into existence (Burnet, 1957). According to the concept of immune editing which is an advanced model idea of immune surveillance, different factors produced due to cancer genetic interaction contribute to tumor response efficiency and facilitate the escape mechanism of the tumor (Dunn et al., 2002). Recently many publications reveal that tumor cells arouse the genesis of suppressor T-cells and other immunosuppressor cells (Fujimoto et al., 1976). Analysis of Tregs presents a milepost in the immunology field and gives us clarification about the Treg immunosuppression (Gershon et al., 1972). It is well studied that T regulatory cells take part in a very significant way in the escaping mechanism regulated by cancer cells (Wang et al., 2008; Schabowsky et al., 2007; Leon et al., 2007; Carreras et al., 2009). Tumor growth generates many mechanisms to activate, proliferate and recruit Treg (tumor Treg) cells and nullify its antitumor activity (Liu et al., 2009; Mir and Umar, 2019). Their role has been seen in multiple settings like in myeloma defense. Grafting acceptance, hypersensitivity reactions, pathogenic defense, and autoimmunity (Waksman, 1977; Zou, 2006).T regulatory cells are part of the family of T-cells- a population that helps in the suppression of immune activation by altering the

activity of other cell types (Shevach, 2001; Mudd et al., 2006). It was primarily identified by (Gershon et al., 1972) and named as suppressor T cells. Although its work was
launched in 1995 by Sakaguchi et al. (1995) published that small patches of T cells with
a specific phenotype (after activation $CD4^+$ cells start releasing Il-2 receptor-alpha
chain, cd25) on their surface can retain self-tolerance. Its malfunction can develop several autoimmune illnesses. Treg cells were named as $Cd4^+cd25^+$ T cell. In 2003, its
performance is significantly characterized after the discovery of the theFoxP3, a
Treg-specific gene (Ziegler, 2006; Huen et al., 2009). Naturally occurring $CD4^+$ Treg
cells contain a specific marker FoxP3, a member of the DNA-binding transcription factor (Forkhead Box P3) (Shevach, 2009).According to new research FOXP3 is critically
paramount for the functionalization and development of the $CD4^+CD25^+$ Tregs factor
(Shevach, 2009; Huen et al., 2009). To date, three T regulatory cells have been identified to show negative feedback in immune response, three subsets of $CD4^+$
T regulatory cells like $Cd4^+Cd25^+FoxP3^+$, three cells secrete TGF-β and type1 Treg
cells (Tγ1) secreting Il-10 (Maggi et al., 2005). Among them, the most prominent is
$Cd4^+Cd25^+FoxP3^+$ T cells, in recent years its decreased level pays much attention
(Fietta et al., 2009; Qin, 2009). As per classification, generally, there are two main
groups of T regulatory cells, inducible Tregs and thymic-derived Tregs (naturally present). At the time of development of T lymphocytes in the thymus, Tregs are formed
termed as naturally occurring Tregs (nTregs) cells which consist of up to 10% of total
T lymphocytes. Admitted it into the peripheral selection and prominently present in
lymph node peripheral reservoirs and spleen (Toda, 2006; Wang and Wang, 2007).
Inducible Tregs (iTregs), on the other hand, and new T cells develop from in the
periphery, in response to several inductive signals such as TGFβ or IL-10 (Riley
et al., 2009; Toda, 2006). Primarily these cells are identified by the presence of
cd4 +, Foxp3$^+$, or cd4$^+$cd25 FoxP3 T cells is characterized by dominant transcription
factor that regulates Treg cells (Ziegler, 2006); Huen et al., 2009) and is considered as a
barrier in immune-oncology (Zou, 2006). Tumor cells can transform conventional
T cells into Treg cells with specific marker Foxp3, and its development leads to
diminishing the effector responses (Fontenot et al., 2005). So, the main outcome of
FoxP3$^+$ Treg cells is to hamper tumor immunosurveillance (Lizee et al., 2006). Despite
the fact that nTreg cells are formed in the thymus it has been addressed that cd4$^+$,
cd25$^+$ T cells in peripheral blood could be transfigured into acquired FoxP3$^+$ T regulatory cells. The most important surface markers on Treg cells are glucocorticoid-
induced TNF-receptors-associated (Gitr) protein and cytotoxic lymphocyte-associated
antigen-four (CTLA-4) in terms of their activity and development (Ha, 2008). Interestingly, plenty of cell types like as bone cells, dendrites, b cells, macrophages, mast
cells, N killer cells, and "NKT" cells are promptly targeted by "FoxP3$^+$ Treg cells
are Cd4$^+$, Cd8$^+$ T cell" (Shevach, 2009; Mir et al., 2022b).

5.6.1 Regulatory T cells in solid tumors

The majority of Treg investigations into cancer are done on patients who have solid tumors. Primarily, it was shown by Carl June that patients suffering from epithelial malignancy, particularly in ovarian and NSCLC had a higher amount of $CD4^+CD25$ in their bloodstream and inside the TILs. CTLA-4 produced by these cells shows an inhibition effect on the multiplication of conventional T cells and the generation of IFN-γ production. In patients with various forms of epithelial malignancies such as "lung, breast, and colorectal cancer," $CD4^+CD25^+$ Tregs have the ability to block the cytotoxicity of NK cells. (Wolf et al., 2003).$CD4^+CD25\ CD127^{low}$ has been recognized as a surface indicator of T regulatory cells in gastric cancer (Shen et al., 2009). They discovered that the abundance of T regulatory cells in stomach carcinoma patients' peripheral blood was considerably greater than in healthy blood circulation. Tumor environment of ascites fluid, tumor tissue, and nearby lymph nodes, Tregs cells are considered to be in higher number. They suggested that $CD4^+CD25CD127^{low}$ might be employed selective marker to enhance human Treg cells in an in vitro experiment in gastric cancer and the tumor is linked to a higher concentration of $Foxp3^+$ T regulatory cells, which has been observed in beginning stage gastric cancer (Mizukami et al., 2008). CCL22 chemokines produced from tumors stimulate the Treg cell migration through CCR4, CCR4 a chemokine protein receptor for Ccl22, and in lung and breast carcinoma decreases the antitumor immunity (Gobert et al., 2009; Mehraj et al., 2022a). Melanoma cells produce Ferritin heavy-chain (H-Ferritin) in huge amounts and were suggested that H-Ferritin mechanisms drive the Treg induction and activation. There is a great connection between blood levels of H-Ferritin and a higher frequency of Treg activation in melanoma patients (Gray et al., 2003). A higher frequency of IL-10 produced by CD5CD25 Tregs is detected in TILS, draining LNs, ascites fluid, and other gastro-esophageal cancers, which were highly related to the disease (Ichihara et al., 2003). It has been studied in 104 patients suffering from ovarian carcinoma the high level of T regulatory cells like $Cd4^+$, $Cd25^+$, and $FoxP3^+$ deemed to be concentrated on cancer, and suppress tumor determined T-cell immunity (Mehraj et al., 2022b, Curiel et al., 2004) and it was detected that the quantity of T regulatory cells found in cancer biopsy of several patients was adversely linked with the survival of patients. These findings provide knowledge about the recruitment of Treg cells mechanism through which tumors harbor the immune privilege and limiting Treg cells migration and actively may aid in the fight against human cancer (Curiel et al., 2004).

5.6.2 Regulatory T cells as biomarkers

The relevance of Tregs is linked with tumor load and the development of disease, their potential was investigated in gastric cancer whose Tregs are circulated in excessive frequencies had the worst living existence (Kono et al., 2006; Mir et al., 2022a;

Sasada et al., 2003). Mortality rate increased with the higher number of Treg cells in circulation and decreased survival rate in patients suffering from HCC (Fu et al., 2007) and also reduces the survival rate in patients with ovarian cancer (Curiel et al., 2004). For the same type of malignancy, its role differs at distinct phases of the disease, this can be elucidated in ovarian cancer where its presence is not favorably investigated in a group of unselected patients (Curiel et al., 2004). It has been revealed that knockout of Tregs before tumor initiation was found to be essential for survival, in comparison to well-established tumors, Tregs can dominate on early evasion immune surveillance mechanisms, not at late stages of cancer growth (Elpek et al., 2007; Mir et al., 2022b). A skewing of CD8$^+$ T-cell/Treg ratio toward Tregs was linked with a worse prediction in 117 patients suffering from epithelial ovarian cancer investigated by Immunohisto-chemical (IHC) research (Sato et al., 2005). In the Same analysis researchers looked at the CD8$^+$ T-cell/Treg ratio and also on Mhc type one expression in cervical cancer (Jordanova et al., 2008). Several researchers evaluated the ratio of CD3$^+$ T-cell/ T regulatory cell ratio (Petersen et al., 2006) and Granzyme B$^+$ CD8$^+$ T cell/Treg in NSCLC and HCC respectively (Gao et al., 2007). As a result, the percentage of negative regulators such as Tregs to effector cells in a tumor invasion is perhaps more significant for diagnosis than the actual quantity of Tregs. For making a better understanding of tumor Tregs infiltration in breast cancer (Mehraj et al., 2021a, 2021b), in tumor tissue and neighboring lymphoid cluster, Tregs were found to be present in two distinct sites. Tregs present in lymphoid infiltrates were recognized as the most detrimental influence on disease and as the result, in this location, they imply the counterbalance of selected lymphoid cells by preventing their activation (Gobert et al., 2009). Insubstantial observation of Tregs and CD8$^+$ T cells was detected in ovarian carcinoma (Curiel et al., 2004). In other studies such as in pancreatic, renal, and colorectal cancers, there is a worse outcome linked with Tregs presence (Griffiths et al., 2007; Hiraoka et al., 2006). Adaptive and innate immunity is greatly responsible for an inflammatory response but it has been verified that T regulatory cells show antiinflammatory properties in both immunities (Tiemessen et al., 2007).In hematological cancers it's likely that T regulatory cells repress tumors and show the anticarcinoma outcome, for example, it is demonstrated that Tregs destroy b cells, and probably malignant b cells are targeted too (Lim et al., 2005; Zhao et al., 2006).Similar fact addresses for T cells and cancers originate from the myeloid, where noncancerous equivalents are found to be restricted by Tregs Fig. 5.5.

5.6.3 T regulatory cells in hematologic malignancies

Different investigations into the function of T regulatory cells in blood related abnormalities have been revealed, contributing to an extra composite mosaic of deep interpretation. The outcome from various investigations into immunological effector cells shows

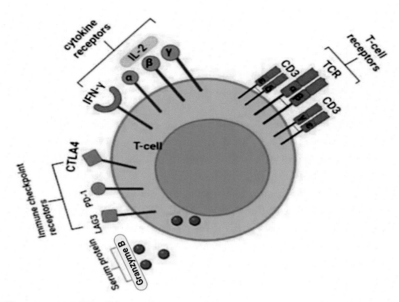

Fig. 5.5 Different types of T-cell biomarkers.

that an additional immune reactive environment is linked to bad results in "Hodgkin's lymphoma" (HL). In line with this, the presence of Foxp3[+] factor regulatory cells emerged to have a constructive effect on costless or disease-free survival in HL, particularly when observed collectively with little penetration of cytotoxic Tia-one[+], cd8[+] T cells (Alvaro et al., 2005). In case of chronic lymphocytic leukemia (CLL), high volume of rounding (cd4[+],cd25[+]) soaring regulatory T cells have been analyzed by arbitrating T-cell repression via CTLA-4 (Bayer et al., 2005). Fascinatingly, CLL, a chronic B cell cancer, is linked with the condition of low globulin which was observed to be inversely connected with regulatory T-cell frequency. This examination depicts a straight repressive outcome of T regulatory cells on immunoglobulin(Ig) concentration; an examination that was additionally applied by central work on the repressive outcome of T regulatory cells on type b cells (Lim et al., 2005) Moreover, victims with (cll) cured by *Fludarabine*, a nucleoside match indicates a particular decline of T regulatory cells (Bayer et al., 2005). B cells extracted during non-Hodgkin lymphomas (bhnls) were as fine as acute myeloid leukemia (AML), and T regulatory cells were also high in volume (Wang et al., 2005b). In AML, the portion of apoptotic (7-Aad[+]) and dividing (Ki-67[+]) cells between T regulatory cells was high in patients in comparison to fit controls. It was confirmed in different investigations that regulatory T cells could have a fast turnover pace and might be produced from quickly growing, extremely dividing memory cd4[+] T cells. They are also comparatively vulnerable to death signal moderately due to gravely stout telomeres and decreased telomerase functioning (Vukmanovic-Stejic et al., 2006).

The collective facts show that the growth of T regulatory cells related to cancer might result from the propagation of an already existing matrix, relatively more than obstruction in full growth. Myelodysplastic syndrome (Mds) is frequently considered the predecessor provision for Aml. Analogous to Aml, Mds. patients display high T regulatory cell density and a distorted cd8$^+$ T-cell/T regulatory cell ratio. In addition, a major-risk subclass of Mds and ailment development to more hostile MDS subtypes were escorted by the growth of T regulatory cell stages, recommending a straight part of T regulatory cells in development and malignant makeover (Hamdi et al., 2009). Several blood related cancer types exhibit numeric and functional shortfall of the T regulatory cell section, for case, cutaneous cell cancer (Tiemessen et al., 2007) and numerous myeloma (Prabhala et al., 2006).

5.7 Cancer vaccines and regulatory T cells

Plenty of confirmations are available for medical feedback related to malignancies and vaccinations are inclined by the phase of abnormality in the instance of vaccination. Carcinoma load and T regulatory cell magnitude, on average, tend to go arm in arm. Patients with high-grade cancer have significantly more T regulatory cell movement than those with the fewest remaining issues (Nicholaou et al., 2009). T regulatory cells might be stretched by malignancy vaccines as shown in tumor research with cancer patients, where immunologic and clinical feedback immunization with either Ny-Eso-one protein or dendrites stimulated with different cell lysate were revealed to be related to the occurrence of "cd4$^+$, cd25$^+$, Foxp3$^+$, cd127" and TGF-beta generating Th-3 cells (Lopez et al., 2009). Computable T-cell feedback has been recorded in patients after vaccination with NY-ESO-one DNA vaccine with assessable T cell responses, which were visibly repressed by Tregs like "cd4$^+$, cd25$^+$, and factor Foxp3$^+$" (Gnjatic et al., 2009).T regulator cells noticeably signify a big hindrance for competent cancer immunological therapies, T regulatory cell reduction has come out as a subordinate therapy that efficiently cooperates with different carcinoma immunization tactics in animal models. Though, the outcome of T regulatory cell diminishes in these models was utmost when completed instantly on pre or postcancer vaccination (Knutson et al., 2006). Exhaustion of regulatory T cells after the institution of tumors often fails to considerably develop the therapeutic results (Elpek et al., 2007) implying a cancer stage reliant effect of T regulatory cells in carcinoma control. Various current clinical works in the tumor are aimed at investigating T regulatory cell depletion in amalgamation with diverse immunotherapeutic ways. In the case of patients suffering from renal carcinoma, eradication of regulatory T cells by using an immunotoxin, followed by immunization with cancer RNA-immunoblotting DCs considerably enhanced the introduction of neoplasm particular T-cell reaction (Dannull et al., 2005). Almost same data can be collected with peptide-based vaccination procedures combine with T regulatory cell depletion in breast and colon carcinoma as well as tumor patients (Mahnke et al., 2007).

Reports from animal models back the idea that cancer-associated regulatory T cells could be prolonged in their reaction to therapeutic immunization and repress the concurrently produced T effector cells (Zhao et al., 2006; Mehraj et al., 2021a, 2021b). Analysis done and studies explained in this part speak about foremost concerns related to the development of cancer vaccines. Furthermore, these interpretations partly recommend that serving the regulatory T-cell compartment is significant as the assessment of the effector cell arm in patients getting immunological therapies.

5.8 Targeting T regulatory cells in cancer therapy

Taken collectively, T regulatory cells, regardless of source, hamper cancer surveillance and come out in various cases to be openly related to the disease etiology. In different studies conducted in the 1980s by Dr. Robert et al. and other researchers, it was found that depletion of T regulatory cells would be a robust approach for enhancing the immune response against cancer. Hitherto, a variety of forms of immunological therapies look up to malignancy healing. It seems unavoidable to work against the repressive impacts of Tregs. However, the effects of regulating T regulatory cells are not unimportant as they might result in useless effects, most notably self-immune phenomena. In addition, the hitting of regulatory T cells has to be controlled for cancer, where T regulatory cells have been revealed to be certainly related to harmful effects. Various approaches meant to reduce T regulatory cells or to functionally inactivate them are presently under progression or in medical trials, outlined in Table 5.2.

Table 5.2 Medical investigations using various approaches to reduce regulatory T cells in tumor patients.

Types of malignancy	Reduction regimen	Responses of treatment
Metastatic melanoma	Cpm (60 mg kg-d 2d) + Flu (25 mg/m^2/d 5d) prior ACT	Objective responses in 6 pts., Aid in 5 pts.
Metastatic melanoma	Cpm (60 mg kg-d 2d) þ Flu (25 mg/m^2/d 5d) prior ACT	Objective responses in 18 pts., Aid in 13 pts.
Chronic lymphocytic leukemia	*Fludarabine*-containing therapies	Reduced T regulatory frequency/function
Metastatic renal cell carcinoma	ONTAK (18 g/kg; single dose) + tumor RNA-transfected DC vaccine	Improved CTL responses, reduced T regulatory levels
Metastatic melanoma, ovarian cancer	*Ipilimumab* (3 mg/kg; successive doses) upon tumor cell vaccination (GVAX)	Sd in 8 pts., Pr in 4 pts., Pd in 8 pts.

Dannull et al. (2005), Mahnke et al. (2007), and Bayer et al. (2005).

5.8.1 Depletion of T regulatory cells

A few current studies have investigated whether the reduction or blockade of T regulatory cells could contribute to improving the immune protection mechanism. Few related studies have depicted the progression of "$cd4^+cd25^+$." T regulatory cells may be associated with tumor development and immunological repression in patients suffering from gastro-related malignancies (Xu et al., 2009). Furthermore, regulatory cell homeostasis is very strong and their levels improve quickly the following reduction to pretreatment degree or even surpass them. To accomplish the most favorable treatment potency, various application procedures and quantity rules had to be cautiously assessed aiming for the perfect equilibrium between depletion of Tregs and improvement of effector T-cell response.

5.8.2 Targeting function of regulatory T cells

CTLA-4 is another target molecule on the surface of Regulatory cells which is taking part in arbitrating suppression as explained earlier.cd-25, CTLA-4 molecules can also be expressed on $cd4^+$ and $cd8^+$ activated T cells (Egen et al., 2002). This viable jamming of CTLA-4 position on plenty of steps, which include T regulatory cells in addition to effector T cells is probably answerable for better effectiveness (Egen et al., 2002). Though it stays nonetheless to be clarified, that's the most important mechanism for checking the discovered anti–CTLA-4 result. At present, two human-based mostly anti–CTLA-4 antibodies, *Ipilimumab* and *Tremelimumab*, have been utilized in stage 1 and 2 medical trials. The outcome from a study carried out on people suffering from the advanced grade of carcinoma and renal tumor means the antitumor impact is because of direct increased activity of $cd4^+$ and $cd8^+$ T cells but not because of regulatory T-cell inhibition (Maker et al., 2005). According to a recent investigation, in patients with advanced stage of skin cell and ovarian carcinoma, the regular combination of anti–CTLA-4 antibodies after immunization with analogous tumor cells producing Gm-Csf developed medical antitumor protection, and notably, did not stimulate any stage third or fourth toxicity (Hodi et al., 2008). Therapeutic influenced cancer death interrelated with intra-tumor $cd8^+$ effector T-cell/T regulatory cell fraction diagnosed after postbiopsy procedures.

Molecules like GITR expressed on n regulatory T cells on lesser levels of stimulated old T cells had been considered a goal for T regulatory cell reduction and functional restriction (Nocentini and Riccardi, 2005). Signaling of GITR under in vitro in murine regulatory T cells resulted in decreased repressive movement, but this couldn't be created in human T regulatory cells (Kanamaru et al., 2004). Coming new investigations are mandatory to look upon the possibility of such a way for the management of malignancy in humans. Broadly expressed TLRs on various human cells, witness the 1st barrier of immune protection by identification of multiple microbes related to molecular patterns.

Their involvement in DC development and working of TLR routes in dendrites had been revealed to control the exchange of old T cells into T regulatory cells (Iwasaki and Medzhitov, 2004). As explained earlier, regulatory T cells express multiple TLRs, and so TLR ligands might have a straight (+ or −) impact on T regulatory cells. Commencement of TLR8 receptor through innate ligands autonomously of the presence of dendrites had been revealed to overturn regulatory T-cell working and alters cancer resistance in rat models (Peng et al., 2005). Activation of TLR stimuli might be of specific value for immunization strategies, since proper TLR activation may tip over T regulatory cell controlled tolerance (Yang et al., 2004).

5.8.3 Targeting the antioxidative ability of T regulatory cells

From the aforesaid explanation, metastatic tumor invasion heightens the volume of stress-regulated by active free oxygen molecules (Kusmartsev et al., 2004). The disastrous effect of RO—species on effector cells of the defense system is well recognized and explained in cancer and other persistent inflammatory dysfunctions (Gringhuis et al., 2000). The details discussed indicate the high resistance of regulatory T cells to oxidation stress is at present vague but seems to be associated with higher cell interior and exterior thiol content. However, the recognition of this route can supply in a very different manner for hitting regulatory T cells to reinstate a "balance of power" among Tregs and traditional T cells as taken into consideration for oxidative pressure vulnerability.

5.8.4 Regulation/modulation of T regulatory cell proliferation

As explained in the earlier part, dendritic cells, regardless of growth rate, are associated with the inauguration and initiation of T regulatory cells. Key particles in that mechanism evolved is the natural catalyst (Ido), which is largely expressed in the tolerogenic bone marrow and PDCs (Chen et al., 2008). Attachment of molecules like CTLA-four on CD-80 induces IDO functioning in DCs (Fallarino et al., 2003). So, the already mentioned anti–CTLA-4 type of cure might interject with the IDO pathway mechanism. Stage I medical attempts to treat diseased folks with a relapsed hard lump of cancer with the Ido blocker one-methyl d-tryptophan are presently continuing. Moreover, animal models have explained that Ido-regulated immunosuppression could be overturned by "*celecoxib*" therapy (Lee et al., 2009). *Celecoxib* is a particular blocker of the Pge two-releasing catalyst Cox-II. The creation of Pge II straightway activates T regulatory cell growth (Akasaki et al., 2004) or indirectly eases T regulatory cell selection by fostering tolerogenic APCs (Bergmann et al., 2007). In addition, T regulatory cells on their own could repress immunological response via Pge-2 production (Mahic et al., 2006), which more helps the assessment of COX-two blockers in the treatment of tumors known to indicate large Cox-2 and T regulatory cell stages such as Hcc and cancer urinary system (Gao et al., 2007). In patients suffering from cancer of the ovary, pDCs directly promote

IL-10–producing CD8$^+$ T regulatory cells (Wei et al., 2005). Cancer cells can generate CXCL-12 and thus magnetize PDCs which express the particular receptor CXCR-4. Inhibiting CXCL-12–CXCR-4 interaction promotes the death of cancer-associated PDCs and destroys their chemotaxis (Zou et al., 2001).

5.9 Conclusion

Voluminous evidence exists from both animals and *Homo sapiens* that T (regs) play a foremost part in the growth of cancer and that Tregs have a vital position in the repression of immunological defense associated with it. Therefore, a comprehensible justification for the creation of medical ways to moderate their dogmatic impact, to develop an immunological defense against tumor development, thus, modification of T regulatory cells, including reduction, decreasing their rate of division and suppressive mechanisms, targeting antioxidant potential, represents novel strategies for carcinoma treatment. Medically, factors that could competently hit regulatory T cells need vast research. The most significant final point for survival is the evaluation of cancer therapy. Over the last 50 years, chemical therapy, particularly cytotoxic, has emerged as one of the centerpieces for the management of malignancies. Whereas the capacity of chemotherapeutic procedures to promote tumor regulation and revocation has persistently developed (particularly in the blood-associated malignancies), chemotherapy usually does not work better to control cancer recurrence. A boom in the blend of chemotherapy and radiotherapy with immunotherapy could prove a remarkable strategy to prevent cancer reemergence and could augment treatment methods for various malignant diseases. Focusing on Tregs would be an amazing choice in curing different types of human and animal malignancies as it is now clear that a key role is played by T regulatory cells in the progression of cancer. So it is exciting and important to decode the complex mechanism behind T regulatory cells in malignancies, which ultimately provides a way to achieve reliable, effective medical treatment and the development of a complete therapy for the regulation and treatment of cancer and other diseases. Furthermore, due to new advancements in technology, like the concept of nanoparticle vehicles used to deliver targets, it might be very useful to regulate T regulatory cells at the base of their actions and to build up host surveillance or foster vaccine-promoted immunity when it is thought to be useful for the medical course of a specific type of cancer in a subject.

References

Akasaki, Y., Liu, G., Chung, N.H., Ehtesham, M., Black, K.L., Yu, J.S., 2004. Induction of a CD4+ T regulatory type 1 response by cyclooxygenase-2-overexpressing glioma. J. Immunol. 173, 4352–4359.
Alvaro, T., Lejeune, M., Salvado, M.T., Bosch, R., Garcia, J.F., Jaen, J., Banham, A.H., 2005. Outcome in Hodgkin's lymphoma can be predicted from the presence of accompanying cytotoxic and regulatory T cells. Clin. Cancer Res. 11, 1467–1473.

Andersen, M.H., Sorensen, R.B., Brimnes, M.K., Svane, I.M., Becker, J.C., thor Straten, P., 2009. Identification of heme oxygenase-1-specific regulatory CD8+ T cells in cancer patients. J. Clin. Investig. 119, 2245–2256.

Azuma, T., Takahashi, T., Kunisato, A., Kitamura, T., Hirai, H., 2003. Human CD4+ CD25+ regulatory T cells suppress NKT cell functions. Cancer Res. 63, 4516–4520.

Bayer, A.L., Yu, A., Adeegbe, D., Malek, T.R., 2005. Essential role for interleukin-2 for CD4(+)CD25(+) T regulatory cell development during the neonatal period. J. Exp. Med. 201, 769–777.

Bergmann, C., Strauss, L., Zeidler, R., Lang, S., Whiteside, T.L., 2007. Expansion of human T regulatory type 1 cells in the microenvironment of cyclooxygenase 2 overexpressing head and neck squamous cell carcinoma. Cancer Res. 67, 8865–8873.

Bettelli, E., Dastrange, M., Oukka, M., 2005. Foxp3 interacts with nuclear factor of activated T cells and NF-kappa B to repress cytokine gene expression and effector functions of T helper cells. Proc. Natl. Acad. Sci. U. S. A. 102, 5138–5143.

Burnet, M., 1957. Cancer: a biological approach. I. The processes of control. Br. Med. J. 1, 779–786.

Carreras, J., Lopez-Guillermo, A., Roncador, G., Vilamor, N., Colomo, L., Marinez, A., Hamoudi, R., Howat, W.J., Montserrat, E., Campo, E., 2009. High numbers of tumor-infiltrating programmed cell death 1-positive regulatory lymphocytes are associated with improved overall survival in follicular lymphoma. J. Clin. Oncol. 27, 1470–1476.

Casares, N., Arribillaga, L., Sarobe, P., et al., 2003. CD4+/CD25+ regulatory cells inhibit activation of tumor-primed CD4+ T cells with IFN-gamma-dependent antiangiogenic activity, as well as long-lasting tumor immunity elicited by peptide vaccination. J. Immunol. 171, 5931–5939.

Chaput, N., Louafi, S., Bardier, A., Charlotte, F., Vaillant, J.C., Menegaux, F., Rosenzwajg, M., Lemoine, F., Klatzmann, D., Taieb, J., 2009. Identification of CD8+CD25+Foxp3+ suppressive T cells in colorectal cancer tissue. Gut 58, 520–529.

Chen, W., Liang, X., Peterson, A.J., Munn, D.H., Blazar, B.R., 2008. The indoleamine 2,3-dioxygenase pathway is essential for human plasmacytoid dendritic cell-induced adaptive T regulatory cell generation. J. Immunol. 181, 5396–5404.

Chen, J., Gingold, J.A., Su, X., 2019. Immunomodulatory TGF-beta signaling in hepatocellular carcinoma. Trends Mol. Med. 25, 1010–1023.

Cortesini, R., LeMaoult, J., Ciubotariu, R., Cortesini, N.S., 2001. CD8+CD28- T suppressor cells and the induction of antigen-specific, antigen-presenting cell-mediated suppression of the reactivity. Immunol. Rev. 182, 201–206.

Cosmi, L., Liotta, F., Lazzeri, E., Francalanci, M., Angeli, R., Mazzinghi, B., Santarlasci, V., Manetti, R., Vanini, V., Romagnani, P., Maggi, E., Romagnani, S., et al., 2003. Human CD8+CD25+ thymocytes share phenotypic and functional features with CD4+CD25+ regulatory thymocytes. J. Blood 102, 4107–4114.

Cullen, S.P., Brunet, M., Martin, S.J., 2010. Granzymes in cancer and immunity. Cell Death Differ. 17, 616–623.

Cupedo, T., Nagasawa, M., Weijer, K., Blom, B., Spits, H., 2005. Development and activation of regulatory T cells in the human fetus. Eur. J. Immunol. 35, 383–390.

Curiel, T.J., Coukos, G., Zou, L., Alvarez, X., Cheng, P., Mottram, P., Evdemon-Hogan, M., Conejo-Garcia, J.R., Zhang, L., Burow, M., Zhu, Y., Wei, S., Kryczek, I., Daniel, B., Gordon, A., Myers, L., Lackner, A., Disis, M.L., Knutson, K.L., Chen, L., Zou, W., 2004. Specific recruitment of regulatory T cells in ovarian carcinoma fosters immune privilege and predicts reduced survival. Nat. Med. 10, 942–949.

Dannull, J., Su, Z., Rizzieri, D., Yang, B.K., Coleman, D., Yancey, D., Zhang, A., Dahm, P., Chao, N., Gilboa, E., Vieweg, J., 2005. Enhancement of vaccine-mediated antitumor immunity in cancer patients after depletion of regulatory T cells. J. Clin. Investig. 115, 3623–3633.

Dunn, G.P., Bruce, A.T., Ikeda, H., Old, L.J., Schreiber, R.D., 2002. Cancer immuno-editing: from immunosurveillance to tumor escape. Nat. Immunol. 2, 991–998.

Egen, J.G., Kuhns, M.S., Allison, J.P., 2002. CTLA-4: new insights into its biological function and use in tumor immunotherapy. Nat. Immunol. 3, 611–618.

Elpek, K.G., Lacelle, C., Singh, N.P., Yolcu, E.S., Shirwan, H., 2007. CD4+CD25+ T regulatory cells dominate multiple immune evasion mechanisms in early but not late phases of tumor development in a B cell lymphoma model. J. Immunol. 178, 6840–6848.

Facciabene, A., Motz, G.T., Coukos, G., 2012. T-regulatory cells: key players in tumor immune escape and angiogenesis. Cancer Res. 72, 2162–2171.

Fallarino, F., Grohmann, U., Hwang, K.W., Orabona, C., Vacca, C., Bianchi, R., Fioretti, M.C., Belladonna, M.L., Alegre, M.L., Puccetti, P., 2003. Modulation of tryptophan catabolism by regulatory T cells. Nat. Immunol. 4, 1206–1212.

Fietta, A.M., Morosini, M., Passadore, I., Cascina, A., Draghi, P., Dore, R., Rossi, S., Pozzi, E., Meloni, F., 2009. Systemic inflammatory response and downmodulation of peripheral CD25+ Foxp3+ T-regulatory cells in patients undergoing raidofrequency thermal ablation for lung cancer. Hum. Immunol. 70, 477–486.

Filaci, G., Fenoglio, D., Fravega, M., Ansaldo, G., Borgonovo, G., Traverso, P., Villaggio, B., Ferrera, A., Kunkl, A., Rizzi, M., Ferrera, F., Balestra, P., et al., 2007. CD8+CD28-T regulatory lymphocytes inhibiting T cell proliferative and cytotoxic functions infiltrate human cancers. J. Immunol. 179, 4323–4334.

Fontenot, J.D., Rasmussen, J.P., Williams, L.M., Dooley, J.L., Farr, A.G., Rudensky, A.Y., 2005. Regulatory T cell lineage specification by the forkhead transcription factor foxp3. Immunity 22, 329–341.

Fu, J., Xu, D., Liu, Z., Shi, M., Zhao, P., Fu, B., Zhang, Z., Yang, H., Zhang, H., Zhou, C., Yao, J., Jin, L., et al., 2007. Increased regulatory T cells correlate with CD8 T-cell impairment and poor survival in hepatocellular carcinoma patients. Gastroenterology 132, 2328–2339.

Fujimoto, S., Greene, M.I., Sehon, A.H., 1976. Regulation of the immune response to tumor antigens. II. The nature of immunosuppressor cells in tumor-bearing hosts. J. Immunol. 116, 800–806.

Gao, Q., Qiu, S.J., Fan, J., Zhou, J., Wang, X.Y., Xiao, Y.S., Xu, Y., Li, Y.W., Tang, Z.Y., 2007. Intratumoral balance of regulatory and cytotoxic T cells is associated with prognosis of hepatocellular carcinoma after resection. J. Clin. Oncol. 25, 2586–2593.

Gasteiger, G., Hemmers, S., Firth, M.A., Le Floc'h, A., Huse, M., et al., 2013. IL-2-dependent tuning of NK cell sensitivity for target cells is controlled by regulatory T cells. J. Exp. Med. 210, 1167–1178.

Gershon, R.K., Cohen, P., Hencin, R., Liebhaber, S.A., 1972. Suppressor T cells. J. Immunol. 108, 586–590.

Gnjatic, S., Altorki, N.K., Tang, D.N., Tu, S.M., Kundra, V., Ritter, G., Old, L.J., Logothetis, C.J., Sharma, P., 2009. NY-ESO-1 DNA vaccine induces T-cell responses that are suppressed by regulatory T cells. Clin. Cancer Res. 15, 2130–2139.

Gobert, M., Treilleux, I., Bendriss-Vermare, N., Bachelot, T., Goddard-Leon, S., Arfi, V., Bitoa, C., Doffin, A.C., Durand, I., Olive, D., Perez, S., Pasqual, N., Faure, C., Ray-Coquard, I., Puisieux, A., Caux, C., Blay, J.Y., Menetrier-Caux, C., 2009. Regulatory T cells recruited through CCL22/CCR4 are selectively activated in lymphoid infiltrates surrounding primary breast tumors and lead to an adverse clinical outcome. Cancer Res. 69, 2000–2009.

Gray, C.P., Arosio, P., Hersey, P., 2003. Association of increased levels of heavy-chain ferritin with increased CD4+ CD25+ regulatory T-cell levels in patients with melanoma. Clin. Cancer Res. 9, 2551–2559.

Griffiths, R.W., Elkor, E., Gilham, D.E., Ramani, V., Clarke, N., Stern, P.L., Hawkins, R.E., 2007. Frequency of regulatory T cells in renal cell carcinoma patients and investigation of correlation with survival. Cancer Immunol. Immunother. 56, 1743–1753.

Gringhuis, S.I., Leow, A., Der, P.-V., Voort, E.A., Remans, P.H., Breedveld, F.C., Verweij, C.L., 2000. Displacement of linker for activation of T cells from the plasma membrane due to redox balance alterations results in hyporesponsiveness of synovial fluid T lymphocytes in rheumatoid arthritis. J. Immunol. 164, 2170–2179.

Ha, T.Y., 2008. Regulatory T cell therapy for autoimmune disease. Immune Netw. 8, 107–123.

Hamdi, W., Ogawara, H., Handa, H., Tsukamoto, N., Nojima, Y., Murakami, H., 2009. Clinical significance of regulatory T cells in patients with myelodysplastic syndrome. Eur. J. Haematol. 82, 201–207.

Hiraoka, N., Onozato, K., Kosuge, T., Hirohashi, S., 2006. Prevalence of FOXP3+ regulatory T cells increases during the progression of pancreatic ductal adenocarcinoma and its premalignant lesions. Clin. Cancer Res. 12, 5423–5434.

Hodi, F.S., Butler, M., Oble, D.A., Seiden, M.V., Haluska, F.G., Kruse, A., Macrae, S., Nelson, M., Canning, C., Lowy, I., Korman, A., Lautz, D., et al., 2008. Immunologic and clinical effects of antibody blockade of cytotoxic T lymphocyte-associated antigen 4 in previously vaccinated cancer patients. Proc. Natl. Acad. Sci. U. S. A. 105, 3005–3010.

Huen, J., Polansky, J.K., Hamann, A., 2009. Epigenetic control of FOXP3 expression: the key to a stable regulatory T-cell lineage? Nat. Rev. Immunol. 9, 83–89. Nat. Rev. Immunol. 9, 83–89.

Ichihara, F., Kono, K., Takahashi, A., Kawaida, H., Sugai, H., Fujii, H., 2003. Increased populations of regulatory T cells in peripheral blood and tumor-infiltrating lymphocytes in patients with gastric and esophageal cancers. Clin. Cancer Res. 9, 4404–4408.

Iwasaki, A., Medzhitov, R., 2004. Toll-like receptor control of the adaptive immune responses. Nat. Immunol. 5, 987–995.

Jordanova, E.S., Gorter, A., Ayachi, O., Prins, F., Durrant, L.G., Kenter, G.G., van der Burg, S.H., Fleuren, G.J., 2008. Human leukocyte antigen class I, MHC class I chain-related molecule A, and CD8 +/regulatory T-cell ratio: which variable determines survival of cervical cancer patients. Clin. Cancer Res. 14, 2028–2035.

Kanamaru, F., Youngnak, P., Hashiguchi, M., Nishioka, T., Takahashi, T., Sakaguchi, S., Ishikawa, I., Azuma, M., 2004. Costimulation via glucocorticoid-induced TNF receptor in both conventional and CD25 + regulatory CD4 + T cells. J. Immunol. 172, 7306–7314.

Ke, X., Wang, J., Li, L., Chen, I.M., Wang, H., Yang, X.F., 2008. Roles of CD4 + CD25(high)FOXP3 T regs in lymphomas and tumors are complete. Front. Biosci. 13, 3986–4001.

Kim, J.M., Rasmussen, J.P., Rudensky, A.Y., 2007. Regulatory T cells prevent catastrophic autoimmunity throughout the lifespan of mice. Nat. Immunol. 8, 191–197.

Kiniwa, Y., Miyahara, Y., Wang, H.Y., Peng, W., Peng, G., Wheeler, T.M., Thompson, T.C., Old, L.J., Wang, R.F., 2003. CD8 + Foxp3 + regulatory T cells mediate immunosuppression in prostate cancer. Clin. Cancer Res. 13, 6947–6958.

Knutson, K.L., Dang, Y., Lu, H., Lukas, J., Almand, B., Gad, E., Azeke, E., Disis, M.L., 2006. IL-2 immunotoxin therapy modulates tumor-associated regulatory T cells and leads to lasting immune-mediated rejection of breast cancers in neu-transgenic mice. J. Immunol. 177, 84–91.

Komatsu, N., Mariotti-Ferrandiz, M.E., Wang, Y., Malissen, B., Waldmann, H., Hori, S., 2009. Heterogeneity of natural Foxp3(+) T cells: a committed regulatory T-cell lineage and an uncommitted minor population retaining plasticity. Proc. Natl. Acad. Sci. U. S. A. 106, 1903–1908.

Kono, K., Kawaida, H., Takahashi, A., Sugai, H., Mimura, K., Miyagawa, N., Omata, H., Fujii, H., 2006. CD4(+)CD25high regulatory T cells increase with tumor stage in patients with gastric and esophageal cancers. Cancer Immunol. Immunother. 55, 1064–1071.

Kusmartsev, S., Nefedova, Y., Yoder, D., Gabrilovich, D.I., 2004. Antigen-specific inhibition of CD8 + T cell response by immature myeloid cells in cancer is mediated by reactive oxygen species. J. Immunol. 172, 989–999.

Lal, G., Bromberg, J.S., 2009. Epigenetic mechanisms of regulation of Foxp3 expression. J. Blood 114, 3727–3735.

Lee, S.Y., Choi, H.K., Lee, K.J., Jung, J.Y., Hur, G.Y., Jung, K.H., Kim, J.H., Shin, C., Shim, J.J., In, K.H., Kang, K.H., Yoo, S.H., 2009. The immune tolerance of cancer is mediated by IDO that is inhibited by COX-2 inhibitors through regulatory T cells. J. Immunol. 32, 22–28.

Leon, K., Carcia, K., Carneiro, J., Lage, A., 2007. How regulatory CD25 + CD4 + T cells impinge on tumor immunobiology: the differential response of tumors to therapies. J. Immunol. 179, 5659–5668.

Levings, M.K., Sangregorio, R., Roncarolo, M.G., 2001. Human cd25(+)cd4(+) t regulatory cells suppress naive and memory T cell proliferation and can be expanded in vitro without loss of function. J. Exp. Med. 193, 1295–1302.

Li, X., Ye, F., Chen, H., Lu, W., Wan, X., Xie, X., 2007. Human ovarian carcinoma cells generate CD4 (+)CD25(+) regulatory T cells from peripheral CD4(+)CD25(−) T cells through secreting TGF-beta. Cancer Lett. 253, 144–153.

Li, Z., Li, D., Tsun, A., Li, B., 2015. FOXP3 + regulatory T cells and their functional regulation. Cell. Mol. Immunol. 12, 558–565.

Lim, H.W., Hillsamer, P., Banham, A.H., Kim, C.H., 2005. Cutting edge: direct suppression of B cells by CD4+ CD25+ regulatory T cells. J. Immunol. 175, 4180–4183.

Liu, V.C., Wong, L.Y., Jang, T., Shah, A.H., Park, I., Yang, X., Zhang, Q., Lonning, S., Teicher, B.A., Lee, C., 2007. Tumor evasion of the immune system by converting CD4+CD25- T cells into CD4+CD25+ T regulatory cells: role of tumor-derived TGF-beta. J. Immunol. 178, 2883–2892.

Liu, Z., Kim, J.H., Falo Jr., L.D., You, Z., 2009. Tumor regulatory T cells potently abrogate antitumor immunity. J. Immunol. 182, 6160–6167.

Lizee, G., Radvanyi, L.G., Overwijk, W.W., Hwu, P., 2006. Improving antitumor immune responses by circumventing immunoregulatory cells and mechanisms. Clin. Cancer Res. 12, 4794–4803.

Lohr, J., Knoechel, B., Abbas, A.K., 2006. Regulatory T cells in the periphery. Immunol. Rev. 212, 149–162.

Lopez, M.N., Pereda, C., Segal, G., Munoz, L., Aguilera, R., Gonzalez, F.E., Escobar, A., Ginesta, A., Reyes, D., Gonzalez, R., Mendoza-Naranjo, A., Larrondo, M., et al., 2009. Prolonged survival of dendritic cell-vaccinated melanoma patients correlates with tumor specific delayed type IV hypersensitivity response and reduction of tumor growth factor beta expressing T cells. J. Clin. Oncol. 27, 945–952.

Maggi, E., Cosmi, L., Liotta, F., Romagnani, P., Romagnani, S., Annunziato, F., 2005. Thymic regulatory T cells. Autoimmun. Rev. 4, 579–586.

Mahic, M., Yaqub, S., Johansson, C.C., Tasken, K., Aandahl, E.M., 2006. FOXP3+CD4+CD25+ adaptive regulatory T cells express cyclooxygenase-2 and suppress effector T cells by a prostaglandin E2-dependent mechanism. J. Immunol. 177, 246–254.

Mahnke, K., Schonfeld, K., Fondel, S., Ring, S., Karakhanova, S., Wiedemeyer, K., Bedke, T., Johnson, T.-S., Storn, V., Schallenberg, S., Enk, A.H., 2007. Depletion of CD4+CD25+ human regulatory T cells in vivo: kinetics of Treg depletion and alterations in immune functions in vivo and in vitro. Int. J. Cancer 120, 2723–2733.

Maker, A.V., Attia, P., Rosenberg, S.A., 2005. Analysis of the cellular mechanism of antitumor responses and autoimmunity in patients treated with CTL A-4 blockade. J. Immunol. 155, 7746–7754.

Malek, T.R., Yu, A., Vincek, V., Scibelli, P., Kong, L., 2002. CD4 regulatory T cells prevent lethal autoimmunity in IL-2Rbeta-deficient mice. Implications for the nonredundant function of IL-2. Immunity 17, 167–178.

Mantel, P.Y., Ouaked, N., Ruckert, B., Karagiannidis, C., Welz, R., Blaser, K., Schmidt-Weber, C.B., 2006. Molecular mechanisms underlying FOXP3 induction in human T cells. J. Immunol. 176, 3593–3602.

Martens, A., Wistuba-Hamprecht, K., GeukesFoppen, M., Yuan, J., Postow, M.A., et al., 2016. Baseline peripheral blood biomarkers associated with clinical outcome of advanced melanoma patients treated with ipilimumab. Clin. Cancer Res. 22, 2908–2918.

Mehraj, U., Dar, A.H., Wani, N.A., et al., 2021a. Tumor microenvironment promotes breast cancer chemoresistance. Cancer Chemother. Pharmacol. 87, 147–158.

Mehraj, U., Qayoom, H., Mir, M.A., 2021b. Prognostic significance and targeting tumor-associated macrophages in cancer: new insights and future perspectives. Breast Cancer 28, 539–555.

Mehraj, U., Aisha, S., Sofi, S., Mir, M.A., 2022a. Expression pattern and prognostic significance of baculoviral inhibitor of apoptosis repeat-containing 5 (BIRC5) in breast cancer: a comprehensive analysis. Adv. Cancer Biol. Metastasis, 100037.

Mehraj, U., Mushtaq, U., Mir, M.A., Saleem, A., Macha, M.A., Lone, M.N., Hamid, A., Zargar, M.A., Ahmad, S.M., Wani, N.A., 2022b. Chemokines in triple-negative breast cancer heterogeneity: new challenges for clinical implications. Semin. Cancer Biol. https://doi.org/10.1016/j.semcancer.2022.03.008.

Mills, K.H., 2004. Regulatory T cells: friend or foe in immunity to infection? Nat. Rev. Immunol. 4, 841–855.

Mir, A.M., Umar, M., 2019. Double-crosser of the immune system: macrophages in tumor progression and metastasis. Curr. Immunol. Rev. 15.

Mir, M., Sofi, S., Qayoom, H., 2022a. Role of Immune System in Triple Negative Breast Cancer (TNBC). Chapter 5, Elsevier.

Mir, M., Sofi, S., Qayoom, H., 2022b. Targeting Biologically Specific Molecules in Triple Negative Breast Cancer (TNBC). Chapter 7, Elsevier.

Misra, N., Bayry, J., Lacroix-Desmazes, S., Kazatchkine, M.D., Kaveri, S.V., 2004. Cutting edge: human CD4+CD25+ T cells restrain the maturation and antigen-presenting function of dendritic cells. J. Immunol. 172, 4676–4680.

Mizukami, Y., Kono, K., Kawaguchi, Y., Akaike, H., Kamimur, K., Sugai, H., Fujii, H., 2008. CCL17 and CCL22 chemokines within tumor environment are related to accumulation of Toxp3+ regulatory T cells in gastric cancer. Int. J. Cancer 122, 2286–2293.

Mudd, P.A., Teague, B.N., Farris, A.D., 2006. Regulatory T cells and systemic lupus erythematosus. Scand. J. Immunol. 64, 211–218.

Nakamura, K., Kitani, A., Fuss, I., Pedersen, A., Harada, N., Nawata, H., Strober, W., 2004. TGF-beta 1 plays an important role in the mechanism of CD4+CD25+ regulatory T cell activity in both humans and mice. J. Immunol. 172, 834–842.

Nicholaou, T., Ebert, L.M., Davis, I.D., McArthur, G.A., Jackson, H., Dimopoulos, N., Tan, B., Maraskovsky, E., Miloradovic, L., Hopkins, W., Pan, L., Venhaus, R., et al., 2009. Regulatory T-cell-mediated attenuation of T-cell responses to the NY-ESO-1 ISCOMATRIX vaccine in patients with advanced malignant melanoma. Clin. Cancer Res. 15, 2166–2173.

Nocentini, G., Riccardi, C., 2005. GITR: a multifaceted regulator of immunity belonging to the tumor necrosis factor receptor superfamily. Eur. J. Immunol. 35, 1016–1022.

Paluskievicz, C.M., Cao, X., Abdi, R., Zheng, P., Liu, Y., Bromberg, J.S., 2019. T regulatory cells and priming the suppressive tumor microenvironment. Front. Immunol. 10, 2453.

Pandiyan, P., Zheng, L., Ishihara, S., Reed, J., Lenardo, M.J., 2007. CD4+CD25+Foxp3+ regulatory T cells induce cytokine deprivation-mediated apoptosis of effector CD4+ T cells. Nat. Immunol. 8, 1353–1362.

Peng, G., Guo, Z., Kiniwa, Y., Voo, K.S., Peng, W., Fu, T., Wang, D.Y., Li, Y., Wang, H.Y., Wang, R.F., 2005. Toll-like receptor 8-mediated reversal of CD4+ regulatory T cell function. Science 309, 1380–1384. Science, 309, 1380–1384.

Petersen, R.P., Campa, M.J., Sperlazza, J., Conlon, D., Joshi, M.B., Harpole Jr., D.H., Patz Jr., E.F., 2006. Tumor infiltrating Foxp3+ regulatory T-cells are associated with recurrence in pathologic stage I NSCLC patients. Cancer 107, 2866–2872.

Piccirillo, C.A., Shevach, E.M., 2001. Cutting edge: control of CD8+ T cell activation by CD4+CD25+ immunoregulatory cells. J. Immunol. 167, 1137–1140.

Prabhala, R.H., Neri, P., Bae, J.E., Tassone, P., Shammas, M.A., Allam, C.K., Daley, J.F., Blanchard, E., Chauhan, D., Thatte, H.S., Anderson, K.C., Munshi, N.C., 2006. Dysfunctional T regulatory cells in multiple myeloma. Blood, 301–304.

Qin, F.X., 2009. Dynamic behavior and function of Foxp3+ regulatory T cells in tumor bearing host. Cell. Mol. Immunol. 6, 3–13.

Quezada, S.A., Peggs, K.S., Simpson, T.R., Allison, J.P., 2011. Shifting the equilibrium in cancer immunoediting: from tumor tolerance to eradication. Immunol. Rev. 241, 104–118.

Qureshi, O.S., Zheng, Y., Nakamura, K., Attridge, K., Manzotti, C., et al., 2011. Trans-endocytosis of CD80 and CD86: a molecular basis for the cell-extrinsic function of CTLA-4. Science 3 (332), 600.

Riley, J.L., June, C.H., Blazar, B.R., 2009. Human T regulatory cell therapy: take a billion or so and call me in the morning. Immunity 30, 656–665.

Romano, M., Tung, S.L., Smyth, L.A., Lombardi, G., 2017. Treg therapy in transplantation: a general overview. Transpl. Int. 30, 745–753.

Sakaguchi, S., 2004. Naturally arising CD4+ regulatory t cells for immunologic self-tolerance and negative control of immune responses. Annu. Rev. Immunol. 22, 531–562.

Sakaguchi, S., Sakaguchi, N., Asano, M., Itoh, M., Toda, M., 1995. Immunological self-tolerance maintained by activated T-cells expressing Il-2 receptor alpha-chains (Cd25)—breakdown of a single mechanism of self-tolerance causes various autoimmune-diseases. J. Immunol. 155, 1151–1164.

Sakaguchi, S., Yamaguchi, T., Nomura, T., Ono, M., 2008. Regulatory T cells and immune tolerance. J. Cell 133, 775–787.

Sanjabi, S., Oh, S.A., Li, M.O., 2017. Regulation of the immune response by TGF-β: from conception to autoimmunity and infection. Cold Spring Harb. Perspect. Biol. 9, a022236.

Sasada, T., Kimura, M., Yoshida, Y., Kanai, M., Takabayashi, A., 2003. CD4 + CD25 + regulatory T cells in patients with gastrointestinal malignancies: possible involvement of regulatory T cells in disease progression. Cancer 98, 1089–1099.

Sato, E., Olson, S.H., Ahn, J., Bundy, B., Nishikawa, H., Qian, F., Jungbluth, A.A., Frosina, D., Gnjatic, S., Ambrosone, C., Kepner, J., Odunsi, T., et al., 2005. Intraepithelial CD8 + tumor-infiltrating lymphocytes and a high CD8 +/regulatory T cell ratio are associated with favorable prognosis in ovarian cancer. Proc. Natl. Acad. Sci. U. S. A. 102, 18538–18543.

Schabowsky, R.H., Madiredii, S., Sharma, R., Yolcu, E.S., Shirwan, H., 2007. Targeting CD4 + CD25 + Foxp3 + regulatory T-cells for the augmentation of cancer immunotherapy. Curr. Opin. Investig. Drugs 8, 1002–1008.

Shen, L.S., Wang, J., Shen, D.F., Yuan, X.L., Dong, P., Li, M.X., Xue, J., Zhang, F.M., Ge, H.L., Xu, D., 2009. CD4 + CD25 + CD127(low/−) regulatory T cells express Foxp3 and suppress effector T cell proliferation and contribute to gastric cancers progression. Clin. Immunol. 131, 109–118.

Shevach, E.M., 2001. Certified professionals: CD4 + CD25 + suppressor T cells. J. Exp. Med. 193, F41–F46.

Shevach, E.M., 2009. Mechanisms of Toxp3 + T regulatory cell-medicated suppression. Immunity 30, 636–645.

Suciu-Foca, N., Cortesini, R., 2007. Central role of ILT3 in the T suppressor cell cascade. Cell. Immunol. 248, 59–67.

Suzuki, H., Kundig, T.M., Furlonger, C., Wakeham, A., Timms, E., Matsuyama, T., Schmits, R., Ohashi, P.S., Simard, J.J., Griesser, H., et al., 1997. Deregulated T cell activation and autoimmunity in mice lacking interleukin-2 receptor beta. Science 268, 1472–1476.

Terabe, M., Swann, J., Ambrosino, E., Sinha, P., Takaku, S., Hayakawa, Y., Godfrey, D., Ostrand-Rosenberg, S., Smyth, M.J., Berzofsky, J.A., 2005. A nonclassical non-Va14Ja18 CD1d-restricted (type II) NKT cell is sufficient for down-regulation of tumor immunosurveillance. J. Exp. Med. 202, 1627–1633.

Tiemessen, M.M., Jagger, A.L., Evans, H.G., van Herwijnen, M.J., John, S., Taams, L.S., 2007. CD4 + CD25 + Foxp3 + regulatory T cells induce alternative activation of human monocytes/macrophages. Proc. Natl. Acad. Sci. U. S. A. 104, 19446–19451.

Toda, A., 2006. Development and function of naturally occurring CD4 + CD25 + regulatory T cells. J. Leukoc. Biol. 80, 458–470.

Tone, Y., Furuuchi, K., Kojima, Y., Tykocinski, M.L., Greene, M.I., Tone, M., 2008. Smad3 and NFAT cooperate to induce Foxp3 expression through its enhancer. Nat. Immunol. 9, 194–202.

Vence, L., Palucka, A.K., Fay, J.W., Ito, T., Liu, Y.J., Banchereau, J., Ueno, H., 2007. Circulating tumor antigen-specific regulatory T cells in patients with metastatic melanoma. Proc. Natl. Acad. Sci. U. S. A. 104, 20884–20889.

Vukmanovic-Stejic, M., Zhang, Y., Cook, J.E., Fletcher, J.M., McQuaid, A., Masters, J.E., Rustin, M.H., Taams, L.S., Beverley, P.C., Macallan, D.C., Akbar, A.N., 2006. Human CD4 + CD25hi Foxp3 + regulatory T cells are derived by rapid turnover of memory populations in vivo. J. Clin. Investig. 116, 2423–2433.

Waksman, B.H., 1977. Tolerance, the thymus, and suppressor T cells. Clin. Exp. Immunol. 28, 363–374.

Wang, H.Y., Wang, R.F., 2007. Regulatory T cells and cancer. Curr. Opin. Immunol. 19, 217.

Wang, H.Y., Lee, D.A., Peng, G., Guo, Z., Li, Y., Kiniwa, Y., Shevach, E.M., Wang, R.F., 2004. Tumor-specific human CD4 + regulatory T cells and their ligands: implications for immunotherapy. Immunity 20, 107–118.

Wang, H.Y., Peng, G., Guo, Z., Shevach, E.M., Wang, R.F., 2005a. Recognition of a new ARTC1 peptide ligand uniquely expressed in tumor cells by antigen-specific CD4 + regulatory T cells. J. Immunol. 174, 2661–2670.

Wang, X., Zheng, J., Liu, J., Yao, J., He, Y., Li, X., Yu, J., Yang, J., Liu, Z., Huang, S., 2005b. Increased population of CD4(+)CD25(high), regulatory T cells with their higher apoptotic and proliferating status in peripheral blood of acute myeloid leukemia patients. Eur. J. Haematol. 75, 468–476.

Wang, K.X., Li, L., Chen, I.M., Wang, H., Yang, X.F., 2008. Roles of CD4 + CD25(high)FOXP3 Tregs in lymphomas and tumors are complex. Front. Biosci. 13, 3986–4001.

Wei, S., Kryczek, I., Zou, L., Daniel, B., Cheng, P., Mottram, P., Curiel, T., Lange, A., Zou, W., 2005. Plasmacytoid dendritic cells induce CD8+ regulatory T cells in human ovarian carcinoma. Cancer Res. 65, 5020–5026.

Whiteside, T.L., 2015. Clinical impact of regulatory T cells (Treg) in Cancer and HIV. Cancer Microenviron. 8, 201–207.

Wolf, M., Schimpl, A., Hunig, T., 2001. Control of T cell hyperactivation in IL-2-deficient mice by CD4 (+)CD25(−) and CD4(+)CD25(+) T cells: evidence for two distinct regulatory mechanisms. Eur. J. Immunol. 31, 1637–1645.

Wolf, A.M., Wolf, D., Steurer, M., Gastl, G., Gunsilius, E., Grubeck-Loebenstein, B., 2003. Increase of regulatory T cells in the peripheral blood of cancer patients. Clin. Cancer Res. 9, 606–612.

Wu, S.P., Liao, R.Q., Tu, H.Y., Wang, W.j., Dong, Z.Y., et al., 2018. Stromal PD-L1-positive regulatory T cells and PD-1-positive CD8-positive T cells define the response of different subsets of non-small cell lung cancer to PD-1/PD-L1 blockade immunotherapy. J. Thorac. Oncol. 13, 521–532.

Xu, H., Mao, Y., Dai, Y., Wang, Q., Zhang, X., 2009. CD4+CD25+ regulatory T cells in patients with advanced gastrointestinal cancer treated with chemotherapy. Onkologie 32, 246–252.

Yang, Y., Huang, C.T., Huang, X., Pardoll, D.M., 2004. Persistent toll-like receptor signals are required for reversal of regulatory T cell-mediated CD8 tolerance. Nat. Immunol. 5, 508–515.

Zhao, D.M., Thornton, A.M., DiPaolo, R.J., Shevach, E.M., 2006. Activated CD4+CD25+ T cells selectively kill B lymphocytes. Blood 107, 3925–3932.

Ziegler, S.F., 2006. Ziegler SF: FOXP3: of mice and men. Annu. Rev. Immunol. 24, 209–226. 2006 ', Annual review of immunology, 24: 209–26.

Zou, W., 2006. Regulatory T cells, tumor immunity and immunotherapy. Nat. Rev. Immunol. 6, 295–307.

Zou, W., Machelon, V., Coulomb-L'Hermin, A., Borvak, J., Nome, F., Isaeva, T., Wei, S., Krzysiek, R., Durand-Gasselin, I., Gordon, A., Pustilnik, T., Curiel, D.T., et al., 2001. Stromal-derived factor-1 in human tumors recruits and alters the function of plasmacytoid precursor dendritic cells. Nat. Med. 7, 1339–1346. https://doi.org/10.1038/nm1201-1339.

Further reading

Mir, M.A., Aisha, S., Mehraj, U., 2022. Chapter 2 - Novel biomarkers in triple-negative breast cancer - role and perspective. In: Mir, M. (Ed.), Combinational Therapy in Triple Negative Breast Cancer. Academic Press, pp. 29–60. https://doi.org/10.1016/B978-0-323-96136-3.

CHAPTER 6

Role of tumor-associated macrophages in the breast tumor microenvironment

Manzoor Ahmad Mir, Abrar Yousuf Mir, and Tabasum Mushtaq
Department of Bioresources, School of Biological Sciences, University of Kashmir, Srinagar, Jammu and Kashmir, India

6.1 Introduction

Breast cancer is the most commonly investigated tumor in females worldwide, and it is the leading cause of death in females (Benson and Jatoi, 2012). In 2012, 1.7 million new cases were estimated, which led to 521,900 deaths. Additionally, in 2018, more than 2 million new breast cancer cases were diagnosed, resulting in 630,000 deaths (Bray et al., 2018; Mehraj et al., 2022a). Predominantly as a result of advancements in medication and detection processes, a remarkable decrease in mortality rate has been observed, though it still accounts for 10%–15% of all malignant deathliness in females, owing to advanced cancers and an impediment to comprehensive therapy (Benson and Jatoi, 2012). Consequently, researchers are looking for potential targets for treatment, for instance, the tumor microenvironment (Cha and Koo, 2020). We know that a tumor is the outcome of the interaction between natural immune cells and cancerous cells, resulting in a fully formed tumor from a single normal cell. Tumor immune cells mainly present in the tumor microenvironment include DCs, NK cells, T cells, MDSCs, mast cells, and TAMs. All these immune cells play a significant role in tumor progression (Mehraj et al., 2021a, b).

Stephen Paget, a pioneer cancer researcher, put forward the "seed and soil" hypothesis in 1889, claiming that cancer cells act as "seeds" that could cause cancer growth only when there is the existence of a conducive microenvironment (Paget, 1889). Despite this fact, cancer detection and intrusion strategies have traditionally focused on cancer-cell–intrinsic factors. Recent research has focused on immune cells such as macrophages, mast cells, and neutrophils, as well as endothelial cells, fibroblasts, adipocytes, and perivascular cells found in TME (Williams et al., 2016). Macrophages are termed "tumor-associated macrophages" and represent the most prominent cells in the breast tumor microenvironment, accounting for greater than 50% of the cell volume in maximum solid malignancy (Vitale et al., 2019; Mehraj et al., 2021a, b). Elie Metchnikoff, in 1882, discovered macrophages as phagocytic immune cells while examining starfish embryos, and demonstrated that macrophages come up with the first line of defense, putting a stop to diseases, upgrading wound healing and maintaining tissue stability, distinguishing

Role of Tumor Microenvironment in Breast Cancer and Targeted Therapies
https://doi.org/10.1016/B978-0-443-18696-7.00003-8

between self and non–self-antigens, as well as solving inflammation processes (Vitale et al., 2019). A higher degree of cellular plasticity has been demonstrated by macrophages when triggered via an innumerable number of signals in TME, and they respond hurriedly to take part in both innate immune response as well as acquired immune response. Signaling proteins like cytokines and chemokines as well as other enzymes present in the TME stimulate chemotaxis in responding to adjacent cells and the TME greatly influences the functional properties of macrophages in the tumor microenvironment (Chanmee et al., 2014). TAM is formed in breast tumors by resident macrophages and the accumulation of disseminating leukocytes (Franklin et al., 2014). With the help of "MCSF" or "CSF1" (monocyte colony stimulating factor) transform recruited monocytes into nonpolarized macrophages (MO) (Fig. 6.1) (Martinez and Gordon, 2014). MO macrophages are extremely plastic, in response to external stimuli they can change their physical composition. Classification of macrophage density within tumor can be categorized on the basis of their functional scale (Mosser and Edwards, 2008). According to the function of macrophages, they are broadly classified into two phenotypes such as the M1/M2 phenotype; M1 phenotype has proinflammatory and antitumor capability, and M2 phenotype led to antiinflammatory as well as tumor-promoting function (Chanmee et al., 2014). These two macrophages are considered as functional spectrum in this classification (Mosser and Edwards, 2008). T helper cell type 1 (Th1) secrete chemokines like "interferon-γ (IFN-γ), either tumor necrosis factor (TNF)" for recruitment of macrophages like M1, and are also termed as classically activated macrophage, leading to the

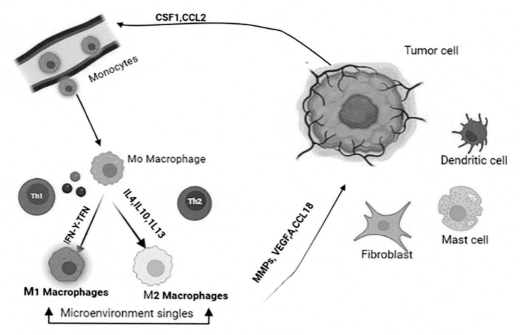

Fig. 6.1 Overview mechanism of recruited macrophages inside the breast tumor microenvironment.

secretion of proinflammatory chemokines namely tumor necrosis factor (TNF) as well as IL-2 (interleukin), along with oxygen radical along with nitrogen intermediates (Biswas and Mantovani, 2010). Contrary to macrophages like M2, which are intensified by cytokines like interleukin-4, interleukin-10, as well as interleukin-13, expressed by T helper cell type 2 (Th2), exhibit protumor properties, and M2 are termed as alternatively activated macrophage (Martinez and Gordon, 2014). Current studies revealed that M2 like macrophages show comparable functionality with TAMs and show response to cytokines like "interleukin-4 (IL-4), interleukin-10 (IL-10), transforming growth factor-beta (TGF-β), and interleukin-13 (IL-13)" stimulating re-grow of tissues (Rhee, 2016). For recruiting macrophages cancer cells release cytokines in the TME and in corresponding M2-like TAMs secrete protumor chemokines in order to enhance tumor cells proliferation (Mantovani et al., 2002) (Fig. 6.1). Tumor-associated-macrophages gain access and hinder the CD8+ T protumor activity, energizing tumor development, proliferation, and metastasis (Ruffell and Coussens, 2015). Furthermore, researchers disclose that the association between tumor cells and TAMs not merely also controls cancer cells toward proliferation and spread but also inhibits the immune response and leads to chemoresistance (Cha and Koo, 2020). So, in a nutshell, TAMs are considered a significant biomarker in cancer detection and a promising target for cancer treatment. Below, we will discuss more about the possible functions of TAMs in cancer proliferation and metastasis.

6.2 Composition

The breast tumor microenvironment may be studied at three distinct levels: local (intratumor), regional (in the breast), and distant (metastatic) levels. Each one is associated with a variety of cells, including fibroblasts, leukocytes, adipocytes, endothelial and basket cells, as well as extracellular matrix (ECM). They also comprise dissolved factors, for instance, estrogen and progesterone. Growth factors, enzymes, chemokines, hormones, as well as other physical observables such as pH, and oxygen percentage, as well (Coleman et al., 2013; Mir, 2021).

6.2.1 Local microenvironment

For the healthy development and proliferation of the breast glands, interferences between stromal and epithelial cells are necessary. Biological stroma keeps epithelial polarity and suppresses excessive cell proliferation and cancer (Folgueira et al., 2013). By the way of illustration basket cells (myoepithelial cells) turned out to be natural inhibitors in the mammary tumor and act as doorkeepers of tumor development, because these cells form the "Basement membrane" and denote an obstruction in the vicinity of luminal epithelial cells (Hu and Polyak, 2008). A breast tumor xenograft study revealed the reduction of myoepithelial cells enhances the transformation of "ductal carcinoma in situ" (DCIS) into "invasive carcinoma" (Hu and Polyak, 2008). Escape and the release study of the Ductal carcinoma in situ carcinoma-to-invasive carcinoma transformation turned out to be represented by these two hypotheses (Hu and Polyak, 2008). "Escape" hypothesis revealed, alteration at the gene level enables cancer epithelial cells to escape the tissue adjoining to the vessels, whereas the "release" hypothesis revealed out, aberrant microenvironment causes BM destruction and metastasis of cancer epithelial cells inside stroma. The essential circumstances of the in situ-to-invasive transformation in breast tumors, is most likely the combination of these two models, underlining the importance of alterations in epithelial and stromal compartments for influencing the cancer development and metastasis. In breast tumor cells, healthy myoepithelial cells also show the suppression in growth, escape, and angiogenesis as well (Barsky and Karlin, 2005). The associated tumor stroma, via paracrine signaling, stimulates myofibroblast as well as fibroblast to influence cancer progression and tumor spread by generating a receptive microenvironment. Despite the fact that tumor-associated stroma simulates a healing wound in many ways with fibroblast proliferation and remodeling of ECM but with no physiological controls (Dvorak, 1986). Correspondingly, several studies demonstrated that IL-6 (interleukin-6) an inflammatory cytokine improves the tumor growth and spread, urge on breast tumor hematopoietic cells (Jiang and Shapiro, 2014). For instance, by recruiting "type 4 C-X-C chemokine receptor (CXCR4)"—stem and precursor cells the chemotactic cytokine "C-X-C motif" ligand (CXCL)12 is physically critical to start tissue renewal and replacement (Cojoc et al., 2013). Tumor-associated stromal cell migration and multiplication are stimulated by "CXCR4/CXCL12" signaling in the mammary TME and the release of "matrix metalloproteinases" (MMP) and subsequent tissue reshaping, further more multiple investigations have shown that—CXCL12—has a direct effect on cancer cell migration and tumor penetrate and also epithelial–mesenchymal transformation through CXCR4 production in tumor cells (Cojoc et al., 2013). However, the high expression of CXCR4 in the breast tumor compartment is correlated with lymphoma and poor analytical prognosis.

6.2.2 Metastatic microenvironment

Spreading of tumor is a complicated mechanism, whereas breast cancer cells exudates via a narrow blood vessels to settle down into the new microenvironment (Coleman et al., 2013). However, cancer cells admit into a "sedentary" state for a long duration of time or initiate design micrometastasis. Emphasize that, from the early tumor, chemokines and cytokines are produced and recruit hematopoietic-mediated cells such are secreted into the blood circulation and afterward supposed to generate premetastasis niche even earlier cancer cell mobilization (Kakonen and Mundy, 2003). Intriguingly, it was illustrated that fibroblast and tumor cells have been seen to migrate to metastasis areas (Place et al., 2011). Bone metastasis is a potentially studied example and increases awareness about metastasis.

Including osteoclasts, bone-developing cells, and blood stem cells "RANKL (receptor activator nuclear factor κβ ligand)" production is increased when breast cancer cells release several kinds of cytokines and growth factors which also lead to the formation of osteoclast and enhance bone-reabsorption (Coleman et al., 2013), destruction of bones that secrete tumor-associating factors, leading to further bone damage, illustrate the self-sufficient process (Kakonen and Mundy, 2003).

Currently, it has been demonstrated that RANKL is correlated with the development of pulmonary metastasis through "CD4+ regulatory T cells" (Tregs), promoting the contribution of well-defined lymphocytes, perhaps essential for boosting metastasis. Furthermore, mice models displayed a better opportunity in breast tumor for multidirectional metastatic cancer, spreading of tumor cells apart from early cancer to the bone besides from bone to distinctive parts and come again to the original site, indicating that the osseous microenvironment is considered an important administrator in the tumor development and metastasis (Coleman et al., 2013).

6.3 Macrophages in the tumor microenvironment

For preserving homeostasis, tissue macrophages perform the main function of destroying microorganisms via the phagocytic process (Cha and Koo, 2020). Frequently, subpopulation of macrophages are characterized as classically activated macrophages (M1) associated with proinflammatory or we can say antitumor properties, that help them to find and kill tumor cells via phagocytosis and cytotoxicity behavior (Prenen and Mazzone, 2019). On the other side, tissue healing and development can be done by alternatively activated macrophages (M2) because they can maintain antiinflammatory characteristics (Atri et al., 2018). In in vitro conditions, macrophage is polarized into M1-like macrophages with the help of "tumor-necrosis-factor alpha," "interferon-gamma," and "lipopolysaccharide" and maintains cancer growth, cancer spread as well as mediates Th1 response (Weagel et al., 2015; Mehraj et al., 2021a, b). Interleukin-4, interleukin-10, and interleukin-13 on the other hand produce M2-type macrophages (Atri et al., 2018) and are important for inhibition of immune response and tissue remodeling, and proper angiogenesis development (Weagel et al., 2015) as illustrated in Fig. 6.1. In TME higher levels of M1 macrophages are correlated with diminished tumor violent behavior, as supported by several studies, instead of a higher number of M2 macrophages are associated with cancer development and weak outcome of tumor (Komohara and Jinushi, 2014). Additionally, macrophage polarization is induced by hormones, and cytokines in TME (Aschenbrenner and Schultze, 2017). Despite the fact several studies have displayed the cryptic result on the polarization of macrophages in TME, that display TAMs may act as both antitumoral and protumoral, depending upon the macrophage phenotype (Cha and Koo, 2020). But once TAMs gain M2 phenotype in TME after being linked with tumor cells, effector T-cells as well as other cells, via the inhibition of adaptive immunity, tumor progression can be suppressed and induce angiogenesis and tumor repair (Mantovani et al., 2009). TAM phenotype particularity relies on tumor development, TAMs mostly contain the M2 phenotype which is proangiogenic (Qian and Pollard, 2010). In the initial phase of the tumor, TAMs gap the "M1-phenotype" to induce antitumor activity and suppress the tumorigenesis, but in an advanced phase of malignancy, TAMs are redirected to the M2-type macrophages and promote tumor progression (Chen et al., 2021). In the course of tumor progression, with a higher concentration of interleukin-12 and a lower concentration of interleukin-10, polarized M1 macrophages infiltrate the tumor and boost immune response, promoting tumor cell destruction. On the other hand, at the advanced period of cancer proliferation, TAMs are polarized into the M2 phenotype, stimulated by reduced interleukin-12 expression levels and higher interleukin-10 expression levels leading to a reduced tumoricidal effect (Cha and Koo, 2020). M2-type macrophages produce a tumor microenvironment that regulates the tumor progression, their life span, and angiogenesis (Chanmee et al., 2014; Williams et al., 2016). Further study manifested that tumor-associated macrophages in mammary tumors have more M2-type macrophages, it has been revealed from different studies that chemicals released from breast tumor cells can polarize macrophages into M2 like. Apart from above discussed cytokines, other signals like "hypoxia-inducible-factor-1 (HIF-1), HIF-2," "nuclear-factor–kappa beta" (NF-kβ) also perform significant part inside TME to re-polarize TAMs, by promoting HIF-1 and HIF-2 signals. TAMs favor to colonize themselves to less vascularized tumor cells and modify to the hypoxia microenvironment (Lewis and Pollard, 2006). Once hypoxia environment gets activity then it upregulates the CXC chemokine receptor 4 (CXCR4) production, and also increases the expression level of chemokine ligand 12 (CXCL12), which plays an essential part in metastasis (Müller et al., 2001), along with activation of another factor such as Nuclear factor–kappa beta (NF-kβ) also involved in modulation of TAMs transcriptional activities. TAMs reduce IL-12 expression levels, and are responsible for defective NF-kβ stimulation and also increased the IL-10 expression levels (Sica et al., 2000). Disability in the switch on of NF-kβ, by the overexposure of nuclear p50 NF-kβ homodimers suppresses the proinflammatory genes transcription, generating factors such as "interleukin-1, interleukin-12, and tumor necrosis factor-α as well as nitric oxide (NO)" (Fig. 6.2) (Sica et al., 2000).

6.4 Recruitment of monocytes and macrophages to breast tumors

Tumor-associated macrophages make up a large inflammatory part in the invasion of breast cancer (O'Sullivan and Lewis, 1994). Chemokines and cytokines are tumor-associated growth factors, aid in the recruitment of monocytes as well as macrophages into tumor sites (Leek and Harris, 2002) "Chemokine (C-C motif) ligand-2 (CCL2)," called "monocyte chemoattractant protein 1 (MCP-1)," is secreted by the

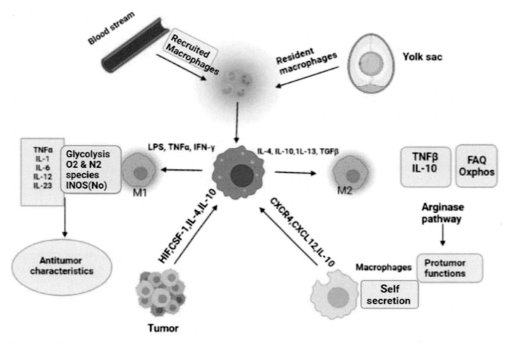

Fig. 6.2 Migration of monocytes from blood stream to tumor site and its differentiation into phenotypes.

tumor as well as stromal cells (Ueno et al., 2000), is considered as one of the best cytokine involved in migration of TAMs into cancer site thus it is related with poor diagnosis in breast-cancer victims (Tsuyada et al., 2012). It has been demonstrated that CCL2 upgrade pulmonary malignancy in animal breast cancer study, by recruiting CCR2-expressing monocytes (Qian et al., 2011). After CCL2-CCR2 switch on, they enhance the CCL3 secretion from macrophages, promoting breast cancer metastasis (Kitamura et al., 2015). Other prominent factors that attract TAMs to the breast tumor microenvironment are "CCL5" also termed as "Regulated-upon-Activation" and RANTES secreted by normal T cells. Malignant epithelial cells also secrete CCL5 in breast cancer and are related to improved disease development.

CCL5 receptors are highly expressed by macrophages and infiltrate the TME in response to CCL5 secreted by tumor cells (An et al., 2019). CCL5 can also change the properties of tumor-associated macrophages by boosting the phenotype of colon cancer (Halama et al., 2016). Tumor cells secrete an additional number of substances for recruitment of macrophages like "colony-stimulating-factor 1" termed as "macrophage-colony-stimulating factor" and "granulocyte-macrophage colony-stimulating factor" and rest factors released by cells in breast cancer (Leek and Harris,

2002; Fu et al., 1992). In breast cancer mouse models, macrophages express poor production of CSF-1 and enhance permeate of the Colony-stimulating factor-1 receptor (CSF-1R) (Lin et al., 2001). Heparin-binding glycoprotein vascular endothelial growth factors are another cytokine linked with macrophage recruitment. This growth factor interplays an essential function in physiological and pathologic improvement of new blood vessels and is considered a powerful mitogen, beyond that it is also examined as the main component in angiogenic processes and plays a significant role in this, and higher expression of this cytokine is found to be in a variety of human malignancies (Table 6.1) (Ferrara and Davis-Smyth, 1997; Sawano et al., 2001). Moreover, in the case of mice embryonic angiogenesis, macrophages lacking the VEGF-receptor expressed dramatically decreased migration with regard to VEGF (Leek et al., 2000), and evaluated increased VEGF production secreted by tumor cells recruit monocytes within TME and more eminently direct the migration of TAMs inside tumors. For tumor angiogenesis, another tissue factor that is vascular permeability factor (VPF), is responsible for attracting monocytes inside TME (Clauss et al., 1990). In agreement herewith, higher levels of

Table 6.1 Chemo-attractants implicated in the recruitment of monocytes to tumors.

Chemoattractant and tumor	Regulated by hypoxia in tumor cells	Method of detection	Positive correlation with TAM accumulation	References
CCL2				
Breast		ELISA/IHC	Y	Ueno et al. (2000)
Ovarian		ISH/ELISA	Y	Negus et al. (1995)
Melanoma		IHC	ND	Graves et al. (1992)
CCL5				
Breast		HC/ELISA	ND	Luboshits et al. (1999)
Melanoma		WB/ELISA	ND	Mrowietz et al. (1999) and Niwa et al. (2001)
Cervical		ELISA	ND	
CSF-1				
Breast	NO	IHC	Y	Tang et al. (1990) and
Ovarian				Kacinski (1995)
		IHC	ND	Kacinski (1995)
Adenocarcinoma		IHC/ELISA	ND	Kacinski (1995)

Mehraj et al. (2021a, b).

VEGF factor inside cancerous cells are linked with scavenger cells permeate in breast cancer in humans (Leek et al., 2000). The establishment of the Hypoxia state in TME leads to one more well-defined part, switching on macrophage activation and assemblage as well as putting a stop to the movement of macrophages out of this zone (Leek et al., 2000). In a breast cancer mouse model, TAMs are attracted into the hypoxia region mediated by "hypoxia-induced *Semaphorin* 3A" through the phosphorylation of VEGF-receptor (VEGF-R1). In tumor angiogenesis both VEGF and hypoxia signaling play a significant job and are shown to be an important trademark of cancer, indicating linkages between tumor angiogenesis and TAMs (Hanahan and Weinberg, 2000). By adding further complexity to TAMs, three lineages of macrophages are present at least that emerge at distinct periods of growth and remain up to maturity (Guerriero, 2018). Every tissue of the body consists of 5%–20% of resident macrophages originating from the yolk sac, formed during embryogenesis. In the course of homeostatic change, like tumor angiogenesis, several phenotypes of macrophage are recruited from bone marrow, spleen, and blood reservoir (Schulz et al., 2012) as well as from resident progenitors or by local recruitment. In different tissues, there is a distinct expression profile of macrophages at the transcriptional level, and is demonstrated that malignant sites vary from the primary tumor region and thus may need to be diagnosed distinctly (Guerriero, 2018). "Endothelial-monocyte-activating polypeptide II (EMAP II)" is another well-determined proinflammatory cytokine that recruits monocytes and macrophages (Kao et al., 1994). Knies et al.'s studies demonstrated that "EMAP II-mRNA" and its messenger protein, "Pro-EMAP II," are produced via various kinds of malignancies (Table 6.1). Although mature-cytokine is predominantly produced by dead tumor cells lysate in in vitro and also persist at the apoptosis site in the mouse embryo development (Knies et al., 2000). This is due to the process of converting proform into a mature form of protein depending on cleavage with the help of protease enzyme and its release is up regulated during necrosis (Knies et al., 2000) after the secretion of mature EMAP II protein, aiding the movement of macrophages to apoptosis and necrosis sites where they are supposed to be capable of removing dead and necrotic debris. This is because tumor is associated with many necrosis sites, and there is the increased number of TAMs with increased necrosis areas (Leek et al., 1999). It is feasible because EMAP II protein plays a significant role in the recruitment of monocytes to some tumors. A wide variety of cell types secrete "endothelins 1-3 (ET-1, -2, and -3)" which are small neuro-peptide and bioactive proteins and function like that of chemokines and show their effect by binding with two "7-trans-membrane-G protein-coupled receptors," "ET-RA and ET-RB," respectively. In vitro endothelins along with their receptors are greatly produced in various cell lines as well as in human tumors (Kusuhara et al., 1990) (Table 6.1). ET-1 act as a chemoattractant for "human-monocytes-binding to ET-RA receptor," although ET-2 act as a chemo attractant for macro-phages binds to "ET-RB receptor," so these data imply that ET-1 may aid monocyte recruitment within tumor, while ET-2 may aid monocyte location within tumor bulk. Notably, descriptive studies revealed their expression level, with assemblage of macrophages in a wide array of human carcinoma, and provided most of the data related to the function of chemotaxis to recruit monocytes as well as macrophages inside TME. Studies using knock-out mice, neutralizing antibodies to disrupt the function of these molecules are uncommon, and they are now needed in order to evaluate whether every molecule is required for recruitment of monocytes and in vivo TAMs localization. However monocytes are recruited by chemoattractant to tumor site and is conceivable, phagocytic cells are recruited also by cell detritus discharged by cell death of malignant cells, so it is shown in cell cultures that cell detritus cannot recruit phagocytes (Bessis and de Boisfleury-Chevance, 1984), although up to now it has been investigated, soluble factors secreted from apoptosis of malignant cells or either through destruction of extracellular matrix (ECM) through necrosis, and may recruit phagocytic cells for instance. Partially degraded collagen proteins aid to be chemo-attractant for monocytes and macrophages.

6.5 Differentiation and maturation of TAMs in breast tumors

The tumor microenvironment (TME) regulates the differentiation and polarization of TAMs resulting in a diversified number of cells, but the subset diversity of cells is still unknown. Typically tumors are less vascularized and malnourished, leading to the differentiation of recruited macrophages into mature wound-healing macrophages. A tumor represents a "wound" that needs to be repaired, because many factors such as "CSF-1, IL-3, IL-4, IL-10, and TGF-β" drive the polarization of tumor-associated macrophages into M2-like macrophages (Italiani and Boraschi, 2014). TAMs promote the survival of cancer cells, proliferation, angiogenesis, and dissemination, all of which are protumor properties of TAMs (Solinas et al., 2009). Monocytes recruited from the bloodstream proliferate in the presence of "LPS/IFN-γ" and mature to "M1/classically polarized-macrophages." They express high qualities of "IL-12, IL-1, IL-23, TNF-α, and CXCL10" and are distinguished by cytotoxicity action toward microorganisms and neoplastic cells as well as higher level of "ROI" production and APC-efficiency. Currently, it's not clear that after assuming a mature phenotype, macrophages can differentiate into M1/M2 repolarization in vivo and acquire their phenotype when recruited to TME and stay the same (Italiani and Boraschi, 2014). In ex vivo condition, M1-macrophages in human is re-polarized into M2 macrophages when exposed to cytokines of M2-like macrophage (Italiani and Boraschi, 2014). Similarly, M2-like macrophages are repolarized to M1-like macrophages after gene alteration via subsequent exposure to IFN-γ or Toll-like receptor ligand (Fig. 6.3.)

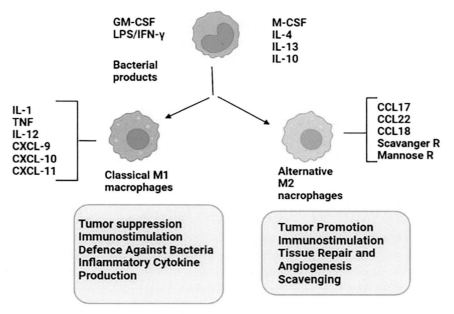

Fig. 6.3 Polarization of macrophages into their respective structures inside TME.

6.6 Relative numbers of macrophages in breast cancer progression

Apart from different subtypes of breast cancer, the abundance of macrophages varies, but it also varies with the developmental stages of cancer. In preclinical studies, it has been demonstrated that macrophages display early breast tumor distribution and progression of HER2+ breast cancer in mouse models, at which place cancer cells and myeloid cells secrete CCL2 and recruit "CD206+/Tie2+" macrophages to proliferate the illness. On the other hand, identical consequences were observed in "MMTV-PyMT luminal B breast cancer" of murine models, by hampering CCL2 production preventing the TAMs recruitment inside the breast tumor site, causing a reduction in metastasis, and persistent mice survival (Qian et al., 2011). Further preclinical models revealed that there is a remarkable link between "CSF-1" and metastatic breast tumors by utilizing the "MMTV-PyMT" ideal (Lin et al., 2001). In "DCIS (ductal-carcinoma *in situ*)" and in IDS (invasive-ductal-carcinoma) number and progression of macrophages are significantly higher than the normal breast tissue. In breast cancer, TAMs displayed a distinct transcriptomic trademark from the normal breast tissue (Cassetta et al., 2019).

The current study proposed by Gil Del Alcazar et al. revealed that in-filtration of Immune cells in the case of "HER2+" and "TNBC" helps in disease proliferation when correlated with DCIS and IDCs (Gil Del Alcazar et al., 2017; Mir et al., 2022a, b, c, d).

It has been shown that IDS contains an abundance of macrophages compared to DCIS. Moreover, a higher frequency of macrophages is present in DCIS when associated with a higher amount of CD8+ T cells. Th1 and Th2 are supplemented with HER2+ IDCS while Th17 and regulatory T cells were enriched in TNBC IDCs, revealed from the gene expression profile. The transition from DCIS to IDCs in TNBC tumors was associated with a substantial quantity of TILs, than in HER2+ tumors, although fewer numbers were seen in an activated state. Well-defined exhaustion of T-cells was seen in advanced stages of TNBC; still, further investigation is needed to understand how macrophages take part in tumor proliferation at various stages.

6.7 Location of macrophages in breast tumors

The placement of macrophages inside the TME, besides disease state and breast tumor subtype, may be a forecast of their properties and are linked with scientific consequences. Nevertheless, scientists have yet to agree on the degree to which region-specific-TAM behavior may be used predictive indicator. Normally, macrophages in tumor stroma are correlated to inhibition of immune response, angiogenesis, and migration of tumor cells. Macrophages in cancer nests, on the other hand, are more heterogeneous among cell kinds, as a consequence, they are associated with worse "overall survival" (OS) as well as "Recurrence-free survival" (RFS) in breast tumor patients (Yang et al., 2018). Merdeck et al. described that stromal-tumor–associated macrophages are significantly associated with tumor progression but not tumor nest TAMs (Medrek et al., 2012a, b). In 60 patients with invasive breast cancer, it has been currently revealed the presence of CD60and CD163 in tumor nests and tumor stroma. In tumor stroma, the highest concentration of CD68+ TAMs was extremely correlated with giant tumor size and positive extranodal spread, moreover higher amount of "CD163+" TAMs in cancer stroma has been linked with good lymphovascular invasion (LBV1) also termed vascular invasion (VI), extranodal extensive, and other molecular subtypes (Mwafy and El-Guindy, 2020). The process is exchangeable, TME modulates the behavior of macrophages, and macrophages, in turn, modulate the tumor location by secreting several signals in breast cancer subtypes for instance macrophages focus on invasive tumor front (ITF) in HER2+ and basal-like subtypes, and utilize "TGF-β signaling" in condensing the extracellular matrix (ECM), and participating in mammary cancer progression (Acerbi et al., 2015). Furthermore, macrophages and TME both of them work altogether by stimulating each other's composition. Both macrophages and the degree of TME infiltration lead to additional complexity by targeting anticancer therapy in breast cancer.

6.7.1 TAMs and hypoxia

6.7.1.1 Hypoxia and macrophage recruitment

Many investigations have confirmed oxygen starvation in malignancies. The chaotic unorganized arrangement of vascularization in solid tumors, with terminated arteries and leaky endothelial lining results in low oxygen tension (hypoxia state) (Brown and Giaccia, 1998).

Breast tumor is correlated with hypoxia condition same as that of other solid tumors, supplying poor oxygen for rapidly developing tumor. Additional to the regions with oxygen starvation, necrotic patches in a tumor microenvironment create an immediate reduction in oxygen level with consequent cell apoptosis. Because debris in this location recruits macrophages and the hypoxia state is considered one of the factors that influence the activity of macrophages. Turner et al. discovered that macrophages once recruited became imprisoned in the tumor necrotic region. One report for this aspect is regulation of MKP-1 (mitogen-activated protein kinase phosphatase) leads to dephosphorylation of chemotaxis receptor "VEGF" and "CCL2" that is VEGFR and CCR2, respectively (Wain et al., 2002). So assemblage of TAMs in the hypoxia region has been linked with truculent deportment in breast tumors (Leek et al., 1999). Other Mechanisms are shown in Fig. 6.4.

6.7.1.2 Hypoxia upregulates VEGF expression in TAMs

It is well-defined that hypoxia stimulates the expression of genes in tumor and inflammatory cells inside TME. Hypoxia causes the upregulation of macrophage transcription factors like "HIF-1α" and "HIF-2α" (Burke et al., 2002). In hypoxia, state HIF-1α act as a label while in breast tumor it has been correlated with truculent tumor behavior (Kimbro and Simons, 2006). In fact, "HIF-1α-dependent genes" show a high mortality rate in breast cancer victims. Until now, "HIF-1α and HIF-2α" upgrade the VEGF gene which is subordinate to hypoxia tension in TME. Lewis et al. demonstrated that VEGF is expressed by TAMs in peri-necrotic tumors and less vascularized regions in breast tumors. Overexpression of HIF-2α in TAMs leads to high vascularization in breast tumor because of the upgrade of VEGF levels.

6.7.1.3 Hypoxia promotes immune evasion by TAMs

Tumor cells promote immune escape by secretingHIF-1α hypoxia factor. Under such circumstances, several immunosuppressive cytokines are secreted by TAMs such as Interleukin-10, which hamper effector T cells (Murata et al., 2002). Currently, Doedens et al. studies that there is a reduction in tumor growth with decreasing *HIF*1α in macrophages apart from VEGF expression and vascularization of tumors, using a murine breast cancer model. In this model, the antitumor activity of TILs (tumor-infiltrating

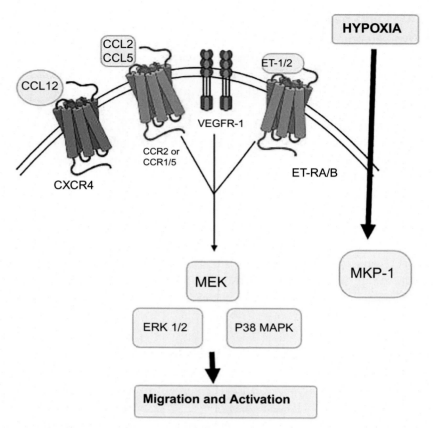

Fig. 6.4 Illustrated process for TAM's imprisoned at hypoxia region: Chemotactic-ligands interact with their specific receptor on TAM's surface, triggering signal-transduction pathway. Chemotaxis-requires the switch on of "ERK1/2 and p38 MAPK" through phosphorylation. Overexpression of "MKP-1" with help of hypoxia condition, "EKR1/2" as well as "p38 MAPK" deactivated through de-Phosphorylation for particular chemotactic receptors. This stops the chemotactic signaling system for working. Hypoxia does not appear to influence the signaling transduction pathway of CXCR4 implying that hypoxia enhance the production and activity of chemotactic receptors "selectively and differentially."

lymphocytes) is inhibited by TAMs (Doedens et al., 2010). In fact, in myeloid cells reduction of HIF-1α overturn the hypoxia–mediated-suppression for activation of T cells, leading to cancer proliferation. The overall study determined that myeloid cells derived from the innate immune system inhibit the T cells of the adaptive immunity in a HIF-1α–dependent manner and hypoxia-induced way with the help of HIF-2α (Leek et al., 2000).

6.7.1.4 Hypoxic TAMs promote metastatic behavior of tumor cells

It is well-defined as macrophages in hypoxia state increases tumor aggressiveness by promoting tumor progression in breast cancer. HIF-1α upregulates the migratory inhibitory factor (MIF) gene in macrophages in the hypoxia state (Schmeisser et al., 2005). Currently, it was demonstrated by Oda et al. that the MIF effect upon HIF is depends on the "p53" process, in a hypoxia state MIF is stabilized by HIF-1α protein. The release of MIFs shows the effect on matrix metalloproteinases; for instance, "MIF–induced increased expression of MMP-7" causes destruction of basement membrane in cancers, opens the door for cancer invasion, and generates a hotbed for metastatic foci. Previous studies tell about, tumor in hypoxia state recruits TAMs into the necrotic area and less vascularized regions of breast tumor. When TME stimulates macrophage recruitment to increase the aggressive tumor behavior, this hypoxia state promotes the protumor actions of TAMs to serve as a possible targeted therapy for cancer. Previously interfering at a different stage of invasive and metastatic tumor function, the proliferation produced by macrophages can be reversed for instance radiation therapy exhibit a hypoxia environment for tumor beds, hampering VEGF and CCL2, and stop the macrophage recruitment to the tumor hypoxia region and hamper tumor proliferation. Other factors are also responsible for tumor progression in hypoxia conditions and are shown in Fig. 6.5.

6.8 Breast cancer cell metastasis

In patients with breast tumors, metastasis is the most common cause of death among them. TAMs play a significant part in breast cancer invasion and spread. For the therapeutic method, TAMs are considered viable for targeting strategy (Chen et al., 2019a, b). With the help of "chemokine (C-C motif) ligand-2, Chemokine (C-C) ligand-5 (CCL5), chemokine (C-C) ligand-18 (CCL18), along with CCL2," TAMs promote breast cancer cell spread to bone and lung tissues, as part of its functional mechanism. Breast cancer cells secrete CCL2 and recruit chemokine "C-C-Receptor 2+ (CCR2+)" macro-phages to get together in lung and production of bone cells from osteoblast, thus take part in cancer cell colonization and building of metastatic niche, as a result inhibiting "CCL2-CCR2" could effectively prevent tumor metastasis. CCL5 released from breast tumor cells acts upon mononuclear macrophages' transition to TAMs whichever stimulates tumor spread as well as infiltration (An et al., 2019). Another factor significantly secreted by TAMs is CCL18, and its function is also linked with metastasis and reduced survival of patients. CCL18 is having a functional receptor that is "PYK2 N-terminal-domain-interacting receptor 1 (PITPNM3)," inhibiting cancer spread and invasive effect of CCL18. Between "malignant-phyllodes-tumors" (PT) in mammary and TAMs, Nie and colleagues discovered a feedback-loop of "CCL5-CCR5" and "CCL18-PIPTNM3," which help preserve TAM phenotype and PT aggressiveness. For the further inhibition of tumor metastasis,

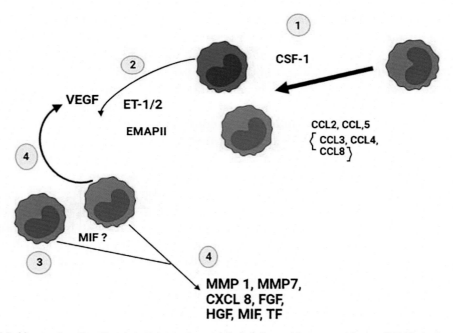

Fig. 6.5 Monocyte migration into tumors is modeled, followed by assemblage of TAMs in hypoxia regions in cancers. (1) Cancer create high qualities of "C-C chemokines and CSF-1" which attract monocytes from the bloodstream (2) once within a cancer TAM's form when a monocyte differentiate. Tumor in hypoxia state release chemo-attractant like "VEGF, endothelin, and EMAP II" which recruit TAMs into tumor inside hypoxia state. (3) Because chemotaxis signal transduction is disrupted, and TAMs are maintained in hypoxia regions, and chemotactic receptors regulation is reduced, "MIF's migratory suppressor" function are also possible, (4) TAMs are mediated to produce VEGF, once they are in hypoxia environment, implying that TAMs are drawn to the location, and also other chemical substances that enhance the progression and cancer angiogenesis.

they used a CCR5 inhibitor and CCL-18-monoclonal antibody and blocked the CCL-5-CCR-5 and CCL-18-PIPTNM-3 pathways. TAMs release both cellular cytokines and their surface receptor, both of which play a key role in stimulating breast tumor metastasis. TAMs lead to the production of epidermal growth factor (EGF) which activates its receptor that is epidermal growth factor receptors (EGFRs) in breast tumors, promoting metastasis and CSF-1 production. TAMs are recruited and activated by CSF-1 causing them to secrete more EGF, implying the presence of an "EGF/CSF-1" regulating a good link between TAMs and tumor cells. EGF causes breast cancer cells to infiltrate blood vessels, resulting in metastasis in blood vessels (Condeelis and Pollard, 2006). TAMs secrete a cluster of "matrix-metallo-proteinases (MMPs)," like MMP-2, MMP-7, and MMP-9, which are linked with the destruction of matrix materials in the TME, stimulating the establishment of metastatic tumor microenvironment by facilitating tumor cell growth. Higher production of Macrophage receptor also termed as scavenger receptor increases tumor development and metastasis with collagenous structure (MARCO). MARCO is linked to epithelial–mesenchymal transition (EMT), gene profiles that drive metastasis, and inhibiting MARCO production could effectively stop EMT (Georgoudaki et al., 2016).

6.9 Breast cancer angiogenesis

Angiogenesis is the process of forming new blood vessels to help cancer grow and develop. Tumor-associated macrophages play a significant role in angiogenesis by being tightly linked to the high-density vascular system that emerged in breast tumors. "vascular-endothelial growth factor (VEGF)" is a vital source for TAMs in TME of breast tumors. Angiogenesis in breast tumors is triggered by the interaction between "VEGF" with "vascular endothelial growth factor receptors" (VEGFRs). As a result blocking interaction between VEGF/VEGFR can dramatically reduce angiogenesis and tumor spread (Song et al., 2018). Macrophage-colony-stimulating factor also termed colony-stimulating factor-1, stimulates the recruitment of macrophages and distinguishes them into the M2 phenotype. "colony-stimulating factor-1 receptor (CSF1-R)" suppressors during neoplasm formation in the breast glands can decrease TAMs, therefore reducing angiogenesis, metastasis, and reducing the risk of recurrence. In TME hypoxia is a trademark that stimulates angiogenesis and helps in macrophage recruitment (LaGory and Giaccia, 2016). Upregulation of hypoxia-inducible factors (HIFs) in hypoxia conditions stimulates the transfer of macrophages into TAMs, which in turn act as transcriptional promoters of VEGF. VEGF promotes the hypoxia environment by stimulating angiogenesis which helps the tumor to receive oxygen and nutrients, for its development (Tamura et al., 2019). The earliest evidence supported that HIF signaling is linked with angiogenesis, suppression in its signaling slows down angiogenesis and tumor development. Suppression of HIF-2α signaling causes highly disordered blood vessels to develop and the hypoxia situation in the TME to worsen (LaGory and Giaccia, 2016). In addition, hypoxia TME upgrade the production of "activating-transcription-factor 4 (ATF4)," one family member of "ATF/cAMP-response-element-binding protein (CREB)," linked with the macrophage recruitment and development of angiogenesis which promotes cancer development indirectly (Liu et al., 2015); therefore, angiogenesis is upregulated by TAMs in tumor malignancy.

6.10 TAMs promote breast cancer cell stemness

The tumor microenvironment is made of a lot of immune-competent cells primarily with TAMs, evidence-supported, that the TAMs promote carcinogenesis, proliferation as well as self-sustain, via inducing and maintaining CSCs (cancer stem cells) (Chen et al., 2019a, b;

Mehraj et al., 2021a, b). Role of several cytokines linked with TAM in the development of breast CSCs is supported by a large body of published data. Previously, it was considered that classical activation of "M1" leads to antitumor benefits through inducing proinflammatory cytokines, which slow tumor growth. Guo and colleagues demonstrated in their current study, that M1's proinflammatory benefits can also drive the CSCs proliferation, and self-sustain. Through inflammatory cytokine stimulation by Lin-28B-let-7-HMGA2 pathway in coculture breast tumor cells with regard to M1 macrophages resulted in the production of aldehyde dehydrogenase 1+ (ALDH1+) breast CSCs. As a result, these CSCs have high drug-resistance ability with increased spheroid formation. They demonstrated that the ALDH1+ breast CSCs population is maintained by the repolarization of the M1 phenotype into M2 (Guo et al., 2019). Both "human and mouse—nonstem cancer cells (NSCC)" change in cancer stem cells (CSCs) by secretion of IL-6 from tumor-associated macrophages and activates JAK/STAT path by promoting the self-sustain and CSCs carcinogenic property (Iliopoulos et al., 2011). M2-like macrophages produce immunosuppressing inflammatory cytokine factors like "interleukin-8 and growth-regulated oncogene (GRO)," leading to activation of the "STAT3-pathway," considered a major regulating agent for the production of CSCs. Tumor-associated macrophages also upregulate cancer cell steaminess by expressing "SRY-related-HMG-box (SOX)" family surface receptors as well as transcription factors (TFs). TAMs in the breast tumor release EGF factor and stimulates "EGFR/STAT3/SOX-2-paracrine-pathway." Subsequent increase of SOX-2 production, further increases the CSC-phenotype in the breast tumor (Yang et al., 2013). The current corpus of knowledge about "SOX-2, OCT-4, and NANOG" reported, in the initial phase of breast cancer, express-SOX-2 not OCT-4 and NANOG expression. A high level of "SOX-2" expression boosts the capability of CSCs to form spheroids and self-renew (Iliopoulos et al., 2011). Implying that SOX-2 expression is the main molecule that upregulates the development of CSCs in initial breast tumors. TGF-β-271 cancer cells (Transforming growth factor-β) polarize into M2 phenotype when they are exposed to TGF. Notch pathway is stimulated by the production of CCL5 secreted by lactate-activated macrophages. In the metabolic connection between TAMs and breast tumors, CCL5 interplay the main role, enhancing aerobic glycolysis, and tumor spread, increasing the number of breast malignancies Glycolytic pathway can be inhibited by the CCL5-CCR5 axis with monoclonal antibodies, as a result, it blocks tumor metastasis. In TME regulating high-lactate level is expressed by TAMs G protein-coupled receptor 132 (Gpr132) and is considered a key detector in the lactate environment, moderating the association between tumor cells and TAMs at the time of metastasis. M2-like macrophage polarization is also done by activated—Lactate Gpr132. HIF production is enhanced by TAMs which aid them in adjusting inside hypoxia TME. HIF has gained the property of upregulating the energy metabolism in tumor cells. In the liver accumulation of cancerous cells and glycolytic metabolic pathway in breast tumor is driven by

HIF-1α and regulate metastasis. RNA is also involved in glycolysis metabolism demonstrated by Chen and colleagues. TAMs also stimulate aerobic glycolysis by secreting "HIF-1α-stabilizing-long noncoding RNA (HISLA)" factor in mammary tumor, in macrophages HISLA are inhibited by lactate, secreted via glycolytic pathway in breast cancer cells, generating an optimistic feedback axis for glycolytic metabolism, increases suppression of treatments in tumor cells. As a result, mitochondrial-oxidative-phosphorylation is regulated by HIF-2α production in cancer cells, so overexpression of mitochondrial oxidative phosphorylation in breast cancer act as hallmark; So HIFs are considered one of the major targets for treating breast tumors.

6.10.1 TAMs modulate t-cell activity to induce an immunosuppressive microenvironment in breast cancer

TAMs having immune-regulatory properties are a fundamental process for the development of cancer and are considered the main area which is targeted, at this spot is the modulation of effector T cell's tumor-killing function. For inhibiting the function of effector T-cells. TAMs perform a crucial role in its suppression by modulating arginine metabolism. ARG-1 (arginine-1), is a molecular signature on M2-like macrophages consisting of a high level of its expression in comparison with controls. When ARG-1 hydrolyzes L-arginine, the concentration of L-arginine falls, suppressing effector T cells' function (de Boniface et al., 2012). Instead of the "ARG-1" marker on M2 macrophages, another marker nitric oxide synthase (iNOS) is present which also leads to the suppression of effector T cells' function by metabolizing L-arginine to generate NO, which ultimately suppresses the function (Choi et al., 2018). In TAMs there is also the modulation of immune checkpoints like PD-1 (programmed cell death-1), which generates a significant pathway for TAMs to promote the effector T cell's tumor-killing function. Through the secretion of various cytokines in the breast, because of these cytokines TAMs increase the production of PD-1 ligand, revealed through many investigations. For instance, TAMs secrete IFN-γ modulates the JAK/STAT3 as well as PI3K/AKT pathways to stimulate the expression of PD-L1 (Zhang et al., 2017). Multifunctional cytokine such as TGF-β stimulates the polarization of macrophages into M2, therefore promoting the TAMs inhibition property although bringing about overexpression of PD-L1–stimulating tumor invasion. Also, its expression was stimulated by IL-6–deficient state when treated with an anti–PD-L1 antibody showing significant effectiveness. Furthermore, "common-lymphatic endothelial and vascular-endothelial receptor-1 (CLEVER-1)," deficiency obstructs cancer progression through stimulation of effector T cell's tumor-killing capability (Vitale et al., 2019). TAMs interplay a key role in cancer progression since destroying CD8[+] T cells leads the way to reduce their capability to remove tumor cells (Farhood et al., 2019), although elucidating the method via which TAMs generate T-cell fatigue, consequently act as a possible therapeutic reason in the immunotherapy development. Utilizing single-cell transcriptome analysis, Xu et al. revealed a connection between TAMs and fatigued T cells in their TNBC based-investigation. In comparison to PD-1 and CTLA-4, the researchers discovered that "Lymphocyte-activating-3 (LAG3)" T-cell immunoglobin as well as "mucin-domain-containing protein 3 (TIM3)" were supplemented after T-lymphocyte fatigue, often targets for new immune related-therapies. TAMs in breast tumors were Calcium/calmodulin-dependent protein kinase kinase (CaMKK2) is significantly expressed, can inhibit the progression and effector T cell's tumor-killing property. Hepatoma also termed hepatocellular carcinoma (HCC) cell lines with higher expression of cyclooxygenase-2 (COX-2) promote polarization of M2 TAM which can devote whichever devote to the fatigue of the antitumor capability in stimulating CD8 + T cells. In tumor stroma population of TAMs increases, and cells start to release STAT3 into their TME giving rise to CD8 + T-cell fatigue (Farhood et al., 2019). Furthermore, in the hepatoma mice model, Pu et al. demonstrated that TAM-linked with extracellular vesicles (EVs) increases CD8 + T-cell fatigue. Although in extracellular vesicles, upregulation of micro-RNA-21-5p (miR-21-5p) that were elevated inside tumor tissues, and TAM's tumor-stimulating function was reduced by inhibiting the miR-21-5p. According to another, T-cell fatigue in HCC is driven by "Exosomal micro-RNA-146a-5p (miR-146a-5p)" from TAMs. TAMs play a significant role in tumor immune control through a variety of ways. Myeloid-derived suppressor cells (MDSCs) and TAMs have an immunosuppressive property that is dependent on cell interaction. MDSCs stimulate the conversion of macrophages into TAMs and were shown to downregulate the production of IL-2. TAMs enhance MDSCs to increase the expression of IL-10, as a result there is the release of IL-12 in macrophages which further downregulates, leading the continuous negative loop destruction of effector T-cell activity (Ugel et al., 2015). Tumor-associated-macrophages reduce effector T-cell activity by secreting IL-10, which suppresses Interleukin-12 synthesis via dendritic cells, resulting in TAMs blunting T-cell function (Ruffell et al., 2014). Tumor-associated macrophages play a crucial part in inhibiting the recruitment of T cells, although the methods by which they do so are certain. Typical-radiation therapy, focusing on CSF1/CSF1R pathway can prevent the recruitment of macrophages and the infiltration of T cells is increased. CCL2/CCR2 leads to the recruitment of macrophages, inhabiting its pathway, producing the same result (DeNardo and Ruffell, 2019). Besides, Th1 secrete cytokines such as "IFN-γ as well as TNF-α" can stimulate the conventional activated macrophages. Th2 secreted cytokines like as IL-13 and IL-4 stimulate alternatively activated macrophages, tumor-associated macrophages are implicated in the immunosuppression of breast tumors well as shield these cells, as previously mentioned.

6.10.2 TAMs regulate energy metabolism in breast cancer cells

By modulating metabolites and metabolic pathways, affecting the cancer progression, in this TAMs greatly influence the allover metabolic state of the TME (Vitale et al., 2019).

Substantial quantities of macrophages are located in the hypoxia cancer area, although lactic acid is synthesized by cancer cells via a glycolytic pathway, causing polarization of macrophages into the M2 phenotype (Choi et al., 2018). Notch pathway triggered by "lactate-activated macrophages," stimulates the release of CCL5, thus performing a significant part by interpreting the metabolic interaction between breast tumors as well as in TAMs, enhancing "aerobic glycolysis," motility, as well as tumor invasion. The glycolytic pathway can be inhibited by suppressing the "CCL-5-CCR-5" axis with recombinant-mono-clonal antibodies, resulting in inhibition of tumor metastasis (Lin et al., 2017). Gpr-132 (G protein-coupled receptor) is the critical sensor for developing lactic acid inside TME, synthesized by TAMs in their environment having a high degree of lactate, promoted the contact between the TAMs and tumor cells during metastasis. Gpr132, which is triggered by lactate, is involved in the polarization of M2-like macrophages (Chen et al., 2017), for its adaptation inside the hypoxia TME, TAMs increase the HIFs expression for its survival. HIFs are essential regulators of cancer-energy metabolism. HIF-1α promotes the glycolytic pathway in breast tumors by promoting metastasis, and accumulation of tumor cells inside the liver. Already discussed above, as demonstrated by Chen and colleagues RNA has a role in aerobic glycolysis as well. Through "HIF-1α-stabilizing long noncoding RNA (HISLA)," TAMs drive aerobic glycolysis in breast tumors. The lactate secreted in the glycolytic pathway from tumor cells, boosts the production of HISLA in macrophages, generating a positive loop of feedback for glycolysis, that increases the resistance against drugs in tumor cells (Chen et al., 2019a, b). In addition, enhancing HIF-2α production promotes mitochondrial oxidative phosphorylation and its higher activation of mitochondrial-oxidative-phosphorylation is a hallmark of the violent phase of breast tumor, here HIFs significantly focus on energy metabolism, for the better therapeutic efficacy of breast cancer.

6.11 Clinical significance of TAMs in breast tumors

In a variety of malignancies, such as breast cancer, TAM infiltration is linked to a weak prognosis (Leek et al., 1996). TAM level was found to be essentially connected with weak prognosis in patients with breast tumors, according to a meta-analysis. TAMs are shown to be the type of immune cell that is linked strongly with weak analytical prognosis in "estrogen-receptor-positive (ER+)" breast cancers in a study involving 11,000 breast cancers (Ali et al., 2016). TAMs have been shown to generate resistance against endocrine therapy in ER+ breast tumor cells in vitro and in vivo via "NF-κB and IL-6-depending on signaling pathways" and have been linked to metastasis and less survival (Medrek et al., 2012a, b). Interestingly, a huge portion of M1-type TAMs in breast tumor ER+ connected with the increased pathological complete response (pCR) rate and longer "disease-free survival (DFS)" and all over survival (OS) (Oshi et al., 2020). The higher frequency of M1-macrophages (iNOS+) was essentially linked to better viability in a cohort of 40 HER2 + breast tumor victim which receive trastuzumab, an anti–HER2 medication, and enhanced survival rate, furthermore increased production of M2-macrophages (CD163 +) were linked to poor prognosis (Honkanen et al., 2019). In addition, a higher frequency of "iNOS +-M1-like macrophages" connected with a higher frequency of CD8[+] T cells found to be greatly linked with good survival, and these mixed markers linked to better victims' capability to set free from proliferation without "trastuzumab" after encountered to initial dose of therapy (Honkanen et al., 2019). Other studies demonstrated that low TAMs and a higher frequency of CD8 + T-cell number are correlated with good re-occurrence and free survival in victims suffering from invasive breast tumors (DeNardo and Ruffell, 2019).

6.12 Preclinical evidence for a role of TAMs in breast cancer treatment resistance

Various tumors such as breast tumors, and fundamentally TAMs affect the efficacy of standard treatments like radiotherapy, chemotherapy, drug target, immunotherapy as well as checkpoint obstruct.

6.12.1 Chemotherapy

In breast tumors of victims and mouse models, TAM showed elevated infiltration when treated with *paclitaxel* in comparison to untreated tumors (DeNardo and Ruffell, 2019). TAM infiltration was moderated in preclinical studies by higher production of CSF1 mRNA in cancer cells after paclitaxel treatment (Mir et al., 2022a, b, c, d; DeNardo and Ruffell, 2019). In breast tumor cells, TAMs inhabited "paclitaxel–produced mitotic arrest" and encouraged initial mitosis. Blocking the recruitment of TAM by inhibiting CSF1-CSF1 receptor (CSF1R) signaling, which resulted in increased effect of paclitaxel and longer mouse life, associated with increased CTL infiltration, reduced vascularization by lowering the expression of VEGF mRNA (DeNardo and Ruffell, 2019). CTL depletion reduced the anti-CSF1R–paclitaxel–medication effect because CTLs were necessary for enhancing paclitaxel efficacy. Chemotherapeutic drugs including "doxorubicin, etoposide, *gemcitabine* and CMF regimen such as *cyclophosphamide, methotrexate, 5-fluorouracil*," macrophages suppress their antitumor efficacy in both in vitro and in vivo studies (Olson et al., 2017; Paulus et al., 2006). CSF1-CSF1R inhibition on the other side, block the recruitment of TAMs, without affecting the number of perivascular TAMs (DeNardo and Ruffell, 2019). Despite the fact, that the phenotype of the rest TAMs has not yet been determined, the minimum fraction of it is perivascular TIE2-expressing TAMs, although was important for the VEGF-A source. These data suggested that TAM-induced chemoresistance in breast tumors may be mediated by VEGF-A expression. One of those methods requires the TAM-induced captains, especially cathepsin S, as well as cathepsin B, which prevent murine breast cancerous cells in ex-vivo subcultures from *paclitaxel-*, *etoposide-*, or *doxorubicin-*mediated cell death. Furthermore, the downstream signaling pathway was poorly defined, cathepsin inhibitor abolished this protective effect both in in vitro and ex vivo cocultures. In ex vivo coculture tests, interleukin-10-antibody changes the interleukin-10, mediated "*paclitaxel*" hindrance in breast tumor, so TAM-induced IL-10 show chemoprotective effect (Yang et al., 2013; Mehraj et al., 2021a, b). Interestingly, "Signal-Transducer and Activator of Transcription-3 (STAT3) signaling pathway," increase gene production of antiapoptotic bcl-2 in cancer cells may be linked to IL-10 induced drug treatment resistance (Yang et al., 2015). IL-10 derived from TAMs has significant importance in chemoresistance, considered as repolarization into an MI-like phenotype could be a viable method for improving chemotherapy efficacy. TAM195, a "selective class IIa histone deacetylase (HDACIIa) inhibitor," has already demonstrated, when coupled with *paclitaxel*, that this medication-induced TAM takes on an MI-type phenotype and reduces cancer burden in MMTV-PyMT mice. TAM-focused treatment, when coupled, could be a viable method for reversing chemoresistance and improving chemotherapeutic efficacy in breast tumor (Mehraj et al., 2022b).

6.12.2 Radiotherapy

Radiation dose-dependently increased tumor CSF1production in MMTV-PyMT mice (DeNardo and Ruffell, 2019). In the same model, TAM reduction by CSF1R inhibition increased the efficacy of breast cancer radiotherapy. CSF1R inhabited enhanced CTL infiltration, reducing the occurrence of CD4+-T-cells in breast cancers. When paired with radiotherapy, CD4+-T-cells depletion show a similar effect as CD4+ T blockade, showing the association between macrophage and other immune cells. TAM-mediated radiotherapy resistance may be due to MMP14 production. MMP14 inhibitor repolarization of M2-type TAMs into M1-type TAMs, in a 4 T1 cancer consisting mice model. Furthermore, MMP14 inhibition decreased angiogenesis, enhanced vascular and improved the radiotherapy efficacy (Ager et al., 2015). The cream imiquimod is applied topically, against a "Toll-like-receptor 7 (TLR7)" on breast cancer, helps in the repolarization of TAMs into M1 phenotype, and improved the local radiation efficacy (Dewan et al., 2012). Briefly, depletion in TAMs repolarization can be a better strategy to improve the efficacy of radiotherapies in breast tumors (Mehraj et al., 2021a, b).

6.12.3 Anti–HER2-targeted therapy

Trastuzumab inhibits HER2 carcinogenic signaling and activates "Antibody-Dependent Cellular Cytotoxicity (ADCC)" to suppress cancer development (Hudis, 2007). Antitumor efficacy of *trastuzumab* is also influenced by the adaptive immune system. CTLs were required for the therapeutic effect of anti-HER2 antibody treatment, in HER2 + TUBO breast cancer mice. After antibody treatment CTL infiltration is enhanced in the tumor, which is associated with tumor development. After CTL reduction, with an anti–CD8-depleting antibody however fast cancer regrowth was observed (Park et al., 2010), implying the T-cell–related method for HER2 antibody resistance therapy, is associated with TAMs because it suppresses CTL infiltration in TUBO animal cancer model (Xu et al., 2015). Elimination of Tumor-associated macrophages, re-polarize M2-type to M1 type TAMS, and considerably enhancing the HER2 antibody therapeutic efficacy, as a result IFN-γ expression and CTL infiltration in cancer significantly improved (Xu et al., 2015). Moreover, enhanced the tumor-infiltrating CTL without eliminating TAMs, TAMs anti-HER2 resistance reversing ability failed. Although, the inhibiting linkage between "CD47 and SIRPα (signal-regulatory protein-alpha)" can be the bacteriophage-induced way to enhance *Trastuzumab* efficiency. Tumor cells "don't eat me" signal production inhibits CD47, improved breast cancer cells' phagocytic activity in vitro. However CD47 antibody suppressed the development of a human breast tumor xenograft (Willingham et al., 2012). Furthermore, using affinity monomers to target SIRP did not increase direct macrophage phagocytosis. The monomers however boosted "macrophage-mediated antibody-dependent cellular phagocytosis (ADCP)" by reducing the ADCP baseline when coupled with trastuzumab. In breast tumor xenograft, the mixture exhibits synergetic antitumor efficacy. Macrophage ADCP ability is dependent on their physical appearance. In vitro M1-type macrophages were potent in phagocytosis in presence of trastuzumab in comparison to M2-type macrophages. Additionally combining CD47 blockade with trastuzumab improved neutrophile-induced ADCC. Furthermore, inhabiting the CD47-SIRPα axis enhanced DNA recognized ability in phagocytic cells, enhanced antitumor immunity, and CTLs-response (Mehraj et al., 2021b). These findings point to a new prototype perspective mixture of therapeutic strategies for breast tumor victims who accept anti-HER2 clinical trials. "Anti-HER2/TAM" targeting strategies in analytical prognosis is illustrated in Table 6.2.

6.12.4 Immunotherapy

In cancer immunotherapy programme-Death-1 (PD-1)/Programmed-Death-Ligand 1 (PDL1) axis, can mediate the immunological tolerance in activating T cells, became a target for immunotherapy. Macrophages caused PD-1 therapeutic resistance by trapping the "PD-1 anti-body" with FC receptor, blocking drug exposure on T cell, according to intra-vital visualization of MC-38-colon-cancer allograft (Mir et al., 2022c, d; Aschenbrenner and Schultze, 2017), however, TAMs produce PD-1 and PD-L1. PD-1 production on TAMS is connected with phagocytosis *in vitro* and *in vivo* conditions (Gordon et al., 2017). This has generated an interest in targeting the macrophage therapy and enhancing the immune checkpoint in breast cancer, demonstrating that the combination of CSFIR inhibitors with PD-1 and CTLA-4 blockade in animals is ideal for generating a Pancreatic-Adenocarcinoma in the mouse. Although relation potentially brings

Table 6.2 Drugs targeting tumor-associated macrophages in clinical trials for breast cancer patients.

Target	Drugs	Clinical trials identifier	Phase	Subtype	Drug combined with
CSF1–CSF1R inhibition	Pexidartinib	NCT01596751 (Active not recruiting)	I/II	All/TN	*Eribulin*
		NCT01525602 (Completed)	Ib	All	*Paclitaxel*
		NCT01042379 (Recruiting; arm closed for. pexidartinib)	II	All	
	Emactuzumab	NCT02323191 (Recruiting)	I	TN	*Atezolizuma*
		NCT02760797 (Completed)	I	TN	*Selicrelumab*
		NCT01494688 (Completed)	I	All/TN	*Paclitaxel*
	LY302285	NCT02265536 (Completed)	I	All	
		NCT02718911 (Recruiting)	I	All	*Durvalumab, tremelimumab*
	ARRY-382	NCT01316822 (Completed)	I	All	
		NCT02880371 (Recruiting)	I/II	TN	*Pembrolizumab*
	Lacnotuzumab	NCT02435680/ EUCTR 2015-000179-29 (Active not recruiting)	II	TN	*Carboplatin, gemcitabin Spartalizumab*
CD47-SIRPα inhibition	TTI-621	NCT02890368 (Recruiting)	I	All	
	ALX148	NCT03013218 (Recruiting)	I	All/HER2+	*Pembrolizumab, trastuzum*
	Ti-061	EUCTR 2016–004372-22 (Prematurely ended)	I/II	All	*Pembrolizumab*
	Hu5F9-G4	NCT02216409 (Active, not recruiting	I	All	
		NCT02953782 (Recruiting	I/II	All	*Cetuximab*

Continued

Table 6.2 Drugs targeting tumor-associated macrophages in clinical trials for breast cancer patients—cont'd

Target	Drugs	Clinical trials identifier	Phase	Subtype	Drug combined with
CD40 stimulation	Selicrelumab	NCT02225002 (Completed)	I	All	
		NCT02157831 (Completed)	I	TN	
		NCT02665416 (Recruiting)	I	TN	*Vanucizumab*
		NCT02760797 (Completed)	I	AlL	*Emactuzumab*
CR3 stimulation	BTH1677	NCT02981303 (NOT Recruiting)	I	All	*Pembrolizumab*
TLR7 stimulation	Imiquimod	NCT00899574 (Completed)	II	AlL	*Cyclophosphamide, radiation*
		NCT01421017 (Active, not recruiting)	I/II	All	
		NCT00821964 (Completed)	II	All	*Nab-paclitaxel*

Qiu et al. (2018).

out cancer regression, during "PD-1, CTLA4" suppressors act as its agent producing controlled efficiency (Zhu et al., 2014). In the MMTV-PyMT mice model, the HDACII a suppressor TMP195 alter the activity of macrophages and repaired the inhibitory TME (Guerriero, 2018). TMP195 in combination with "PD-1 antibody" results in cancer reduction, not seen in PD-1 inhibitor alone. This study demonstrated TAMs created immune-compromised environment causes anti–PD-1 hindrance in animal model, due to the immunological suppressive milieu they create, agonistic antibodies stimulated macrophages through the costimulatory CD40 protein, resulting in macrophage-induced tumor regression. Furthermore, stimulation of CD40 resulted in an increase in "PD-L1" production in TAMS. Joining both CD40-activation and "PD-L1" suppression had a synergistic anticancer effect shown in EMT-6 mouse model breast cancers (Zippelius et al., 2015). HER2/neu-production in breast cancer allograft, this relation exhibited synergetic antitumor effect as well as enhanced infiltrating of dendritic cells, monocytes, and T-lymphocytes. "Pathogen-Associated-Molecular Patterns (PAMPs)" can stimulate innate immune cells like macrophages, for instance, BTH1677, a fungal-obtained "1,3–1,6 beta-glucan" boosts macrophage destruction of antibody-targeting cancer cell in vitro by increasing "Fcγ-receptors and Complement-Receptor-3 (CR3)" (Bose et al., 2016; Mir et al., 2022c, d). BTH1677 in vitro cause repolarization of M2-type TAMs into M1-type TAMs and Rapid increase of $CD4^+$ T-cell and IFN-γ expression. In 4-T1-tumor–bearing animals, ideal BTH1677 had shown synergistic antitumor effects with PD-L1antibodies as well as anti–PD-1 (Bose et al., 2016). In preclinical breast cancer models, macrophage-focused therapy can improve immune checkpoint suppression efficiency. Table 6.2 summarizes ongoing findings on the relationship between patients linked with mammary tumors.

6.13 Conclusion

In TME, tumor-associated macrophages are the most common inflammatory mediators, besides other mediators are also present, such as "chemokines, growth factors, pro- and antiinflammatory cytokines." TAM protease is also one of the inflammatory mediators implicated modulation of tumor angiogenesis and tumor progression. TAMs also play an important role in chronic inflammation, ECM remolding, and immune response inhibition by interacting with the "NFB, Jak-STAT chemokine receptor" and the TGF-mediated-signaling pathway. Furthermore, it has been demonstrated that TAMs are distinct from normal phagocytes in a controlled physiological milieu, as TAMs are the result of the tumor microenvironment's reprogramming of macrophages like tumor-mediated "exosomes, cytokines, and other immune cells," resulting in distinct TAM cytokine production. So, the association between other cells and macrophages in TME can be changed and generate a new place to promote tumor cell life span and its progression. So TAMs play an essential part in breast-cancer progression by enhancing TME angiogenesis and metastasis, initiating tumor cell steaminess, energy metabolism, and supporting immune response inhibition. In TME, several factors regulate macrophage activity and its polarization. So, as a result, TAMs are essential components in cancer development and have the aim of generating a viable treatment strategy. TAM repolarization into antitumor MI-type macrophages is a possible therapeutic method. Xiao et al. demonstrate that the higher expression of M2-type TAMs was found in the control group, reaching 43.1%, and M2-type TAMs were reduced by up to 10.7% in therapy by repolarization-M2 into M1. Additionally, the concentration of MI-type macrophages was enhanced from 10.2% to 58%, which probably allows for the efficient suppression of cancer development and metastasis with reduced immune side issues. At the time, mixing diagnosed procedures associated with conventional chemotherapeutic drugs and "herbal-Chinese medication" focused on enhancing the TAMs repolarization and serving as the original therapeutic procedure for breast cancer treatment. Hence, examining the activity and methods of tumor-associated macrophages in the progression of breast tumors produces a better infrastructure for therapy.

References

Acerbi, I., Cassereau, L., Dean, I., Shi, Q., Au, A., Park, C., et al., 2015. Human breast cancer invasion and aggression correlates with ECM stiffening and immune cell infiltration. Integr. Biol. 7, 1120–1134.

Ager, E.I., Kozin, S.V., Kirkpatrick, N.D., Seano, G., Kodack, D.P., Askoxylakis, V., et al., 2015. Blockade of MMP14 activity in murine breast carcinomas: implications for macrophages, vessels, and radiotherapy. J. Natl. Cancer Inst. 107, 1–12.

Ali, H.R., Chlon, L., Pharoah, P.D., Markowetz, F., Caldas, C., 2016. Patterns of immune infiltration in breast cancer and their clinical implications: a gene-expression-based retrospective study. PLoS Med. 13 (e1002194).

An, G., Wu, F., Huang, S., Feng, L., Bai, J., Gu, S., et al., 2019. Effects of CCL5 on the biological behavior of breast cancer and the mechanisms of its interaction with tumor-associated macrophages. Oncol. Rep. 42, 2499–2511.

Aschenbrenner, A.C., Schultze, J.L., 2017. New "programmers" in tissue macrophage activation. Pflugers Arch. - Eur. J. Physiol. 469, 375–383.

Atri, C., Guerfali, F.Z., Laouini, D., 2018. Role of human macrophage polarization in inflammation during infectious diseases. Int. J. Mol. Sci. 19, 1801.

Barsky, S.H., Karlin, N.J., 2005. Myoepithelial cells: autocrine and paracrine suppressors of breast cancer progression. J. Mammary Gland Biol. Neoplasia 10, 249–260.

Benson, J.R., Jatoi, I., 2012. The global breast cancer burden. Future Oncol. 8, 697–702.

Bessis, M., de Boisfleury-Chevance, A., 1984. Facts and speculation about necrotaxis (chemotaxis toward a dying cell). Blood Cells 10, 5–22.

Biswas, S.K., Mantovani, A., 2010. Macrophage plasticity and interaction with lymphocyte subsets: cancer as a paradigm. Nat. Immunol. 11, 889–896.

Bose, N., Jonas, A.B., Qiu, X., Chan, A.S., Ottoson, N.R., Graffff, J.R., 2016. Imprime PGG treatment enhances antibody-dependent cellular phagocytosis (ADCP) of tumor cells by monocyte-derived macrophages. Immunol. Res. 4.

Bray, F., Ferlay, J., Soerjomataram, I., Siegel, R.L., Torre, L.A., Jemal, A., 2018. GLOBOCAN estimates of incidence and mortality worldwide for 36 cancers in 185 countries. CA Cancer J. Clin. 68 (6), 394–424.

Brown, J.M., Giaccia, A.J., 1998. The unique physiology of solid tumors: opportunities (and problems) for cancer therapy. Cancer Res. 58, 1408–1416.

Burke, B., Tang, N., Corke, K.P., et al., 2002. Expression of HIF-1alpha by human macrophages: implications for the use of macrophages in hypoxia-regulated cancer gene therapy. J. Pathol. 204, 204–212.

Cassetta, L., Fragkogianni, S., Sims, A.H., Swierczak, A., Forrester, L.M., Zhang, H., et al., 2019. Human tumor-associated macrophage and monocyte transcriptional landscapes reveal cancer-specific reprogramming, biomarkers, and therapeutic targets. Cancer Cell 35, 588–602.

Cha, Y.J., Koo, J.S., 2020. Role of tumor-associated myeloid cells in breast cancer. Cell 9, 1785.

Chanmee, T., Ontong, P., Konno, K., Itano, N., 2014. Tumor-associated macrophages as major players in the tumor microenvironment. Cancer 6, 1670–1690.

Chen, D., Zhang, X., Li, Z., Zhu, B., 2021. Metabolic regulatory crosstalk between tumor microenvironment and tumor-associated macrophages. Theranostics 11, 1016.

Chen, F., Chen, J., Yang, L., et al., 2019a. Extracellular vesicle-packaged HIF-1α- stabilizing lncRNA from tumour-associated macrophages regulates aerobic glycolysis of breast cancer cells. Nat. Cell Biol. 21 (4), 498–510.

Chen, P., Zuo, H., Xiong, H., et al., 2017. Gpr132 sensing of lactate mediates tumor–macrophage interplay to promote breast cancer metastasis. Proc. Natl. Acad. Sci. U. S. A. 114 (3), 580–585.

Chen, Y., Song, Y., Du, W., et al., 2019b. Tumor-associated macrophages: an accomplice in solid tumor progression. J. Biomed. Sci. 26 (1), 78.

Choi, J., Gyamfi, J., Jang, H., et al., 2018. The role of tumor-associated macrophage in breast cancer biology. Histol. Histopathol. 33 (2), 133–145.

Clauss, M., Gerlach, M., Gerlach, H., Brett, J., Wang, F., Familletti, P.C., et al., 1990. Vascular permeability factor: a tumor-derived polypeptide that induces endothelial cell and monocyte procoagulant activity, and promotes monocyte migration. J. Exp. Med. 172, 1535–1545.

Cojoc, M., Peitzsch, C., Trautmann, F., Polishchuk, L., Telegeev, G.D., Dubrovska, A., 2013. Emerging targets in cancer management: role of the CXCL12/CXCR4 axis. Onco. Targets. Ther. 6, 1347–1361.

Coleman, R.E., Gregory, W., Marshall, H., Wilson, C., Holen, I., 2013. The metastatic microenvironment of breast cancer: clinical implications. Breast 22, s50–s56.

Condeelis, J., Pollard, J.W., 2006. Macrophages: obligate partners for tumor cell migration, invasion, and metastasis. Cell 124 (2), 263–266.

de Boniface, J., Mao, Y., Schmidt-Mende, J., et al., 2012. Expression patterns of the immunomodulatory enzyme arginase 1 in blood, lymph nodes and tumor tissue of early-stage breast cancer patients. Oncoimmunology 1 (18).

DeNardo, D.G., Ruffell, B., 2019. Macrophages as regulators of tumour immunity and immunotherapy. Nat. Rev. Immunol. 19 (6), 369–382.

Dewan, M.Z., Vanpouille-Box, C., Kawashima, N., Di Napoli, S., Babb, J.S., Formenti, S.C., et al., 2012. Synergy of topical toll-like receptor 7 agonist with radiation and low-dose cyclophosphamide in a mouse model of cutaneous breast cancer. Clin. Cancer Res. 18, 6668–6678.

Doedens, A.L., Stockmann, C., Rubinstein, M.P., et al., 2010. Macrophage expression of hypoxia-inducible factor-1 alpha suppresses T-cell function and promotes tumor progression. Cancer Res. 70, 7465–7475.

Dvorak, H.F., 1986. Tumors: wounds that do not heal. Similarities between tumor stroma generation and wound healing. N. Engl. J. Med. 315, 1650–1659.

Farhood, B., Najafi, M., Mortezaee, K., 2019. CD8(+) cytotoxic T lymphocytes in cancer immunotherapy: a review. J. Cell. Physiol. 234 (6), 8509–8521.

Ferrara, N., Davis-Smyth, T., 1997. The biology of vascular endothelial growth factor. Endocr. Rev. 18, 4–25.

Folgueira, M.A., Maistro, S., Katayama, M.L., Roela, R.A., Mundim, F.G., Nanogaki, S., de Bock, G.H., Brentani, M.M., 2013. Markers of breast cancer stromal fibroblasts in the primary tumour site associated with lymph node metastasis: a systematic review including our case series. Biosci. Rep. 33, e00085.

Franklin, R.A., Liao, W., Sarkar, A., Kim, M.V., Bivona, M.R., Liu, K., Pamer, E.G., Li, M.O., 2014. The cellular and molecular origin of tumor-associated macrophages. Science 344 (6186), 921–925. https://doi.org/10.1126/science.1252510. Epub.

Fu, Y.X., Cai, J.P., Chin, Y.H., Watson, G.A., Lopez, D.M., 1992. Regulation of leukocyte binding to endothelial tissues by tumor-derived GM-CSF. Int. J. Cancer 50, 585–588.

Georgoudaki, A.M., Prokopec, K.E., Boura, V.F., et al., 2016. Reprogramming tumor-associated macrophages by antibody targeting inhibits cancer progression and metastasis. Cell Rep. 15 (9), 2000–2011.

Gil Del Alcazar, C.R., Huh, S.J., Ekram, M.B., Trinh, A., Liu, L.L., Beca, F., et al., 2017. Immune escape in breast cancer during in situ to invasive carcinoma transition. Cancer Discov. 7, 1098–1115.

Gordon, S.R., Maute, R.L., Dulken, B.W., 2017. PD-1 expression by tumour-associated macrophages inhibits phagocytosis and tumour immunity. Nature 545, 495–499.

Graves, D.T., Barnhill, R., Galanopoulos, T., Antoniades, H.N., 1992. Expression of monocyte chemotactic protein-1 in human melanoma in vivo. Am. J. Pathol. 140, 9–14.

Guerriero, J.L., 2018. Macrophages: the road less traveled, changing anticancer therapy. Trends Mol. Med. 24, 472–489.

Guo, L., Cheng, X., Chen, H., et al., 2019. Induction of breast cancer stem cells by M1 macrophages through Lin-28B-let-7-HMGA2 axis. Cancer Lett. 452, 213–225.

Halama, N., Zoernig, I., Berthel, A., Kahlert, C., Klupp, F., Suarez-Carmona, M., et al., 2016. Tumoral immune cell exploitation in colorectal cancer metastases can be targeted effectively by anti-CCR5 therapy in cancer patients. Cancer Cell 29, 587–601.

Hanahan, D., Weinberg, R.A., 2000. The hallmarks of cancer. Cell 100, 57–70.

Honkanen, T.J., Tikkanen, A., Karihtala, P., Mäkinen, M., Väyrynen, J.P., Koivunen, J.P., 2019. Prognostic and predictive role of tumour-associated macrophages in HER2 positive breast cancer. Sci. Rep. 9, 10961.

Hu, M., Polyak, K., 2008. Microenvironmental regulation of cancer development. Curr. Opin. Genet. Dev. 18, 27–34.

Hudis, C.A., 2007. Trastuzumab-mechanism of action and use in clinical practice. New England J. Med. 357, 39–51.

Iliopoulos, D., Hirsch, H.A., Wang, G., et al., 2011. Inducible formation of breast cancer stem cells and their dynamic equilibrium with non-stem cancer cells via IL6 secretion. Proc. Natl. Acad. Sci. U. S. A. 108 (4), 1397–1402.

Italiani, P., Boraschi, D., 2014. From monocytes to M1/m2 macrophages: phenotypical vs. functional differentiation. Front. Immunol. 5, 514.

Jiang, X., Shapiro, D.J., 2014. The immune system and inflammation in breast cancer. Mol. Cell. Endocrinol. 382, 6673–6682.

Kacinski, B.M., 1995. CSF-1 and its receptor in ovarian, endometrial and breast cancer. Ann. Med. 27, 79–85.

Kakonen, S.M., Mundy, G.R., 2003. Mechanisms of osteolytic bone metastases in breast carcinoma. Cancer 97, 834–839.

Kao, J., Houck, K., Fan, Y., et al., 1994. Characterization of a novel tumor-derived cytokine. Endothelial monocyte activating polypeptide II. J. Biol. Chem. 269, 25106–25119.

Kimbro, K.S., Simons, J.W., 2006. Hypoxia-inducible factor-1 in human breast and prostate cancer. Endocr. Relat. Cancer 13, 739–749.

Kitamura, T., Qian, B.Z., Soong, D., Cassetta, L., Noy, R., Sugano, G., et al., 2015. CCL2-induced chemokine cascade promotes breast cancer metastasis by enhancing retention of metastasis-associated macrophages. J. Exp. Med. 212, 1043–1059.

Knies, U.E., Kroger, S., Clauss, M., 2000. Expression of EMAP II in the developing and adult mouse. Apoptosis 5, 141–151.

Komohara, Y., Jinushi, M., 2014. Clinical significance of macrophage heterogeneity in human malignant tumors. Cancer Sci. 105, 1–8.

Kusuhara, M., Yamaguchi, K., Nagasaki, K., et al., 1990. Production of endothelin in human cancer cell lines. Cancer Res. 50, 3257–3261.

LaGory, E.L., Giaccia, A.J., 2016. The ever-expanding role of HIF in tumour and stromal biology. Nat. Cell Biol. 18 (4), 356–365.

Leek, R.D., Harris, A.L., 2002. Tumor-associated macrophages in breast cancer. J. Mammary Gland Biol. Neoplasia 7, 177–189.

Leek, R.D., Hunt, N.C., Landers, R.J., Lewis, C.E., Royds, J.A., Harris, A.L., 2000. Macrophage infiltration is associated with VEGF and EGFR expression in breast cancer. J. Pathol. 190, 430–436.

Leek, R.D., Lewis, C.E., Whitehouse, R., Greenall, M., Clarke, J., Harris, A.L., 1996. Association of macrophage infiltration with angiogenesis and prognosis in invasive breast carcinoma. Cancer Res. 56, 4625–4629.

Leek, R.D., Landers, R.J., Harris, A.L., Lewis, C.E., 1999. Necrosis correlates with high vascular density and focal macrophage infiltration in invasive carcinoma of the breast. Br. J. Cancer 79, 991–995.

Lewis, C.E., Pollard, J.W., 2006. Distinct role of macrophages in different tumor microenvironments. Cancer Res. 66, 605–612.

Lin, E.Y., Nguyen, A.V., Russell, R.G., Pollard, J.W., 2001. Colony-stimulating factor 1 promotes progression of mammary tumors to malignancy. J. Exp. Med. 193 (727–40).

Lin, S., Sun, L., Lyu, X., et al., 2017. Lactate-activated macrophages induced aerobic glycolysis and epithelial-mesenchymal transition in breast cancer by regulation of CCL5-CCR5 axis: a positive metabolic feedback loop. Oncotarget 8 (66), 110426–110443.

Liu, C., Li, Z., Wang, L., et al., 2015. Activating transcription factor 4 promotes angiogenesis of breast cancer through enhanced macrophage recruitment. Biomed. Res. Int. 2015 (974615).

Luboshits, G., Shina, S., Kaplan, O., et al., 1999. Elevated expression of the CC chemokine regulated on activation, normal T cell expressed and secreted (RANTES) in advanced breast carcinoma. Cancer Res. 59, 4681–4687.

Mantovani, A., Sica, A., Allavena, P., Garlanda, C., Locati, M., 2009. Tumor-associated macrophages and the related myeloid-derived suppressor cells as a paradigm of the diversity of macrophage activation. Hum. Immunol. 70, 325–330.

Mantovani, A., Sozzani, S., Locati, M., Allavena, P., Sica, A., 2002. Macrophage polarization: tumor-associated macrophages as a paradigm for polarized M2 mononuclear phagocytes. Trends Immunol. 23, 549–555.

Martinez, F.O., Gordon, S., 2014. The M1 and M2 paradigm of macrophage activation: time for reassessment. F1000Prime Rep 6, 13.

Medrek, C., Ponten, F., Jirstrom, K., Leandersson, K., 2012a. The presence of tumor associated macrophages in tumor stroma as a prognostic marker for breast cancer patients. BMC Cancer 12, 306.

Medrek, C., Ponten, F., Jirstrom, K., Leandersson, K., 2012b. The presence of tumor associated macrophages in tumor stroma as a prognostic marker for breast cancer patient. BMC Cancer 12, 306.

Mehraj, U., Aisha, S., Sofi, S., Mir, M.A., 2022a. Expression pattern and prognostic significance of baculoviral inhibitor of apoptosis repeat-containing 5 (BIRC5) in breast cancer: A comprehensive analysis. Adv. Cancer Biol.-Metastasis 100037.

Mehraj, U., Alshehri, B., Khan, A.A., Bhat, A.A., Bagga, P., Wani, N.A., Mir, M.A., 2022b. Expression pattern and prognostic significance of chemokines in breast cancer: an integrated bioinformatics analysis. Clin. Breast Cancer. https://doi.org/10.1016/j.clbc.2022.04.008.

Mehraj, U., Ganai, R.A., Macha, M.A., et al., 2021a. The tumor microenvironment as driver of stemness and therapeutic resistance in breast cancer: new challenges and therapeutic opportunities. Cell. Oncol. 44, 1209–1229.

Mehraj, U., Qayoom, H., Mir, M.A., 2021b. Prognostic significance and targeting tumor-associated macrophages in cancer: new insights and future perspectives. Breast Cancer 28, 539–555.

Mir, A.M., 2021. Cancer etiology, diagnosis and treatments. Combination Therapies and their Effectiveness in Breast Cancer Treatment. vol. 1 NOVA Biomedical Publishers, New York, USA, pp. 1–411.

Mir, M., Jan, S., Mehraj, U., 2022a. Current Therapeutics and Treatment Options in TNBC (Chapter 3). Elsevier Science Publishers USA, pp. 73–144.

Mir, M., Jan, S., Mehraj, U., 2022b. Triple-Negative Breast Cancer—An Aggressive Subtype of Breast Cancer. Elsevier Science Publishers, USA, pp. 1–28.

Mir, M., Sofi, S., Qayoom, H., 2022c. Different Drug Delivery Approaches in Combinational Therapy in TNBC (Chapter 8). Elsevier Science Publishers USA, pp. 201–230.

Mir, M., Sofi, S., Qayoom, H., 2022d. Role of Immune System in Triple Negative Breast Cancer (TNBC) (Chapter 5). Elsevier Science Publishers USA, pp. 177–201.

Mosser, D.M., Edwards, J.P., 2008. Exploring the full spectrum of macrophage activation. Nat. Rev. Immunol. 8, 958–969.

Mrowietz, U., Schwenk, U., Maune, S., et al., 1999. The chemokine RANTES is secreted by human melanoma cells and is associated with enhanced tumour formation in nude mice. Br. J. Cancer 79, 1025–1031.

Müller, A., Homey, B., Soto, H., Ge, N., Catron, D., Buchanan, M.E., McClanahan, T., Murphy, E., Yuan, W., Wagner, S.N., et al., 2001. Involvement of chemokine receptors in breast cancer metastasis. Nuture 410, 50–56.

Murata, Y., Ohteki, T., Koyasu, S., Hamuro, J., 2002. IFN-gamma and pro-inflammatory cytokine production by antigen-presenting cells is dictated by intracellular thiol redox status regulated by oxygen tension. Eur. J. Immunol. 32, 2866–2873.

Mwafy, S.E., El-Guindy, D.M., 2020. Pathologic assessment of tumor-associated macrophages and their histologic localization in invasive breast carcinoma. J. Egypt. Natl. Canc. Inst. 32, 6.

Negus, R.P., Stamp, G.W., Relf, M.G., et al., 1995. The detection and localization of monocyte chemoattractant protein-1 (MCP-1) in human ovarian cancer. J. Clin. Investig., 95.

Niwa, Y., Akamatsu, H., Niwa, H., Sumi, H., Ozaki, Y., Abe, A., 2001. Correlation of tissue and plasma RANTES levels with disease course in patients with breast or cervical cancer. Clin. Cancer Res. 7, 285–289.

Olson, O.C., Kim, H., Quail, D.F., Foley, E.A., Joyce, J.A., 2017. Tumor-associated macrophages suppress the cytotoxic activity of antimitotic agents. Cell Rep. 19 (1), 101–113. https://doi.org/10.1016/j.celrep.2017.03.038.

Oshi, M., Tokumaru, Y., Asaoka, M., Yan, L., Satyananda, V., Matsuyama, R., Matsuhashi, N., Futamura, M., Ishikawa, T., Yoshida, K., Endo, I., Takabe, K., 2020. M1 Macrophage and M1/M2 ratio defined by transcriptomic signatures resemble only part of their conventional clinical characteristics in breast cancer. Sci Rep. 10 (1), 16554. https://doi.org/10.1038/s41598-020-73624-w.

O'Sullivan, C., Lewis, C.E., 1994. Tumour-associated leucocytes: friends or foes in breast carcinoma. J. Pathol. 172, 229–235.

Paget, S., 1889. The distribution of secondary growths in cancer of the breast. Lancet 133, 571–573.

Park, S., Jiang, Z., Mortenson, E.D., Deng, L., Radkevich-Brown, O., Yang, X., et al., 2010. The therapeutic effect of anti-HER2/neu antibody depends on both innate and adaptive immunity. Cancer Cell 18, 160–170.

Paulus, P., Stanley, E.R., Schäfer, R., Abraham, D., Aharinejad, S., 2006. Colony-stimulating factor-1 antibody reverses chemoresistance in human MCF-7 breast cancer xenografts. Cancer Res. 66, 4349–4356.

Place, A.E., Jin Huh, S., Polyak, K., 2011. The microenvironment in breast cancer progression: biology and implications for treatment. Breast Cancer Res. 13, 227.

Prenen, H., Mazzone, M., 2019. Tumor-associated macrophages: a short compendium. Cell. Mol. Life Sci. 76, 1447–1458.

Qian, B.-Z., Li, J., Zhang, H., Kitamura, T., Zhang, J., Campion, L.R., et al., 2011. CCL2 recruits inflammatory monocytes to facilitate breast-tumour metastasis. Nature 475, 222–225.

Qian, B.Z., Pollard, J.W., 2010. Macrophage diversity enhances tumor progression and metastasis. Cell 141, 39–51.

Qiu, Q.S., Waaijer, J.H., de Elisabeth, V.G.E., et al., 2018. Tumor associated macrophages in breast Cancer: innocent bystander or important player. Cancer Treat. Rev. 70, 178–189.

Rhee, L., 2016. Diverse macrophages polarization in tumor microenvironment. Arch. Pharm. Res. 39, 1588–1596.

Ruffell, B., Chang-Strachan, D., Chan, V., et al., 2014. Macrophage IL-10 blocks CD8 + T cell-dependent responses to chemotherapy by suppressing IL-12 expression in intratumoral dendritic cells. Cancer Cell 27526 (5), 623–637.

Ruffell, B., Coussens, L.M., 2015. Macrophages and therapeutic resistance in cancer. Cancer Cell 27, 462–472.

Sawano, A., Iwai, S., Sakurai, Y., et al., 2001. Vascular endothelial growth factor receptor 1, is a novel cell surface marker for the lineage of monocyte macrophages in humans. Blood 97, 785–791.

Schmeisser, A., Marquetant, R., Illmer, T., et al., 2005. The expression of macrophage migration inhibitory factor 1alpha (MIF 1alpha) in human atherosclerotic plaques is induced by different proatherogenic stimuli and associated with plaque instability. Artherosclerosis 178, 83–94.

Schulz, C., Gomez Perdiguero, E., Chorro, L., Szabo-Rogers, H., Cagnard, N., Kierdorf, K., et al., 2012. A lineage of myeloid cells independent of Myb and hematopoietic stem cells. Science 336, 86–90. https://doi.org/10.1126/science.1219179.

Sica, A., Saccani, A., Bottazzi, B., Polentarutti, N., Vecchi, A., van Damme, J., Mantovani, A., 2000. Autocrine production of IL-10 mediates defective IL-12 production and NF-kappa B activation in tumor-associated macrophages. J. Immunol. 164, 762–767.

Solinas, G., Germano, G., Mantovani, A., Allavena, P., 2009. Tumor-associated macrophages (TAM) as major players of the cancer-related inflammation. J. Leukoc. Biol. 86, 1065–1073.

Song, Y., Tang, C., Yin, C., 2018. Combination antitumor immunotherapy with VEGF and PlGF siRNA via systemic delivery of multi-functionalized nanoparticles to tumor-associated macrophages and breast cancer cells. Biomaterials 185, 117–132.

Tamura, R., Tanaka, T., Akasaki, Y., Murayama, Y., Yoshida, K., Sasaki, H., 2019. The role of vascular endothelial growth factor in the hypoxic and immunosuppressive tumor microenvironment: perspectives for therapeutic implications. Med. Oncol. 37 (1), 2. https://doi.org/10.1007/s12032-019-1329-2.

Tang, R.P., Kacinski, B., Validire, P., et al., 1990. Oncogene amplification correlates with dense lymphocyte infiltration in human breast cancers: a role for hematopoietic growth factor release by tumor cells. J. Cell. Biochem. 44, 189–198.

Tsuyada, A., Chow, A., Wu, J., Somlo, G., Chu, P., Loera, S., et al., 2012. CCL2 mediates cross-talk between cancer cells and stromal fibroblasts that regulates breast cancer stem cells. Cancer Res. 72, 2768–2779.

Ueno, T., Toi, M., Saji, H., Muta, M., Bando, H., Kuroi, K., 2000. Significance of macrophage chemoattractant protein-1 in macrophage recruitment, angiogenesis, and survival in human breast cancer. Clin. Cancer Res. 6, 3282–3289.

Ugel, S., de Sanctis, F., Mandruzzato, S., et al., 2015. Tumor-induced myeloid deviation: when myeloid-derived suppressor cells meet tumor associated macrophages. J. Clin. Investig. 125 (9), 3365–3376.

Vitale, I., Manic, G., Coussens, L.M., Kroemer, G., Galluzzi, L., 2019. Macrophages and metabolism in the tumor microenvironment. Cell Metab. 30, 36–50.

Wain, J.H., Kirby, J.A., Ali, S., 2002. Leucocyte chemotaxis: examination of mitogen-activated protein kinase and phosphoinositide 3-kinase activation by monocyte chemoattractant proteins-1, −2, −3 and −4. Clin. Exp. Immunol. 127, 436–444.

Weagel, E., Smith, C., Liu, P.G., Robison, R., O'Neill, K., 2015. Macrophage polarization and its role in cancer. J Clin Cell Immunol 6, 338.

Williams, C.B., Yeh, E.S., Soloff, A.C., 2016. Tumor-associated macrophages: unwitting accomplices in breast cancer malignancy. NPJ Breast Cancer 2, 15025.

Willingham, S.B., Volkmer, J.-P., Gentles, A.J., Sahoo, D., Dalerba, P., Mitra, S.S., et al., 2012. The CD47-signal regulatory protein alpha (SIRPa) interaction is a therapeutic target for human solid tumors. Proc. Natl. Acad. Sci. U. S. A. 109, 6662–6667.

Xu, M., Liu, M., Du, X., Li, S., Li, H., Li, X., et al., 2015. Intratumoral delivery of IL-21 overcomes anti-Her2/Neu resistance through shifting tumor-associated macrophages from M2 to M1 phenotype. J. Immunol. 194, 4997–5006.

Yang, C., He, L., He, P., Liu, Y., Wang, W., He, Y., et al., 2015. Increased drug resistance in breast cancer by tumor-associated macrophages through IL-10/STAT3/bcl-2 signaling pathway. Med. Oncol. 32, 352.

Yang, J., Liao, D., Chen, C., et al., 2013. Tumor-associated macrophages regulate murine breast cancer stem cells through a novel paracrine EGFR/Stat3/sox-2 signaling pathway. Stem Cells (Dayton, Ohio) 31 (2), 248–258.

Yang, M., McKay, D., Pollard, J.W., Lewis, C.E., 2018. Diverse functions of macrophages in different tumor microenvironments. Cancer Res. 78, 5492–5503.

Zhang, X., Zeng, Y., Qu, Q., Zhu, J., Liu, Z., Ning, W., Zeng, H., Zhang, N., Du, W., Chen, C., Huang, J.A., 2017. PD-L1 induced by IFN-γ from tumor-associated macrophages via the JAK/STAT3 and PI3K/AKT signaling pathways promoted progression of lung cancer. Int. J. Clin. Oncol. 22 (6), 1026–1033. https://doi.org/10.1007/s10147-017-1161-7.1.

Zhu, Y., Knolhoff, B.L., Meyer, M.A., Nywening, T.M., West, B.L., Luo, J., et al., 2014. CSF1/CSF1R blockade reprograms tumor-infiltrating macrophages and improves response to T cell checkpoint immunotherapy in pancreatic cancer models. Cancer Res. 74, 5057–5069.

Zippelius, A., Schreiner, J., Herzig, P., Müller, P., 2015. Induced PD-L1 expression mediates acquired resistance to agonistic anti-CD40 treatment. Cancer Immunol. Res. 3, 236–244.

Further reading

Arlauckas, S.P., Garris, C.S., Kohler, R.H., Kitaoka, M., Cuccarese, M.F., 2017. In vivo imaging reveals a tumor-associated macrophage-mediated resistance pathway in anti-PD-1 therapy. Sci. Transl. Med. 9, 3604.

Martinez, F.O., Gordon, S., Locati, M., Mantovani, A., 2006. Transcriptional profiling of the human monocyte-to-macrophage differentiation and polarization: new molecules and patterns of gene expression. J. Immunol. 177, 7303–7311.

Stout, R.D., Jiang, C., Matta, B., Tietzel, I., Watkins, S.K., Suttles, J., 2005. Macrophages sequentially change their functional phenotype in response to changes in microenvironmental influences. J. Immunol. 175, 342–349.

CHAPTER 7

Role of Tumor-associated neutrophils in the breast tumor microenvironment

Manzoor Ahmad Mir and Ulfat Jan
Department of Bioresources, School of Biological Sciences, University of Kashmir, Srinagar, Jammu and Kashmir, India

7.1 Introduction

A well-defined leukocyte called a neutrophil, is known to have a main function in the host immune response by extravasating from the bloodstream and entering multiple organs. These immune cells are the most frequent form of systemic leukocytes accounting for about 50%–70% of all systemic leukocytes. The main role of these immune cells is phagocytosis by producing various types of cytokines, dangerous chemicals, and oxygen radicals, as well as antimicrobial peptides (Fridlender and Albelda, 2012). These cells are produced from hematopoietic progenitor cells and play a critical role in innate immune responses. The immune cell that links inflammation with cancer is the neutrophil. Based on classical immunological studies, these innate immune components are principally important for immune surveillance, immunological regulation, and inflammatory processes. Due to the classical immunological studies and the shorter life span of the neutrophils, their roles in cancer progression were ignored. Recent findings have demonstrated that neutrophils possess two main characteristics of phenotypic variability and functional adaptability based on which it has been proved that neutrophils take an active part in cancer progression, especially in the cancer microenvironments (Wu et al., 2019). Emerging research has uncovered critical routes, whereby tumors impair typical neutrophil balance. These routes are polarization and activation of the neutrophils by tumors; life span of the neutrophils; preservation and migration of neutrophils from the basal cells; and granulopoiesis. From the past 40 years, it has been seen that the abnormalities in the healthy cells/tissues are not the ample cause for the formation of the tumors. But it has been seen that the process of inflammation acts as an important factor for tumor growth by causing harm to certain tissues, and neutrophils are the essential cells of the process of inflammation which means that neutrophils directly/indirectly are associated with cancers (Coffelt et al., 2016). There are several types of cancers, but in case of females, breast cancer is the leading cause of mortality. Uncontrolled and abnormal cell division in breast cancer cells is the most dreadful cancer in women population all over the world (Siegel et al., 2014; Mir et al., 2022c). Globally, breast cancer accounts for about a 17 lakh rise in new cases and about 520,000 deaths yearly (Mehraj et al., 2021a, 2022a). There are numerous agents that lead to breast cancer

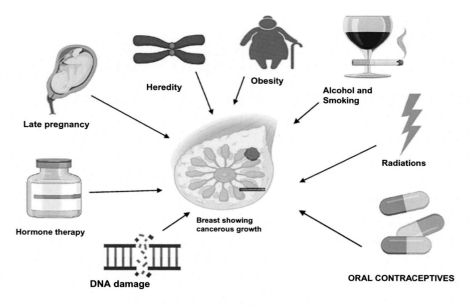

Late pregnancy

Heredity

Obesity

Alcohol and Smoking

Radiations

Hormone therapy

Breast showing cancerous growth

DNA damage

ORAL CONTRACEPTIVES

MAIN CAUSES/RISK FACTORS OF THE BREAST CANCER

Fig. 7.1 Diagrammatic illustration of the various risk factors or causes of the breast cancer.

including DNA damage, heredity, late pregnancy, hormone therapy, radiations, etc. (Fig. 7.1; MacMahon, 2006; Thomson et al., 2014).

The mortality rate of breast cancer in case of women in the United States is more than 40,000/per year (Al-Hajj et al., 2003). There are four subgroups of breast cancer depending on transcriptomes and biochemical depictions: luminal A, luminal B, HER2-enriched, and triple-negative breast cancer (Perou et al., 2000; Sørlie et al., 2001; Mir et al., 2022d). Because breast cancer is polymorphic, malignancies with almost the same clinicopathological condition might well have varying tumor progression, leading to variable outcomes (Fan et al., 2006). Breast cancer cell dissemination necessitates reduced cell to cell attachment but elevated cell to ECM attachment, as well as increased pervasiveness and mobility through matrix-degrading protease release and cytoskeletal remodeling (Kalluri and Weinberg, 2009). A well-known strategy for commencing migratory and protruding characteristic properties of breast cancer is the epithelial-mesenchymal transition in which stratified breast cancer cells develop a multipotent morphological phenotype (Kalluri and Weinberg, 2009). The tumor microenvironment (TME) is the basis of advanced cancer stages in the case of breast cancer that is TME plays a leading role in breast cancer metastasis (Yu et al., 2014; Mehraj et al., 2021a). In the TME of diverse breast cancer tissues, the fibroblast is the most common kind of stromal cell. Through the encouragement of peripheral immune growth factors, cancer cells turn stromal fibroblast cells into cancer-associated fibroblasts (CAFs). With the help of paracrine growth factors, tumor cells possess the power of bracing stromal fibroblast cells into the

CAFs and these CAFs are responsible mainly for the endurance, growth, and progression of the cancer cells (Yu et al., 2014; Kalluri and Zeisberg, 2006).

7.2 Immunity and cancer

As tumor immunology research progresses at a breakneck pace, a significant effort and time are being put into elucidating the reasons that underpin the immune system's identification and eradication of tumors, as well as the repercussions of these activities. It has always been obvious that the immune system's detection ability is not confined to the standard models of self versus nonself and includes the nuanced variations across self and modified self. This finding bolstered the case for rethinking the tumor immunosurveillance concept, which had been largely neglected. Burnet and Thomas suggested this concept 50 years ago (Dunn et al., 2006). About 50–100 years ago, it was suggested that the immune system must be able to recognize and destroy cancerous cells same as pathogens as the immune system possess the ability to recognize and kill foreign pathogens along with cancer immunosurveillance. Our immune system can recognize nascent cancerous cells as antigens through specific immune cells either innate or inborn, effector molecules, and various tumor suppression strategies. Although the immune system can aid tumor growth through a process called immunoediting (Vesely et al., 2011; Mir et al., 2022f). Over the past 50 years it has been proved that cancer is a genetic abnormality in which body cells undergoes mutations that typically prevent their unmanageable proliferation. Malignant cells could do a lot of damage, but there are a lot of internal and external tumor-suppressor systems that could really stop them from spreading (Vesely et al., 2011). There are numerous internal tumor-suppression techniques including cellular senescence; p53 protein; mitochondria associated proapoptotic proteins of the Bcl-2 family, caspases, cytotoxicity, phagocytosis, and mitotic collapse (Xue et al., 2007; Danial and Korsmeyer, 2004). The external tumor-suppression methods include cells' inextricable reliance on certain regulatory cues in the surroundings to suppress the inherent symptoms, including the epithelial cell–extracellular matrix relationship, which causes apoptosis once interrupted (Janes and Watt, 2006), presence of dysfunctional intercellular structures, crucial linkages among cell polarity genes responsible for cellular junctions and proliferation hinder cell cycle progression (Humbert et al., 2003); immunoregulatory leukocytes directly affect the transformation of a normal cell to cancerous cell (Vesely et al., 2011).

Our immune system possesses three major roles to prevent cancer development and progression:

1. By reducing or clearing the infections caused by the viruses that can develop or propagate cancer/tumor.
2. Clearance of various disease-causing organisms by preventing the persistence of the inflammation that helps tumor formation.

3. Immunosurveillance by identification and elimination of transformed cells.

There are numerous pathways to manage cancer targets such as, mitochondria-induced apoptosis and death-receptor apoptotic pathway (Vesely et al., 2011) and there are numerous components of the immune system that control the protective system against external antigens and autoantigens that can lead to cancer, these components include committed cells such as Treg cells, immune checkpoint inhibitors in the form of CTLA-4 and PD-1, immunosuppressive cytokines such transforming growth factor (TGF)-β (Li and Flavell, 2008; Qayoom et al., 2021). TGF-β directs the growth of regulatory T cells and inhibits the formation as well as activity of effector T lymphocytes and dendritic cells (DCs) in specific immunity (Sanjabi et al., 2017; Flavell et al., 2010). It not only directs adaptive immunity, but it also controls the inborn immunity by suppressing the NK cells and also monitors the activities of neutrophils and macrophages, as a result, there is a formation of an antagonistic immunological regulatory response system. Dysregulation in the functioning of the TGF-β leads to various types of abnormalities such as malfunctioning of the immune system, cancer, and various other defects (Batlle and Massagué, 2019). Inherent lymphoid cells, such as natural killer (NK) cells, depend on germline-encoded pattern recognition receptors as well as other signaling molecules to efficiently recognize pathogenic antigens or membranous molecules on tumor cells to regulate downstretching. The above cells mount one's regulatory defenses, including phagocytosis by monocytes as well as inherent cytotoxic reactions of the NK cells, while initiating host defenses (Woo et al., 2015). The potential of antigen-presenting cells to entrap tumor cells through the use of the process of phagocytosis, a procedure that includes specific cell identification, cellular endocytosis, and lysosomal digestion which is governed by signaling pathways between the target cell and the phagocyte, is critical to this process is necessary for the interconnection of the innate and adaptive immune system (Feng et al., 2019; Khan et al., 2022). Throughout this situation, systemic immune phagocytic cells (TAMs), leukocytes (TANs), antigen-presenting cells (DCs), myeloid-derived suppressor cells (MDSCs), and NK cells are the major factors of cancer-related inflammation and, due to their functional plasticity, can play pivotal pro- or antitumorigenic roles at various stages of cancer progression. In reality, innate immune system could either prevent cancer progression by killing tumor cells and/or slowing their development, or it can promote the self-renewal of altered cells by shaping overall antigenicity and/or suppressing the host's antitumor defenses (Fridman et al., 2017; Coussens et al., 2013; De Visser et al., 2006; Hinshaw and Shevde, 2019). NK cells have strong proapoptotic behavior, killing latently infected or cancerous cells without regard for MHC-I, as well as slowly release a variety of immunoregulatory cytokines and chemokines, such as interferon (IFN), TNF-α, granulocyte macrophage colony-stimulating factor, CCL5, and IL-22, which are associated within upregulation of DCs and tumor-associated macrophages (TAMs). Stimulation of these cells depends on the assimilation of innate cytotoxicity arbitrating receptors and the inhibition of accompanying receptors (Castriconi et al., 2009; Vitale et al., 2005; Mehraj et al., 2022b). Immune cells sustain strong immunosurveillance capacities during the early stages of cancer formation (elimination phase), and antitumor immunity predominate. Inherent immune cells (monocytes, neutrophils, DCs, and NK cells) work in tandem alongside specific immunity (T and B lymphocytes) to provide a strong initial defense against tumor cells, recognizing and destroying more immuno-modulatory cancerous cells while also preventing uncontrolled tumor growth (Schreiber et al., 2011; Teng et al., 2015). Surprisingly, the array of TCRs in migrating T cells from individuals having breast, pulmonary, and ovarian malignancies is less diverse. Moreover, because a reduced cell receptor repertoire in individuals is linked to aging and other past inflammatory responses including persistent infections, such alterations could be a factor in cancer expansion. Well-defined information about the TCRs and cancer is needed (Hiam-Galvez et al., 2021). Polyclonal memory $CD4^+$ and $CD8^+$ T lymphocytes of blood plasma show lower capability to deliver interleukin (IL)-2 and IFN-γ in response to specific stimuli with PMA and ionomycin among individual women possessing breast cancer, indicating that distant T lymphocytes also are physiologically disturbed (Verronèse et al., 2016). In metastatic breast cancer, distal virgin $CD4^+$ T lymphocytes showed reduced sensitivity following IL-6 activation was evaluated via activation of STAT1 and STAT3 (Hiam-Galvez et al., 2021). Regulatory B cells, which are defined by the synthesis of the antiinflammatory molecule IL-10, are another inhibitory lymphocyte type that participates in tumorigen-esis. In the same way that regulatory T cells have expanded, IL-10-producing Bregs have expanded in the blood plasma of gastric cancer patients and lung cancer, while overall B cell populations remains steady. Repressive $CD25^+$ regulatory B cells were increased inside the spleen, lymph nodes, and bloodstream in the 4T1-treated mice with breast cancer (Yuen et al., 2016; Wang et al., 2015; Murakami et al., 2019; Zhou et al., 2014; Olkhanud et al., 2011). Another immune cell called NK cell provides an antitumor immunity by killing tumor cells and enhancing the antitumor activities of the other immune cells (Hiam-Galvez et al., 2021). Peripheral NK cells from breast cancer patients show different morphologies, having lower production of activating receptors like NKp30, NKG2D, DNAM-1, and CD16, and higher expression of the inhibiting target NKG2A, and also a reduced ability to kill cancer cells and degra-nulate in vitro (Mamessier et al., 2011). Overall, such findings endorse the concept that cell-mediated immune organization degradation arises in a variety of tumors. To apprise medicinal growth and current studies of the factors that cause these systemic interrup-tions, more effort is necessary to completely comprehend the different immunoreac-tions in cancer patients, and the relationships between such immune checkpoints and the tumor stage, developmental state, and disease prevalence. It also is crucial to comprehend how overall immunological alterations are just so profound in certain sit-uations but so mild in many others (Hiam-Galvez et al., 2021).

7.3 Cells associated with breast cancer

It has been seen that the mature adult tissues are maintained by the coordinated multi-plication of precursor cells that are capable of giving rise to progenitor cells capable of producing specialized cell populations. Cancer is a widespread illness that affects the tumor cells as well as the stromal cells that surround them and it has been seen that the stromal cells present in the TME play a main role in cancer progression and disease expansion (Mao et al., 2013). It has been seen that the cancer progression and disease development are associated with various host cells including inflammatory infiltrate, angiogenesis, stromal cells, etc. A large number of immune cells play a major role in the cancer progression and cancer development, mainly the infiltrate that usually consists of macrophages and neutrophils as well as immunosuppressive cells called MDSCs. These two immune infiltrate cells possess duplicate functioning in the case of breast cancer, pos-sessing both beneficial and harmful effects (Galdiero et al., 2013). The majority of cancer stroma are made up of CAFs which influence the cancer cell by promoting disease devel-opment, genesis, infiltration, and dissemination. CAFs not only enhance tumor growth in breast cancer but often cause treatment resistance. As a result, addressing CAFs offers a fresh strategy to manage cancers that have developed treatment resistance and it has been suggested that these CAFs not only help in cancer progression but prompt remedial resis-tance (Mao et al., 2013; Mir et al., 2022b). For the past 40 years, scientists have mainly focused on the cells that are present in the TMEs and according to modern studies, TMEs are composed mainly of tumor parenchyma and stroma. In the case of breast and pan-creatic cancer, stromal cells associated with cancer are the major cell types present that aid in cancer progression and disease expansion. It has been proved by the cocultured examinations that CAFs affect the drug susceptibility to cancerous cells (Kalluri and Zeisberg, 2006; Östman and Augsten, 2009). It has been seen that the TGF-β and CXCL12/SDF-1 are mainly considered the major tumor-cell-derived elements, usually influencing the stimulation of CAFs (Kojima et al., 2010; Löhr et al., 2001). The TME contains a diverse range of leukocytes that could play a double function in tumor forma-tion and dissemination. The immune system can kill tumor cells immediately or contrib-ute to the generation of an antitumor immune reaction, but they are also solicited and programmed by cancer cells enhancing the activity of tumor propagation. Caveolin-1 is a familiar hallmark of malignant transformation in fibroblasts, and the result indicates Cav-1 as a facilitator of CAF activation. Furthermore, numerous oncogenes (v-abl, bcr-abl, and crkl) alter NIH 3T3 stromal cells, resulting in reduced caveolins (Cav-1,2,3), that coincides very well with bigger size of clusters generated by such oncogenes (Koleske et al., 1995). In breast cancer, CAFs have just a reduced amount of Caveolin-1 protein in contrast to NAFs, whereas CAFs generally grow more quickly than NAFs, indicating that Cav-1 reduction indicates CAF stimulation. Furthermore, the explana-tion for the loss of Caveolin-1 expression in CAFs is yet unknown. Caveolin-1 dysre-gulation in CAFs is primarily thought to be the result of proteolytic breakdown and phagocytosis (Mao et al., 2013). After CAFs, a class of WBCs that are associated with the breast cancer microenvironment are macrophages. These are the well-studied leukocytes mainly in the case of breast cancer, and these cells are thought to play a basic role in the cancer vasculature, infiltration, and metastases usually called TAMs. Perhaps crucially, employing an immunization method to eliminate TAMs reduced tumor progress in breast as well as other cancers, suggesting potentially addressing the TME could be a viable treatment option (Polyak, 2007; Mir and Mehraj, 2019). There are several key players in this immune cell infiltration, namely neutrophils and macrophages. TAMs are a well-known member of the cellular infiltration in various tumors, along with major makers of many messengers (e.g., chemokines) that play a role in the initiation as well as management of the severe inflammatory phase (Mantovani et al., 1992; Mehraj et al., 2021b). Macrophages are usually involved in inflammatory reactions because they produce chemicals like IL-6, tumor necrosis factor-α, and IFN-γ (Brown et al., 2008; Grivennikov et al., 2010). Colony-stimulating factor-1 (CSF-1) overexpression is frequently observed trailing edge of tumors, as high CSF-1 concentrations in tumors are linked to a bad outcome (Laoui et al., 2011; Qian and Pollard, 2010). It was experimentally proved in murine models that CSF-1 plays a major role in the recruitment of macrophages toward tumors and acts as a factor in tumor progression as well as metastasis. Under the influence of the IL-4, VEGFA also takes part in the progression as well as the metastasis of cancer (Fig. 7.2; Noy and Pollard, 2014). Whenever there is the recruitment of the monocytes

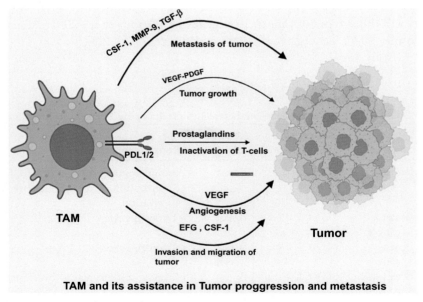

TAM and its assistance in Tumor proggression and metastasis

Fig. 7.2 Tumor-associated macrophage and its assistance in tumor progression and metastasis through various chemical mediators.

toward the tumor site, these cells are reprogrammed to TAMs, gaining specific activities including encouraging tumor development, vasculature, tumor progression, and metastasis, as well as inhibiting antineoplastic T cells (Netea-Maier et al., 2018). TAM secrete cytokines, chemokines, and proteases all point to them playing a key role both T-regulatory cell hyperactivation, as well as suppressing cytotoxic T cells in the TME (Noy and Pollard, 2014). When comparing monocytes invading tumor-bearing lungs to monocytes from naive lungs, macrophage invading tumor-bearing lungs possess higher Cox2 expression and higher PGE2 synthesis. It has been observed in in-vitro experiments. Research shows that when cancer progresses, both cancerous cells as well as immune cells seem to be capable of enhancing overall production of prostaglandins, culminating in a progressive increase in prostaglandin synthesis, as seen in lung tumors (Poczobutt et al., 2016). Vast proportion of the genes, shown to be improperly activated in tumor epithelium and fibroblast cells by Allinen and colleagues express extruded proteins as well as sensors, suggesting that aberrant immunoregulatory signaling may play a significant role in breast tumor growth. Numerous CXC chemokine family members, such as CXCL12 and CXCL14, which are highly expressed in tumor epithelium and myofibroblasts, increase tumorigenesis, movement, and infiltration, as well as vasculature and distant dissemination. CXCL1, IL-8, CCL5/RANTES, and MCP1 are some of the additional chemokines that have been linked to breast cancer (Table 7.1). Breast and other kinds of malignancies have been explored for treatments because of the fact that these chemokine receptors belong to serpentine receptor family that can act as best drug targets, and there is a possibility that inhibiting these chemokines can fairly help in treating breast and other types of cancers in near future (Orimo et al., 2005; Allinen et al., 2004; Zlotnik, 2006; Taborga et al., 2007; Mehraj et al., 2022b).

Table 7.1 Different types of chemokines and cytokines produced by TME cells in breast cancer.

S. no.	Type of cancer	Chemokine or cytokine	Affected cell	Consequence
1.	Breast cancer	OSM	Breast cells	Stimulates the synthesis of VEGF, cellular separation, and raises the risk of invasion
2.	Breast cancer	CXCL 12	Breast cells	Tumorigenesis
3.	Breast cancer	CXCL 14	Breast cells	Tumorigenesis
4.	Breast cancer	CXCL 1	Breast cells	Cancer cell survival and metastasis
5.	Breast cancer	RANTES	Breast cells	Cancer progression

7.4 Neutrophils and cancer

Neutrophils are the most common type of leukocyte within human blood, and they play an important role in the first layer of defense against microbial infections. The function in cancer-related inflammatory response had also generally regarded dismissed due to their short life span as well as completely distinct appearance. TANs can have both protumoral and antitumoral activities, similar to macrophages, and findings across experimental animals suggest that neutrophils could be polarized toward genetic variants in response to various tumor-derived signals (Mantovani et al., 2011; Fridlender et al., 2009). There is a strong suggestion that tumor-associated neutrophils (TANs) do not act as a strong host defense system likewise normal neutrophils, it was first time experimentally proved by Sparmann and Bar-Sagi, and they demonstrated that mice with a mutation in the K-ras signaling pathway promoted the IL-8 production through nuclear factor-κB signaling pathway. They also discovered that the LSL-K-ras mice's benign growths attract TANs via producing MIP-2 and KC, which are the murine analogs of IL-8. Concluding that, simple neutrophil restriction investigations utilizing Gr-1 immunoglobulin were found to diminish vascular endothelial adhesion to tumors, restrict tumor development, as well as restrict metastatic quantity (Sparmann and Bar-Sagi, 2004; Ji et al., 2006; Pekarek et al., 1995; Tazawa et al., 2003). Neutrophils, like macrophages, can help either in promoting the development of a tumor or having anticarcinogenic activities. Breast cancer is characterized by gene mutations, and research shows that neutrophils play a role in tumorigenesis by releasing nitrogen dioxide and peroxynitrite and oxygen radicals (ROS) (Güngör et al., 2010; Hanahan and Weinberg, 2011; Sandhu et al., 2000). As a result, neutrophil-derived antioxidants, such as hypochlorous acid produced by myeloperoxidase, have been linked to genetic alterations as well as damage to DNA (Güngör et al., 2010). Hypochlorous acid in turn activates certain proteases like MMP-2, MMP-7, MMP-8, and MMP-9 and also deactivates TIMP-1, a tissue deactivator of the metalloprotease 1 that consecutively enhances the action of matrix metallopeptidase-9 that assists the invasion of cancer to other cells and tissues (Galdiero et al., 2013). Neutrophil-derived mediators and granule-stored peptides may indeed play a variety of roles in tumor growth. For example, neighboring epithelium lung cancerous cells took up neutrophil elastase (NE), which encouraged tumor progression by hydrolyzing the insulin receptor substrate-1 (IRS-1), which normally limits phosphoinositide-3-kinase activity and lowers PDGFR signaling (Houghton et al., 2010). This enzyme also takes part in the epithelial to mesenchymal transformation intervened by neutrophils (Galdiero et al., 2013). On the other hand in the case of breast cancer, NE cleaves cyclin-E into a shortened variant that is expressed in presence of human leukocyte antigen-1 and increased breast cancer cell breakdown by T lymphocytes. Granulocyte-macrophage colony-stimulating factor (GM-CSF) produced from cancerous cells of breast stimulated neutrophils to produce oncostatin M (OSM), that in return prompted breast cancerous cells to produce VEGF, promoting cancer cell dissociation and enhancing overall aggressive activity (Galdiero et al., 2013). Cancer-associated neutrophils additionally produce a diverse range of angiogenic factors that can influence tumor angiogenesis. CXCL1/ MIP-2, for example, attracts neutrophils, which then produce physiologically active vascular endothelial growth factor A, culminating in revascularization in person (Scapini et al., 2004). In the case of breast cancer, GM-CSF levels increase that in turn increases neutrophil count and results in lower chances of recovery (McGary et al., 1995). According to investigations, TANs establish a protumorigenic (N2) phenotype in un-treated tumors, which is mostly mediated more by availability of TGF-β, and in reverse process via inhibiting TGF—or increasing IFN—can also change the phenotypic behavior of TANs to a more antagonistic (N1) one. Lack of TGF-β, anticancer "N1-like" create considerable high degrees of TNF-α, MIP-1α, H_2O_2, and NO, who were deadly to cancerous cells both in vivo and in vitro (Gregory and Houghton, 2011; Jablonska et al., 2010; Fridlender et al., 2012). Protumorigenic phenotype like neutrophils may work in tandem with tumor-resident mesenchymal stem cells to accelerate cancer growth (Fig. 7.3; Zhang et al., 2014).

The latest discovery of TAN unique markers (CD62L^{lo}, CD54^{hi}) in a patient with lung cancer, including such appearance with a different array of chemokine receptors

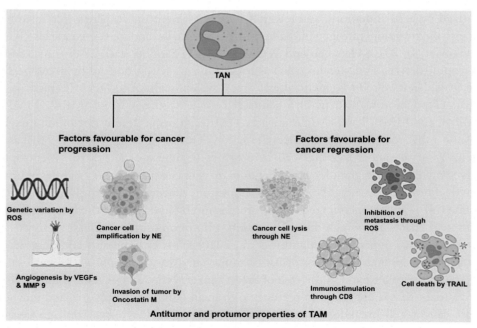

Fig. 7.3 Diagrammatic representation of antitumoral and protumoral properties of the tumor-associated macrophages.

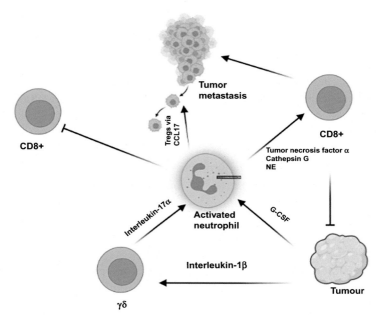

Fig. 7.4 Various outcomes of the interplay among T lymphocytes and neutrophils against tumor progression and metastasis.

including CCR5, CCR7, CXCR3, and CXCR4, suggests further scientific research confirm TAN-specific NETosis could be achievable (Eruslanov et al., 2014). TANs from developed tumors release CCL17 or CCL22, which attracts immunosuppressive regulatory T cells (Tregs) exhibiting faulty destructive capabilities to the tumor, suppressing potential anticancer defense. TANs from nascent tumors have been more lethal against tumor cells, comparable to TAMs, whereas TANs-derived mature tumors gain a rather more protumoral character, demonstrating how TME evolution affects TAN behavior (Fig. 7.4; Mishalian et al., 2013, 2014). Regarding TAMs, it is indeed unclear whether TAN activation is bidirectional, and it has been proposed that perhaps the N1- and N2-like morphologies of neutrophil populations are caused by various intensities of stimulation instead of polarization. A vital issue around whether TANs can be regulated to endure stark permanent stimulation or perhaps reverse activating phases goes unresolved, and much more studies are needed (Kim and Bae, 2016).

7.5 Factors affecting recruitment of TANs into the tumor

TAM and TAN progenitors are believed to be localized inside the spleen, wherefrom these leukocytes physically move toward the TME, and also that CXCL8 (IL-8), a neutrophil chemoattractant, is indeed important for TAN mobilization. TANs are also not "stem-cell G-MDSCs" regulated by the TME, according to new transcriptomics, there is a distinct subpopulation of neutrophils through both bones hematopoietic stem cell-derived neutrophils and G-MDSCs derived. Furthermore, it is unclear yet if the bulk of TANs is G-MDSCs that have already been attracted toward the tumor or bone marrow/blood-derived neutrophils that have been transformed to N2 TANs in the TME particularly owing to excessive local TGF levels (Fridlender et al., 2009; Fridlender et al., 2012; Cortez-Retamozo et al., 2012).

There are three main stages of the assemblage of the neutrophils toward tumor sites from bone marrow that are as under

➤ Proliferation and maturity of the immature neutrophil cells.
➤ Invasion of the neutrophils into the blood by attaching themselves to the endothelium.
➤ Neutrophil chemotaxis toward tumor environments (Wu et al., 2019).

HSCs are the mother cells from which immature neutrophils are obtained. There is vital management of granulocyte-colony-stimulating factor (G-CSF) and GM-CSF for the expansion and maturation of these cells. The nuclear morphological transformation of the neutrophil development includes the original round-shape nucleus eventually becoming a segment-shaped nucleus—as well as modifications in membrane antigen presentation, such as CD65 and CD16—are all part of neutrophil maturity (Wu et al., 2019). The interaction of CXCR4 and CXCR2, as well as their substrates, is crucial for neutrophil translocation in stem cells. These two effectors are part of the CXC chemokine receptor superfamily as GPCRs. CXCR4 and CXCR2 are found on the neutrophil's interface and cross seven times the bilayer. CXCR4 helps neutrophils find their way back to the stem cells. CXCR4 as well as its substrates (such as CXCL12) with elevated amounts would limit neutrophil motility (Martin et al., 2003; Chow and Luster, 2014; Eash et al., 2010). The CXCR2 receptor, on the other hand, is solely accountable for regulating neutrophil discharge to the vasculature, whereas CXCR2, CXCR2 ligands, and G-CSF work with each other to promote neutrophils mobilization (Furze and Rankin, 2008). The neutrophil gradient is regulated by hostile communication between CXCR2 and CXCR4 (Martin et al., 2003; Eash et al., 2010). The overexpression of CXCR2 implies that developed neutrophils have been mobilized toward the bloodstream. Conversely, as CXCR4 levels rise within older neutrophils, they would retreat toward the bone marrow and then be eaten via phagocytosis (Hong, 2017). Interaction among CXCR2 with its substrates CXCL1–3 and CXCL5–8 is indeed required for neutrophils recruitment toward tumor locations (Belperio et al., 2002; Sharma et al., 2013). CXCR2 component is indeed the main member in neutrophils mobilization to tumor locations in disease cancer (Fridlender and Albelda, 2012). There are various cellular subtypes in the TME that usually give rise to CXCR2 chemokines such cells are CAFs, various immune cell types, and tumor cells (Wu et al., 2019). The above collaborators would then generate CXCR2 chemokines into the bloodstream when neutrophil mobilization is required. These neutrophils would then travel along a favorable chemo-tactic shift toward the CXCR2 agonists with greater quantities. Such chemotaxis requires both of the activation of CXCR2 on the surface of neutrophils and the synthesis of CXCR2 mediators. If CXCR2 levels are inhibited, it will result in the retentivity of the neutrophils inside bone marrow. It also results in reduction of neutrophil congrega-tion (Eash et al., 2010; Wu et al., 2019).

According to the prior findings it has been well established that a number of helpful promoters including IL-17 and G-CSF that increase the infiltration of the neutrophils. Macrophages and various types of endothelial cells as well as cancerous cells can give rise to a cytokine called G-CSF-1 (Wu et al., 2019). Along with neutrophil deployment, G-CSF is recognized to play a key function in neutrophil multiplication, development, and efficiency (Chow and Luster, 2014; Yang et al., 2014; Gentles et al., 2015; Fridlender and Albelda, 2012; Lorente et al., 2015; Mir et al., 2022a). Via downregulation of CXCR4 as well as its mediator, CXCL12, G-CSF promotes neutrophils movement (Gabrilovich and Nagaraj, 2009). Here, we can say that recruitment of the neutrophils toward tumor sites depends on the CXCR2, CXCR4 and their corresponding ligands (Eash et al., 2010). IL-17 is another important component in neutrophil mobilization. IL-17A-F are the 6 representatives of the IL-17 family. Because IL-17A is perhaps the eminently well-known component of this superfamily, its often referred to as IL-17. G-CSF, IL-6, CCL2 (MCP-1), and CXCR2 substrates are among the growth factors and cytokines that have been identified to be upregulated by IL-17. The amount of neu-trophils inside the TME is strongly correlated to IL-17. It has been reported to promote the overall release of CXCL1 and CXCL5 of breast carcinoma cells in breast cancer dis-ease models, that aids tumorigenesis. As a result, elevated concentrations of IL-17 in breast cancers are associated with shorter overall life expectancies (Wu et al., 2019).

7.6 Mechanism behind TANs

Inside the TME, there is a constant interplay among "immune cells, stromal cells, and malignant cells" as well (Pietras and Östman, 2010). In a variety of solid tumors, infil-trated neutrophils are observed, which were once thought to be suggestive of a protective immunological response (Ilkovitch and Lopez, 2009; Sionov et al., 2015), there is signif-icant evidence that neutrophils stimulate local tumor development via different signaling pathways like paracrine regulation, take part in cancer proliferation to outlying metastasis (Swierczak et al., 2015; Lechner et al., 2010). According to a new study, cancer cells mediate distinct phenotypic alterations in peripheral blood, these modifications include the transformation of "MDSCs" (Lechner et al., 2010). "CD11b[+], CD33[+], CD66[+]" (Serafini et al., 2006; Zea et al., 2005; Mir and Agrewala, 2008). Myeloid-derived inhib-itor cells have been found to infiltrate tumors and help them grow. These cells migrate inside the tumor and develop into "TANs" (Kusmartsev et al., 2005), which vary from

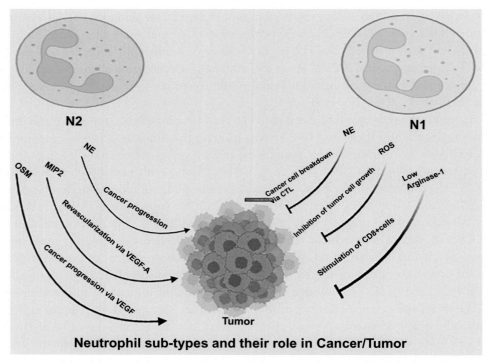

Fig. 7.5 The N1 and N2 neutrophil subtypes and their role in cancer/tumor through various mediators.

normal neutrophils transcriptionally and immunologically. TANs are subgrouped category of neutrophils that are tumor-dependent and diverse, depended on "anti- or protumor" characteristics. N1,N2 are the names for antitumor and protumor phenotypes of TANs, respectively (Fig. 7.5; Fridlender et al., 2009). "IL-1β, TNF-α, IL-6, and IL-12" cytokines are secreted by N1 which cause inflammation along with oxygen radical which kill cancer cells (Uribe-Querol and Rosales, 2015), its functions, on the other hand, gets depleted as cancer progression elevates as well as phenotype N2 shows dominance (Mishalian et al., 2013). Tumor cells influence invading neutrophils inside TME according to many investigations. Genetic variation, cancer disintegration, chemokine, and cytokine signals all attract neutrophils inside TME (Liang and Ferrara, 2016). Particularly through "NF-κB pathway, mutant K-ras" cause IL-8 production in invading neutrophils. Cancer-related signaling pathway is triggered by IL-8 which results in a decrease in "CD8+ and T-cell antitumor responses." PMN degranulation of Arginase-1 is triggered by IL-8 which transfer extracellular "arginine to ornithine to urea." CD3 production is boosted by extracellular arginine in case of T lymphocytes, as a result T lymphocyte become more activated and proliferate, Arginine-1 is required. The immunological response is slowed when extracellular arginine is decreased (Zea et al.,

2005; Rodriguez et al., 2002; Rotondo et al., 2009). Serine proteases, NE, matrix metalloprotease (MMP-9), and cathepsin G are present in TAN's granules, and all are responsible for modulation of cancer development (Houghton et al., 2010; Yui et al., 2014). Especially NE from TANs inside cancer cells attaches to IRS-1. This binding leads to reduce regulative effect of IRS-1 on "Phosphatidylinositol 3-kinase (PI3K)" increase the cancer development via "AKT-dependent pathways" a well-defined mechanism that is elevated in several tumors (Vivanco and Sawyers, 2002; Wadhwa et al., 2020). IL-8 released from tumor cell resulting in TAN, degrading Arginase-1 inside TME. Local $CD8^+$ cells are signaled to enhance their CD3 production, which is a constituent of "T-lymphocyte-TCR-complex" which allow T cells to scan antigens on MHC-1, inhabiting this receptor, T cells are unable to participate in immunological response. So that the Arginnase-1 introduced inside TME by TANs reduces the quantity of Arginine as well as its production, and eventually the stimulation of local $CD8^+$ T cells (Deng et al., 2021).

Two main receptors play a major role in neutrophil chemotaxis including CXCR-1 and CXCR-2. For cancer progression, cancerous cells show different ligands for CXCR-1 and CXCR-2 that in turn assists the employment of TANs toward the tumor site. It has been seen in mouse models that the cytokines like TNF-α are also taking part in the process of neutrophil appointment as well perseverance in the TME. It has separately been studied in two mice breast cancer models that γ and Δ T lymphocytes produce IL-17, that aids in tumor progression, neutrophil employment as well as tumor metastasis (Powell and Huttenlocher, 2016). A chemotactic concentration of tumor-secreted substances continuously recruits neutrophils toward the TME. CXCL8/IL-8 as well as similar proinflammatory cytokines are produced in response to cancer progression (Lazennec and Richmond, 2010; Sparmann and Bar-Sagi, 2004). It has been well studied by Bellocq et al. that there is an intimate relationship in-between the neutrophil number and IL-8, while observing bronchioloalveolar cancer patients, this experiment suggests that IL-8 plays a significant role in the neutrophil recruitment along the cancer microenvironments (Bellocq et al., 1998). Neutrophils also secrete MMP-9 which also aids in neutrophil recruitment along with the tumor sites via CXCL5 (Song et al., 2013).

There is a restricted number of immune secretions by which normal neutrophils get converted into TANs and then affect tumor progression and metastasis which are discussed as follows (Gregory and Houghton, 2011).

7.6.1 Various types of chemokines/cytokines acting as immunoeditors

There have already been documented cases of tumor-mediated stimuli inducing protumor actions within leukocytes including neutrophils. In a cell culture experiment, tumor cells produced GM-CSF, which elicited potent synthesis of the IL-6 like mediator OSM by neutrophils that aid in tumor development, progression as well as metastasis of the breast tumor (Queen et al., 2005). On the other hand, OSM stimulates the breast tumor cells to produce more VEGF and was more aggressive in Matrigel infiltration experiments. Additionally, it was also found in another experiment that a component present in established culture derived from HCC tissues stimulated neutrophils to produce hepatocyte growth factor, which boosted tumor cell invasion and metastasis (Imai et al., 2005).

7.6.2 Production of ROS by neutrophils is carcinogenic to humans

There are numerous phagocytic enzymes present in neutrophil phagolysosomes including myeloperoxidase, and NADPH oxidases, that can reduce O_2 to O_2^-. Along with it these O_2^- radicals can be transformed into H_2O_2, a vigorous reactive oxygen species, and afterward, these species are rather converted into a prophylactic HOCl (hypochlorous acid) through myeloperoxidase. Though this mechanism was devised by the host immune system against bacterial membranes it also damages body cells as well resulting in DNA damage and tumor initiation as well as cancer relapse (Gregory and Houghton, 2011; Mir et al., 2022f). Hypochlorous acid, for example, has been found to be carcinogenic in lung epithelial A549 cell lines, with considerable production of abnormalities in HPRT near therapeutic doses (Güngör et al., 2010). On coculturing of neutrophil cell lines with a diverse range of different selected cells, auxiliary point mutations, DNA strand breaks, as well as 8-OHdG precancerous tumors were identified (Knaapen et al., 2006). Additionally hypochlorous acid shows direct antitumor effects through tumor cell membrane disruptions (Dallegri et al., 1991).

7.6.3 Proteolytic enzymes generated from leucocytes help malignancies in both matrix-independent as well as matrix-dependent ways

There are three main proteolytic enzymes produced from neutrophils that play a key role in the tumor amplification, disease progression as well as tumor metastasis including NE, MMP-8, and MMP-9 (Gregory and Houghton, 2011). NE seems to be the most important mediator of neutrophils functioning, accounting for around 2% of the dry weight of neutrophils. Its primary metabolic function appears to be the elimination of intruding microbes (Belaaouaj et al., 1998). NE recognizes a wide range of substances, including cytokines, their receptors, and integrins, plus practically most ECM elements, such as the relatively innocuous elastic fiber (Lee and Downey, 2001). Expansion experiments revealed that NE entered tumors via clathrin-coated pits and traveled via intracellular compartments, marking the very first confirmation of a soluble proteinase's capacity to penetrate a particular cell's lipid bilayer. NE has ingress to a vast range of possible targets between endosomal and endosome associated proteins after it has gained access to the tumor cell. Expansion experiments revealed that NE entered tumors via clathrin-coated pits and traveled via intracellular compartments, marking the very first confirmation of a soluble proteinase's capacity to penetrate a particular cell's lipid bilayer. NE has ingressed a vast range of possible targets between endosomal and endosome-associated proteins after it has gained access to the tumor cell. Researchers discovered IRS-1 a target for NE-mediated degradation between these putative components. IRS-1 is a recognized PI3K regulatory element p85. This reservoir of accessible p85 increases when IRS-1 is degraded, allowing this to bind with much more robust growth factors, especially platelet-derived growth factor receptor (PDGFR). The phosphoinositide 3-kinase pathway's activation promotes abnormal lung tumor progression (Houghton et al., 2010; Mir et al., 2022g). MMPs are catalysts that have broad substrate specificity, link basic elements, and are inhibited via tissue metalloproteinase inhibitors. Several varieties of the cells inside the TME, such as all hematopoietic cells and fibroblast cells, express matrix metalloproteinase-9 also called gelatinase B (Kessenbrock et al., 2010). Coussens and his colleagues were the first to fully describe the fact that MMP-9 majorly contributes to tumor proliferation and they reveal that MMP-9 deficient epidermal tumor model exhibited abased keratinocyte hyperproliferation in HPV16 (Coussens et al., 2000). Using the neutrophil specific 7/4 antibodies in immunofluorescence and flow cytometry assays, this research reveals that neutrophils are the exclusive makers of matrix metalloproteinase-9 in the TME, giving credible proof favoring TAN as the production of organic matrix metalloproteinase-9 within the TME (Gregory and Houghton, 2011). There is further need of studies to fully understand the dual roles of TANs in TMEs and their recruitments toward TME via various signaling pathways (Table 7.2).

Table 7.2 Various kinds of strategies employed by the cells of TME to subvert and evade various immune mechanisms used by the host body against tumor.

S. no.	Strategy	Effector molecule	Effect on host cell
1.	Stimulation of CAFs	TGF-β and CXCL12	Cancer progression
2.	Transformation of fibroblasts into CAFs	Caveolin-1	Facilitator of CAF activation
3.	Recruitment of neutrophils toward tumor site	CXCL12 and CXCL14	Tumorigenesis
4.	Increase in neutrophil count	GM-CSF	Lowers the chances of breast cancer recovery
5.	Modulation of the apoptosis	p53	Reduces apoptosis and enhances tumor growth
6.	Neutrophil chemoattractant	CXCL8	TAN mobilization
7.	Conversion of extracellular arginine to ornithine to urea	Arginase-1	Immunological suppression
8.	Activation of STAT-1 and STAT-3	IL-6	Tumor proliferation and metastasis
9.	Conversion of stromal cells onto the CAFs	Paracrine growth factors	Growth and progression of tumor

7.7 Summary

In the current era, despite having advanced comprehensive medical facilities, cancer is rising at an alarming rate especially breast cancer in females and various other types of cancers whose mortality rate is increasing at an alarming rate. Scientists are anxiously studying the TME and the associated cells so that they can even lessen the cancer burden on the earth. There are several cellular subtypes associated with the TME, but neutrophils are gaining a lot of attention as these are basic immune cells that are produced upon the early onset of inflammation. There is further need for research to target neutrophils as a medication against tumors and cancers as these are basic immune cells present in the TMEs. There are several types of antitumor or anticancer drugs, but they are unable to level down such a cancer rate due to various circumstances including the ineffectiveness of drugs, host-self cells, and host own immune cells that help in cancer progression and metastasis. So, there is an urgent need for specific medications in the form of immunotherapy, magic bullets, etc. that can help to tackle such a dreadful disease in the future (Mir et al., 2022e). We hope that new therapeutic approaches would be beneficial for mankind and advancements in cancer or tumor treatments will be seen in near future.

References

Al-Hajj, M., Wicha, M.S., Benito-Hernandez, A., Morrison, S.J., Clarke, M.F., 2003. Prospective identification of tumorigenic breast cancer cells. Proc. Natl. Acad. Sci. U. S. A. 100, 3983–3988.

Allinen, M., Beroukhim, R., Cai, L., Brennan, C., Lahti-Domenici, J., Huang, H., Porter, D., Hu, M., Chin, L., Richardson, A., 2004. Molecular characterization of the tumor microenvironment in breast cancer. Cancer Cell 6, 17–32.

Batlle, E., Massagué, J., 2019. Transforming growth factor-β signaling in immunity and cancer. Immunity 50, 924–940.

Belaaouaj, A., McCarthy, R., Baumann, M., Gao, Z., Ley, T.J., Abraham, S.N., Shapiro, S.D., 1998. Mice lacking neutrophil elastase reveal impaired host defense against gram negative bacterial sepsis. Nat. Med. 4, 615–618.

Bellocq, A., Antoine, M., Flahault, A., Philippe, C., Crestani, B., Bernaudin, J.-F., Mayaud, C., Milleron, B., Baud, L., Cadranel, J., 1998. Neutrophil alveolitis in bronchioloalveolar carcinoma: induction by tumor-derived interleukin-8 and relation to clinical outcome. Am. J. Pathol. 152, 83.

Belperio, J.A., Keane, M.P., Burdick, M.D., Londhe, V., Xue, Y.Y., Li, K., Phillips, R.J., Strieter, R.M., 2002. Critical role for CXCR2 and CXCR2 ligands during the pathogenesis of ventilator-induced lung injury. J. Clin. Invest. 110, 1703–1716.

Brown, E., Charles, K., Hoare, S., Rye, R., Jodrell, D., Aird, R., Vora, R., Prabhakar, U., Nakada, M., Corringham, R., 2008. A clinical study assessing the tolerability and biological effects of infliximab, a TNF-α inhibitor, in patients with advanced cancer. Ann. Oncol. 19, 1340–1346.

Castriconi, R., Daga, A., Dondero, A., Zona, G., Poliani, P.L., Melotti, A., Griffero, F., Marubbi, D., Spaziante, R., Bellora, F., 2009. NK cells recognize and kill human glioblastoma cells with stem cell-like properties. J. Immunol. 182, 3530–3539.

Chow, M.T., Luster, A.D., 2014. Chemokines in cancer. Cancer Immunol. Res. 2, 1125–1131.

Coffelt, S.B., Wellenstein, M.D., De Visser, K.E., 2016. Neutrophils in cancer: neutral no more. Nat. Rev. Cancer 16, 431–446.

Cortez-Retamozo, V., Etzrodt, M., Newton, A., Rauch, P.J., Chudnovskiy, A., Berger, C., Ryan, R.J., Iwamoto, Y., Marinelli, B., Gorbatov, R., 2012. Origins of tumor-associated macrophages and neutrophils. Proc. Natl. Acad. Sci. U. S. A. 109, 2491–2496.

Coussens, L.M., Tinkle, C.L., Hanahan, D., Werb, Z., 2000. MMP-9 supplied by bone marrow-derived cells contributes to skin carcinogenesis. Cell 103, 481–490.

Coussens, L.M., Zitvogel, L., Palucka, A.K., 2013. Neutralizing tumor-promoting chronic inflammation: a magic bullet? Science 339, 286–291.

Dallegri, F., Ottonello, L., Ballestrero, A., Dapino, P., Ferrando, F., Patrone, F., Sacchetti, C., 1991. Tumor cell lysis by activated human neutrophils: analysis of neutrophil-delivered oxidative attack and role of leukocyte function-associated antigen 1. Inflammation 15, 15–30.

Danial, N.N., Korsmeyer, S.J., 2004. Cell death: critical control points. Cell 116, 205–219.

De Visser, K.E., Eichten, A., Coussens, L.M., 2006. Paradoxical roles of the immune system during cancer development. Nat. Rev. Cancer 6, 24–37.

Deng, X.-X., Jiao, Y.-N., Hao, H.-F., Xue, D., Bai, C.-C., Han, S.-Y., 2021. Taraxacum mongolicum extract inhibited malignant phenotype of triple-negative breast cancer cells in tumor-associated macrophages microenvironment through suppressing IL-10/STAT3/PD-L1 signaling pathways. J. Ethnopharmacol. 274, 113978.

Dunn, G.P., Koebel, C.M., Schreiber, R.D., 2006. Interferons, immunity and cancer immunoediting. Nat. Rev. Immunol. 6, 836–848.

Eash, K.J., Greenbaum, A.M., Gopalan, P.K., Link, D.C., 2010. Cxcr2 and CXCR4 antagonistically regulate neutrophil trafficking from murine bone marrow. J. Clin. Invest. 120, 2423–2431.

Eruslanov, E.B., Bhojnagarwala, P.S., Quatromoni, J.G., Stephen, T.L., Ranganathan, A., Deshpande, C., Akimova, T., Vachani, A., Litzky, L., Hancock, W.W., 2014. Tumor-associated neutrophils stimulate T cell responses in early-stage human lung cancer. J. Clin. Invest. 124, 5466–5480.

Fan, C., Oh, D.S., Wessels, L., Weigelt, B., Nuyten, D.S., Nobel, A.B., Van'T Veer, L.J., Perou, C.M., 2006. Concordance among gene-expression-based predictors for breast cancer. N. Engl. J. Med. 355, 560–569.

Feng, M., Jiang, W., Kim, B., Zhang, C.C., Fu, Y.-X., Weissman, I.L., 2019. Phagocytosis checkpoints as new targets for cancer immunotherapy. Nat. Rev. Cancer 19, 568–586.

Flavell, R.A., Sanjabi, S., Wrzesinski, S.H., Licona-Limón, P., 2010. The polarization of immune cells in the tumour environment by Tgfβ. Nat. Rev. Immunol. 10, 554–567.

Fridlender, Z.G., Albelda, S.M., 2012. Tumor-associated neutrophils: friend or foe? Carcinogenesis 33, 949–955.

Fridlender, Z.G., Sun, J., Kim, S., Kapoor, V., Cheng, G., Ling, L., Worthen, G.S., Albelda, S.M., 2009. Polarization of tumor-associated neutrophil phenotype by TGF-β:"N1" versus "N2" TAN. Cancer Cell 16, 183–194.

Fridlender, Z.G., Sun, J., Mishalian, I., Singhal, S., Cheng, G., Kapoor, V., Horng, W., Fridlender, G., Bayuh, R., Worthen, G.S., 2012. Transcriptomic analysis comparing tumor-associated neutrophils with granulocytic myeloid-derived suppressor cells and normal neutrophils. PLoS One 7, e31524.

Fridman, W.H., Zitvogel, L., Sautès-Fridman, C., Kroemer, G., 2017. The immune contexture in cancer prognosis and treatment. Nat. Rev. Clin. Oncol. 14, 717–734.

Furze, R.C., Rankin, S.M., 2008. Neutrophil mobilization and clearance in the bone marrow. Immunology 125, 281–288.

Gabrilovich, D.I., Nagaraj, S., 2009. Myeloid-derived suppressor cells as regulators of the immune system. Nat. Rev. Immunol. 9, 162–174.

Galdiero, M.R., Bonavita, E., Barajon, I., Garlanda, C., Mantovani, A., Jaillon, S., 2013. Tumor associated macrophages and neutrophils in cancer. Immunobiology 218, 1402–1410.

Gentles, A.J., Newman, A.M., Liu, C.L., Bratman, S.V., Feng, W., Kim, D., Nair, V.S., Xu, Y., Khuong, A., Hoang, C.D., 2015. The prognostic landscape of genes and infiltrating immune cells across human cancers. Nat. Med. 21, 938–945.

Gregory, A.D., Houghton, A.M., 2011. Tumor-associated neutrophils: new targets for cancer therapy. Cancer Res. 71, 2411–2416.

Grivennikov, S.I., Greten, F.R., Karin, M., 2010. Immunity, inflammation, and cancer. Cell 140, 883–899.

Güngör, N., Knaapen, A.M., Munnia, A., Peluso, M., Haenen, G.R., Chiu, R.K., Godschalk, R.W., Van Schooten, F.J., 2010. Genotoxic effects of neutrophils and hypochlorous acid. Mutagenesis 25, 149–154.

Hanahan, D., Weinberg, R.A., 2011. Hallmarks of cancer: the next generation. Cell 144, 646–674.

Hiam-Galvez, K.J., Allen, B.M., Spitzer, M.H., 2021. Systemic immunity in cancer. Nat. Rev. Cancer 21, 345–359.

Hinshaw, D.C., Shevde, L.A., 2019. The tumor microenvironment innately modulates cancer progression. Cancer Res. 79, 4557–4566.

Hong, C.-W., 2017. Current understanding in neutrophil differentiation and heterogeneity. Immune Netw. 17, 298–306.

Houghton, A.M., Rzymkiewicz, D.M., Ji, H., Gregory, A.D., Egea, E.E., Metz, H.E., Stolz, D.B., Land, S.-R., Marconcini, L.A., Kliment, C.R., 2010. Neutrophil elastase–mediated degradation of IRS-1 accelerates lung tumor growth. Nat. Med. 16, 219–223.

Humbert, P., Russell, S., Richardson, H., 2003. Dlg, Scribble and Lgl in cell polarity, cell proliferation and cancer. Bioessays 25, 542–553.

Ilkovitch, D., Lopez, D.M., 2009. The liver is a site for tumor-induced myeloid-derived suppressor cell accumulation and immunosuppression. Cancer Res. 69, 5514–5521.

Imai, Y., Kubota, Y., Yamamoto, S., Tsuji, K., Shimatani, M., Shibatani, N., Takamido, S., Matsushita, M., Okazaki, K., 2005. Neutrophils enhance invasion activity of human cholangiocellular carcinoma and hepatocellular carcinoma cells: an in vitro study. J. Gastroenterol. Hepatol. 20, 287–293.

Jablonska, J., Leschner, S., Westphal, K., Lienenklaus, S., Weiss, S., 2010. Neutrophils responsive to endogenous IFN-β regulate tumor angiogenesis and growth in a mouse tumor model. J. Clin. Invest. 120, 1151–1164.

Janes, S.M., Watt, F.M., 2006. New roles for integrins in squamous-cell carcinoma. Nat. Rev. Cancer 6, 175–183.

Ji, H., Houghton, A., Mariani, T., Perera, S., Kim, C., Padera, R., Tonon, G., McNamara, K., Marconcini, L., Hezel, A., 2006. K-ras activation generates an inflammatory response in lung tumors. Oncogene 25, 2105–2112.

Kalluri, R., Weinberg, R.A., 2009. The basics of epithelial-mesenchymal transition. J1786. Clin. Invest. 119 (6), 1420–1428.

Kalluri, R., Zeisberg, M., 2006. Fibroblasts in cancer. Nat. Rev. Cancer 6, 392–401.

Kessenbrock, K., Plaks, V., Werb, Z., 2010. Matrix metalloproteinases: regulators of the tumor microenvironment. Cell 141, 52–67.

Khan, S.U., Pathania, A.S., Wani, A., Fatima, K., Mintoo, M.J., Hamza, B., Paddar, M.A., Bhumika, W., Anand, L.K., Maqbool, M.S., 2022. Activation of lysosomal mediated cell death in the course of autophagy by mTORC1 inhibitor. Sci. Rep. 12, 1–13.

Kim, J., Bae, J.-S., 2016. Tumor-associated macrophages and neutrophils in tumor microenvironment. Mediators Inflamm. 2016.

Knaapen, A.M., Güngör, N., Schins, R.P., Borm, P.J., Van Schooten, F.J., 2006. Neutrophils and respiratory tract DNA damage and mutagenesis: a review. Mutagenesis 21, 225–236.

Kojima, Y., Acar, A., Eaton, E.N., Mellody, K.T., Scheel, C., Ben-Porath, I., Onder, T.T., Wang, Z.C., Richardson, A.L., Weinberg, R.A., 2010. Autocrine TGF-β and stromal cell-derived factor-1 (Sdf-1) signaling drives the evolution of tumor-promoting mammary stromal myofibroblasts. Proc. Natl. Acad. Sci. U. S. A. 107, 20009–20014.

Koleske, A.J., Baltimore, D., Lisanti, M.P., 1995. Reduction of caveolin and caveolae in oncogenically transformed cells. Proc. Natl. Acad. Sci. U. S. A. 92, 1381–1385.

Kusmartsev, S., Nagaraj, S., Gabrilovich, D.I., 2005. Tumor-associated CD8+ T cell tolerance induced by bone marrow-derived immature myeloid cells. J. Immunol. 175, 4583–4592.

Laoui, D., Movahedi, K., Van Overmeire, E., Van Den Bossche, J., Schouppe, E., Mommer, C., Nikolaou, A., Morias, Y., De Baetselier, P., Van Ginderachter, J.A., 2011. Tumor-associated macrophages in breast cancer: distinct subsets, distinct functions. Int. J. Dev. Biol. 55, 861–867.

Lazennec, G., Richmond, A., 2010. Chemokines and chemokine receptors: new insights into cancer-related inflammation. Trends Mol. Med. 16, 133–144.

Lechner, M.G., Liebertz, D.J., Epstein, A.L., 2010. Characterization of cytokine-induced myeloid-derived suppressor cells from normal human peripheral blood mononuclear cells. J. Immunol. 185, 2273–2284.

Lee, W.L., Downey, G.P., 2001. Leukocyte elastase: physiological functions and role in acute lung injury. Am. J. Respir. Crit. Care Med. 164, 896–904.

Li, M.O., Flavell, R.A., 2008. Contextual regulation of inflammation: a duet by transforming growth factor-β and interleukin-10. Immunity 28, 468–476.

Liang, W., Ferrara, N., 2016. The complex role of neutrophils in tumor angiogenesis and metastasis. Cancer Immunol. Res. 4, 83–91.

Löhr, M., Schmidt, C., Ringel, J., Kluth, M., Müller, P., Nizze, H., Jesnowski, R., 2001. Transforming growth factor-β1 induces desmoplasia in an experimental model of human pancreatic carcinoma. Cancer Res. 61, 550–555.

Lorente, D., Mateo, J., Templeton, A., Zafeiriou, Z., Bianchini, D., Ferraldeschi, R., Bahl, A., Shen, L., Su, Z., Sartor, O., 2015. Baseline neutrophil–lymphocyte ratio (NLR) is associated with survival and response to treatment with second-line chemotherapy for advanced prostate cancer independent of baseline steroid use. Ann. Oncol. 26, 750–755.

MacMahon, B., 2006. Epidemiology and the causes of breast cancer. Int. J. Cancer 118, 2373–2378.

Mamessier, E., Sylvain, A., Thibult, M.-L., Houvenaeghel, G., Jacquemier, J., Castellano, R., Gonçalves, A., André, P., Romagné, F., Thibault, G., 2011. Human breast cancer cells enhance self tolerance by promoting evasion from NK cell antitumor immunity. J. Clin. Invest. 121, 3609–3622.

Mantovani, A., Bottazzi, B., Colotta, F., Sozzani, S., Ruco, L., 1992. The origin and function of tumor-associated macrophages. Immunol. Today 13, 265–270.

Mantovani, A., Cassatella, M.A., Costantini, C., Jaillon, S., 2011. Neutrophils in the activation and regulation of innate and adaptive immunity. Nat. Rev. Immunol. 11, 519–531.

Mao, Y., Keller, E.T., Garfield, D.H., Shen, K., Wang, J., 2013. Stromal cells in tumor microenvironment and breast cancer. Cancer Metastasis Rev. 32, 303–315.

Martin, C., Burdon, P.C., Bridger, G., Gutierrez-Ramos, J.-C., Williams, T.J., Rankin, S.M., 2003. Chemokines acting via CXCR2 and CXCR4 control the release of neutrophils from the bone marrow and their return following senescence. Immunity 19, 583–593.

McGary, C.T., Miele, M.E., Welch, D.R., 1995. Highly metastatic 13762NF rat mammary adenocarcinoma cell clones stimulate bone marrow by secretion of granulocyte-macrophage colony-stimulating factor/interleukin-3 activity. Am. J. Pathol. 147, 1668.

Mehraj, U., Dar, A.H., Wani, N.A., Mir, M.A., 2021a. Tumor microenvironment promotes breast cancer chemoresistance. Cancer Chemother. Pharmacol. 87, 147–158.

Mehraj, U., Qayoom, H., Mir, M.A., 2021b. Prognostic significance and targeting tumor-associated macrophages in cancer: new insights and future perspectives. Breast Cancer 28, 539–555.

Mehraj, U., Aisha, S., Sofi, S., Mir, M.A., 2022a. Expression pattern and prognostic significance of baculoviral inhibitor of apoptosis repeat-containing 5 (BIRC5) in breast cancer: a comprehensive analysis. Adv. Cancer Biol. Metastasis, 100037.

Mehraj, U., Mushtaq, U., Mir, M.A., Saleem, A., Macha, M.A., Lone, M.N., Hamid, A., Zargar, M.A., Ahmad, S.M., Wani, N.A., 2022b. Chemokines in triple-negative breast cancer heterogeneity: new challenges for clinical implications. Semin. Cancer Biol. https://doi.org/10.1016/j.semcancer.2022.03.008. Elsevier.

Mir, M.A., Agrewala, J.N., 2008. Signaling through CD80: an approach for treating lymphomas. Expert Opin. Ther. Targets 12, 969–979.

Mir, M.A., Mehraj, U., 2019. Double-crosser of the immune system: macrophages in tumor progression and metastasis. Curr. Immunol. Rev. 15, 172–184.

Mir, M., Jan, S., Mehraj, U., 2022a. Conventional Adjuvant Chemotherapy in Combination With Surgery, Radiotherapy and Other Specific Targets. Elsevier (Chapter 4).

Mir, M., Jan, S., Mehraj, U., 2022b. Current Therapeutics and Treatment Options in TNBC. Elsevier (Chapter 3).

Mir, M., Jan, S., Mehraj, U., 2022c. Novel Biomarkers In Triple-Negative Breast Cancer—Role and Perspective. Elsevier (Chapter 2).

Mir, M., Jan, S., Mehraj, U., 2022d. Triple-Negative Breast Cancer—An Aggressive Subtype of Breast Cancer. Elsevier.

Mir, M., Sofi, S., Qayoom, H., 2022e. Different Drug Delivery Approaches in Combinational Therapy in TNBC. Elsevier (Chapter 8).

Mir, M., Sofi, S., Qayoom, H., 2022f. Role of Immune System in Triple Negative Breast Cancer (TNBC). Elsevier (Chapter 5).

Mir, M., Sofi, S., Qayoom, H., 2022g. Targeting Biologically Specific Molecules in Triple Negative Breast Cancer (TNBC). Elsevier (Chapter 7).

Mishalian, I., Bayuh, R., Levy, L., Zolotarov, L., Michaeli, J., Fridlender, Z.G., 2013. Tumor-associated neutrophils (TAN) develop pro-tumorigenic properties during tumor progression. Cancer Immunol. Immunother. 62, 1745–1756.

Mishalian, I., Bayuh, R., Eruslanov, E., Michaeli, J., Levy, L., Zolotarov, L., Singhal, S., Albelda, S.M., Granot, Z., Fridlender, Z.G., 2014. Neutrophils recruit regulatory T-cells into tumors via secretion of CCL17—a new mechanism of impaired antitumor immunity. Int. J. Cancer 135, 1178–1186.

Murakami, Y., Saito, H., Shimizu, S., Kono, Y., Shishido, Y., Miyatani, K., Matsunaga, T., Fukumoto, Y., Ashida, K., Sakabe, T., 2019. Increased regulatory B cells are involved in immune evasion in patients with gastric cancer. Sci. Rep. 9, 1–9.

Netea-Maier, R.T., Smit, J.W., Netea, M.G., 2018. Metabolic changes in tumor cells and tumor-associated macrophages: a mutual relationship. Cancer Lett. 413, 102–109.

Noy, R., Pollard, J.W., 2014. Tumor-associated macrophages: from mechanisms to therapy. Immunity 41, 49–61.

Olkhanud, P.B., Damdinsuren, B., Bodogai, M., Gress, R.E., Sen, R., Wejksza, K., Malchinkhuu, E., Wersto, R.P., Biragyn, A., 2011. Tumor-evoked regulatory B cells promote breast cancer metastasis by converting resting CD4 + T cells to T-regulatory cells. Cancer Res. 71, 3505–3515.

Orimo, A., Gupta, P.B., Sgroi, D.C., Arenzana-Seisdedos, F., Delaunay, T., Naeem, R., Carey, V.J., Richardson, A.L., Weinberg, R.A., 2005. Stromal fibroblasts present in invasive human breast carcinomas promote tumor growth and angiogenesis through elevated SDF-1/Cxcl12 secretion. Cell 121, 335–348.

Östman, A., Augsten, M., 2009. Cancer-associated fibroblasts and tumor growth—bystanders turning into key players. Curr. Opin. Genet. Dev. 19, 67–73.

Pekarek, L.A., Starr, B.A., Toledano, A.Y., Schreiber, H., 1995. Inhibition of tumor growth by elimination of granulocytes. J. Exp. Med. 181, 435–440.

Perou, C.M., Sørlie, T., Eisen, M.B., Van De Rijn, M., Jeffrey, S.S., Rees, C.A., Pollack, J.R., Ross, D.T., Johnsen, H., Akslen, L.A., 2000. Molecular portraits of human breast tumours. Nature 406, 747–752.

Pietras, K., Östman, A., 2010. Hallmarks of cancer: interactions with the tumor stroma. Exp. Cell Res. 316, 1324–1331.

Poczobutt, J.M., De, S., Yadav, V.K., Nguyen, T.T., Li, H., Sippel, T.R., Weiser-Evans, M.C., Nemenoff, R.A., 2016. Expression profiling of macrophages reveals multiple populations with distinct biological roles in an immunocompetent orthotopic model of lung cancer. J. Immunol. 196, 2847–2859.

Polyak, K., 2007. Breast cancer: origins and evolution. J. Clin. Invest. 117, 3155–3163.

Powell, D.R., Huttenlocher, A., 2016. Neutrophils in the tumor microenvironment. Trends Immunol. 37, 41–52.

Qayoom, H., Mehraj, U., Aisha, S., Sofi, S., Mir, M.A., 2021. Integrating immunotherapy with chemotherapy: a new approach to drug repurposing. Drug Repurposing, first ed. vol. 1 IntechOpen, UK, pp. 1–37.

Qian, B.-Z., Pollard, J.W., 2010. Macrophage diversity enhances tumor progression and metastasis. Cell 141, 39–51.

Queen, M.M., Ryan, R.E., Holzer, R.G., Keller-Peck, C.R., Jorcyk, C.L., 2005. Breast cancer cells stimulate neutrophils to produce oncostatin M: potential implications for tumor progression. Cancer Res. 65, 8896–8904.

Rodriguez, P.C., Zea, A.H., Culotta, K.S., Zabaleta, J., Ochoa, J.B., Ochoa, A.C., 2002. Regulation of t cell receptor cd3ζ chain expression by L-arginine. J. Biol. Chem. 277, 21123–21129.

Rotondo, R., Barisione, G., Mastracci, L., Grossi, F., Orengo, A.M., Costa, R., Truini, M., Fabbi, M., Ferrini, S., Barbieri, O., 2009. IL-8 induces exocytosis of arginase 1 by neutrophil polymorphonuclears in nonsmall cell lung cancer. Int. J. Cancer 125, 887–893.

Sandhu, J.K., Privora, H.F., Wenckebach, G., Birnboim, H.C., 2000. Neutrophils, nitric oxide synthase, and mutations in the mutatect murine tumor model. Am. J. Pathol. 156, 509–518.

Sanjabi, S., Oh, S.A., Li, M.O., 2017. Regulation of the immune response by TGF-β: from conception to autoimmunity and infection. Cold Spring Harb. Perspect. Biol. 9, a022236.

Scapini, P., Morini, M., Tecchio, C., Minghelli, S., Di Carlo, E., Tanghetti, E., Albini, A., Lowell, C., Berton, G., Noonan, D.M., 2004. CXCL1/macrophage inflammatory protein-2-induced angiogenesis in vivo is mediated by neutrophil-derived vascular endothelial growth factor-A. J. Immunol. 172, 5034–5040.

Schreiber, R.D., Old, L.J., Smyth, M.J., 2011. Cancer immunoediting: integrating immunity's roles in cancer suppression and promotion. Science 331, 1565–1570.

Serafini, P., Borrello, I., Bronte, V., 2006. Myeloid suppressor cells in cancer: recruitment, phenotype, properties, and mechanisms of immune suppression. Semin. Cancer Biol., 53–65. Elsevier.

Sharma, B., Nawandar, D.M., Nannuru, K.C., Varney, M.L., Singh, R.K., 2013. Targeting CXCR2 enhances chemotherapeutic response, inhibits mammary tumor growth, angiogenesis, and lung metastasis. Mol. Cancer Ther. 12, 799–808.

Siegel, R., Ma, J., Zou, Z., Jemal, A., 2014. Cancer statistics, 2014. CA Cancer J. Clin. 64, 9–29.

Sionov, R.V., Fridlender, Z.G., Granot, Z., 2015. The multifaceted roles neutrophils play in the tumor microenviron. Cancer Microenviron. 8, 125–158.

Song, J., Wu, C., Zhang, X., Sorokin, L.M., 2013. In vivo processing of CXCL5 (LIX) by matrix metalloproteinase (MMP)-2 and MMP-9 promotes early neutrophil recruitment in IL-1β–induced peritonitis. J. Immunol. 190, 401–410.

Sørlie, T., Perou, C.M., Tibshirani, R., Aas, T., Geisler, S., Johnsen, H., Hastie, T., Eisen, M.B., Van De Rijn, M., Jeffrey, S.S., 2001. Gene expression patterns of breast carcinomas distinguish tumor subclasses with clinical implications. Proc. Natl. Acad. Sci. U. S. A. 98, 10869–10874.

Sparmann, A., Bar-Sagi, D., 2004. Ras-induced interleukin-8 expression plays a critical role in tumor growth and angiogenesis. Cancer Cell 6, 447–458.

Swierczak, A., Mouchemore, K.A., Hamilton, J.A., Anderson, R.L., 2015. Neutrophils: important contributors to tumor progression and metastasis. Cancer Metastasis Rev. 34, 735–751.

Taborga, M., Corcoran, K.E., Fernandes, N., Ramkissoon, S.H., Rameshwar, P., 2007. G-coupled protein receptors and breast cancer progression: potential drug targets. Mini Rev. Med. Chem. 7, 245–251.

Tazawa, H., Okada, F., Kobayashi, T., Tada, M., Mori, Y., Une, Y., Sendo, F., Kobayashi, M., Hosokawa, M., 2003. Infiltration of neutrophils is required for acquisition of metastatic phenotype of benign murine fibrosarcoma cells: implication of inflammation-associated carcinogenesis and tumor progression. Am. J. Pathol. 163, 2221–2232.

Teng, M.W., Galon, J., Fridman, W.-H., Smyth, M.J., 2015. From mice to humans: developments in cancer immunoediting. J. Clin. Invest. 125, 3338–3346.

Thomson, A.K., Heyworth, J.S., Girschik, J., Slevin, T., Saunders, C., Fritschi, L., 2014. Beliefs and perceptions about the causes of breast cancer: a case-control study. BMC Res. Notes 7, 1–8.

Uribe-Querol, E., Rosales, C., 2015. Neutrophils in cancer: two sides of the same coin. J. Immunol. Res. 2015, 983698. https://doi.org/10.1155/2015/983698.

Verronèse, E., Delgado, A., Valladeau-Guilemond, J., Garin, G., Guillemaut, S., Tredan, O., Ray-Coquard, I., Bachelot, T., N'kodia, A., Bardin-Dit-Courageot, C., 2016. Immune cell dysfunctions in breast cancer patients detected through whole blood multi-parametric flow cytometry assay. Oncoimmunology 5, e1100791.

Vesely, M.D., Kershaw, M.H., Schreiber, R.D., Smyth, M.J., 2011. Natural innate and adaptive immunity to cancer. Annu. Rev. Immunol. 29, 235–271.

Vitale, M., Chiesa, M.D., Carlomagno, S., Pende, D., Arico, M., Moretta, L., Moretta, A., 2005. NK-dependent Dc maturation is mediated by TNFα and IFNγ released upon engagement of the NKp30 triggering receptor. Blood 106, 566–571.

Vivanco, I., Sawyers, C.L., 2002. The phosphatidylinositol 3-kinase–AKT pathway in human cancer. Nat. Rev. Cancer 2, 489–501.

Wadhwa, B., Paddar, M., Khan, S., Mir, S., Clarke, P.A., Grabowska, A.M., Vijay, D.G., Malik, F., 2020. AKT isoforms have discrete expression in triple negative breast cancers and roles in cisplatin sensitivity. Oncotarget 11, 4178.

Wang, W., Yuan, X., Chen, H., Xie, G., Ma, Y., Zheng, Y., Zhou, Y., Shen, L., 2015. CD19+ CD24hiCD38hiBregs involved in downregulate helper T cells and upregulate regulatory T cells in gastric cancer. Oncotarget 6, 33486.

Woo, S.-R., Corrales, L., Gajewski, T.F., 2015. Innate immune recognition of cancer. Annu. Rev. Immunol. 33, 445–474.

Wu, L., Saxena, S., Awaji, M., Singh, R.K., 2019. Tumor-associated neutrophils in cancer: going pro. Cancer 11, 564.

Xue, W., Zender, L., Miething, C., Dickins, R.A., Hernando, E., Krizhanovsky, V., Cordon-Cardo, C., Lowe, S.W., 2007. Senescence and tumour clearance is triggered by p53 restoration in murine liver carcinomas. Nature 445, 656–660.

Yang, B., Kang, H., Fung, A., Zhao, H., Wang, T., Ma, D., 2014. The role of interleukin 17 in tumour proliferation, angiogenesis, and metastasis. Mediators Inflamm. 2014, 623759. https://doi.org/10.1155/2014/623759.

Yu, Y., Xiao, C., Tan, L., Wang, Q., Li, X., Feng, Y., 2014. Cancer-associated fibroblasts induce epithelial–mesenchymal transition of breast cancer cells through paracrine TGF-β signalling. Br. J. Cancer 110, 724–732.

Yuen, G.J., Demissie, E., Pillai, S., 2016. B lymphocytes and cancer: a love–hate relationship. Trends Cancer 2, 747–757.

Yui, S., Osawa, Y., Ichisugi, T., Morimoto-Kamata, R., 2014. Neutrophil cathepsin G, but not elastase, induces aggregation of MCF-7 mammary carcinoma cells by a protease activity-dependent cell-oriented mechanism. Mediators Inflamm. 2014.

Zea, A.H., Rodriguez, P.C., Atkins, M.B., Hernandez, C., Signoretti, S., Zabaleta, J., McDermott, D., Quiceno, D., Youmans, A., O'neill, A., 2005. Arginase-producing myeloid suppressor cells in renal cell carcinoma patients: a mechanism of tumor evasion. Cancer Res. 65, 3044–3048.

Zhang, X., Zhu, Q., Yuan, X., Qian, H., Xu, W., 2014. Mesenchymal stem cells in cancer: a new link to neutrophils. Cancer Cell Microenviron. 1.

Zhou, J., Min, Z., Zhang, D., Wang, W., Marincola, F., Wang, X., 2014. Enhanced frequency and potential mechanism of B regulatory cells in patients with lung cancer. J. Transl. Med. 12, 1–11.

Zlotnik, A., 2006. Chemokines and cancer. Int. J. Cancer 119, 2026–2029.

CHAPTER 8

The extracellular matrix in breast cancer

Manzoor Ahmad Mir and Aabida Gul
Department of Bioresources, School of Biological Sciences, University of Kashmir, Srinagar, Jammu and Kashmir, India

8.1 Introduction

The ability of breast tissue to change structurally during embryonic development, puberty, and pregnancy is notable. Breast development and differentiation at various stages are controlled by the extracellular matrix (ECM) of a breast which is a guiding factor (Wiseman and Werb, 2002). Collagens and glycosaminoglycans, for example, play an essential role in mammary gland development (Wicha et al., 1980). During branching morphogenesis, the ECM constitution is elegantly stabilized between ECM component deposition and matrix metalloproteinase (MMP) destruction (Fata et al., 2003). The ECM is very charged during lactation, which is a structural need for mammary epithelial cell development (Paszek and Weaver, 2004). Involution is marked by increased collagen deposition, as well as laminin and fibronectin proteolysis and MMP expression (Schedin and Keely, 2011). As a result, the ECM's function extends in excess providing structural support to cells. The ECM controls a range of cellular functions, along with proliferation, differentiation, and migration (Hynes, 2009). It influences endothelial cell differentiation and survival and also helps in tissue-specific immune responses (Sorokin, 2010; Mir et al., 2022d,e,f). The ECM also helps in maintaining the cell–cell communication and any disruptions in this mechanism result in breast cancer (Mir et al., 2022d,e,f; Fig. 8.1).

8.2 The breast tissue's ECM architecture

The fundamental mammary structure is constructed of epithelial cells encircling a central space called the lumen, with contractible myoepithelial cells, all of which are encased in the basement membrane (BM), which divides the epithelium from the stroma. The interstitial matrix, also known as the Stromal compartment, surrounds the cells and the BM, contributing to the tissue's tensile strength. The ECM is made up of the interstitial matrix and the BM. Type IV collagens, laminin, fibronectin, and linker proteins like nidogen and entactin make up the majority of the BM, and epithelial, endothelial, and stromal cells collaborate to make it (Lu et al., 2012; Mehraj et al., 2021b). Proteoglycans, fibrillar collagen, glycoprotein (such as tenascin C), and fibronectin are copious in the interstitial matrix. Fibrillar collagen makes up the mass of the stroma that surrounds normal

Role of Tumor Microenvironment in Breast Cancer and Targeted Therapies
https://doi.org/10.1016/B978-0-443-18696-7.00006-3

195

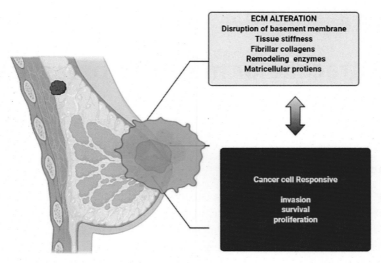

Fig. 8.1 Numerous changes in composition and organization in breast cancer development featured by ECM.

mammary cells. The composition of the ECM, on the other hand, is hugely altered throughout pathogenesis (Huijbers et al., 2010; Table 8.1; Fig. 8.2).

8.3 ECM changes as breast cancer progresses

The ECM of a normal mammary gland is flexible, but as the tumor progresses, it stiffens and gets richer in collagen Fig. 8.3, a procedure known as "desmoplasia" (Paszek et al., 2005). Cancer-associated fibroblasts (CAFs) are primarily responsible for abnormal ECM remodeling, after then, epithelial cells and pro-tumor immune cells play a role in tumor growth (Lu et al., 2011). Tissue stiffness is commonly used as a marker of breast

Table 8.1 Involvement of extracellular matrix constituents in breast cancer.

Collagens		Glycoproteins		Glycosaminoglycan's	
Type I collagen	+	Laminin	−	Hyaluronan	+
Type I trimer collagen	+	Fibronectin	+	Chondroitin sulfate	+
Type III collagen	+	Vitronectin	+	Dermatan sulfate	−
Type IV collagen	−	Elastin	+	Heparan sulfate	−
Type V collagen	+	Thrombospondin	+		
OF/LB collagen	+	Tenascin	+		

Components of the ECM that are expressed more (+) or less (−) frequently in breast tumor tissues or tumor cell lines compared to healthy breast tissues or cell lines.

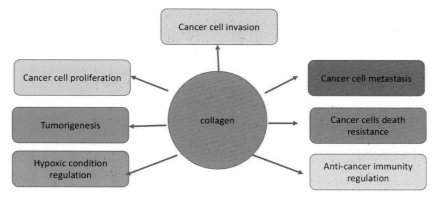

Fig. 8.2 Role of collagen in breast cancer.

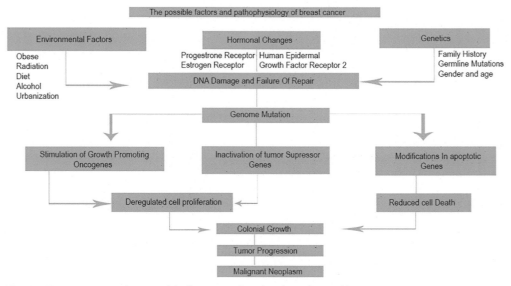

Fig. 8.3 Demonstrates the possible factors and pathophysiology of breast cancer.

carcinogenesis in imaging modalities such as MRI elastography, sonoelastography, TDI analysis, and physical palpitation. While the resolution of these approaches in distinguishing various cellular and acellular components is limited, they do demonstrate a convincing relationship between stiffness and malignancy (Lopez et al., 2011). Major interstitial compulsion within the tumor, condensing stress as a consequence of increased tumor cell proliferation, ECM stiffness due to cross-linking of ECM components and enhanced deposition, and increased cellular stiffness all cause changes in the mechanics of breast tumor tissue.

8.4 Rigidity of the ECM and tumor development

While it is becoming progressively fair that altered ECM stiffness plays a role in tumor growth, shall now concentrate on some of the mechanisms at work (Mehraj et al., 2021a). Changes in mechanosignaling result from enhanced ECM rigidity, a changed vascular environment, and pro-tumorigenic immune infiltration, which together could assist the cell convert to an invasive phenotype.

8.5 In morphological breast tumor subtypes, ECM dynamics are studied

Mammary tumor progression can be divided into two major stages based on morphological characteristics: DCIS (ductal in situ carcinoma) is a premalignant stage, IDC (invasive ductal carcinoma), which has destructive nature that involves BM breaching and tumor cell migration into neighboring tissues (Hugh et al., 2009). IDC and DCIS are distinguished by the loss of the myoepithelial layer and the presence of BM. Changes in the ECM accompany each step, allowing pro-tumorigenic cells to infiltrate and colonize the tumor, allowing it to develop into malignancy Fig. 8.4. DCIS develops in areas of the breast that are thick on mammography (Ursin et al., 2005). Its evolution entails gradual increases in collagen deposition, linearization, and collagen fiber thickening (Acerbi et al., 2015). All of these factors contribute to increased ECM stiffness. As breast cancer advances, certain collagens such as collagen I, II, III, V, and IX show increasing accumulation (Huijbers et al., 2010). In MMTV-PyMT mice, the mammary gland elastic modulus (tissue stiffness measurement) was around 400 Pa in normal, noninvasive breast tissue according to AFM studies. In premalignant tumors, it was 12×100 Pa, and in malignant tumors, it was 3×1000 Pa (Lopez et al., 2011), demonstrating a considerable enhancement in tumor tissue rigidity at various stages of breast cancer. According to human studies, as breast cancers advance from DCIS to IDC, the ECM undergoes enhanced collagen fiber linearization and thickness and result in collagen deposition and cross-linking (Acerbi et al., 2015). In addition, the collagen fibers orientation is significantly altered (Conklin et al., 2011). Collagen I fibers that have been linearized and thickened are orientated adjacent to the tumor boundaries in DCIS (Levental et al., 2009). Additional collagen fiber thickening and linearization are reported in IDC (Acerbi et al., 2015). In addition, the collagen fibers in IDC are positioned perpendicular to the tumor margin, generating migratory paths for invasive tumor cells to escape the tumor tissue and enter the bloodstream (Provenzano et al., 2006).

A fourfold increase in stiffness was seen within the tumor tissue, Especially near the IDC phenotype's invasive front normal tissue has an elastic modulus of roughly 400 Pa, however invasive portions have an elastic modulus of over 5000 Pa. Furthermore, when compared to the invasive front (Acerbi et al., 2015), the tumor core was shown to be less rigid, showing that trespass cells require a stiffer platform than proliferating cells (Acerbi

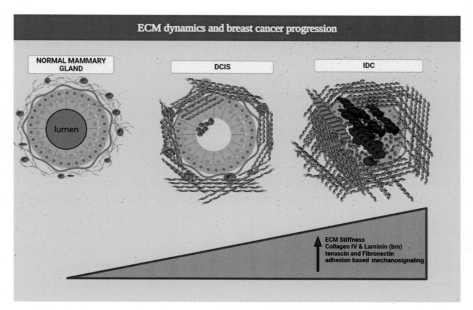

Fig. 8.4 Breast cancer progression and ECM dynamics. A layer of epithelial cells surrounds a central lumen in a typical mammary gland. It is contained by the basement membrane, which is bordered by a layer of contractile myoepithelial cells. The stroma, or interstitial matrix, surrounds this structure and is constructed up of Fibrillar collagen that is arbitrary organized. Moreover, to ECM maintenance, immunological monitoring, and mammary homeostasis, the stroma houses fibroblasts and immune cells. The epithelial cells of ductal carcinoma in situ (DCIS) experience uncontrolled growth and infiltrate into the central lumen. Cross-linked extracellular matrix fibrils (collagen) are structured in bundles parallel to the tumor border. The presence of cancer-associated fibroblasts and immune cells changes the stromal makeup. The lumen gets mostly filled by epithelial cancerous cells during invasive ductal carcinoma (IDC). The Extracellular matrix fibrils are cross-linked further and organized perpendicular to the tumor boundaries to give migration paths for tumor cells to penetrate nearby tissue and blood vessels. Overall, increasing ECM rigidity, changed ECM composition, and aberrant mechanosignaling accompany the transition from normal mammary tissue to IDC.

et al., 2015), the difference in elastic moduli between stable and destructive breast cancer morphologies was dramatically reduced (2×100 and 3×100 Pa, respectively) When cells were newly separated from mice when compared in-situ computation (Lopez et al., 2011). The question of whether these separated cells have varied tumorigenic potential in vitro remains unresolved. These findings insinuate that the ECM is critical for tumor cells, to sense and respond to mechanical stresses that are different from those seen in stable breast tissue so to earn oncogenic and malignant characteristics (Lopez et al., 2011).

8.6 The dynamics of the ECM in molecular breast tumor subtypes

Furthermore, to their histological characteristics, hormone receptor expression is used to categorize breast cancer subtypes Table 8.2 (Mir et al., 2022a,b,c). The reduced aggressive luminal A and luminal B, as well as the increased aggressive HER2+ and basal (TNBC) often known as triple-negative breast cancer, are among them. Former research on breast density and tumor subtypes yielded uncertain and frequently contradictory outcomes. For example, estrogen receptor (ER) expression has been observed to be both enhanced and astray in bulk breast tissue in distinct investigations (Ding et al., 2010; Mir et al., 2022a,b,c). The stroma of HER2+ and TNBC breast cancer subtypes has significantly more collagen deposition and matrix rigidity than luminal subtypes, according to a closer investigation of the stroma. Upholding the theory that greater tissue stiffness is linked to tumor aggressiveness (Acerbi et al., 2015). In addition, the tumor epithelium had higher levels of Integrins expression and mechanosignaling. These two subtypes render the high risk of death and have a much short time to relapse in breast cancer patients, understanding the role of the stroma and tissue mechanics in this phenotype is critical (Hugh et al., 2009).

While a strongly rich milieu can aid disease progression, different subtypes are expected to produce these environments in unique ways. Triple-negative breast cancers have an enhancement in the number of fibroblasts and a substantial influx of myeloid cells, both of which induce ECM remodeling by increasing matrix stiffness (Park et al., 2015; Mir et al., 2022d,e,f).

Breast tumors that are HER2 positive have a higher number of fibroblasts and a reduced inflammatory response, stromal desmoplasia is thought to be caused by increased direct fibroblast-tumor cell contact (Acerbi et al., 2015). HER2+ CAFs are strongly

Table 8.2 Molecular/intrinsic subtype of breast cancer.

Subtypes	Molecular signatures	Characteristics	Treatment option
Luminal A	ER+, PR±, HER2−, Low Ki67	~70%, the most common best prognosis	Hormonal therapy Targeted therapy
Luminal B	ER+, PR±, HER2±, High Ki67	10%–20% Lower survival than luminal A	Hormonal therapy Targeted therapy
HER2	ER−, PR−, HER2+	5%–20%	Targeted therapy
Triple negative	ER−, PR−, HER2−	15%–20% More common in black women Diagnosed at a younger age Worst prognosis	Limited targeted therapy
Normal-like	ER+, PR±, HER2−, Low Ki67	Rare Low proliferation gene cluster expression	Hormonal therapy Targeted therapy

associated with interaction and modulation of the ECM, as well as integrins signaling and actin cytoskeleton modulation, according to gene expression analyses of CAFs (Tchou et al., 2012). As a result, increased ECM rigidity appears to be a familiar denominator in aggressive breast tumors, which can be classified visually and molecularly. The ways via which a rigid ECM can aid tumor growth are numerous and frequently interconnected.

8.7 Mechanosignaling changes

Tumor cells respond biochemically and physically to mechanical alterations in the ECM in a procedure named as "mechanosignaling," which involves tumor cells responding biochemically and physically to mechanical alterations in the ECM (Schedin and Keely, 2011; Mir et al., 2020). Tumor cells use mechanosensors like the Integrins family of receptors to detect biophysical changes in the ECM (Galbraith, 2002). Integrins are heterodimeric transmembrane receptors that act as conduits between the ECM and tumor cells (White et al., 2004). Up regulation and clustering of Integrins, such as 1 Integrins, occurs as the ECM stiffens which can both bring about carcinogenesis and maintain the proliferation of advanced stage of tumor cells. The levels of pY397 FAK—active form of focal adhesion kinase (FAK) are higher in stiffer matrices, is a downstream effector of 1 Integrin's (Paszek et al., 2005). Through the Rho-ROCK pathway, increasing levels ofpY397 FAK lead to enhanced intracellular contractility (Provenzano et al., 2009). During the invasion, tumor cells can tug on the matrix. Increased FAK also activates the MAP kinase pathway, which promotes tumor cell growth (Provenzano et al., 2009). High levels of 1 Integrin and FAK are seen in high-grade DCIS (Acerbi et al., 2015). In high-grade DCIS, activation of another mechanically activated kinase, p130Cas, is also enhanced. The functional ramifications of this, on the other hand, are still unclear. The mechanosensing proteins 1 integrin, vinculum, activated Akt, and FAK colocalize at the stiffest invasive tumor front, from normal to DCIS to IDC phenotypes the degree of expression and colocalization increases progressively (Rubashkin et al., 2014). Increased breast tissue stiffness also promotes invasion by up regulating oncogenic microRNAs that disrupt tumor-suppressive pathways and a slew of other proliferative/invasive mechanisms linked to breast cancer (Gehler et al., 2013).

8.8 Immune system changes

By allowing greater adherence and movement of immune cells, ECM stiffness controls the amount and character of immunological infiltrates in tumor tissue (Qayoom et al., 2021a). Collagen that is stiff and linear, for example, creates paths for immune cells to go into the tumor (Lu et al., 2012). It works in the same way that it helps tumor cells spread outward. ECM components also contain 1 integrins, and leukocyte-associated LAIR-binding sites, nonintegrin receptor DDR1, which serve to anchor immune cells and allow them to enter the tumor microenvironment (Franco et al., 2008). Immune

T cells' activation, maturation, and differentiation are all regulated by ECM stiffness. ECM breakdown produces particles, like elastin, that are chemo attractive to monocytes (Houghton, 2006) particularly and has been connected to the development of breast cancer (Krishnan and Cleary, 1990). Due to altered cytokine signaling, a collagen–dense breast tumor surrounding recruits tumor-associated neutrophils, and its reduction inhibits metastasis in a stiffness–dependent manner. However, the exact mechanism is unknown (García–Mendoza et al., 2016). Rest immune cells including T cells and myeloid cells were not observed in this investigation (Coussens and Werb, 2002). In breast cancer, at the advanced stages, macrophages are frequently recruited wit increased inflammation, stiffness, and infiltration of CD45 + cells. The most prevalent subpopulation of CD45 + are CD163 + macrophage cells, that express TGF-β, which promotes migration and ECM accumulation (Acerbi et al., 2015; Mir et al., 2022a,b,c), most likely as part of a tumor feedback loop.

8.9 Vasculature changes

The development of new blood vessels is required for tumor proliferation and invasion. Endothelial cells that line blood arteries are extremely mechanosensitive, implying that ECM rigidity and vascular remodeling are linked (Sieminski et al., 2004). When invasive DCIS is compared to low-grade DCIS, micro vascular density is consistently higher (Teo et al., 2002). The vascular of a tumor is stiffer than the vasculature of a healthy person, in addition to vascular density (Lopez et al., 2011). Further blood vessels within the tumor core are harder and finer than those at the destructive front. They do not stain positive for lectin, indicating that the tumor core has no vascular activity (Lopez et al., 2011). When grown on stiff collagen matrices, endothelial cells branch more than cells grown on softer collagen matrices (Kohn et al., 2015). Endothelial permeability and leukocyte transmigration are both increased as stiffness increases (Kohn et al., 2015) which could help tumors progress and trespass. In breast cancer, the methods by which the ECM modulates the vascular network are still unknown. To forecast patient response to antiangiogenic therapy, more research is required to setup the molecular underpinnings of breast tumor rigidity and angiogenesis/vasculogenesis.

8.10 ECM and metastasis
8.10.1 The initiation of the premetastatic niche is aided by ECM

To metastasize to different organs, the original tumors must now acquire additional features. For metastasis to occur, the premetastatic niche must be established. Premetastatic niche creation is a process of preparing remote locations for oncogenic colonization before the arrival of disseminated tumor cells (Qayoom et al., 2021b). Most of the time,

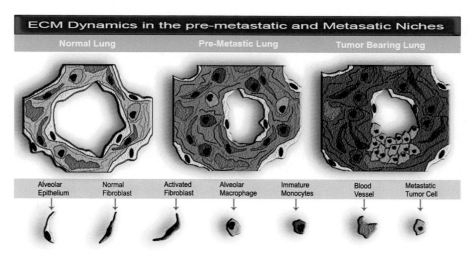

Fig. 8.5 This figure shows ECM dynamics in metastatic niches and premetastatic.

tumor cells from one primary site to a secondary metastasis site in a predictable fashion (Kaplan et al., 2006). When breast cancer cells break through the BM, they enter systemic circulation and populate organs like lungs, brain, bones or liver, etc. (Chambers, 2002; Mir et al., 2022a,b,c). What makes these secondary organs so attractive to initial tumor cells is an important question. The ECM may have a performance in the formation of tumor-friendly premetastatic niches Fig. 8.5, according to new data For example, the collagen cross-linking protein, LOX is required for invasion and its inhibition inhibits metastasis (Cox et al., 2015). Furthermore, enhanced fibronectin expression at secondary sites governs the premetastatic niche's growth (Erler and Weaver, 2009).

MDSCs (myeloid-derived suppressor cells) must be recruited to the premetastatic location in breast cancer for the ECM to be remodeled and potentially become "prometastatic." The MDSCs that have been deployed to the premetastatic niche help to build an immune-suppressive milieu in the lung, which aids tumor cell proliferation (Giles et al., 2016). The ECM proteoglycans versican is secreted by $CD11b^+ Ly6C^{high}$ MDSCs recruited to the premetastatic lung in mice models of breast cancer, facilitating the mesenchymal-to-epithelial transition of breast tumor cells, enhancing their proliferation, and speeding up metastases (Gao et al., 2012).

Versican knockdown reduces lung metastatic burden considerably, and in metastatic lungs of patients versican is observed to be elevated as compared to healthy conditions (Gao et al., 2012), implying the purpose of ECM in establishing a tumor-hospitable niche (Erler et al., 2009). In the premetastatic niche, fibronectin is frequently increased. Fibronectin produced by fibroblast binds to the integrin $\alpha4\beta1/VLA-4$, which is expressed by invading VEGFR1 + cells in distant target organs (HPCs) (Kaplan et al., 2005). Fibronectin-α4β1 interaction is required for the development of VEGFR1 + HPC clusters, and suppression of these collections limits the process of metastasis (Kaplan et al., 2005).

In premetastatic clusters, fibronectin-integrin interaction leads to MMP over expression, this further remodels the ECM, making it more amenable to tumor cell infiltration (Kaplan et al., 2006). The tumor cells' homing in to the premetastatic niche is aided by ECM-integrin interactions.

Exosomal integrins (ITGs) guide metastasis in an organ-specific manner (Hoshino et al., 2015). Exosomes destined for the lungs include integrin alpha 6 (ITGα6), whereas those destined for the liver have ITGβ5. Within laminin-rich lung microenvironments, lung-tropic ITGs united with local S100A4$^+$ fibroblasts. These Exosomes "train" the lungs by permitting ITGs to cling to certain ECM environments, preparing them for the entry of breast cancer cells (Hoshino et al., 2015).

8.10.2 ECM and the growth of tumors

Tumor cells that are on the verge of transitioning from a normal to metastatic phenotype take on few of the characteristics of unicellular organisms (Shubik, 1994; Jan et al., 2021). They become motile after breaking up their rigid connections with neighboring cells and forcing their way through hindrances such as dense interstitial mesenchymal and BMs. This mechanism involves crosstalk between cancer cells and tumor stroma of the tumor, which has been associated to a change in the expression of cytoskeleton proteins, cadherin family cell adhesion molecules, matrix-degrading proteases, and integrins (Haslam, 1991; Sakakura, 1991). Tumor growth preferentially occurs at orthotropic, rather than ectopic, sites, according to transplantation experiments with breast tumor tissues (Bao et al., 1994). Surprisingly, when tumor cells are coinjected with EHS matrix, the results are considerably improved. Raise the likelihood of tumor growth and metastatic behavior, which could be attributed to EHS-induced angiogenesis (Daniel Bonfil et al., 1994). The reexpression of embryonic features including oncofetal fibronectin, OF/LB collagen type I-triple collagen, and tenascin, which are an indication of the stromal fibrotic response to tumor cells, suggests that ECM has a similar tumor-promoting role. Reexpression of embryonic characteristics, in theory, should aid cell proliferation and motility, promoting tumor growth and metastasis. In spite of evident impacts of EHS matrix on tumor and metastasis development in vivo, as well as the unexpected reappearance of embryonic forms of ECM elements, it is still unclear the role of ECM components deposited in the tumor environment in situ.

A short while ago, it was discovered that stromelysin-1 over expressing mice (Sympson et al., 1994) develop mammary tumors at a much higher rate, implying that a healthy ECM serves a protective rather than a tumor-promoting function, at least in the initial stages of tumor development. In breast cancer patients, increased fibronectin and elastin expression has also been related to a better prognosis and a lower risk of metastasis. Tumor development and progression can be understood as the consequence of an imbalance between tumor-suppressing and tumor-promoting microenvironmental stimuli, as evidenced by the expression of ECM molecules in tumor tissues.

8.10.3 Proliferation

One of the most important indications of malignant transformation in vivo is cell cycle escape and unregulated proliferation. The molecular processes that prohibit stable cells from proliferating and overcome by tumor cells remain unknown yet again. Although paracrine, autocrine, cytokines and systemic growth factors are supposed to be the primary determinants of growth, ECM molecules additionally play a role.

The ability of a mammary cancer cell line to respond to PDGF and bFGF was determined by the ECM substrate utilized for growing the cells, with fibronectin exhibiting more proliferative activity than collagen (type-I) (Elliott et al., 1992). ECM molecules bind to growth factors and limit their transport and diffusion. But there are certain growth factors that are activated when attached to the ECM; others must be activated by proteolysis and removal of ECM ligand. As a result, the matrix environment dictates where, when, and how development factors can operate on cells. Furthermore, the ECM regulates growth factor production, potentially leading to the accumulation of a specific set of growth factors. It has been manifested, for example, that when mammary epithelial cells are exposed to EHS matrix or have opportunity to build their own BM, TGF β synthesis is inhibited (Streuli et al., 1993). Breast epithelial cells remain spherical and stop multiplying, When are plated in a flexible matrix gel, nevertheless, they continue to develop on a substrate that allows for cell spreading. A breast cancer cell line is also inhibited by type V collagen. As a result of the ECM's effect on cell adherence and form, cytoskeleton/nuclear skeletal topologies that prevent proliferation may emerge. Other ECM molecules, contrastingly, encode signals that, in the lack of dramatic alterations in cellular shape, can control cell proliferation. It's tempting to think that when tumors' BMs are broken down by proteolysis, the liberated fragments could influence the activity of cells in local tissues and others after reaching them via circulation.

Stromelysin-1 transgenic mice develop breast tumors as well as lymphomas (Sympson et al., 1994). The BM and interstitial matrix are repositories for concealed, potentially mitogenic or otherwise effective sites, the conformation of ECM molecules is crucial for their interaction with their ligand, as it is well known that particular motifs of ECM molecules can be cryptic. As a result, deterioration of ECM in certain locations may expose a diversity of novel stimuli while also increasing the concentration of those that currently exist. Although there is no experimental proof for this concept, since laminin is a key component of the BM and contains patterns of possible mitogenic activation of tumor growth in the aftermath of BM disintegration, it looks conceivable.

8.10.4 Angiogenesis

The formation of new blood vessels (angiogenesis) in the area of the tumor tissue is essential for the tumor to develop and metastasize (Folkman, 1971). ECM compounds directly influence on the development of new blood vessels, in addition to the various growth factors and cytokines implicated in angiogenesis. ECM components, not surprisingly, can both promote and prevent angiogenesis. Endothelial cells placed in type I collagen gels produced more tubes when given chondroitin sulfate and hyaluronan. Fibronectin has been shown to both stimulate and inhibit angiogenesis (Tolsma et al., 1993). Thrombospondin, which is usually thought to be an antiangiogenic agent, has a short while ago discovered to indirectly induce angiogenesis by stimulating the proliferation of endothelial cells. When the stroma responds to the increased appearance of myofibroblasts during carcinogenesis, Thrombospondin, which normally inhibits angiogenesis, may stimulate it. In angiogenesis, laminin and its binding protein, entactin, play similar dual roles. The concentration dependency of laminin-entactin complexes on vessel development, on the other hand, provides some insight. Angiogenesis is stimulated when laminin entactin is applied to cells at low concentrations, whereas angiogenesis is inhibited when laminin entactin is applied at high doses.

8.10.5 Metastasis

The desertion of cells from their local environment would be the first step in a simple story of steps of events leading to tumor cell dispersion. The initial phase in the life of a newly motile tumor cell disrupts all normal physical interactions with nearby cells, which allows this to happen. Cells then migrate toward the BM and blood vessels that surround it and pass through them. In the destruction of BMs around epithelial cells, tumor cells produced proteases, whose expression is controlled by ECM elements (Mackay et al., 1994), which are responsible. They also help penetrate physical obstacles like dense mesenchymal. Newly generated blood vessels, on other hand, may not need infiltration because BMs are regularly fenestrated, infiltration of freshly created blood vessels may not necessitate BM breakdown. Tumor cell migration is a complicated process that includes the establishment of stable substrate connections at the leading end to apply tensional forces for directional movement, as well as releasing substrate attachment points to facilitate cell body displacement. Depending on the particular composition of the ECM, a balance of sticky and antiadhesive matrix qualities is likely to operate as a promoter or inhibitor of migration. Different ECM molecules have adhesive and antiadhesive qualities, with, collagens laminin and fibronectin having adhesive properties and tenascin, chondroitin sulfate proteoglycans and Thrombospondin having antiadhesive properties Fig. 8.6. Tenascin and Thrombospondin can have adhesive properties, while collagens and laminin can have antiadhesive properties (Bornstein, 1992).

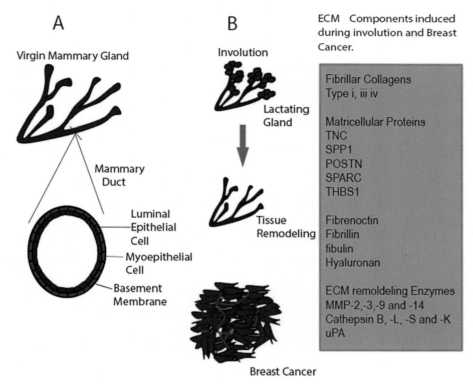

Fig. 8.6 This figure shows ECM constitution in breast cancer development and metastasis and ECM components induced during involution and breast cancer.

Migratory signals influence tumor cell motility as well. Laminin, hyaluronan, type-IV collagen, fibronectin and type I-trimer collagen, not a regular type I collagen, are ECM molecules that can increase tumor cell motility and/or chemo- and hypotaxis. As previously stated, BM degradation leads to the solubilization of ECM fragments, which may have chemotactic effects. This is especially essential in light of the fact that different Thrombospondin domains exhibit chemo- and hypotactic actions. Tenascin has been shown to hinder and stimulate cell migration in the past. Concentration dependence, and soluble vs substrate (matrix)–bound presentation, could all be factors (Halfter et al., 1989).

Vast of tumor cells present in the blood do not play a part in the establishment of metastasis. The few exceptions control the challenge of adherence to and entrance through the BMs of blood vessels. This extravasation requires ECM receptors. Experiments with synthetic peptides containing the RGD motif, a portion of the peptide sequence recognized by several integrins, were carried out, showing that they suppressed tumor cell invasion in culture trials, an action that is most likely mediated through the $\alpha5\beta1$ fibronectin receptor. In tissue culture, however, ligands for the $\alpha v\beta3$ vitronectin receptor boosted tumor cell invasiveness of BMs. Furthermore, synthesized RGD and YIGSR peptides, the latter compete for laminin binding to its receptors, successfully inhibited tumor cell dispersion and metastasis development when given intravenously. When cells were coinjected with laminin into blood arteries, however, tumor metastases increased. Surprisingly, the active site that causes the enhancement in metastatic potential is situated in a different part of the laminin molecule than the YIGSR inhibitory site (Kanemoto et al., 1990).

8.11 Stromal remodeling is required for metastasis

Premetastatic niche creates a tumor-friendly surrounding at the secondary metastatic location prior to metastatic colonization. Once they reach a second growth site, tumor cells modify the surrounding around them to develop favorable growth factors. The role of the ECM in the development of metastatic and premetastatic niches is represented in. Investigational proof insinuates that tumor cell distribution occurs too soon in tumorigenesis, and a huge proportion of patients present with metastatic disease, at the time of diagnosis. Interestingly, remodeling of lymph node ECM develops in computational metastasis models without a primary tumor mass, implying that these changes are mediated straightly by the tumor cell secretome (Rizwan et al., 2015). ECM proteins like fibronectin, Collagen, tenascin C, and versican, have a role in the establishment of a metastatic niche in breast cancer. Collagen deposition has been observed in secondary sites of organs common to breast cancer metastasis, such as bone and the lymph node. It has been suggested that metastasis to the lung requires the acquirement of stem-like characteristics, a phenotype promoted by optimal stromal cues. Tenascin C regulates this stem-like phenotype by the notch and wnt pathways, and its expression by metastatic tumor cells is critical for colonization success (Oskarsson et al., 2011). S100A4+ fibroblasts are involved in the deposition of stromal tenascin C in the lung as well as the metastatic spread of breast cancer cells (O'Connell et al., 2011). Likewise, periostin expression is increased in the lungs leads to metastatic colonization, and is required for tumor cell outgrowth via wnt signaling. Interactions between tumor cell integrins and the recently formed ECM of the secondary site are disrupted, preventing the acquirement of a stem-like phenotype and limiting metastatic tumor growth (Aguirre-Ghiso et al., 2001).

While the roles of various ECM components in the establishment of premetastatic and metastatic niches are understood better, little is known about how tissue rigidity aids metastasis. It is known that LOX is required for the development of the premetastatic niche (Erler and Weaver, 2009) and that LOX causes enhanced rigidity, the mechanical properties of the target site are unknown. Do increased LOX, tenascin C, versican, periostin, fibronectin, and collagen deposition stiffen the premetastatic lung? Is it possible that this stiffness contributes to, or even initiates, tumor cells, prometastatic immune and stromal cells, infiltrate? What role do these components play in the topology and architecture of premetastatic and metastatic ECMs, individually or in combination? What is the relationship between matrix-building ECM elements (LOX) and matrix-degrading MMPs, how is it fine turned to fine-tune the metastatic process spatially and temporally? Understanding the biophysical nature of the ECM in the premetastatic and metastatic niches, including stiffness, porosity, linearization, and cross-linking, will permit observation of the degree of metastatic, and shed light on ECM-mediated therapeutic resistance.

8.12 Treatment resistance mediated by ECM

The ECM's biophysical properties can have an impact on breast cancer patients' treatment outcomes. Patients with soft breast tumors were found to be more sensitive to treatment using shear-wave elastography than those with rigid tumors (Hayashi et al., 2012). Furthermore, in Her2 + breast tumors, the ECM secreted protein acidic and rich in cysteine (SPARC) profile was linked to chemotherapy resistance (Fig. 8.7; Giussani et al., 2015). A firmer substrate can, as previously stated, promote cell invasion, proliferation,

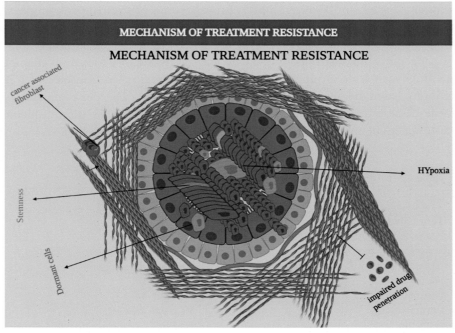

Fig. 8.7 This figure represents the Mechanism of treatment resistance. In a variety of mechanisms, the breast cancer extracellular matrix mediates resistance to radiation therapy and chemotherapy therapy. Conversion of stable fibroblasts to cancer-associated fibroblasts is mediated by chemotherapeutic medications. These release collagen and fibronectin and, which causes substantial extracellular matrix remodeling, and aids chemotherapy-induced ECM changes and treatment resistance.

pro-oncogenic immune infiltration, and vasculogenesis. As a result, it is reasonable to conclude that a rigid tumor micro-surrounding supports therapeutic resistance, permitting the tumor niche to thrive despite cytotoxic assault. Treatment resistance can be mediated in a variety of ways by the ECM.

8.13 Limiting the entry of drugs

ECM components such as collagen, glycosaminoglycans, and decorin form a protective framework surrounding and throughout the tumor, restricting the diffusion of chemotherapeutic drugs (Magzoub et al., 2008). This could be attributed to enhancing ECM rigidity as a consequence of enhanced component cross-linking and deposition, such as collagen. When collagenase was used to treat tumors that were high in collagen, drug penetrance was improved. Unexpectedly, the amount of collagen, but not its direction, was discovered to be crucial in preventing drug penetration (Erikson et al., 2008). Furthermore, increased ECM rigidity and poor drug delivery to the target site might be caused by high interstitial compulsion and compression forces inside the tumor microenvironment (Paszek and Weaver, 2004). An expression of stromal gene profile comprised of ECM proteins like collagens was found in breast cancer patients treated with anthracycline-based treatment (Farmer et al., 2009), SPARC, thrombospondins and periostin, decorin is linked to a poor therapeutic result. Resistance to various chemotherapeutic drugs such as doxorubicin (Misra et al., 2008), tamoxifen (Jansen et al., 2005), and antibody-based therapies have also been linked to ECM (Thurber et al., 2008). As a result, the ECM is believed to act as a protective encasement for the tumor, shielding it from anticancer chemicals and fostering carcinogenic growth Table 8.3.

Table 8.3 Drugs used for breast cancer treatment.

Drugs	Molecular targets
Tamoxifen	ER
Raloxifene	ER
Steroidal Al: Exemestane	Aromatase/estrogen
Nonsteroidal Al: Anastrozole and Letrozole	Aromatase/estrogen
Herceptin	HER-2
Pertuzumab	HER-2
Bevacizumab	VEGF/VEGFR
Gefitinib	EGFR
Zactima	VEGFR/EGFR
Doxorubicin	DNA, Topoisomerase II complex
Taxane (Paclitaxel, docetaxel)	B subunit of tubulin, Bcl-2
5-Fluorouracil, Capecitabine (prodrug)	Thymidylate synthase

8.14 Resistance mediated through contact

Nonintegrin and integrin and adhesions bind tumor cells to the ECM and signal invasion, differentiation, and proliferation. Also, they support chemo resistance in tumors (Holle et al., 2016). In breast cancer the degree of tumor aggression is determined by the differential expression of specific integrins (Chrenek et al., 2001), αVβ3 integrin, For example, is knotted in breast cancer metastases to the bone. Additionally to generating a stem-like phenotype, β3 integrins induce resistance to the EGFR inhibitors erlotinib and lapatinib (Seguin et al., 2014). β1 integrin is linked to Dormant cells, which are extremely rebellious to radiation and chemotherapy, are related with. It is unclear the role of nonintegrin discoidin receptors in mediating treatment resistance in breast cancer. The discoidin receptor, DDR1, has been found to facilitate chemo resistance by the NF-κβ pathway. Explains that discoidin receptors promote tumor growth both independently and through interactions with integrins like α2β1 integrin (Rammal et al., 2016), it will be beneficial to explore their involvement in increasing chemo resistance alongside that of integrins.

8.15 Hypoxia and stemness levels are both on the rise

Breast tumor cells release LOX, which hardens the ECM, and promotes the establishment of a lung premetastatic niche (Erler et al., 2009). Also, for the hypoxia–induced metastasis, LOX is required, as indicated by the use of LOX inhibitors, which prevent metastasis even when hypoxia is present (Erler et al., 2006). While hypoxia-inducible factor-1 regulates LOX expression, it is impossible to rule out the chances of a feedback loop in which hypoxia stimulates LOX expression and vice versa (Erler et al., 2006). Tumor rigidity can lead to the enhanced tumor cell, and vascular remodeling, which can keep a hypoxic environment going, if not initiated.

   Hypoxia has been associated with a weak prognosis and treatment resistance in breast cancer patients. Breast cancer stem-like cells have been shown to proliferate in hypoxia and stiff breast tumors, which influences therapy resistance (Al-Ejeh et al., 2011).

8.16 Dormancy induction

When primary tumor cells leave the proliferative cell cycle and penetrate a nondividing, quiescent state tumor dormancy occurs. Chemotherapy treatments, which primarily target rapidly proliferating cells, are highly resistant to dormant breast tumor cells, allowing them to remain and produce micro metastases at a later date (Naumov et al., 2003). The transformation from dormant to proliferative state is mediated by β1 integrin fibronectin synthesis, and phosphorylated myosin light chain kinase (pMLCK). Actin stress fibers appear in the proliferating cells, making them efficiently rigid; apparently in response to the hardening ECM caused by fibronectin deposition and enhanced β1 integrin-mediated adhesion. Softer substrates have been shown to induce cellular dormancy in hepatocellular carcinoma, whereas stiffer substrates can facilitate therapeutic resistance and proliferation (Schrader et al., 2011). This has also been demonstrated in vitro in lung and breast cancer cell lines.

The tumor cells are thought to face a stiff matrix at the main site, which aids invasion, and a softer matrix at the secondary site, which causes them to switch to dormancy (Schrader et al., 2011). These investigations shed light on ECM variability in new ways. They further support the idea that not all medicines targeting a rigid ECM will result in successful treatment outcomes, because smooth matrices may play a role in treatment resistance. As a result, when creating therapeutic options, it's critical to take into account the oncogenic ECM's heterogeneity rather than single traits like increased rigidity.

8.17 ECM remodeling as a result of treatment

ECM remodeling can be induced by a variety of anticancer drugs, which act as a compensatory mechanism to encourage treatment resistance. In breast cancer models Doxorubicin enhances the expression of the ECM protein fibulin, which may promote doxorubicin resistance in breast cancer cells (Pupa et al., 2007). Chemotherapeutic drugs may also influence ECM remodeling indirectly, for example, by encouraging the conversion of stable stromal fibroblasts to CAFs (Peiris-Pagès et al., 2015), which release fibronectin and collagen and cause substantial ECM remodeling (Kalluri and Zeisberg, 2006). Additionally to chemotherapy, radiation therapy has been shown to cause tumor tissue stiffness, which leads to treatment resistance (Shen et al., 2014).

Increased LOX secretion is induced by ionizing radiation in a hypoxia-dependent way (Shen et al., 2014), which could explain why tumor recurrence is more common following radiation treatment. Thus, chemotherapeutic medicines, in combination with radiation, can cause ECM remodeling, promoting tumor development, treatment resistance, and the possibility of disease recurrence.

8.18 The role of enzymes in ECM remodeling

Induced ECM-remodeling enzymes encourage stem/progenitor signaling pathways and metastasis in BC. Wnt, PI3K/AKT, ERK, JNK, Src-FAK, and other pathways are controlled by ECM during remodeling in BC formation. Fibronectin, Fibrillar collagens, certain laminins, proteoglycans, and matricellular proteins are major ECM proteins activated, and they could be potential therapeutic targets for therapy. MMPs destroy ECM proteins, allowing cancer cells to invade and spread. MMP-11 (stromelysin-3) appears to aid tumor formation by inhibiting apoptosis (Mehraj et al., 2022a). In animal models, however, it suppresses metastasis, indicating that it has dual roles in tumor progression.

MMP-2 and MMP-9, entangled in metastasis, angiogenesis, and invasion, are inhibited by BDM (β-D-mannuronic acid). BDM has antimetastatic properties and suppresses tumor growth by reducing pro-tumor inflammatory chemokines and cytokines (Mehraj et al., 2022b). MMP-14, which is found on the cell surface and is a potential target for preventing metastasis, and a new antibody-mediated MMP-14 inhibition, appears to decrease metastasis and hypoxia in TNBC mice.

Upregulation of MMPs such as MMP-2, MMP-11, MMP-13, and MMP-14 was related to invasion and ECM remodeling throughout the transition from DCIS (ductal carcinoma in situ) to IDC. MMPs, in conjunction with cross-linking enzymes such as (LOX) Lysil oxidase, aid collagen maturation and govern the production and use of soluble factors like TGF-β, which in turn regulates the expression of various ECM proteins and modifying enzymes, including LOXs. Lox causes intramolecular and intermolecular collagen and is a copper-dependent amine oxidase that crosses linking by oxidative deamination of lysine and hydroxylysine residues in the telopeptide domains.

This cross-linking hardens the matrix and enhances focal adhesions integrin clustering, and PI3K signaling, all of which aid ErbB2 dependent breast tumor invasion. When compared to individuals with soft breast carcinomas, patients with higher matrix stiffness (measured by elastography) had lower feedback to neoadjuvant chemotherapy. Women with a higher mammographic density are more likely to evolve BC than women with a lower mammographic density. In mice, it appears that LOXL4 down regulation enhances lung metastasis and BC growth.

By catalyzing cross-linking of extracellular components collagen and elastin, the LOXL2 protein is implicated in cancer growth and metastasis. E-cadherin downregulation mediated by LOXL-2/Snail-1 boosts lung metastasis of BC without affecting ECM stiffness, and LOXL-2/Snail-1-mediated E-cadherin downregulation promotes lung metastasis of BC without affecting ECM stiffness. Collagen is a significant scaffolding protein in the stroma that gives the tissue tensile strength, and its metabolism is disrupted in cancer, resulting in high expression and deposition. Although type I collagen is assumed to act as a barrier against tumor invasion, increased collagen expression has been linked to a high risk of metastasis.

Collagen synthesis is aided by the enzyme collagen prolyl hydroxylase, which is overexpressed in BC tissues with a bad prognosis. Furthermore, collagen production enzyme procollagen lysyl hydroxylase-2 enhances breast tumor rigidity and facilitates metastatic cancers in the lungs and lymph nodes. Tumor development and invasion of ER + type BC are aided by matrix stiffness. Through ERK1/2 signal Upregulation and JAK2/STAT5 signal downregulation, the hardened ECM promotes invasion and metastasis. Heparanase is an enzyme that cleaves heparan sulfate and promotes tumor invasion and metastasis.

Heparanase activity is increased by ER stress during chemotherapy. The MMTV-Heparanase animals enhanced breast tumor cell proliferation and metastasis to the lungs, implying that Heparanase plays a part in BC development. Element (an extract of the Curcumae rhizoma plant) is an anticarcinogenic phytochemical that works by inhibiting the expression of Heparanase (a possible target for Heparanase). The anticancer properties of heparin and nanoheparin derivatives are demonstrated by their ability to reduce BC cell development and metastasis. The deprivation of ECM integrity caused by plasmin promotes cancer cell spread, and plasmin-induced ECM degradation can be inhibited by lipoprotein-A (plasminogen competitive inhibitor). Vitamin C appears to be critical in preventing tumor growth and metastasis because ECM integrity necessitates vitamin C.

ECM proteins like COL-I, III, IV, VI, fibronectin, laminin 332, periostin, and vitronectin promote tumor progression and metastasis, but proteins like DMBT1 and SPARC prevent BC formation and metastasis.

8.19 The ECM of tumors can be targeted therapeutically

Given the importance of the ECM and matrix mechanics in tumor development, targeting the ECM may be a viable option. This can be accomplished in two ways: (i) by targeting the stroma and (ii) by targeting the stroma's biological responses. To control enhanced tissue dynamics and likely tumor growth, targeting the stroma entails correcting tumor-induced alterations to the ECM. Normalizing the tumor stroma by inhibiting TGF-β signaling reduces the deposition of collagen and promotes vascular permeability in preclinical animals, dramatically decreasing tumor development and improving therapeutic response (Liu et al., 2012). While preclinical systems show promising results, clinical trials are significantly more difficult because of the pleiotropic nature of TGF-β signaling. The use of medicines that target ECM constituents directly to diminish tissue stiffness has also been proven to slow tumor development (Erler et al., 2006). The enzyme hyaluronidase, which degrades extracellular hyaluronic acid, is useful in not only suppressing tumor development but also easing confined pressures to improve chemotherapy entrance and responsiveness (Beckenlehner et al., 1992). Numerous clinical trials using neoadjuvant hyaluronidase have been constituted, especially for metastatic breast cancer, due to the promising results of preclinical investigations in breast and other types of cancer (NCT02753595). In preclinical animals, approaches that target collagen maturation by inhibiting cross-linking enzymes have also showed potential. In orthotopic models of breast cancer, the enzymatic LOX inhibitor Beta-aminopropionitrile (BAPN) dramatically inhibits collagen formation, tumor cell invasion, and metastasis (Pickup et al., 2014). In different types of cancer, the allosteric inhibitor (LOXL2) reduces desmoplastic response and limits tumor cell spread. In phase I and phase II clinical experiment, copper depletion uses tetrathiomolybdate reduced LOX activity, and lung metastasis in breast cancer patients (Chan et al., 2017). These methods have not yet been tested in clinical trials; they represent novel approaches with substantial therapeutic potential. Inhibiting cellular responses to these cues is a second way to minimize the possible pro-tumorigenic effects of ECM tissue mechanics and deposition. Integrin-mediated FAK phosphorylation is the most common method of translating mechanical inputs into metabolic reactions. The stimulation of downstream signaling events is prevented when this phosphorylation process is inhibited. Through genetic and pharmacological modifications, FAK inhibitors appear remarkable preclinical success. In phase I therapeutic trials, targeted decrease of FAK activity using either direct phosphorylation blocking or kinase blocking showed significant promise (NCT00666926 and NCT00996671). Mislaying of FAK activity in tumor cells offers tremendous potential in a neoadjuvant context, but the systemic implications and compensatory mechanisms adopted by the tumor have yet to be determined.

8.20 Conclusion

Breast cancer's heterogeneity is partly attributable to the dynamic nature of its ECM. The ECM undergoes continual remodeling throughout normal mammary growth, albeit under strictly controlled settings. When this mechanism is disrupted, the ECM becomes dysregulated and disordered, resulting in breast cancer. In terms of stiffness, constitution, structure, and cross-linking, the ECM of a normal breast differs significantly from that of a breast tumor. It is now commonly known that the ECM is not a bystander in the evolution of cancer. Rather, it plays an active role in the progression from premalignant DCIS to metastatic IDC, both physically and biochemically. It can also supply the elements for the formation of a premetastatic niche in some organs including the brain, bone, lungs, etc., leading to primary tumor cell malignant colonization.

When there is stability between ECM deposition and breakdown, tumor development and invasion can occur. ECM components like fibronectin and collagen are secreted by CAFs and epithelial cells, which aid in a deposition. When the tumor cells are ready to break down the BM and begin the invasion process, these cells additionally secrete ECM-degrading enzymes such as MMPs and collagenase. Although dysregulated in cancer, ECM homeostasis is nonetheless maintained by feedback mechanisms that stabilize deposition and degradation. Comprehension of the feedback mechanisms that command ECM architecture can help and assist in designing the optimal options for the treatment to target various dynamics for potentially preventing the progression of breast tumors to malignant stages, i.e., cancer.

References

Acerbi, I., Cassereau, L., Dean, I., Shi, Q., Au, A., Park, C., Chen, Y.Y., Liphardt, J., Hwang, E.S., Weaver, V.M., 2015. Human breast cancer invasion and aggression correlates with ECM stiffening and immune cell infiltration. Integr. Biol. 7 (10), 1120–1134.

Aguirre-Ghiso, J.A., Liu, D., Mignatti, A., Kovalski, K., Ossowski, L., 2001. Urokinase receptor and fibronectin regulate the ERKMAPK to p38MAPK activity ratios that determine carcinoma cell proliferation or dormancy in vivo. Mol. Biol. Cell 12 (4), 863–879.

Al-Ejeh, F., Smart, C.E., Morrison, B.J., Chenevix-Trench, G., López, J.A., Lakhani, S.R., Brown, M.P., Khanna, K.K., 2011. Breast cancer stem cells: treatment resistance and therapeutic opportunities. Carcinogenesis 32 (5), 650–658.

Bao, L., Matsumura, Y., Baban, D., Sun, Y., Tarin, D., 1994. Effects of inoculation site and Matrigel on growth and metastasis of human breast cancer cells. Br. J. Cancer 70 (2), 228–232.

Beckenlehner, K., Bannke, S., Spruß, T., Bernhardt, G., Schönenberger, H., Schiess, W., 1992. Hyaluronidase enhances the activity of adriamycin in breast cancer models in vitro and in vivo. J. Cancer Res. Clin. Oncol. 118 (8), 591–596.

Bornstein, P., 1992. Thrombospondins: structure and regulation of expression. FASEB J. 6 (14), 3290–3299.

Chambers, A.F., Groom, A.C., IC, M.D., 2002. Dissemination and growth of cancer cells in metastatic sites. Nat. Rev. Cancer 2, 563–572.

Chan, N., Willis, A., Kornhauser, N., Ward, M.M., Lee, S.B., Nackos, E., Seo, B.R., Chuang, E., Cigler, T., Moore, A., 2017. Influencing the tumor microenvironment: a phase II study of copper-depletion using tetrathiomolybdate (TM) in patients with breast cancer at high risk for recurrence and in preclinical models of lung metastases. 23, 666–676.

Chrenek, M.A., Wong, P., Weaver, V.M., 2001. Tumour-stromal interactions: integrins and cell adhesions as modulators of mammary cell survival and transformation. Breast Cancer Res. 3 (4), 1–6.

Conklin, M.W., Eickhoff, J.C., Riching, K.M., Pehlke, C.A., Eliceiri, K.W., Provenzano, P.P., Friedl, A., Keely, P.J., 2011. Aligned collagen is a prognostic signature for survival in human breast carcinoma. Am. J. Pathol. 178 (3), 1221–1232.

Coussens, L.M., Werb, Z., 2002. Inflammation and cancer. Nature 420 (6917), 860–867.

Cox, T.R., Rumney, R.M.H., Schoof, E.M., Perryman, L., Høye, A.M., Agrawal, A., Bird, D., Latif, N.A., Forrest, H., Evans, H.R., 2015. The hypoxic cancer secretome induces pre-metastatic bone lesions through lysyl oxidase. Nature 522 (7554), 106–110.

Daniel Bonfil, R., Vinyals, A., Bustuoabad, O.D., Llorens, A., Benavides, F.J., Gonzalez-Garrigues, M., Fabra, A., 1994. Stimulation of angiogenesis as an explanation of matrigel-enhanced tumorigenicity. Int. J. Cancer 58 (2), 233–239.

Ding, J., Warren, R., Girling, A., Thompson, D., Easton, D., 2010. Mammographic density, estrogen receptor status and other breast cancer tumor characteristics. Breast J. 16 (3), 279–289.

Elliott, B., Östman, A., Westermark, B., Rubin, K., 1992. Modulation of growth factor responsiveness of murine mammary carcinoma cells by cell matrix interactions: correlation of cell proliferation and spreading. J. Cell. Physiol. 152 (2), 292–301.

Erikson, A., Andersen, H.N., Naess, S.N., Sikorski, P., Davies Cde, L., 2008. Physical and chemical modifications of collagen gels: impact on diffusion. Biopolymers 89 (2), 135–143.

Erler, J.T., Weaver, V.M., 2009. Three-dimensional context regulation of metastasis. Clin. Exp. Metastasis 26 (1), 35–49.

Erler, J.T., Bennewith, K.L., Nicolau, M., Dornhöfer, N., Kong, C., Le, Q.-T., Chi, J.-T.A., Jeffrey, S.S., Giaccia, A.J., 2006. Lysyl oxidase is essential for hypoxia-induced metastasis. Nature 440 (7088), 1222–1226.

Erler, J.T., Bennewith, K.L., Cox, T.R., Lang, G., Bird, D., Koong, A., Le, Q.-T., Giaccia, A.J., 2009. Hypoxia-induced lysyl oxidase is a critical mediator of bone marrow cell recruitment to form the pre-metastatic niche. Cancer Cell 15 (1), 35–44.

Farmer, P., Bonnefoi, H., Anderle, P., Cameron, D., Wirapati, P., Becette, V., André, S., Piccart, M., Campone, M., Brain, E., 2009. A stroma-related gene signature predicts resistance to neoadjuvant chemotherapy in breast cancer. Nat. Med. 15 (1), 68–74.

Fata, J.E., Werb, Z., Bissell, M.J., 2003. Regulation of mammary gland branching morphogenesis by the extracellular matrix and its remodeling enzymes. Breast Cancer Res. 6 (1), 1–11.

Folkman, J., 1971. Tumor angiogenesis: therapeutic implications. N. Engl. J. Med. 285 (21), 1182–1186.

Franco, C., Hou, G., Ahmad, P.J., Fu, E.Y.K., Koh, L., Vogel, W.F., Bendeck, M.P., 2008. Discoidin domain receptor 1 (ddr1) deletion decreases atherosclerosis by accelerating matrix accumulation and reducing inflammation in low-density lipoprotein receptor–deficient mice. Circ. Res. 102 (10), 1202–1211.

Galbraith, C.G., Yamada, K., Sheetz, M.P., 2002. The relationship betweenforce and focal complex development. J. Cell Biol., 695–705.

Gao, D., Joshi, N., Choi, H., Ryu, S., Hahn, M., Catena, R., Sadik, H., Argani, P., Wagner, P., Vahdat, L.-T., Port, J.L., Stiles, B., Sukumar, S., Altorki, N.K., Rafii, S., Mittal, V., 2012. Myeloid progenitor cells in the premetastatic lung promote metastases by inducing mesenchymal to epithelial transition. Cancer Res. 72 (6), 1384–1394.

García-Mendoza, M.G., Inman, D.R., Ponik, S.M., Jeffery, J.J., Sheerar, D.S., Van Doorn, R.R., Keely, P.-J., 2016. Neutrophils drive accelerated tumor progression in the collagen-dense mammary tumor microenvironment. Breast Cancer Res. 18 (1), 49.

Gehler, S., Ponik, S.M., Riching, K.M., Keely, P.J., 2013. Bi-directional signaling: extracellular matrix and integrin regulation of breast tumor progression. Crit. Rev. Eukaryot. Gene Expr. 23 (2).

Giles, A.J., Reid, C.M., Evans, J.D., Murgai, M., Vicioso, Y., Highfill, S.L., Kasai, M., Vahdat, L., Mackall, C.L., Lyden, D., Wexler, L., Kaplan, R.N., 2016. Activation of hematopoietic stem/progenitor cells promotes immunosuppression within the pre-metastatic niche. Cancer Res. 76 (6), 1335–1347.

Giussani, M., Merlino, G., Cappelletti, V., Tagliabue, E., Daidone, M.G., 2015. Tumor-extracellular matrix interactions: identification of tools associated with breast cancer progression. Semin. Cancer Biol. 35, 3–10.

Halfter, W., Chiquet-Ehrismann, R., Tucker, R.P., 1989. The effect of tenascin and embryonic basal lamina on the behavior and morphology of neural crest cells in vitro. Dev. Biol. 132 (1), 14–25.

Haslam, S.Z., 1991. Stromal–epithelial interactions in normal and neoplastic mammary gland. Cancer Treat. Res. 53, 401–420.

Hayashi, M., Yamamoto, Y., Ibusuki, M., Fujiwara, S., Yamamoto, S., Tomita, S., Nakano, M., Murakami, K., Iyama, K.-I., Iwase, H., 2012. Evaluation of tumor stiffness by elastography is predictive for pathologic complete response to neoadjuvant chemotherapy in patients with breast cancer. Ann. Surg. Oncol. 19 (9), 3042–3049.

Holle, A.W., Young, J.L., Spatz, J.P., 2016. In vitro cancer cell-ECM interactions inform in vivo cancer treatment. Adv. Drug Deliv. Rev. 97.

Hoshino, A., Costa-Silva, B., Shen, T.L., Rodrigues, G., Hashimoto, A., Tesic Mark, M., Lyden, D., 2015. Tumour exosome integrins determine organotropic metastasis. Nature 527, 329–335.

Houghton, A.M., Quintero, P.A., Perkins, D.L., Kobayashi, D.K., Kelley, D.G., Marconcini, L.A., Mecham, R.P., Senior, R.M., Shapiro, S.D., 2006. Elastin fragments drive disease progression in a murine model of emphysema. J. Clin. Invest. 116, 753–759.

Hugh, J., Hanson, J., Cheang, M.C.U., Nielsen, T.O., Perou, C.M., Dumontet, C., Reed, J., Krajewska, M., Treilleux, I., Rupin, M., 2009. Breast cancer subtypes and response to docetaxel in node-positive breast cancer: use of an immunohistochemical definition in the BCIRG 001 trial. J. Clin. Oncol. 27 (8), 1168.

Huijbers, I.J., Iravani, M., Popov, S., Robertson, D., Al-Sarraj, S., Jones, C., Isacke, C.M., 2010. A role for fibrillar collagen deposition and the collagen internalization receptor endo180 in glioma invasion. PLoS One 5 (3), e9808.

Hynes, R.O., 2009. The extracellular matrix: not just pretty fibrils. Science 326 (5957), 1216–1219.

Jan, S., Qayoom, H., Mehraj, U., Mir, M., 2021. Therapeutic Options for Breast Cancer. Nova Science.

Jansen, M.P.H.M., Foekens, J.A., van Staveren, I.L., Dirkzwager-Kiel, M.M., Ritstier, K., Look, M.P., Meijer-van Gelder, M.E., Sieuwerts, A.M., Portengen, H., Dorssers, L.C.J., 2005. Molecular classification of tamoxifen-resistant breast carcinomas by gene expression profiling. J. Clin. Oncol. 23 (4), 732–740.

Kalluri, R., Zeisberg, M., 2006. Fibroblasts in cancer. Nat. Rev. Cancer 6 (5), 392–401.

Kanemoto, T., Reich, R., Royce, L., Greatorex, D., Adler, S.H., Shiraishi, N., Martin, G.R., Yamada, Y., Kleinman, H.K., 1990. Identification of an amino acid sequence from the laminin A chain that stimulates metastasis and collagenase IV production. Proc. Natl. Acad. Sci. U. S. A. 87 (6), 2279–2283.

Kaplan, R.N., Riba, R.D., Zacharoulis, S., Bramley, A.H., Vincent, L., Costa, C., MacDonald, D.D., Jin, D.K., Shido, K., Kerns, S.A., Zhu, Z., Hicklin, D., Wu, Y., Port, J.L., Altorki, N., Port, E.R.,

Ruggero, D., Shmelkov, S.V., Jensen, K.K., Rafii, S., Lyden, D., 2005. VEGFR1-positive haematopoietic bone marrow progenitors initiate the pre-metastatic niche. Nature 438 (7069), 820–827.

Kaplan, R.N., Rafii, S., Lyden, D., 2006. Preparing the "soil": the premetastatic niche. Cancer Res. 66 (23), 11089–11093.

Kohn, J.C., Zhou, D.W., Bordeleau, F., Zhou, A.L., Mason, B.N., Mitchell, M.J., King, M.R., Reinhart-King, C.A., 2015. Cooperative effects of matrix stiffness and fluid shear stress on endothelial cell behavior. Biophys. J. 108 (3), 471–478.

Krishnan, R., Cleary, E.G., 1990. Elastin gene expression in elastotic human breast cancers and epithelial cell lines. Cancer Res. 50 (7), 2164–2171.

Levental, K.R., Yu, H., Kass, L., Lakins, J.N., Egeblad, M., Erler, J.T., Fong, S.F.T., Csiszar, K., Giaccia, A., Weninger, W., 2009. Matrix crosslinking forces tumor progression by enhancing integrin signaling. Cell 139 (5), 891–906.

Liu, J., Liao, S., Diop-Frimpong, B., Chen, W., Goel, S., Naxerova, K., Ancukiewicz, M., Boucher, Y., Jain, R.K., Xu, L., 2012. TGF-β blockade improves the distribution and efficacy of therapeutics in breast carcinoma by normalizing the tumor stroma. Proc. Natl. Acad. Sci. U. S. A. 109 (41), 16618–16623.

Lopez, J.I., Kang, I., You, W.-K., McDonald, D.M., Weaver, V.M., 2011. In situ force mapping of mammary gland transformation. Integr. Biol. 3 (9), 910–921.

Lu, P., Takai, K., Weaver, V.M., Werb, Z., 2011. Extracellular matrix degradation and remodeling in development and disease. Cold Spring Harb. Perspect. Biol. 3 (12).

Lu, P., Weaver, V.M., Werb, Z., 2012. The extracellular matrix: a dynamic niche in cancer progression. J. Cell Biol. 196 (4), 395–406.

Mackay, A.R., Gomez, D.E., Nason, A.M., Thorgeirsson, U.P., 1994. Studies on the effects of laminin, E-8 fragment of laminin and synthetic laminin peptides PA22-2 and YIGSR on matrix metalloproteinases and tissue inhibitor of metalloproteinase expression. Lab. Invest. 70 (6), 800–806.

Magzoub, M., Jin, S., Verkman, A.S., 2008. Enhanced macromolecule diffusion deep in tumors after enzymatic digestion of extracellular matrix collagen and its associated proteoglycan decorin. FASEB J. 22 (1), 276–284.

Mehraj, U., Dar, A.H., Wani, N.A., Mir, M.A., 2021a. Tumor microenvironment promotes breast cancer chemoresistance. Cancer Chemother. Pharmacol. 87 (2), 147–158.

Mehraj, U., Ganai, R.A., Macha, M.A., Hamid, A., Zargar, M.A., Bhat, A.A., Nasser, M.W., Haris, M., Batra, S.K., Alshehri, B., 2021b. The tumor microenvironment as driver of stemness and therapeutic resistance in breast cancer: new challenges and therapeutic opportunities. Cell. Oncol., 1–21.

Mehraj, U., Aisha, S., Sofi, S., Mir, M.A., 2022a. Expression pattern and prognostic significance of baculoviral inhibitor of apoptosis repeat-containing 5 (BIRC5) in breast cancer: a comprehensive analysis. Adv. Cancer Biol. Metastasis, 100037.

Mehraj, U., Mushtaq, U., Mir, M.A., Saleem, A., Macha, M.A., Lone, M.N., Hamid, A., Zargar, M.A., Ahmad, S.M., Wani, N.A., 2022b. Chemokines in Triple-Negative Breast Cancer Heterogeneity: New Challenges for Clinical Implications. Elsevier.

Mir, M.A., Qayoom, H., Mehraj, U., Nisar, S., Bhat, B., Wani, N.A., 2020. Targeting different pathways using novel combination therapy in triple negative breast cancer. Curr. Cancer Drug Targets 20 (8), 586–602.

Mir, M., Jan, S., Mehraj, U., 2022a. Conventional Adjuvant Chemotherapy in Combination With Surgery, Radiotherapy and Other Specific Targets (Chapter-4 Elsevier). Elsevier Science Publishers USA, pp. 145–176.

Mir, M., Jan, S., Mehraj, U., 2022b. Current Therapeutics and Treatment Options in TNBC (Chapter-3 Elsevier). Elsevier Science Publishers, USA, pp. 73–144.

Mir, M., Jan, S., Mehraj, U., 2022c. Triple-Negative Breast Cancer—An Aggressive Subtype of Breast Cancer. pp. 1–35.

Mir, M., Sofi, S., Qayoom, H., 2022d. Different Drug Delivery Approaches in Combinational Therapy in TNBC (Chapter-8 Elsevier). Elsevier Science Publishers, USA, pp. 278–311.

Mir, M., Sofi, S., Qayoom, H., 2022e. Role of Immune System in Triple Negative Breast Cancer (TNBC) Chapter-5 Elsevier. Elsevier Science Publishers, USA, pp. 177–201.

Mir, M., Sofi, S., Qayoom, H., 2022f. Targeting Biologically Specific Molecules in Triple Negative Breast Cancer (TNBC) Chapter-7 Elsevier. Elsevier Science Publishers, USA, pp. 245–277.

Misra, S., Obeid, L.M., Hannun, Y.A., Minamisawa, S., Berger, F.G., Markwald, R.R., Toole, B.P., Ghatak, S., 2008. Hyaluronan constitutively regulates activation of COX-2-mediated cell survival activity in intestinal epithelial and colon carcinoma cells. J. Biol. Chem. 283 (21), 14335–14344.

Naumov, G.N., Townson, J.L., MacDonald, I.C., Wilson, S.M., Bramwell, V.H.C., Groom, A.C., Chambers, A.F., 2003. Ineffectiveness of doxorubicin treatment on solitary dormant mammary carcinoma cells or late-developing metastases. Breast Cancer Res. Treat. 82 (3), 199–206.

O'Connell, J.T., Sugimoto, H., Cooke, V.G., MacDonald, B.A., Mehta, A.I., LeBleu, V.S., Dewar, R., Rocha, R.M., Brentani, R.R., Resnick, M.B., 2011. VEGF-A and tenascin-C produced by S100A4 + stromal cells are important for metastatic colonization. Proc. Natl. Acad. Sci. U. S. A. 108 (38), 16002–16007.

Oskarsson, T., Acharyya, S., Zhang, X.H.F., Vanharanta, S., Tavazoie, S.F., Morris, P.G., Downey, R.J., Manova-Todorova, K., Brogi, E., Massagué, J., 2011. Breast cancer cells produce tenascin C as a metastatic niche component to colonize the lungs. Nat. Med. 17 (7), 867–874.

Park, S.Y., Kim, H.M., Koo, J.S., 2015. Differential expression of cancer-associated fibroblast-related proteins according to molecular subtype and stromal histology in breast cancer. Breast Cancer Res. Treat. 149 (3), 727–741.

Paszek, M.J., Weaver, V.M., 2004. The tension mounts: mechanics meets morphogenesis and malignancy. J. Mammary Gland Biol. Neoplasia 9 (4), 325–342.

Paszek, M.J., Zahir, N., Johnson, K.R., Lakins, J.N., Rozenberg, G.I., Gefen, A., Reinhart-King, C.A., Margulies, S.S., Dembo, M., Boettiger, D., Hammer, D.A., Weaver, V.M., 2005. Tensional homeostasis and the malignant phenotype. Cancer Cell 8 (3), 241–254.

Peiris-Pagès, M., Sotgia, F., Lisanti, M.P., 2015. Chemotherapy induces the cancer-associated fibroblast phenotype, activating paracrine Hedgehog-GLI signalling in breast cancer cells. Oncotarget 6 (13), 10728.

Pickup, M.W., Mouw, J.K., Weaver, V.M., 2014. The extracellular matrix modulates the hallmarks of cancer. EMBO Rep. 15 (12), 1243–1253.

Provenzano, P.P., Eliceiri, K.W., Campbell, J.M., Inman, D.R., White, J.G., Keely, P.J., 2006. Collagen reorganization at the tumor-stromal interface facilitates local invasion. BMC Med. 4 (1), 1–15.

Provenzano, P.P., Inman, D.R., Eliceiri, K.W., Keely, P.J., 2009. Matrix density-induced mechanoregulation of breast cell phenotype, signaling and gene expression through a FAK–ERK linkage. Oncogene 28 (49), 4326–4343.

Pupa, S.M., Giuffré, S., Castiglioni, F., Bertola, L., Cantú, M., Bongarzone, I., Baldassari, P., Mortarini, R., Argraves, W.S., Anichini, A., 2007. Regulation of breast cancer response to chemotherapy by fibulin-1. Cancer Res. 67 (9), 4271–4277.

Qayoom, H., Mehraj, U., Aisha, S., Sofi, S., Mir, M.A., 2021a. Integrating Immunotherapy With Chemotherapy: A New Approach to Drug Repurposing. Nova Science.

Qayoom, H., Wani, N.A., Alshehri, B., Mir, M.A., 2021b. An insight into the cancer stem cell survival pathways involved in chemoresistance in triple-negative breast cancer. Future Oncol. 17 (31), 4185–4206.

Rammal, H., Saby, C., Magnien, K., Van-Gulick, L., Garnotel, R., Buache, E., El Btaouri, H., Jeannesson, P., Morjani, H., 2016. Discoidin domain receptors: potential actors and targets in cancer. Front. Pharmacol. 7, 55.

Rizwan, A., Bulte, C., Kalaichelvan, A., Cheng, M., Krishnamachary, B., Bhujwalla, Z.M., Jiang, L., Glunde, K., 2015. Metastatic breast cancer cells in lymph nodes increase nodal collagen density. Sci. Rep. 5 (1), 1–6.

Rubashkin, M.G., Cassereau, L., Bainer, R., DuFort, C.C., Yui, Y., Ou, G., Paszek, M.J., Davidson, M.W., Chen, Y.-Y., Weaver, V.M., 2014. Force engages vinculin and promotes tumor progression by enhancing PI3K activation of phosphatidylinositol (3, 4, 5)-triphosphate. Cancer Res. 74 (17), 4597–4611.

Sakakura, T., 1991. New aspects of stroma-parenchyma relations in mammary gland differentiation. Int. Rev. Cytol. 125, 165–202.

Schedin, P., Keely, P.J., 2011. Mammary gland ECM remodeling, stiffness, and mechanosignaling in normal development and tumor progression. Cold Spring Harb. Perspect. Biol. 3 (1), a003228.

Schrader, J., Gordon-Walker, T.T., Aucott, R.L., van Deemter, M., Quaas, A., Walsh, S., Benten, D., Forbes, S.J., Wells, R.G., Iredale, J.P., 2011. Matrix stiffness modulates proliferation, chemotherapeutic response, and dormancy in hepatocellular carcinoma cells. Hepatology 53 (4), 1192–1205.

Seguin, L., Kato, S., Franovic, A., Camargo, M.F., Lesperance, J., Elliott, K.C., Yebra, M., Mielgo, A., Lowy, A.M., Husain, H., 2014. An integrin β3–KRAS–RalB complex drives tumour stemness and resistance to EGFR inhibition. Nat. Cell Biol. 16 (5), 457–468.

Shen, C.J., Sharma, A., Vuong, D.-V., Erler, J.T., Pruschy, M., Broggini-Tenzer, A., 2014. Ionizing radiation induces tumor cell lysyl oxidase secretion. BMC Cancer 14 (1), 1–10.

Shubik, P., 1994. Neoplasia: a general pathological reaction. Cancer Lett. 83 (1–2), 3–7.

Sieminski, A.L., Hebbel, R.P., Gooch, K.J., 2004. The relative magnitudes of endothelial force generation and matrix stiffness modulate capillary morphogenesis in vitro. Exp. Cell Res. 297 (2), 574–584.

Sorokin, L., 2010. The impact of the extracellular matrix on inflammation. Nat. Rev. Immunol. 10 (10), 712–723.

Streuli, C.H., Schmidhauser, C., Kobrin, M., Bissell, M.J., Derynck, R., 1993. Extracellular matrix regulates expression of the TGF-beta 1 gene. J. Cell Biol. 120 (1), 253–260.

Sympson, C.J., Talhouk, R.S., Alexander, C.M., Chin, J.R., Clift, S.M., Bissell, M.J., Werb, Z., 1994. Targeted expression of stromelysin-1 in mammary gland provides evidence for a role of proteinases in branching morphogenesis and the requirement for an intact basement membrane for tissue-specific gene expression. J. Cell Biol. 125 (3), 681–693.

Tchou, J., Kossenkov, A.V., Chang, L., Satija, C., Herlyn, M., Showe, L.C., Puré, E., 2012. Human breast cancer associated fibroblasts exhibit subtype specific gene expression profiles. BMC Med. Genet. 5 (1), 1–13.

Teo, N.B., Shoker, B.S., Jarvis, C., Martin, L., Sloane, J.P., Holcombe, C., 2002. Vascular density and phenotype around ductal carcinoma in situ (DCIS) of the breast. Br. J. Cancer 86 (6), 905–911.

Thurber, G.M., Schmidt, M.M., Wittrup, K.D., 2008. Antibody tumor penetration: transport opposed by systemic and antigen-mediated clearance. Adv. Drug Deliv. Rev. 60 (12), 1421–1434.

Tolsma, S.S., Volpert, O.V., Good, D.J., Frazier, W.A., Polverini, P.J., Bouck, N., 1993. Peptides derived from two separate domains of the matrix protein thrombospondin-1 have anti-angiogenic activity. J. Cell Biol. 122 (2), 497–511.

Ursin, G., Hovanessian-Larsen, L., Parisky, Y.R., Pike, M.C., Wu, A.H., 2005. Greatly increased occurrence of breast cancers in areas of mammographically dense tissue. Breast Cancer Res. 7 (5), 1–4.

White, D.E., Kurpios, N.A., Zuo, D., Hassell, J.A., Blaess, S., Mueller, U., Muller, W.J., 2004. Targeted disruption of β1-integrin in a transgenic mouse model of human breast cancer reveals an essential role in mammary tumor induction. Cancer Cell 6 (2), 159–170.

Wicha, M.S., Liotta, L.A., Vonderhaar, B.K., Kidwell, W.R., 1980. Effects of inhibition of basement membrane collagen deposition on rat mammary gland development. Dev. Biol. 80 (2), 253–266.

Wiseman, B.S., Werb, Z., 2002. Stromal effects on mammary gland development and breast cancer. Science 296 (5570), 1046–1049.

CHAPTER 9

Breast cancer stem cells and their role in tumor microenvironment

Manzoor Ahmad Mir[a] and Ab Qayoom Naik[b]
[a]Department of Bioresources, School of Biological Sciences, University of Kashmir, Srinagar, Jammu and Kashmir, India
[b]Laboratory of Endocrinology, Department of Biosciences, Barkatullah University, Bhopal, MP, India

9.1 Introduction

Breast cancer, one of the most common and major causes of morbidity and mortality, results in more than 1 in 10 new cancer diagnoses per year (Mir et al., 2020; Mehraj et al., 2021a, Qayoom et al., 2021). It is also the leading cause of cancer death among the female population worldwide. According to an estimate, the global prevalence of breast tumors will reach 2.3 million by 2030 (Sung et al., 2021; Zafar et al., 2022). Nonspecific ductal carcinoma and specific invasive breast cancer subtypes are presently considered for the invasive breast cancer classifications (Mehraj et al., 2021b). The nonspecific type of breast cancer is a dumpster full of carcinomas that aren't defined as particular subtypes but aren't categorized as special subtypes. Nonspecific invasive ductal carcinomas account for 60% to 75% of all breast cancers. The most common types are lobular, tubular, papillary, and mucinous tumors, which account for 20% to 25% of all cancers (Fig. 9.1). Due to the slow progression of the disease, routine screening is of utmost vital for the timely identification of its development (Tudoran et al., 2016; Zhou et al., 2019; Mehraj et al., 2022a; Song and Farzaneh, 2021). There is a continuous replenishment of epithelial cells in the breast tissue of an adult woman throughout the reproductive life during pregnancy and the estrous cycle which is regulated by mammary stem cells in their primordial state (MaSCs) (Fig. 9.2). MaSCs are characterized by proliferation and differentiation into biopotential lineage-specific progenitors, which eventually give rise to functional breast epithelial cells (Tharmapalan et al., 2019). The management of these cellular functions is guided by brightly-regulated paracrine cues and interplay between breast epithelium cells and their tissue microenvironment, as well as disruption to the interaction among MaSCs, epithelial progenitors, and their microenvironment (Bissell et al., 2003; Mehraj et al., 2022a, b). To understand the involvement of the milieu of the breast tissue in controlling the activities of both normal and tumor stem cells, as well as MaSC-microenvironment crosstalk is believed to open a new window of identifying

Role of Tumor Microenvironment in Breast Cancer and Targeted Therapies
https://doi.org/10.1016/B978-0-443-18696-7.00005-1

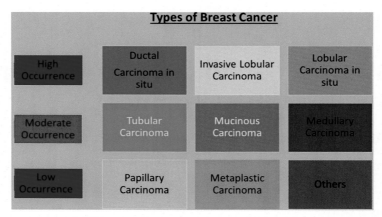

Fig. 9.1 No special type (NST) invasive breast carcinoma and its most common specific subtypes including invasive lobular, tubular, cribriform, metaplastic, apocrine, mucinous, and papillary.

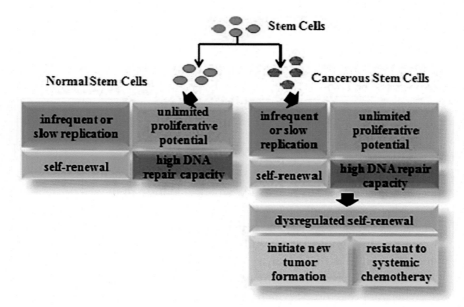

Fig. 9.2 Characteristic features of cancer stem cells (CSCs) including ability to self-renew, differentiate into defined progenies, and initiate and sustain tumor growth in vivo.

how a modified breast tissue microenvironment contributes to the development of breast tumor, its proliferation, and reaction to the therapy (Mir and Mehraj, 2019). Besides, efforts are to be made to study its implications for the evolution of innovative therapeutic approaches focused on cancer stem cells (CSCs) (Bhat et al., 2019; Campbell and Polyak, 2007).

9.2 Origin of BCSCs

The generation of BCSCs from regular stem cells, mutation-induced pluripotency of precursor cells into CSCs, and the dedifferentiation of adult breast cells into stem cells via the EMTs are presently the three main hypothesis (Scheel and Weinberg, 2012). Given the current knowledge of BCSCs, it appears that BCSCs can arise from either mammary stem cells or progenitor cells (Bao et al., 2015; Lim et al., 2009). This model, referred to as a hierarchical or CSC model posits that only a small number of stem/progenitor cells inside a tumor have the tumor-propagating capacity and can repeat tumor hierarchy. BCSCs can be distinguished from normal stem cells by the presence of increased ALDH1 expression (Ginestier et al., 2007b). In both in vivo and in vitro investigations, healthy and cancerous human breast epithelium cells with high ALDH1 activity have been found to have stem/progenitor cell features that can lead to tumor formation. The expression of the CD44+/CD24 cell marker on progenitor cells has also been discovered to mimic the CD44+/CD24/Lin phenotype found in BCSCs (Liu et al., 2014). Furthermore, gene expression analysis demonstrated that basal breast cancers resembled healthy luminal progenitor cells than any other epithelium component, such as the stem cell-enriched population (Lim et al., 2009). In terms of self-renewal, multiplication, and differentiation, BCSCs are similar to mammary stem cells and poorly differentiated progenitor cells (Bao et al., 2015; Liu et al., 2014). BCSCs create mammospheres in vitro (Ponti et al., 2005), develop tumors with phenotypic heterogeneity similar to the primary tumor (Al-Hajj et al., 2003), are implicated in tumor metastasis and resistant to conventional treatment (Sin and Lim, 2017).

Despite the evidence presented above, when subjected to deleterious environmental stimuli such as radiotherapy and chemotherapy, differentiated mammary cells can change into BCSCs. Besides, cell dedifferentiation can trigger genetic mutations in cells, allowing them to recover stem cell-like capabilities (Van Keymeulen et al., 2015; Meyer et al., 2011). In this model, all tumor cells are believed to have comparable tumorigenic potential, and tumor heterogeneity is formed via intratumoral clonal evolution via sequential alterations, referred to as stochastic clonal evolution. It was found that a PIK3CA mutant in luminal cells generated both basal-like and luminal malignancies, but in basal cells its expression induced luminal tumors, demonstrating the multipotency reactivation from differentiated breast cells (Van Keymeulen et al., 2015). Another study discovered that tumor cells with stem cell, luminal and basal-like phenotypes were all tumorigenic in the presence of specific environmental stressors, such as when coinoculated with irradiated cells, and that each tumor cell subpopulation could form xenografts (Meyer et al., 2011). However, only stem cells efficiently formed tumors. According to this research, interconversion can occur in some conditions because the CSC and non-CSC states are not hardwired (Meyer et al., 2011).

9.3 Breast cancer markers and targeted pathways involved in stem cell-mediated breast cancer progression

New approaches are being explored because of the complex and heterogeneous nature of breast cancer which renders its treatment challenging and increases morbidity and mortality associated to breast cancer. Gene expression profiling described breast tumors as HER2-positive, luminal-like, or basal-like by displaying a detailed molecular depiction of the breast tumor (Perou et al., 2000). The clinical categorization of heterogeneous breast cancer (Table 9.1) includes four prominent molecular subgroups, i.e., luminal A and luminal B characterized by positive expression of estrogen receptors (ERs); HER2 positive breast tumor is defined as those with significant HER2 transcriptional activation and TNBC, which is identified by the lack of ER, PR, and HER2, as well as an elevated frequency of germline BRCA1/2 mutations (Foulkes et al., 2003; Lord and Ashworth, 2016). TNBC is linked to increased prevalence of hematogenous

Table 9.1 Molecular subtypes of breast cancer characterized by specific markers and their global prevalence.

S. no.	Type	Hormone receptors	Treatment therapies	Prevalence	References
1.	Luminal A	HR +/ HER2−(HR-positive/HER2-negative)	Hormonal therapy	50%–60%	Cheang et al. (2008), Carey (2010)
2.	Luminal B	HR +/HER2 +(HR-positive/HER2-positive)	Chemotherapy and HER2 protein target therapy	15%–20%	Creighton (2012)
3.	Triple-negative	HR-/HER2−(HR/HER2-negative)	Surgery, chemotherapy, radiation therapy, (PARP inhibitors, platinum chemotherapy, or immunotherapy; for advanced BC)	8%–37%	Rakha et al. (2009)
4.	HER2-positive	ER −/PR −/HER2 +(ER-negative/PR-negative/HER2 +positive)	HER2 protein target therapy using monoclonal antibodies; chemotherapy	15%–20%	Tsutsui et al. (2003), Parker et al. (2009)
5.	Normal-like breast cancer	ER +/PR +/ HER2 −	Hormonal therapy	5%–10%	Hu et al. (2006), Weigelt et al. (2010)

metastasis, with higher heterogeneity compared to other types. They have been subdivided into transcriptome-based subtypes such as basal-like immune-suppressed, immunomodulatory, luminal androgen receptor, and mesenchymal-like (Jiang et al., 2019). Some of the important factors for breast tumor progression include elevated exhibition level of estrogen, ER, PR, HER2. However, the principal factor responsible for familial breast cancer is mutation in BRCA1 and BRCA2 genes (Kaminska et al., 2015). The common BC types include ductal and lobular while as several subtypes of BC are luminal A and B, HER2+, claudin-low, and TNBC. These subtypes are categorized by molecular and histological characterization into noninvasive and invasive (Nounou et al., 2015; Semenza, 2015; Yousefnia et al., 2019, 2020).

The concept of breast tumor heterogeneity is based on two distinct models, i.e., clonal modulation model suggests random mutation and clonal selection responsible for breast cancer cellular heterogeneity, and the CSC model which propounds that BCSCs account for cellular complexity and tumor progression. Interestingly, the tumor microenvironment plays a vital part in facilitating the evolution of breast cancer cells in both models (Vermeulen et al., 2008; Greaves and Maley, 2012; Brooks et al., 2015). BCSCs though are low in number but significant enough because of posttreatment recurrence potential. The population of BC cells is characterized by diverse phenotypes like migration, self-renewal, invasion, and chemotherapy and radiotherapy resistance. The identification of molecular processes and transcription factors are associated with characteristic BCSCs stemness traits resulting in the creation of novel therapeutic options for BCSCs (Nounou et al., 2015).

9.4 BCSCs and associated cellular markers

BCSCs form 2% of breast tumors and their potential opposition to treatment may lead to treatment failure and tumor recurrence (Lin et al., 2016). The BCSCs genesis is still a topic of discussion, wherein typical stem cells, progenitors, or differentiated cells may all be thought of as a precursor of BCSCs (Sin and Lim, 2017). Researchers believe that signaling pathway deregulation in normal stem cells can change BCSCs to CSCs because of genetic and epigenetic modifications (Suyama et al., 2016; Wang et al., 2014). Besides, many researchers have found that the manifestation of individual molecules in such pathways can be unregulated in BCSCs, as can the expression of microRNAs (miRNAs), as many studies have found that various miRNAs have been elevated in BCSCs including miR-10b, miR-21, and miR-125 (Ma et al., 2007; Han et al., 2012a,b, Song et al., 2013). Consequently, downregulation of these miRNAs (miR-7, miR-9, miR-16, miR-23b) is propounded as a novel treatment approach for breast tumors along with other alternative strategies (Zhang et al., 2010; Okuda et al., 2013; Mohammadi-Yeganeh et al., 2015).

BCSCs in different breast tumor types express several specific markers including CD_{326} (EpCAM), ESA, $CD44^+/CD24^-$, and ALDH activity. CD44 is the characteristic

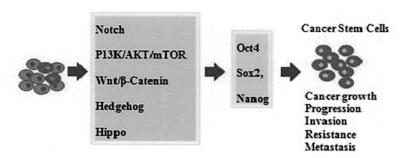

Fig. 9.3 Description of the activation of various pathways involved in the stemness, tumor development and enrichment of cancer stem cells (CSCs) population.

surface marker of stemness expressed by the BCSCs linked to HA and ECM proteins OPN and MMP (Idowu et al., 2012) while CD24 marker is the differentiation breast tumor cells marker. In BCSCs, CD44 and RTK can regulate cell attachment, movement, and proliferative signal dissemination. Besides, signaling pathways like Rho GTPases, Ras-MAPK, and PI3K/Akt responsible for cell attachment, movement, progression, and EMT control are also regulated by CD44 (Zöller, 2011; Al-Othman et al., 2020).

Despite being an important marker, CD44[+] is not considered very helpful in BCSCs sorting and identification in every type of breast tumor (Yousefnia et al., 2019; Ricardo et al., 2011; Liu et al., 2014). CD44-/CD24+ and CD44+/CD24− phenotypes are characteristic of luminal and basal breast tumors respectively, while basal/epithelial breast tumors show positive expression toward both (Feifei et al., 2012). BCSCs with the higher frequency of CD44+/CD24− are more significant in TNBCs (Idowu et al., 2012). In addition, ALDH activity is vital in stem cells differentiation and is considered a preferable prognostic identifier along with greater carcinogenic potential in vivo compared to CD44/CD24 (Tanei et al., 2009; Ginestier et al., 2007). An important observation about the cancerous cells is that postsurgery use of radiation therapy can transform differentiated CSCs with the help of Oct4/Sox2/KLF4 expression (Fig. 9.3). As a result, in certain tumor patients, radiation is not advised because of recurrence and metastases risk (Wang et al., 2014). Hypoxia, which is caused by a shortage of oxygen and blood arteries in the depths of the tumor, may influence the manifestation of CSCs genes. It has the potential to boost the amount of CSCs by converting differentiated cancer cells to CSCs (Semenza, 2015). Some of the important BCSCs markers (Fig. 9.4) are given below.

The surface biomarkers of BCSCs are used to identify or isolate BC. Emerging research suggests that distinct BCSCs are decided by the kind of surface markers present (Dey et al., 2019; Sridharan et al., 2019); BCSC activities are dictated by the kind of identifiers present on the surface (Table 9.2).

Breast Cancer Stem Cells (BCSCs) Markers

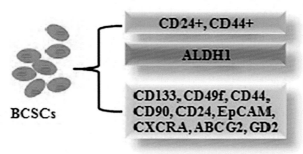

Fig. 9.4 Breast cancer stem cells (BCSCs) and associated cellular markers characteristic of specific type of BCSC used for the separation and identification of BCSCs for treatment therapy.

Table 9.2 Breast cancer stem cells surface markers and their functions in breast cancer.

S. no.	Surface marker	Role in breast cancer
1.	CD44	CD44 mediates tumor activation, proliferation, metastasis and drug resistance; regulate cell-cell interaction, movement, survival, invasion, and EMT (Al-Hajj et al., 2003; Palomeras et al., 2018; Al-Othman et al., 2020)
2.	ALDH1	ALDH1 is a strong candidate for breast cancer stem cells because of its role in the oxidation of retinol to retinoic acid, which governs early stem cell differentiation (Fleisher et al., 2016; Panigoro et al., 2020)
3.	CD133	CD133 provides drug resistance, metastasis, self-renewal, identification of BCSCs (Tume et al., 2016; Nadal et al., 2013)
4.	EpCAM	Regulation of cancer cell growth and potential prognostic marker in breast cancer (Kimbung et al., 2015; Gao et al., 2017)
5.	BCRP/ ABCG2	ABCG2 promotes breast cancer multidrug chemoresistance, tumorigenicity, and metastasis (Nakanishi and Ross, 2012; Bai et al., 2018)
6.	GD2	Promotes tumorigenesis, identifies BCSCs, associated with GD3S-mediated EMT (Battula et al., 2012; Liang et al., 2017)
7.	CXCR4	CXCR4 promotes cell progression, promotes metastasis (Luker et al., 2012; Okuyama Kishima et al., 2015)
8.	CD49f	CD49f regulates several stem cell-like activities, such as CD29- and CD49f-mediated metastasis (Ye et al., 2015, 2017)
9.	CD90	CD90 promotes cell migration, tumorigenesis, metastasis (Perou et al., 2000; Lobba et al., 2018)

9.5 BCSCs and associated signaling pathways

Several studies have observed CSCs pathways (Table 9.3) responsible for stemness, metastasis, self-renewal, and therapeutic resistance (Suyama et al., 2016; Eckert et al., 2015; Woosley et al., 2019; Evans et al., 2018). In typical SCs, pathway deregulation may convert these cells to CSCs, besides; CSCs specific proteins also regulate several signaling pathways. A close association between Sonic hedgehog (SHh and CD24 revealed that through the increased manifestation of SHh GLI1, and MMP2, knocking down CD24 in breast tumor cells resulted in enhanced progression, spread, and tumorigenicity.

Table 9.3 Various factors and pathways affecting cancer stem cells.

S. no.	Factors/ pathways	Function	References
1.	Hedgehog	Manages self-renewal-potential of SCs by activating BMI-1; transcription factors (GLI1/GLI2) are responsible for mammosphere formation and CSC growth; upregulation of markers (c-myc, Nanog, Oct 4) due to Hh signaling; invasion	Cochrane et al. (2015), Sari et al. (2018)
2.	PI3K	Causes enhanced survival of BCSCs due to differential expression in CSCs; PI3K and programmed cell death–ligand 1 share a close association that accounts for stemness in claudin low breast cancer subtypes due to upregulation of Nanog, Oct-4A, and Bmil genes (responsible for self-renewal of BCSCs)	Madsen (2020) Yoon et al. (2021)
3.	Wnt	Tumorigenicity and metastases due to increased Wnt signaling in BCSCs; decreased Wnt decreases tumorigenicity; Wnt downstream molecules (LEF1, β-catenin and TCF–4. β-catenin complexes with the TCF/LEF) overexpressed in CSCs results in transcription of several target genes responsible for invasion, maintenance and metastases including c–Myc, Igr5, cyclin D1, fibronectin, c-Jun, MMP7	De Sousa e Melo and Vermeulen (2016), Zhang and Wang, (2020)

Table 9.3 Various factors and pathways affecting cancer stem cells—cont'd

S. no.	Factors/pathways	Function	References
4.	BRCA1	Loss of BRCA1 causes aggressive basal-like BC along with BCSCs expansion; BRCA1 expression silencing via siRNA transforms cells to acquire stemness	Rassi (2009), Kim et al. (2019)
5.	MicroRNAs	Modulates CSC pathway linked genes (Notch, Wnt/β-catenin, hedgehog, PI3K, NF-κB); upregulation of miR-22, miR-9, miR-181, miR-155 in CSCs; assists in stemness and tumor invasion	Garg (2015), Khan et al. (2019)
6.	HER2	Heterodimers containing HER2 activate signaling proliferative pathways (RAS/Raf/MAPL pathway) along with PI3K/Akt pathway; overexpression of HER2 leads to multidrug resistance	Korkaya and Wicha (2013), Pupa et al. (2021)
7.	Notch	Increased self-renewal potential of CSCs attributed to abnormal Notch expression in CSCs via stemness genes (ALDH, Sox2, Oct4) upregulation; manages RTK ErbB2 gene transcription which affects CSCS self-renewal capacity; induces Snail homolog 2 expression which induces quiescent mesenchymal characteristic in BCSCs	Wang et al. (2009), Xiao et al. (2017), Venkatesh et al., (2018)
8.	Hypoxia	Genes associated with CSCs are upregulated by hypoxia resulting in self-renewal capability and differentiation blocking; inhibits BRCA1 expression and BRCA1 protein downregulation; besides upregulates BCSCs pool	Emami Nejad et al. (2021), Zhang et al. (2021)
9.	NF-kB	Overexpression of CD44 (target of NF-kB) increases in CSCs; regulates MMP9 (ECM modifying matrix); NF-kB inhibition causes CD44 and MMP9 repression resulting in low invasiveness in BCSCs	Rinkenbaugh and Baldwin (2016), Zakaria et al. (2018)

In addition, through STAT1 inhibition, CD24 reduces the malignant BCSCs by decreasing SHh expression (Suyama et al., 2016). It has been observed that increased CD44 expression increases the manifestation of β-catenin along with Notch1 and Ki67 (Cui et al., 2015). Human breast tumor cells and BCSC activities are regulated by CD44 binding to PKC, which is regulated by hyaluronan. Nanog is phosphorylated more when PKC is activated. Nanog that has been phosphorylated is located into the nucleus, where it boosts miR-21 expression and lowers the expression of the tumor suppressor program cell death protein 4 (PDCD4). IAPs and MD11 are increased as a result of this mechanism, resulting in antiapoptosis and chemotherapeutic resistance in BCSCs (Bourguignon et al., 2009). Furthermore, the link between HA and CD44 stimulates c-Src kinase activation and Twist phosphorylation. The twist is phosphorylated and translocated into the nucleus, where it binds to the Twist binding site and stimulates miR-10a expression(s). The tumor suppressor HOXD10 is downregulated, RhoA/RhoC is upregulated, and RhoGTPase-Rho-kinase is stimulated as an outcome of this pathway (ROK). The stimulation of ROK results in the stimulation of the cytoskeleton and the attack on breast cancer cells (Bourguignon et al., 2010).

9.5.1 Hedgehog signaling pathway

EMT is a phenomenon in which epithelium cells become mesenchymal cells by reducing cell-cell interaction and enhancing cell metastasis. In both normal and malignant cells, EMT can result in CSCs with enhanced marker expression, colony formation, mammosphere formation, metastasis, and invasion (Mani et al., 2008). One of the most essential steps in the regulation of EMT is the management of EMT-inducing transcription factors including Snail, ZEB, Twist, and Slug. These transcription factors cause EMT by activating certain molecular programs in various signaling pathways, which inhibit epithelium markers such as E-cadherin while promoting mesenchymal markers including vimentin (Simeone et al., 2019; Brabletz et al., 2018). Excessive ZEB1 manifestation has been linked to the function of numerous particular molecules involved in EMT and BCSC malignancy, including FOXC2, NFB, SOX2, BCL6, and HIF1 (Simeone et al., 2019). In general, EMT transcription factors were associated in the management of signaling pathways in CSCs in general (Stefania and Vergara, 2017).

To maintain tissue homeostasis and self-renewal in breast tumors, the function of the hedgehog (Hh) signaling pathway is very crucial. The Hh signaling cascade involved in maintenance of stemness is usually upregulated in BCSCs. The aberrant stimulation of the Hh pathway in BCSCs, on the other hand, is defined based on certain pieces of evidence. The stimulation of Hh signaling by Sonic Hedgehog (SHh) released by BCSCs governs tumor-related fibroblasts (CAFs) (Valenti et al., 2017) thereby fostering BCSCs self-renewal and proliferation. Besides, salinomycin resistance is caused via SHh-mediated signaling activation. Inhibition of the Hh signaling pathway, on the other hand, could make BCSCs more sensitive to paclitaxel when combined with cyclopamine

(He et al., 2015). The activation mechanism must be identified to create drugs specific to Hh signaling pathway to reverse drug resistance.

9.5.2 Wnt/β-catenin signaling pathway

The Wnt/β-catenin signaling pathway has a critical function in the BCSCs self-renewal potential since the pathway was thought to be a key component of Sam68-mediated self-renewal in BC cells (Wang et al., 2015). Studies also suggest that BCSCs self-renewal is significantly inhibited by Gomisin M2 by undermining the Wnt/β-catenin signaling cascade (Yang et al., 2019). BCSC has a higher degree of Wnt/−catenin signaling, which leads to their high resilience compared to other cells. Suppression of BCSCs proliferation by CWP232228 (Wnt/β-Catenin inhibitor) occurs by the suppression of β-catenin-mediated transcription. Due to drug resistance to BCSCs' self-renewal or growth, Wnt/−catenin is being recommended as a therapeutic focus for BCSCs treatment (Jang et al., 2015).

9.5.3 PI3K/AKT/mTOR signaling pathway

BC treatment resistance is hypothesized to be linked to the phosphatidylinositol 3-kinase (PI3K)-related signaling cascade initiation in BCSCs. According to new research, the PI3K/AKT/mTOR signaling cascade may have a role in ET resistance in ER + breast tumors (Droog et al., 2013). The interaction of Wnt/−catenin and PI3k signaling promotes BCSC stemness and self-renewal by modulating Wnt/−catenin signaling, whereas the association of PI3k and Wnt/−catenin signaling stimulates BCSC self-renewal and stemness by influencing Wnt/−catenin signaling (Solzak et al., 2017). The PI3K/AKT/mTOR signaling pathway inhibitors reduce BCSC self-renewal potential and survival, i.e., they influence BCSC activity similar to IGF-IR, which is connected to breast tumor growth. IGF-IR inhibitors, as well as PI3K/Akt/mTOR signaling pathway inhibitors, minimize the frequency of BCSCs (Chang et al., 2013). As a result, rapalogs like NVPBGT226 and NVP-BEZ235 were identified as PI3K and mTOR inhibitors that might trigger GLP1-mediated stem-like properties in BC cells lines (Posada et al., 2017).

9.5.4 Notch signaling pathway

Among the several signaling pathways, self-renewal and survival are aided by the Notch signaling pathway. The regulation of Notch signaling is maintained by Cytokine-IL-6, and the detection of elevated IL-6 in HT-treated breast tumors is linked with the stimulation of Notch3 signaling in breast tumor cells. This in turn provides the breast tumor cells to self-renew rather than relying on an ER-dependent survival mechanism, which reduces the therapeutic efficacy of HT. On the other hand, the self-renewal potential of CD133^{high}ER^{low} BCSCs was remarkably decreased due to the inhibition of Notch signaling in HT-resistant cells (Sansone et al., 2016). It was reported that the combination of MK-0752 and Tocilizumab significantly reduces the number of BCSCs and prevents proliferation of tumor growth in breast tumor via the Notch3 signaling cascade (Wang et al., 2018). According to recent studies, BCSCs promote drug resistance in breast cancers via Notch-related signaling pathways, such as the formation of stem cell phenotypes in ER/ESR1+ BC cell lines via activation of the Notch signaling system (Gelsomino et al., 2018). Increased BCSC activity as a result of activation of the JAG1-NOTCH4 signaling pathway causes antiestrogen resistance in breast cancers. Therefore, by lowering PTEN expression and enhancing ERK1/2 signaling, BCSCs can overcome Notch1-mediated trastuzumab resistance. The Notch1-PTEN-ERK1/2 signaling pathway is regarded to be a promising target for novel trastuzumab resistance treatments (Simões et al., 2015; Baker et al., 2018).

9.6 BCSCs as a predictive marker

A subpopulation of cells known as BCSCs characterized by stemness, self-renewal ability, and regenerative potential to form bulk tumor cells, has been identified beside the tumor cells which are responsible for the major cellular load in BC. As a result, functional description and research into BCSCs' potential as prognostic markers and therapeutic indicators are ongoing (Vargo-Gogola and Rosen, 2007; Koren and Bentires-Alj, 2015). BCSCs actively participate in dysregulated pathways in the EMT and their over expression in circulating tumor cells (CTCs), which are shed into the vasculature and spread throughout the body, resulting in metastasis. Due to the dormant status of BCSCs, conventional therapies are not successful in the elimination of BCSCs which makes them resistant to treatment. Therefore, efforts including clinical trials are being made to design novel therapy intended to eradicate BCSCs based on their quiescent nature (Scioli et al., 2019).

An important step in breast tumor progression is the EMT; an embryonic program that is reactivated in tumor cells and gives epithelial (nonmotile) cells mesenchymal cell characteristics. Therefore, epithelial cells are provided with the ability to attack surrounding tissues and spread (Kalluri, 2009). CSCs play a very crucial role in this process including their transformation into CTCs (KsiąŻkiewicz et al., 2012). Such a close association of CTCs to metastasis is studied as a possible marker of metastasis and is correlated to severe metastatic breast tumor prognosis (Cristofanilli et al., 2004). Multicentric prospective studies concluded that five CTCs per 7.5 mL of peripheral blood was the optimum cut-off value for the identification of patients having poor prognosis along with poor overall survival (OS), progression-free survival (PFS), and to develop a stronger prediction model (Bidard et al., 2014).

The initial presence of CTCs has been reported in a pooled data analysis of 3173 non-metastatic BC patients which revealed that one or more CTCs were found in 20.2% of patients, that could be used as a nonrestricted prognostic predictor for OS and DFS (Janni et al., 2016). Currently, several ongoing clinical trials including DETECT III, CirCe T-DM1, Treat CTC trial have measured CTCs for the orientation of therapeutic decisions (Ignatiadis et al., 2016; Bidard et al., 2014). However, results published till the data are still conflicting.

The analysis of tumor specimens is crucial for the characterization of CSCs and to unfold the mechanism of the prognosis of diseases and how they respond to treatments. Some of the first markers like CD44, ALDH-1, and CD24, were evaluated in primary tumors through immunohistochemistry for the identification of CSC population. A retrospective study carried out on 639 patients with a follow-up of 12.6 years evaluated ALDH-1$^+$ and CD44$^+$/CD24$^-$ with the help of quantitative immunofluorescence. Although ALDH-1 + alone was not able to significantly predict a result, there was a strong link between the simultaneous manifestation of these markers and a poor result, regardless of grade, nodal status, receptor status, tumor size, and HER2/neu (Neumeister et al., 2010). There was no link between immunohistochemistry ALDH-1 + or CD44 +/CD24 and the difference in OS in a study of 144 individuals with invasive ductal carcinoma (Rabinovich et al., 2018). ALDH and CD44/CD24 positive immunohistochemical staining for ALDH-1 was related with an increased risk of recurrence and metastasis, according to the findings (Zhong et al., 2014). Even while an increased cell number in the tumor was associated with metastatic disease and recurrences, CD44 +/CD24 cell labeling had no connection with metastasis or recurrence on its own. According to several researches, ALDH-1 is a marker of tumor invasiveness and tumor progression, but the CD44 +/CD24 ratio suggests primarily a "self-renewal" ability, meaning that these two markers have distinct functions as tumors grow. As a result, they advocated for integrating the use of both markers whenever possible to develop a greater understanding of the stem population. Therefore, detailed insight of CSCs in the basic tumor mass, both circulating and quiescent, could lead to a better prognosis.

9.7 BCSC metabolism and tumor microenvironment

For the survival of BCSCs, GPCRs are crucial in chemotherapy. In a physiological setting, receptors like CXCR1 and CXCR2 are involved in the chemotaxis of neutrophils, macrophages, and endothelial cells. CXCR1-neutralizing antibody or repertaxin (inhibitor) acts as an antagonist against CXCR1 responsible for selective depletion of BCSCs greater than bulk tumor cells in vitro (Ginestier et al., 2010). Interestingly, CXCR4 manifested in BCSCs serves as a target in the restraining or elimination of BCSCs in Phase I studies. CXCR4 activation is thought to aid mesenchymal BCSC metastasis by activating the PKA/MAPKAP2 pathway, which activates the extracellular signal-regulated kinase (ERK) pathway in BCSCs (Yi et al., 2014).

Anticancer drugs rely on the development of oxidative stress as a key mechanism of action. BCSC contains a very active DNA repair system that helps to repair DNA damage, which is particularly important following chemotherapy. BCSCs' ability to repair DNA damage has previously been connected to ROS, as ROS levels in BCSCs are much lower than in noncancerous stem cells (NCSCs). This is because BCSCs have high levels of free radical scavenging mechanisms such as SOD, CAT, and GPx, which protect them from ROS-induced genotoxicity. Reduced ROS scavengers in BCSCs led to therapeutic sensitization and a significant decrease in clonogenicity Diehn et al., 2009). Medicines responsible for the generation of ROS- may have the therapeutic capacity to eliminate drug-resistant BCSCs by inducing premature senescence via H2O2-induced BCSC loss of function ((Phillips et al., 2006; Zhong et al., 2019). Glucose and mitochondrial metabolism are important to BCSCs. BCL-2 is a well-known mediator of mitochondrial metabolism; inhibiting BCL-2 can prevent oxidative phosphorylation (OXPHOS), resulting in a reduction in BCSCs that rely on OXPHOS (Deshmukh et al., 2016). By upregulating autophagic pathways, BCSCs can resemble dormancy. Salinomycin is an ionophore antibiotic that has been demonstrated to induce autophagy and thereby eliminate BCSCs (Jiang et al., 2018). Breast cancer metastasis is dependent on the epithelial-mesenchymal transition (EMT), which has recently been linked to Spleen Tyrosine Kinase (SYK) in the EMT. Fostamatinib, an SYK inhibitor, prevents metastatic tumors from spreading by blocking the mesenchymal-epithelial transition (MET) (Shinde et al., 2019).

9.8 BCSCs targeting in therapy resistance and drug development

CSCs because of their potential stemness, self-renewal and regenerative ability are resistant (Fig. 9.5) to conventional medicines that target the tumor bulk (Creighton et al., 2009). It has been found that traditional drugs specific to tumor bulk are not effective in CSCs elimination. Antimitotic agents like taxanes (paclitaxel and docetaxel), are ineffective against dormant CSCs within the tumor bulk (Hernández-Vargas et al., 2007), resulting in the reconstruction of the earlier tumor cell number. This increases disease progression and the CTCs adhesiveness (Li et al., 2008; Balzer et al., 2010). These findings have made some researchers focus on the CSC subpopulation, with encouraging

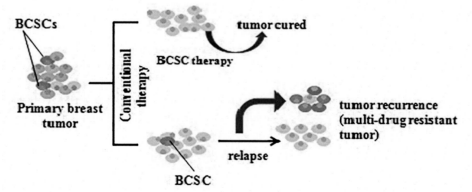

Fig. 9.5 Breast cancer stem cells (BCSCs) are responsible for the BC drugs resistance, causing relapse and metastasis in BC patients.

preclinical and clinical trial results (Holmes et al., 2013; Ning et al., 2012). The use of new and traditional medications in combination is a novel therapeutic strategy for BCSC-targeting. Signaling pathways discussed earlier are the key targets for BCSCs, as they are implicated in the self-renewal and survival of BCSCs (Chiotaki et al., 2015).

There are some surface proteins expressed by CSCs in multidrug resistance including ATP binding cassette (ABC) transporters (Dean, 2009). The resistance developed by CSCs against several drugs is attributed to the activation of the ABC of BCSCs which successfully pumps out chemotherapeutic drugs including taxanes and anthracyclines, the most important drugs for breast tumor treatment (Cojoc et al., 2015). Besides, cellular resistance to antitumor drugs is also attributed to elevated ABCG2 levels in BCSCs allowing cytotoxic medicines to be expelled quickly (Hirschmann-Jax et al., 2004). The SOX2-ABCG2-TWIST1 axis promotes stemness and treatment resistance in TNBC, according to a new study, implying that ABC proteins could be employed to remove BCSCs (Mukherjee et al., 2017). When used with other chemotherapeutic agents like cyclophosphamide, ABC transporter inhibitors like Dofequidar have been shown to increase BCSC responsiveness to anticancer treatments in individuals with advanced or recurrent BC (Saeki et al., 2007). SOX2 is a critical transcription factor involved in stemness maintenance and drug resistance potential. In BC cells, MLN4924 suppresses SOX2 expression, inducing stemness suppression and tamoxifen sensitivity.

9.9 BCSCs: Current developments and therapeutic significance

Research studies investigating the origin, characteristic properties, and role of BCSCs have provided credible evidence that breast cancer besides many other cancers are directed by cells having stemness and were called as CSCs or tumor-initiating cells. These cells are responsible for tumor mediating tumor metastasis and therapeutic resistance in addition to tumor initiation and growth. The therapeutic significance of addressing BCSCs for breast cancer treatment, such as identifying critical pathways that control BCSC self-renewal and developing effective approaches to invade BCSCs, have the potential to significantly enhance breast cancer patient outcomes (Luo et al., 2015).

The presence of stem-like cells with mammary epithelium is indicated by the active status of the mammary glands. According to preliminary transplantation experiments employing mouse mammary fat pad sections and retroviral tagging of mammary epithelium cells, multipotent mammary stem cells maintain the mammary epithelium (Kordon and Smith, 1998; Smith, 1996). The potential characterization and isolation of MaSCs and progenitor cell populations in mice and humans (Keller et al., 2012; Shipitsin et al., 2007; Asselin-Labat et al., 2007), supports the stemness and hierarchical architecture of mammary epithelium, as well as the potential of a single MaSC located in the basal/myoepithelial layer to functionally reconstruct a breast gland by activating differentiated progenies via lineage-restricted progenitor cell (Stingl et al., 2006; Shackleton et al., 2006).

Recent advances in stem cell biology have established a direct relationship between tumorigenesis and stem cells based on the first evidence wherein it was found that acute myeloid leukemia develops from a primitive hematopoietic cell capable of self-renewal (Bonnet and Dick, 1997). BC is a highly heterogeneous disease manifested by its classification into various subtypes each with a distinct transcriptome and molecular expression marker (Visvader, 2009). Breast cancer is now well-known to be organized hierarchically and controlled by a limited section of tumor cells exhibiting stem cell characteristics (Charafe-Jauffret et al., 2008; Wicha et al., 2006). This tiny group of BCSCs, also known as BC initiation cells, was originally discovered among solid tumors by the expression of the cell surface markers CD24+, EpCAM+, and CD44+ (Al-Hajj et al., 2003).

The discovery of leukemia-initiating cells fueled efforts to characterize and isolate CSCs in solid tumors, leading to the identification of stem cell-like populations in malignant and benign tumors of the brain, breast, colon, head, and other organs, as well as melanoma (Ginestier et al., 2007; Patrawala et al., 2006; Krishnamurthy et al., 2010).

There is a basic difference between CSC model of tumorigenesis and the clonal evolution model which supports tumor initiation through random mutation and clonal selection. Besides, it proposes that all tumor cells are equally potential to attain genetic mutations vital to tumor activation and development. An indiscriminate buildup of genomic abnormalities results in divergent but coexisting tumor cell clones significant to intratumoral heterogeneity (Quintana et al., 2008; Murray et al., 2012; Joosse and Pantel, 2013).

The presence and expression of markers, as well as other molecular events generated by CSCs, seems to have a potential impact on the development of cancer-targeting drugs. As CSCs are believed to be involved in commonly seen radiotherapy and chemotherapy resistance in many tumors, clinical targeting of the CSC may result in metastasis decrease (Zielske et al., 2011). The potential resistance by stem cells to chemotherapeutic drugs is attributed to the dormant and slower cell cycles. Further, these cells have a lot of drug transporters, especially exporters. CSCs are also characterized by high ALDH enzyme activity, known for metabolizing several chemotherapeutic drugs like cyclophosphamide into low cytotoxic metabolites.

Because CSCs are more potent, aggressive, and subject to metastasis than bulk tumorigenic cells, the CSC model contends that tumor recurrence after routine excision and/or chemo/radiotherapy could be prevented by removing repopulating cells using CSC-targeting medications (Liu et al., 2012). Aldefluor + cells from breast cancer cell lines revealed higher invasiveness and metastasizing capacity in NOD/SCID mice after intracardiac injection (Liu et al., 2011). Furthermore, patients with breast carcinomas showed a larger CD24− CD44+ breast CSC population (Balic et al., 2006). In order to amplify the efficiency of drugs targeting CSCs, it is recommended to supplement these drugs with radiation or standard chemotherapy. CSC-specific drugs are not usually specific to destroy several bulk numbers of differentiated bulk tumor cells resulting in a complicated prognosis. Therefore, unconventional methods are required to be developed and

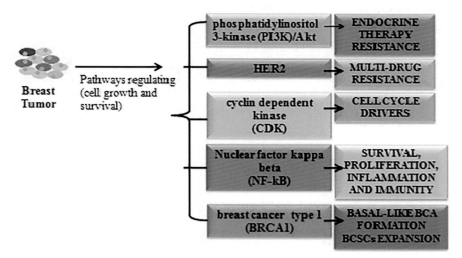

Fig. 9.6 Different signaling pathways involved in cancer cell growth and survival and their role in treatment therapies.

implemented for precise and successful CSC target outcomes. The use of the RECIST method for the measurement of tumor shrinkage in clinical trials reveals that tumor regression often fails to match with better survival rates (Brekelmans et al., 2007). After chemotherapy, CD24— CD44+ breast CSCs were found to rise; however, combining chemotherapy with a BCSC-specific drug such as the HER2 prevented the BCSCs elevation (Li et al., 2008).

Another treatment option in this procedure is to administer a CSC specific drug before surgery, after that, CSC biomarker profiling on chosen patient biopsies are done and the cells obtained could be grown as tumor spheres to ascertain drug CSCs target ability besides characteristic signaling pathways involved. Recent developments in gene therapy indicate that microRNAs play a significant role in gene regulation mediating self-renewal, proliferation and CSC pathways (Liu et al., 2012). For the successful eradication of CSCs, It is critical to figure out how signaling pathways interact with these cells (Fig. 9.6) to control CSC-specific processes like growth, renewal, differentiation, and death. Several pathways involved in successful regulation of normal and malignant stem cells include the Notch, Hedgehog, p53, and Wnt signaling pathways (Korkaya and Wicha, 2007; Korkaya et al., 2009; Liu and Wicha, 2010; Markey, 2009).

9.10 Summary

Developments in stem cell biology, gene therapy, and associated treatment techniques suggest the potential significance of BCSCs in breast tumor carcinogenesis, therapeutic resistance, and recurrence. Efforts to isolate and characterize BCSCs, as well as the development of unique markers, are ongoing to target and destroy this cell type using CSC-targeting drugs. The identification of targets for the development of BSCS-specific medicines suggests that a combined approach aiming at several different pharmacological targets would have more benefits and be more promising. However, because to difficulties experienced by the identified markers in identifying a single tiny cell population with significant plasticity, there are still some inconsistencies in these therapeutic approaches. Due to the variability of BCSC cells, the therapy approach using a combination of many targets is sustained. New circulating indicators for evaluating the action of anti–BCSC medicines are also being investigated all the time.

The possible significance of CSCs in tumor initiation, development, and recurrence has piqued researchers' attention, prompting them to investigate critical signaling pathways governing CSC features such as self-renewal and stemness, as well as create therapeutic techniques to eliminate CSCs. The CSC therapeutic strategy is expensive, so new funding mechanisms are needed, so that disease foundations, academic researchers, donors, government sponsors, philanthropists, and industry partners will collaborate to transform promising advancements in stem cell biology into practical and relevant clinical therapies (Liu and Wicha, 2010). Recent advances in this sector, such as targeted medicines paired with traditional procedures, have shown promise in eradicating the disease with little chance of recurrence. However, some challenges in the CSC approach must be overcome before the disease can be completely eradicated, including more basic CSC research, a thorough understanding of the disease's genetic basis, and the different signaling pathways particular to each cancer type and subtype. For better discrimination and quantification of CSCs, new trial designs and separation and characterization approaches are badly needed. To evaluate patient responses and clearly detect CSCs before or after treatment, imaging modalities such as ultrasonic, magnetic resonance, and conventional microscopy are required. Approaches that exploit unique cell cycling traits, epigenetics, apoptotic programs, miRNA modulation of EMT/MET states, or other characteristics of tumor-initiating cells while protecting normal stem cells would be particularly intriguing.

References

Al-Hajj, M., Wicha, M.S., Benito-Hernandez, A., Morrison, S.J., Clarke, M.F., 2003. Prospective identification of tumorigenic breast cancer cells. Proc. Natl. Acad. Sci. U. S. A. 100, 3983–3988.

Al-Othman, N., Alhendi, A., Ihbaisha, M., Barahmeh, M., Alqaraleh, M., Al-Momany, B.Z., 2020. Role of CD44 in breast cancer. Breast Dis. 39, 1–13.

Asselin-Labat, M.-L., Sutherland, K.D., Barker, H., Thomas, R., Shackleton, M., Forrest, N.C., Hartley, L., Robb, L., Grosveld, F.G., Van Der Wees, J., 2007. Gata-3 is an essential regulator of mammary-gland morphogenesis and luminal-cell differentiation. Nat. Cell Biol. 9, 201–209.

Bai, X., Ni, J., Beretov, J., Graham, P., Li, Y., 2018. Cancer stem cell in breast cancer therapeutic resistance. Cancer Treat. Rev. 69, 152–163.

Baker, A., Wyatt, D., Bocchetta, M., Li, J., Filipovic, A., Green, A., Peiffer, D.S., Fuqua, S., Miele, L., Albain, K.S., 2018. Notch-1-PTEN-ERK1/2 signaling axis promotes HER2+ breast cancer cell proliferation and stem cell survival. Oncogene 37, 4489–4504.

Balic, M., Lin, H., Young, L., Hawes, D., Giuliano, A., McNamara, G., Datar, R.H., Cote, R.J., 2006. Most early disseminated cancer cells detected in bone marrow of breast cancer patients have a putative breast cancer stem cell phenotype. Clin. Cancer Res. 12, 5615–5621.

Balzer, E.M., Whipple, R.A., Cho, E.H., Matrone, M.A., Martin, S.S., 2010. Antimitotic chemotherapeutics promote adhesive responses in detached and circulating tumor cells. Breast Cancer Res. Treat. 121, 65–78.

Bao, L., Cardiff, R.D., Steinbach, P., Messer, K.S., Ellies, L.G., 2015. Multipotent luminal mammary cancer stem cells model tumor heterogeneity. Breast Cancer Res. 17, 1–14.

Battula, V.L., Shi, Y., Evans, K.W., Wang, R.-Y., Spaeth, E.L., Jacamo, R.O., Guerra, R., Sahin, A.A., Marini, F.C., Hortobagyi, G., 2012. Ganglioside GD2 identifies breast cancer stem cells and promotes tumorigenesis. J. Clin. Invest. 122, 2066–2078.

Bhat, V., Allan, A.L., Raouf, A., 2019. Role of the microenvironment in regulating normal and cancer stem cell activity: implications for breast cancer progression and therapy response. Cancer 11, 1240.

Bidard, F.C., Peeters, D.J., Fehm, T., Nolé, F., Gisbert-Criado, R., Mavroudis, D., Grisanti, S., Generali, D., Garcia-Saenz, J.A., Stebbing, J., Caldas, C., Gazzaniga, P., Manso, L., Zamarchi, R., De Lascoiti, A.F., De Mattos-Arruda, L., Ignatiadis, M., Lebofsky, R., Van Laere, S.J., Meier-Stiegen, F., Sandri, M.T., Vidal-Martinez, J., Politaki, E., Consoli, F., Bottini, A., Diaz-Rubio, E., Krell, J., Dawson, S.J., Raimondi, C., Rutten, A., Janni, W., Munzone, E., Carañana, V., Agelaki, S., Almici, C., Dirix, L., Solomayer, E.F., Zorzino, L., Johannes, H., Reis-Filho, J.S., Pantel, K., Pierga, J.Y., Michiels, S., 2014. Clinical validity of circulating tumour cells in patients with metastatic breast cancer: a pooled analysis of individual patient data. Lancet Oncol. 15, 406–414.

Bissell, M.J., Rizki, A., Mian, I.S., 2003. Tissue architecture: the ultimate regulator of breast epithelial function. Curr. Opin. Cell Biol. 15, 753.

Bonnet, D., Dick, J.E., 1997. Human acute myeloid leukemia is organized as a hierarchy that originates from a primitive hematopoietic cell. Nat. Med. 3, 730–737.

Bourguignon, L.Y.W., Spevak, C.C., Wong, G., Xia, W., Gilad, E., 2009. Hyaluronan-CD44 interaction with protein kinase Cε promotes oncogenic signaling by the stem cell marker Nanog and the production of microRNA-21, leading to down-regulation of the tumor suppressor protein PDCD4, anti-apoptosis, and chemotherapy resistance in breast tumor cells. J. Biol. Chem. 284, 26533–26546.

Bourguignon, L.Y.W., Wong, G., Earle, C., Krueger, K., Spevak, C.C., 2010. Hyaluronan-CD44 interaction promotes c-Src-mediated twist signaling, microRNA-10b expression, and RhoA/RhoC up-regulation, leading to rho-kinase-associated cytoskeleton activation and breast tumor cell invasion. J. Biol. Chem. 285, 36721–36735.

Brabletz, T., Kalluri, R., Nieto, M.A., Weinberg, R.A., 2018. EMT in cancer. Nat. Rev. Cancer 18, 128–134.

Brekelmans, C.T., Tilanus-Linthorst, M.M., Seynaeve, C., vd Ouweland, A., Menke-Pluymers, M.B., Bartels, C.C., et al., 2007. Tumour characteristics, survival and prognostic factors of hereditary breast cancer from BRCA2-, BRCA1-and non-BRCA1/2 families as compared to sporadic breast cancer cases. Eur. J. Cancer 43, 867–876.

Brooks, M.D., Burness, M.L., Wicha, M.S., 2015. Therapeutic implications of cellular heterogeneity and plasticity in breast cancer. Cell Stem Cell 17, 260–271.

Campbell, L.L., Polyak, K., 2007. Breast tumor heterogeneity: cancer stem cells or clonal evolution? Cell Cycle 6, 2332–2338.

Carey, L.A., 2010. Through a glass darkly: advances in understanding breast cancer biology, 2000–2010. Clin. Breast Cancer 10, 188–195.

Chang, W.-W., Lin, R.-J., Yu, J., Chang, W.-Y., Fu, C.-H., Lai, A.C.-Y., Yu, J.-C., Yu, A.L., 2013. The expression and significance of insulin-like growth factor-1 receptor and its pathway on breast cancer stem/progenitors. Breast Cancer Res. 15, 1–16.

Charafe-Jauffret, E., Monville, F., Ginestier, C., Dontu, G., Birnbaum, D., Wicha, M.S., 2008. Cancer stem cells in breast: current opinion and future challenges. Pathobiology 75, 75–84.

Cheang, M.C.U., Voduc, D., Bajdik, C., Leung, S., McKinney, S., Chia, S.K., Perou, C.M., Nielsen, T.O., 2008. Basal-like breast cancer defined by five biomarkers has superior prognostic value than triple-negative phenotype. Clin. Cancer Res. 14, 1368–1376.

Chiotaki, R., Polioudaki, H., A Theodoropoulos, P., 2015. Cancer stem cells in solid and liquid tissues of breast cancer patients: characterization and therapeutic perspectives. Curr. Cancer Drug Targets 15, 256–269.

Cochrane, C.R., Szczepny, A., Watkins, D.N., Cain, J.E., 2015. Hedgehog signaling in the maintenance of cancer stem cells. Cancer 7, 1554–1585.

Cojoc, M., Mäbert, K., Muders, M.H., Dubrovska, A., 2015. A Role for Cancer Stem Cells in Therapy Resistance: Cellular and Molecular Mechanisms. Elsevier, pp. 16–27.

Creighton, C.J., 2012. The molecular profile of luminal B breast cancer. Biologics 6, 289.

Creighton, C.J., Li, X., Landis, M., Dixon, J.M., Neumeister, V.M., Sjolund, A., Rimm, D.L., Wong, H., Rodriguez, A., Herschkowitz, J.I., 2009. Residual breast cancers after conventional therapy display mesenchymal as well as tumor-initiating features. Proc. Natl. Acad. Sci. U. S. A. 106, 13820–13825.

Cristofanilli, M., Budd, G.T., Ellis, M.J., Stopeck, A., Matera, J., Miller, M.C., Reuben, J.M., Doyle, G.V., Allard, W.J., Terstappen, L.W.M.M., 2004. Circulating tumor cells, disease progression, and survival in metastatic breast cancer. N. Engl. J. Med. 351, 781–791.

Cui, J., Li, P., Liu, X., Hu, H., Wei, W., 2015. Abnormal expression of the Notch and Wnt/β-catenin signaling pathways in stem-like ALDHhiCD44 + cells correlates highly with Ki-67 expression in breast cancer. Oncol. Lett. 9, 1600–1606.

De Sousa e Melo, F., Vermeulen, L., 2016. Wnt signaling in cancer stem cell biology. Cancer 8, 60.

Dean, M., 2009. ABC transporters, drug resistance, and cancer stem cells. J. Mammary Gland Biol. Neoplasia 14, 3–9.

Deshmukh, A., Deshpande, K., Arfuso, F., Newsholme, P., Dharmarajan, A., 2016. Cancer stem cell metabolism: a potential target for cancer therapy. Mol. Cancer 15, 1–10.

Dey, P., Rathod, M., De, A., 2019. Targeting stem cells in the realm of drug-resistant breast cancer. Breast Cancer 11, 115.

Diehn, M., Cho, R.W., Lobo, N.A., Kalisky, T., Dorie, M.J., Kulp, A.N., Qian, D., Lam, J.S., Ailles, L.E., Wong, M., 2009. Association of reactive oxygen species levels and radioresistance in cancer stem cells. Nature 458, 780–783.

Droog, M., Beelen, K., Linn, S., Zwart, W., 2013. Tamoxifen resistance: from bench to bedside. Eur. J. Pharmacol. 717, 47–57.

Eckert, R.L., Fisher, M.L., Grun, D., Adhikary, G., Xu, W., Kerr, C., 2015. Transglutaminase is a tumor cell and cancer stem cell survival factor. Mol. Carcinog. 54, 947–958.

Emami Nejad, A., Najafgholian, S., Rostami, A., Sistani, A., Shojaeifar, S., Esparvarinha, M., Nedaeinia, R., Haghjooy Javanmard, S., Taherian, M., Ahmadlou, M., 2021. The role of hypoxia in the tumor microenvironment and development of cancer stem cell: a novel approach to developing treatment. Cancer Cell Int. 21, 1–26.

Evans, M.K., Brown, M.C., Geradts, J., Bao, X., Robinson, T.J., Jolly, M.K., Vermeulen, P.B., Palmer, G.M., Gromeier, M., Levine, H., 2018. XIAP regulation by MNK links MAPK and NFκB signaling to determine an aggressive breast cancer phenotype. Cancer Res. 78, 1726–1738.

Feifei, N., Mingzhi, Z., Yanyun, Z., Huanle, Z., Fang, R., Mingzhu, H., Mingzhi, C., Yafei, S., Fengchun, Z., 2012. MicroRNA expression analysis of mammospheres cultured from human breast cancers. J. Cancer Res. Clin. Oncol. 138, 1937–1944.

Fleisher, B., Clarke, C., Ait-Oudhia, S., 2016. Current advances in biomarkers for targeted therapy in triple-negative breast cancer. Breast Cancer 8, 183.

Foulkes, W.D., Stefansson, I.M., Chappuis, P.O., Bégin, L.R., Goffin, J.R., Wong, N., Trudel, M., Akslen, L.A., 2003. Germline BRCA1 mutations and a basal epithelial phenotype in breast cancer. J. Natl. Cancer Inst. 95, 1482–1485.

Gao, S., Sun, Y., Liu, X., Zhang, D., Yang, X., 2017. EpCAM and COX-2 expression are positively correlated in human breast cancer. Mol. Med. Rep. 15, 3755–3760.

Garg, M., 2015. Emerging role of microRNAs in cancer stem cells: implications in cancer therapy. World J. Stem Cells 7, 1078.

Gelsomino, L., Panza, S., Giordano, C., Barone, I., Gu, G., Spina, E., Catalano, S., Fuqua, S., Andò, S., 2018. Mutations in the estrogen receptor alpha hormone binding domain promote stem cell phenotype through notch activation in breast cancer cell lines. Cancer Lett. 428, 12–20.

Ginestier, C., Hur, M.H., Charafe-Jauffret, E., Monville, F., Dutcher, J., Brown, M., Jacquemier, J., Viens, P., Kleer, C.G., Liu, S., et al., 2007. ALDH1 is a marker of normal and malignant human mammary stem cells and a predictor of poor clinical outcome. Cell Stem Cell 1, 555–567.

Ginestier, C., Liu, S., Diebel, M.E., Korkaya, H., Luo, M., Brown, M., Wicinski, J., Cabaud, O., Charafe-Jauffret, E., Birnbaum, D., 2010. CXCR1 blockade selectively targets human breast cancer stem cells in vitro and in xenografts. J. Clin. Invest. 120, 485–497.

Greaves, M., Maley, C.C., 2012. Clonal evolution in cancer. Nature 481, 306–313.

Han, M., Liu, M., Wang, Y., Chen, X., Xu, J., Sun, Y., Zhao, L., Qu, H., Fan, Y., Wu, C., 2012a. Antagonism of miR-21 reverses epithelial-mesenchymal transition and cancer stem cell phenotype through AKT/ERK1/2 inactivation by targeting PTEN. PLoS One 7, e39520.

Han, M., Liu, M., Wang, Y., Mo, Z., Bi, X., Liu, Z., Fan, Y., Chen, X., Wu, C., 2012b. Re-expression of miR-21 contributes to migration and invasion by inducing epithelial-mesenchymal transition consistent with cancer stem cell characteristics in MCF-7 cells. Mol. Cell. Biochem. 363, 427–436.

He, M., Fu, Y., Yan, Y., Xiao, Q., Wu, H., Yao, W., Zhao, H., Zhao, L., Jiang, Q., Yu, Z., 2015. The Hedgehog signalling pathway mediates drug response of MCF-7 mammosphere cells in breast cancer patients. Clin. Sci. 129, 809–822.

Hernández-Vargas, H., Von Kobbe, C., Sánchez-Estévez, C., Julián-Tendero, M., Palacios, J., Moreno-Bueno, G., 2007. Inhibition of paclitaxel-induced proteasome activation influences paclitaxel cytotoxicity in breast cancer cells in a sequence-dependent manner. Cell Cycle 6, 2662–2668.

Hirschmann-Jax, C., Foster, A.E., Wulf, G.G., Nuchtern, J.G., Jax, T.W., Gobel, U., Goodell, M.A., Brenner, M.K., 2004. A distinct "side population" of cells with high drug efflux capacity in human tumor cells. Proc. Natl. Acad. Sci. U. S. A. 101, 14228–14233.

Holmes, F.A., Espina, V., Liotta, L.A., Nagarwala, Y.M., Danso, M., McIntyre, K.J., Osborne, C.R., Anderson, T., Krekow, L., Blum, J.L., Pippen, J., Florance, A., Mahoney, J., O'shaughnessy, J.A., 2013. Pathologic complete response after preoperative anti-HER2 therapy correlates with alterations in PTEN, FOXO, phosphorylated Stat5, and autophagy protein signaling. BMC. Res. Notes 6, 507.

Hu, Z., Fan, C., Oh, D.S., Marron, J.S., He, X., Qaqish, B.F., Livasy, C., Carey, L.A., Reynolds, E., Dressler, L., 2006. The molecular portraits of breast tumors are conserved across microarray platforms. BMC Genomics 7, 1–12.

Idowu, M.O., Kmieciak, M., Dumur, C., Burton, R.S., Grimes, M.M., Powers, C.N., Manjili, M.H., 2012. CD44+/CD24−/low cancer stem/progenitor cells are more abundant in triple-negative invasive breast carcinoma phenotype and are associated with poor outcome. Hum. Pathol. 43, 364–373.

Ignatiadis, M., Rack, B., Rothé, F., Riethdorf, S., Decraene, C., Bonnefoi, H., Dittrich, C., Messina, C., Beauvois, M., Trapp, E., 2016. Liquid biopsy-based clinical research in early breast cancer: the EORTC 90091-10093 treat CTC trial. Eur. J. Cancer 63, 97–104.

Jang, G.-B., Hong, I.-S., Kim, R.-J., Lee, S.-Y., Park, S.-J., Lee, E.-S., Park, J.H., Yun, C.-H., Chung, J.U., Lee, K.-J., 2015. Wnt/β-catenin small-molecule inhibitor CWP232228 preferentially inhibits the growth of breast cancer stem-like cells. Cancer Res. 75, 1691–1702.

Janni, W.J., Rack, B., Terstappen, L.W.M.M., Pierga, J.-Y., Taran, F.-A., Fehm, T., Hall, C., De Groot, M.R., Bidard, F.-C., Friedl, T.W.P., 2016. Pooled analysis of the prognostic relevance of circulating tumor cells in primary breast cancer. Clin. Cancer Res. 22, 2583–2593.

Jiang, J., Li, H., Qaed, E., Zhang, J., Song, Y., Wu, R., Bu, X., Wang, Q., Tang, Z., 2018. Salinomycin, as an autophagy modulator—a new avenue to anticancer: a review. J. Exp. Clin. Cancer Res. 37, 1–13.

Jiang, Y.Z., Ma, D., Suo, C., Shi, J., Xue, M., Hu, X., Xiao, Y., Yu, K.D., Liu, Y.R., Yu, Y., Zheng, Y., Li, X., Zhang, C., Hu, P., Zhang, J., Hua, Q., Zhang, J., Hou, W., Ren, L., Bao, D., Shao, Z.M., 2019. Genomic and transcriptomic landscape of triple-negative breast cancers: subtypes and treatment strategies. Cancer cell 35 (3), 428–440.e5. https://doi.org/10.1016/j.ccell.2019.02.001.

Joosse, S.A., Pantel, K., 2013. Biologic challenges in the detection of circulating tumor cells. Cancer Res. 73, 8–11.

Kalluri, R., 2009. EMT: when epithelial cells decide to become mesenchymal-like cells. J. Clin. Invest. 119, 1417–1419.

Kaminska, M., Ciszewski, T., Lopacka-Szatan, K., Miotła, P., Starosławska, E., 2015. Breast cancer risk factors. Prz. Menopauzalny 14, 196–202.

Keller, P.J., Arendt, L.M., Skibinski, A., Logvinenko, T., Klebba, I., Dong, S., Smith, A.E., Prat, A., Perou, C.M., Gilmore, H., 2012. Defining the cellular precursors to human breast cancer. Proc. Natl. Acad. Sci. U. S. A. 109, 2772–2777.

Khan, A.Q., Ahmed, E.I., Elareer, N.R., Junejo, K., Steinhoff, M., Uddin, S., 2019. Role of miRNA-regulated cancer stem cells in the pathogenesis of human malignancies. Cell 8, 840.

Kim, H., Lin, Q., Yun, Z., 2019. BRCA1 regulates the cancer stem cell fate of breast cancer cells in the context of hypoxia and histone deacetylase inhibitors. Sci. Rep. 9, 1–11.

Kimbung, S., Loman, N., Hedenfalk, I., 2015. Clinical and Molecular Complexity of Breast Cancer Metastases. Elsevier, pp. 85–95.

Kordon, E.C., Smith, G.H., 1998. An entire functional mammary gland may comprise the progeny from a single cell. Development 125, 1921–1930.

Koren, S., Bentires-Alj, M., 2015. Breast tumor heterogeneity: source of fitness, hurdle for therapy. Mol. Cell 60, 537–546.

Korkaya, H., Wicha, M.S., 2007. Selective targeting of cancer stem cells. BioDrugs 21, 299–310.

Korkaya, H., Wicha, M.S., 2013. HER2 and breast cancer stem cells: more than meets the eye. Cancer Res. 73, 3489–3493.

Korkaya, H., Paulson, A., Charafe-Jauffret, E., Ginestier, C., Brown, M., Dutcher, J., Clouthier, S.G., Wicha, M.S., 2009. Regulation of mammary stem/progenitor cells by PTEN/Akt/β-catenin signaling. PLoS Biol. 7, e1000121.

Krishnamurthy, S., Dong, Z., Vodopyanov, D., Imai, A., Helman, J.I., Prince, M.E., Wicha, M.S., Nör, J.E., 2010. Endothelial cell-initiated signaling promotes the survival and self-renewal of cancer stem cells. Cancer Res. 70, 9969–9978.

KsiążKiewicz, M., Markiewicz, A., Żaczek, A.J., 2012. Epithelial-mesenchymal transition: a hallmark in metastasis formation linking circulating tumor cells and cancer stem cells. Pathobiology 79, 195–208.

Li, X., Lewis, M.T., Huang, J., Gutierrez, C., Osborne, C.K., Wu, M.-F., Hilsenbeck, S.G., Pavlick, A., Zhang, X., Chamness, G.C., 2008. Intrinsic resistance of tumorigenic breast cancer cells to chemotherapy. J. Natl. Cancer Inst. 100, 672–679.

Liang, Y.-J., Wang, C.-Y., Wang, I.A., Chen, Y.-W., Li, L.-T., Lin, C.-Y., Ho, M.-Y., Chou, T.-L., Wang, Y.-H., Chiou, S.-P., 2017. Interaction of glycosphingolipids GD3 and GD2 with growth factor receptors maintains breast cancer stem cell phenotype. Oncotarget 8, 47454.

Lim, E., Vaillant, F., Wu, D., Forrest, N.C., Pal, B., Hart, A.H., Asselin-Labat, M.-L., Gyorki, D.E., Ward, T., Partanen, A., 2009. Aberrant luminal progenitors as the candidate target population for basal tumor development in BRCA1 mutation carriers. Nat. Med. 15, 907–913.

Lin, C.Y., Barry-Holson, K.Q., Allison, K.H., 2016. Breast cancer stem cells: are we ready to go from bench to bedside? Histopathology 68, 119–137.

Liu, S., Wicha, M.S., 2010. Targeting breast cancer stem cells. J. Clin. Oncol. 28, 4006–4012.

Liu, S., Ginestier, C., Ou, S.J., Clouthier, S.G., Patel, S.H., Monville, F., Korkaya, H., Heath, A., Dutcher, J., Kleer, C.G., 2011. Breast cancer stem cells are regulated by mesenchymal stem cells through cytokine networks. Cancer Res. 71, 614–624.

Liu, S., Clouthier, S.G., Wicha, M.S., 2012. Role of microRNAs in the regulation of breast cancer stem cells. J. Mammary Gland Biol. Neoplasia 17, 15–21.

Liu, Y., Nenutil, R., Appleyard, M.V., Murray, K., Boylan, M., Thompson, A.M., Coates, P.J., 2014. Lack of correlation of stem cell markers in breast cancer stem cells. Br. J. Cancer 110, 2063–2071.

Lobba, A.R.M., Carreira, A.C.O., Cerqueira, O.L.D., Fujita, A., Deocesano-Pereira, C., Osorio, C.A.B., Soares, F.A., Rameshwar, P., Sogayar, M.C., 2018. High CD90 (THY-1) expression positively correlates with cell transformation and worse prognosis in basal-like breast cancer tumors. PLoS One 13, e0199254.

Lord, C.J., Ashworth, A., 2016. BRCAness revisited. Nat. Rev. Cancer 16, 110–120.

Luker, K.E., Lewin, S.A., Mihalko, L.A., Schmidt, B.T., Winkler, J.S., Coggins, N.L., Thomas, D.G., Luker, G.D., 2012. Scavenging of CXCL12 by CXCR7 promotes tumor growth and metastasis of CXCR4-positive breast cancer cells. Oncogene 31, 4750–4758.

Luo, M., Clouthier, S.G., Deol, Y., Liu, S., Nagrath, S., Azizi, E., Wicha, M.S., 2015. Breast cancer stem cells: current advances and clinical implications. Methods Mol. Biol. 1293, 1–49.

Ma, L., Teruya-Feldstein, J., Weinberg, R.A., 2007. Tumour invasion and metastasis initiated by microRNA-10b in breast cancer. Nature 449, 682–688.

Madsen, R.R., 2020. PI3K in stemness regulation: from development to cancer. Biochem. Soc. Trans. 48, 301–315.

Mani, S.A., Guo, W., Liao, M.-J., Eaton, E.N., Ayyanan, A., Zhou, A.Y., Brooks, M., Reinhard, F., Zhang, C.C., Shipitsin, M., 2008. The epithelial-mesenchymal transition generates cells with properties of stem cells. Cell 133, 704–715.

Markey, K.A., 2009. Firms seek to prove Cancer stem cell hypothesis. Genet. Eng. Biotechnol. News 29, 16–17.

Mehraj, U., Dar, A.H., Wani, N.A., Mir, M.A., 2021a. Tumor microenvironment promotes breast cancer chemoresistance. Cancer Chemother. Pharmacol., 1–12.

Mehraj, U., Ganai, R.A., Macha, M.A., Hamid, A., Zargar, M.A., Bhat, A.A., Nasser, M.W., Haris, M., Batra, S.K., Alshehri, B., 2021b. The tumor microenvironment as driver of stemness and therapeutic resistance in breast cancer: new challenges and therapeutic opportunities. Cell. Oncol., 1–21.

Mehraj, U., Aisha, S., Sofi, S., Mir, M.A., 2022a. Expression pattern and prognostic significance of baculoviral inhibitor of apoptosis repeat-containing 5 (BIRC5) in breast cancer: a comprehensive analysis. Adv. Cancer Biol. Metastasis, 100037.

Mehraj, U., Mushtaq, U., Mir, M.A., Saleem, A., Macha, M.A., Lone, M.N., Hamid, A., Zargar, M.A., Ahmad, S.M., Wani, N.A., 2022b. Chemokines in Triple-Negative Breast Cancer Heterogeneity: New Challenges for Clinical Implications. Elsevier.

Meyer, D.S., Brinkhaus, H., Müller, U., Müller, M., Cardiff, R.D., Bentires-Alj, M., 2011. Luminal expression of PIK3CA mutant H1047R in the mammary gland induces heterogeneous tumors. Cancer Res. 71, 4344–4351.

Mir, M.A., Mehraj, U., 2019. Double-crosser of the immune system: macrophages in tumor progression and metastasis. Curr. Immunol. Rev. 15, 172–184.

Mir, M.A., Qayoom, H., Mehraj, U., Nisar, S., Bhat, B., Wani, N.A., 2020. Targeting different pathways using novel combination therapy in triple negative breast Cancer. Curr. Cancer Drug Targets 20, 586–602.

Mohammadi-Yeganeh, S., Mansouri, A., Paryan, M., 2015. Targeting of miR9/NOTCH1 interaction reduces metastatic behavior in triple-negative breast cancer. Chem. Biol. Drug Des. 86, 1185–1191.

Mukherjee, P., Gupta, A., Chattopadhyay, D., Chatterji, U., 2017. Modulation of SOX2 expression delineates an end-point for paclitaxel-effectiveness in breast cancer stem cells. Sci. Rep. 7, 1–16.

Murray, N.P., Reyes, E., Tapia, P., Badinez, L., Orellana, N., Fuentealba, C., Olivares, R., Porcell, J., Dueñas, R., 2012. Redefining micrometastasis in prostate cancer—a comparison of circulating prostate cells, bone marrow disseminated tumor cells and micrometastasis: implications in determining local or systemic treatment for biochemical failure after radical prostatectomy. Int. J. Mol. Med. 30, 896–904.

Nadal, R., Ortega, F.G., Salido, M., Lorente, J.A., Rodríguez-Rivera, M., Delgado-Rodríguez, M., Macià, M., Fernández, A., Corominas, J.M., García-Puche, J.L., Sánchez-Rovira, P., Solé, F., Serrano, M.J., 2013. CD133 expression in circulating tumor cells from breast cancer patients: potential role in resistance to chemotherapy. Int. J. Cancer 133, 2398–2407.

Nakanishi, T., Ross, D.D., 2012. Breast cancer resistance protein (BCRP/ABCG2): its role in multidrug resistance and regulation of its gene expression. Chin. J. Cancer 31, 73.

Neumeister, V., Agarwal, S., Bordeaux, J., Camp, R.L., Rimm, D.L., 2010. In situ identification of putative cancer stem cells by multiplexing ALDH1, CD44, and cytokeratin identifies breast cancer patients with poor prognosis. Am. J. Pathol. 176, 2131–2138.

Ning, N., Pan, Q., Zheng, F., Teitz-Tennenbaum, S., Egenti, M., Yet, J., Li, M., Ginestier, C., Wicha, M.S., Moyer, J.S., 2012. Cancer stem cell vaccination confers significant antitumor immunity. Cancer Res. 72, 1853–1864.

Nounou, M.I., Elamrawy, F., Ahmed, N., Abdelraouf, K., Goda, S., Syed-Sha-Qhattal, H., 2015. Breast cancer: conventional diagnosis and treatment modalities and recent patents and technologies. Breast Cancer 9, S29420.

Okuda, H., Xing, F., Pandey, P.R., Sharma, S., Watabe, M., Pai, S.K., Mo, Y.-Y., Iiizumi-Gairani, M., Hirota, S., Liu, Y., 2013. miR-7 suppresses brain metastasis of breast cancer stem-like cells by modulating KLF4. Cancer Res. 73, 1434–1444.

Okuyama Kishima, M., Oliveira, C.E.C.D., Banin-Hirata, B.K., Losi-Guembarovski, R., Brajão De Oliveira, K., Amarante, M.K., Watanabe, M.A.E., 2015. Immunohistochemical expression of CXCR4 on breast cancer and its clinical significance. Anal. Cell. Pathol. 2015.

Palomeras, S., Ruiz-Martínez, S., Puig, T., 2018. Targeting breast cancer stem cells to overcome treatment resistance. Molecules 23, 2193.

Panigoro, S.S., Kurnia, D., Kurnia, A., Haryono, S.J., Albar, Z.A., 2020. ALDH1 cancer stem cell marker as a prognostic factor in triple-negative breast cancer. Int. J. Surg. Oncol. 2020.

Parker, J.S., Mullins, M., Cheang, M.C.U., Leung, S., Voduc, D., Vickery, T., Davies, S., Fauron, C., He, X., Hu, Z., 2009. Supervised risk predictor of breast cancer based on intrinsic subtypes. J. Clin. Oncol. 27, 1160.

Patrawala, L., Calhoun, T., Schneider-Broussard, R., Li, H., Bhatia, B., Tang, S., Reilly, J.G., Chandra, D., Zhou, J., Claypool, K., 2006. Highly purified CD44 + prostate cancer cells from xenograft human tumors are enriched in tumorigenic and metastatic progenitor cells. Oncogene 25, 1696–1708.

Perou, C.M., Sørlie, T., Eisen, M.B., Van De Rijn, M., Jeffrey, S.S., Rees, C.A., Pollack, J.R., Ross, D.T., Johnsen, H., Akslen, L.A., 2000. Molecular portraits of human breast tumours. Nature 406, 747–752.

Phillips, T.M., McBride, W.H., Pajonk, F., 2006. The response of CD24−/low/CD44 + breast cancer–initiating cells to radiation. J. Natl. Cancer Inst. 98, 1777–1785.

Ponti, D., Costa, A., Zaffaroni, N., Pratesi, G., Petrangolini, G., Coradini, D., Pilotti, S., Pierotti, M.A., Daidone, M.G., 2005. Isolation and in vitro propagation of tumorigenic breast cancer cells with stem/progenitor cell properties. Cancer Res. 65, 5506–5511.

Posada, I.M.D., Lectez, B., Sharma, M., Oetken-Lindholm, C., Yetukuri, L., Zhou, Y., Aittokallio, T., Abankwa, D., 2017. Rapalogs can promote cancer cell stemness in vitro in a Galectin-1 and H-ras-dependent manner. Oncotarget 8, 44550.

Pupa, S.M., Ligorio, F., Cancila, V., Franceschini, A., Tripodo, C., Vernieri, C., Castagnoli, L., 2021. HER2 signaling and breast cancer stem cells: the bridge behind HER2-positive breast cancer aggressiveness and therapy refractoriness. Cancer 13, 4778.

Qayoom, H., Wani, N.A., Alshehri, B., Mir, M.A., 2021. An insight into the cancer stem cell survival pathways involved in chemoresistance in triple-negative breast cancer. Future Oncol. 17, 4185–4206.

Quintana, E., Shackleton, M., Sabel, M.S., Fullen, D.R., Johnson, T.M., Morrison, S.J., 2008. Efficient tumour formation by single human melanoma cells. Nature 456, 593–598.

Rabinovich, I., Sebastião, A.P.M., Lima, R.S., De Andrade Urban, C., Schunemann Jr., E., Anselmi, K.F., Elifio-Esposito, S., De Noronha, L., Moreno-Amaral, A.N., 2018. Cancer stem cell markers ALDH1 and CD44 +/CD24−phenotype and their prognosis impact in invasive ductal carcinoma. Eur. J. Histochem. 62.

Rakha, E.A., Elsheikh, S.E., Aleskandarany, M.A., Habashi, H.O., Green, A.R., Powe, D.G., El-Sayed, M.E., Benhasouna, A., Brunet, J.-S., Akslen, L.A., 2009. Triple-negative breast cancer: distinguishing between basal and nonbasal subtypes. Clin. Cancer Res. 15, 2302–2310.

Rassi, H., 2009. Role of the BRCA1 gene in stem cells and treatment of mammary gland cancer. Breast Cancer Res. 11, 1–2.

Ricardo, S., Vieira, A.F., Gerhard, R., Leitão, D., Pinto, R., Cameselle-Teijeiro, J.F., Milanezi, F., Schmitt, F., Paredes, J., 2011. Breast cancer stem cell markers CD44, CD24 and ALDH1: expression distribution within intrinsic molecular subtype. J. Clin. Pathol. 64, 937–946.

Rinkenbaugh, A.L., Baldwin, A.S., 2016. The NF-κB pathway and cancer stem cells. Cell 5, 16.

Saeki, T., Nomizu, T., Toi, M., Ito, Y., Noguchi, S., Kobayashi, T., Asaga, T., Minami, H., Yamamoto, N., Aogi, K., 2007. Dofequidar fumarate (MS-209) in combination with cyclophosphamide, doxorubicin, and fluorouracil for patients with advanced or recurrent breast cancer. J. Clin. Oncol. 25, 411–417.

Sansone, P., Ceccarelli, C., Berishaj, M., Chang, Q., Rajasekhar, V.K., Perna, F., Bowman, R.L., Vidone, M., Daly, L., Nnoli, J., 2016. Self-renewal of CD133hi cells by IL6/Notch3 signalling regulates endocrine resistance in metastatic breast cancer. Nat. Commun. 7, 1–10.

Sari, I.N., Phi, L.T.H., Jun, N., Wijaya, Y.T., Lee, S., Kwon, H.Y., 2018. Hedgehog signaling in cancer: a prospective therapeutic target for eradicating cancer stem cells. Cell 7, 208.

Scheel, C., Weinberg, R.A., 2012. Cancer Stem Cells and Epithelial–Mesenchymal Transition: Concepts and Molecular Links. Elsevier, pp. 396–403.

Scioli, M.G., Storti, G., D'amico, F., Gentile, P., Fabbri, G., Cervelli, V., Orlandi, A., 2019. The role of breast cancer stem cells as a prognostic marker and a target to improve the efficacy of breast cancer therapy. Cancer 11, 1021.

Semenza, G.L., 2015. Regulation of the breast cancer stem cell phenotype by hypoxia-inducible factors. Clin. Sci. 129, 1037–1045.

Shackleton, M., Vaillant, F., Simpson, K.J., Stingl, J., Smyth, G.K., Asselin-Labat, M.-L., Wu, L., Lindeman, G.J., Visvader, J.E., 2006. Generation of a functional mammary gland from a single stem cell. Nature 439, 84–88.

Shinde, A., Hardy, S.D., Kim, D., Akhand, S.S., Jolly, M.K., Wang, W.H., Anderson, J.C., Khodadadi, R.B., Brown, W.S., George, J.T., Liu, S., Wan, J., Levine, H., Willey, C.D., Krusemark, C.J., Geahlen, R.L., Wendt, M.K., 2019. Spleen tyrosine kinase-mediated autophagy is required for epithelial-mesenchymal plasticity and metastasis in breast cancer. Cancer Res. 79, 1831–1843.

Shipitsin, M., Campbell, L.L., Argani, P., Weremowicz, S., Bloushtain-Qimron, N., Yao, J., Nikolskaya, T., Serebryiskaya, T., Beroukhim, R., Hu, M., Halushka, M.K., Sukumar, S., Parker, L.M., Anderson, K.S., Harris, L.N., Garber, J.E., Richardson, A.L., Schnitt, S.J., Nikolsky, Y., Gelman, R.S., Polyak, K., 2007. Molecular definition of breast tumor heterogeneity. Cancer Cell 11, 259–273.

Simeone, P., Trerotola, M., Franck, J., Cardon, T., Marchisio, M., Fournier, I., Salzet, M., Maffia, M., Vergara, D., 2019. The Multiverse Nature of Epithelial to Mesenchymal Transition. Elsevier, pp. 1–10.

Simões, B.M., O'brien, C.S., Eyre, R., Silva, A., Yu, L., Sarmiento-Castro, A., Alférez, D.G., Spence, K., Santiago-Gómez, A., Chemi, F., Acar, A., Gandhi, A., Howell, A., Brennan, K., Rydén, L., Catalano, S., Andó, S., Gee, J., Ucar, A., Sims, A.H., Marangoni, E., Farnie, G., Landberg, G., Howell, S.J., Clarke, R.B., 2015. Anti-estrogen resistance in human breast tumors is driven by JAG1-NOTCH4-dependent cancer stem cell activity. Cell Rep. 12, 1968–1977.

Sin, W.C., Lim, C.L., 2017. Breast cancer stem cells—from origins to targeted therapy. Stem Cell Investig. 4.

Smith, G.H., 1996. Experimental mammary epithelial morphogenesis in an in vivo model: evidence for distinct cellular progenitors of the ductal and lobular phenotype. Breast Cancer Res. Treat. 39, 21–31.

Solzak, J.P., Atale, R.V., Hancock, B.A., Sinn, A.L., Pollok, K.E., Jones, D.R., Radovich, M., 2017. Dual PI3K and Wnt pathway inhibition is a synergistic combination against triple negative breast cancer. NPJ Breast Cancer 3, 1–8.

Song, K., Farzaneh, M., 2021. Signaling pathways governing breast cancer stem cells behavior. Stem Cell Res. Ther. 12, 1–11.

Song, S.J., Poliseno, L., Song, M.S., Ala, U., Webster, K., Ng, C., Beringer, G., Brikbak, N.J., Yuan, X., Cantley, L.C., 2013. MicroRNA-antagonism regulates breast cancer stemness and metastasis via TET-family-dependent chromatin remodeling. Cell 154, 311–324.

Sridharan, S., Howard, C.M., Tilley, A., Subramaniyan, B., Tiwari, A.K., Ruch, R.J., Raman, D., 2019. Novel and alternative targets against breast cancer stemness to combat chemoresistance. Front. Oncol., 1003.

Stefania, D.D., Vergara, D., 2017. The many-faced program of epithelial–mesenchymal transition: a system biology-based view. Front. Oncol. 7, 274.

Stingl, J., Eirew, P., Ricketson, I., Shackleton, M., Vaillant, F., Choi, D., Li, H.I., Eaves, C.J., 2006. Purification and unique properties of mammary epithelial stem cells. Nature 439, 993–997.

Sung, H., Ferlay, J., Siegel, R.L., Laversanne, M., Soerjomataram, I., Jemal, A., Bray, F., 2021. Global cancer statistics 2020: GLOBOCAN estimates of incidence and mortality worldwide for 36 cancers in 185 countries. CA Cancer J. Clin. 71, 209–249.

Suyama, K., Onishi, H., Imaizumi, A., Shinkai, K., Umebayashi, M., Kubo, M., Mizuuchi, Y., Oda, Y., Tanaka, M., Nakamura, M., 2016. CD24 suppresses malignant phenotype by downregulation of SHH transcription through STAT1 inhibition in breast cancer cells. Cancer Lett. 374, 44–53.

Tanei, T., Morimoto, K., Shimazu, K., Kim, S.J., Tanji, Y., Taguchi, T., Tamaki, Y., Noguchi, S., 2009. Association of breast cancer stem cells identified by aldehyde dehydrogenase 1 expression with resistance to sequential Paclitaxel and epirubicin-based chemotherapy for breast cancers. Clin. Cancer Res. 15, 4234–4241.

Tharmapalan, P., Mahendralingam, M., Berman, H.K., Khokha, R., 2019. Mammary stem cells and progenitors: targeting the roots of breast cancer for prevention. EMBO J. 38, e100852.

Tsutsui, S., Ohno, S., Murakami, S., Kataoka, A., Kinoshita, J., Hachitanda, Y., 2003. Prognostic significance of the coexpression of p53 protein and c-erbB2 in breast cancer. Am. J. Surg. 185, 165–167.

Tudoran, O.M., Balacescu, O., Berindan-Neagoe, I., 2016. Breast cancer stem-like cells: clinical implications and therapeutic strategies. Clujul Med. 89, 193–198.

Tume, L., Paco, K., Ubidia-Incio, R., Moya, J., 2016. CD133 in breast cancer cells and in breast cancer stem cells as another target for immunotherapy. Gac. Mex. Oncol. 15, 22–30.

Valenti, G., Quinn, H.M., Heynen, G.J.J.E., Lan, L., Holland, J.D., Vogel, R., Wulf-Goldenberg, A., Birchmeier, W., 2017. Cancer stem cells regulate cancer-associated fibroblasts via activation of hedgehog signaling in mammary gland tumors. Cancer Res. 77, 2134–2147.

Van Keymeulen, A., Lee, M.Y., Ousset, M., Brohée, S., Rorive, S., Giraddi, R.R., Wuidart, A., Bouvencourt, G., Dubois, C., Salmon, I., 2015. Reactivation of multipotency by oncogenic PIK3CA induces breast tumour heterogeneity. Nature 525, 119–123.

Vargo-Gogola, T., Rosen, J.M., 2007. Modelling breast cancer: one size does not fit all. Nat. Rev. Cancer 7, 659–672.

Venkatesh, V., Nataraj, R., Thangaraj, G.S., Karthikeyan, M., Gnanasekaran, A., Kaginelli, S.B., Kuppanna, G., Kallappa, C.G., Basalingappa, K.M., 2018. Targeting Notch signalling pathway of cancer stem cells. Stem Cell Investig. 5.

Vermeulen, L., Sprick, M.R., Kemper, K., Stassi, G., Medema, J.P., 2008. Cancer stem cells–old concepts, new insights. Cell Death Differ. 15, 947–958.

Visvader, J.E., 2009. Keeping abreast of the mammary epithelial hierarchy and breast tumorigenesis. Genes Dev. 23, 2563–2577.

Wang, Z., Li, Y., Banerjee, S., Sarkar, F.H., 2009. Emerging role of Notch in stem cells and cancer. Cancer Lett. 279, 8–12.

Wang, Y., Li, W., Patel, S.S., Cong, J., Zhang, N., Sabbatino, F., Liu, X., Qi, Y., Huang, P., Lee, H., Taghian, A., Li, J.J., Deleo, A.B., Ferrone, S., Epperly, M.W., Ferrone, C.R., Ly, A., Brachtel, E.F., Wang, X., 2014. Blocking the formation of radiation-induced breast cancer stem cells. Oncotarget 5, 3743–3755.

Wang, L., Tian, H., Yuan, J., Wu, H., Wu, J., Zhu, X., 2015. CONSORT: Sam68 is directly regulated by miR-204 and promotes the self-renewal potential of breast cancer cells by activating the Wnt/beta-catenin signaling pathway. Medicine 94.

Wang, T., Fahrmann, J.F., Lee, H., Li, Y.-J., Tripathi, S.C., Yue, C., Zhang, C., Lifshitz, V., Song, J., Yuan, Y., 2018. JAK/STAT3-regulated fatty acid β-oxidation is critical for breast cancer stem cell self-renewal and chemoresistance. Cell Metab. 27, 136–150.

Weigelt, B., Mackay, A., A'hern, R., Natrajan, R., Tan, D.S.P., Dowsett, M., Ashworth, A., Reis-Filho, J.S., 2010. Breast cancer molecular profiling with single sample predictors: a retrospective analysis. Lancet Oncol. 11, 339–349.

Wicha, M.S., Liu, S., Dontu, G., 2006. Cancer stem cells: an old idea—a paradigm shift. Cancer Res. 66, 1883–1890.

Woosley, A.N., Dalton, A.C., Hussey, G.S., Howley, B.V., Mohanty, B.K., Grelet, S., Dincman, T., Bloos, S., Olsen, S.K., Howe, P.H., 2019. TGFβ promotes breast cancer stem cell self-renewal through an ILEI/LIFR signaling axis. Oncogene 38, 3794–3811.

Xiao, W., Gao, Z., Duan, Y., Yuan, W., Ke, Y., 2017. Notch signaling plays a crucial role in cancer stem-like cells maintaining stemness and mediating chemotaxis in renal cell carcinoma. J. Exp. Clin. Cancer Res. 36, 1–13.

Yang, Y., Hao, E., Pan, X., Tan, D., Du, Z., Xie, J., Hou, X., Deng, J., Wei, K., 2019. Gomisin M2 from Baizuan suppresses breast cancer stem cell proliferation in a zebrafish xenograft model. Aging (Albany NY) 11, 8347.

Ye, F., Qiu, Y., Li, L., Yang, L., Cheng, F., Zhang, H., Wei, B., Zhang, Z., Sun, L., Bu, H., 2015. The presence of EpCAM-/CD49f+ cells in breast cancer is associated with a poor clinical outcome. J. Breast Cancer 18, 242–248.

Ye, F., Zhong, X., Qiu, Y., Yang, L., Wei, B., Zhang, Z., Bu, H., 2017. CD49f can act as a biomarker for local or distant recurrence in breast cancer. J. Breast Cancer 20, 142–149.

Yi, T., Zhai, B., Yu, Y., Kiyotsugu, Y., Raschle, T., Etzkorn, M., Seo, H.-C., Nagiec, M., Luna, R.E., Reinherz, E.L., 2014. Quantitative phosphoproteomic analysis reveals system-wide signaling pathways downstream of SDF-1/CXCR4 in breast cancer stem cells. Proc. Natl. Acad. Sci. U. S. A. 111, E2182–E2190.

Yoon, C., Lu, J., Yi, B.C., Chang, K.K., Simon, M.C., Ryeom, S., Yoon, S.S., 2021. PI3K/Akt pathway and Nanog maintain cancer stem cells in sarcomas. Oncogene 10, 1–14.

Yousefnia, S., Ghaedi, K., Seyed Forootan, F., Nasr Esfahani, M.H., 2019. Characterization of the stemness potency of mammospheres isolated from the breast cancer cell lines. Tumor Biol. 41, 1010428319869101.

Yousefnia, S., Seyed Forootan, F., Seyed Forootan, S., Nasr Esfahani, M.H., Gure, A.O., Ghaedi, K., 2020. Mechanical pathways of malignancy in breast cancer stem cells. Front. Oncol. 10, 452.

Zafar, T., Naik, A.Q., Shrivastava, V.K., 2022. Epidemology and risk factors of breast cancer. In: Malik, S.S., Masood, N. (Eds.), Breast Cancer: From Bead to Personalized Medicine. Springer Nature, Singapore Pte Ltd.

Zakaria, N., Mohd Yusoff, N., Zakaria, Z., Widera, D., Yahaya, B.H., 2018. Inhibition of NF-κB signaling reduces the stemness characteristics of lung cancer stem cells. Front. Oncol. 8, 166.

Zhang, Y., Wang, X., 2020. Targeting the Wnt/β-catenin signaling pathway in cancer. J. Hematol. Oncol. 13, 1–16.

Zhang, X., Wan, G., Mlotshwa, S., Vance, V., Berger, F.G., Chen, H., Lu, X., 2010. Oncogenic Wip1 phosphatase is inhibited by miR-16 in the DNA damage signaling pathway. Cancer Res. 70, 7176–7186.

Zhang, Q., Han, Z., Zhu, Y., Chen, J., Li, W., 2021. Role of hypoxia inducible factor-1 in cancer stem cells. Mol. Med. Rep. 23 (1), 17. https://doi.org/10.3892/mmr.2020.11655.

Zhong, Y., Shen, S., Zhou, Y., Mao, F., Guan, J., Lin, Y., Xu, Y., Sun, Q., 2014. ALDH1 is a better clinical indicator for relapse of invasive ductal breast cancer than the CD44+/CD24− phenotype. Med. Oncol. 31, 1–8.

Zhong, G., Qin, S., Townsend, D., Schulte, B.A., Tew, K.D., Wang, G.Y., 2019. Oxidative stress induces senescence in breast cancer stem cells. Biochem. Biophys. Res. Commun. 514, 1204–1209.

Zhou, J., Chen, Q., Zou, Y., Chen, H., Qi, L., Chen, Y., 2019. Stem cells and cellular origins of breast cancer: updates in the rationale, controversies, and therapeutic implications. Front. Oncol. 9, 820.

Zielske, S.P., Spalding, A.C., Wicha, M.S., Lawrence, T.S., 2011. Ablation of breast cancer stem cells with radiation. Transl. Oncol. 4, 227–233.

Zöller, M., 2011. CD44: can a cancer-initiating cell profit from an abundantly expressed molecule? Nat. Rev. Cancer 11, 254–267.

Further reading

Baccelli, I., Stenzinger, A., Vogel, V., Pfitzner, B.M., Klein, C., Wallwiener, M., Scharpff, M., Saini, M., Holland-Letz, T., Sinn, H.P., Schneeweiss, A., Denkert, C., Weichert, W., Trumpp, A., 2014. Co-expression of MET and CD47 is a novel prognosticator for survival of luminal breast cancer patients. Oncotarget 5, 8147–8160.

Bensimon, J., Altmeyer-Morel, S., Benjelloun, H., Chevillard, S., Lebeau, J., 2013. CD24−/low stem-like breast cancer marker defines the radiation-resistant cells involved in memorization and transmission of radiation-induced genomic instability. Oncogene 32, 251–258.

Bourguignon, L.Y.W., Singleton, P.A., Diedrich, F., Stern, R., Gilad, E., 2004. CD44 interaction with Na +-H+ exchanger (NHE1) creates acidic microenvironments leading to hyaluronidase-2 and cathepsin B activation and breast tumor cell invasion. J. Biol. Chem. 279, 26991–27007.

Charafe-Jauffret, E., Ginestier, C., Iovino, F., Tarpin, C., Diebel, M., Esterni, B., Houvenaeghel, G., Extra, J.-M., Bertucci, F., Jacquemier, J., 2010. Aldehyde dehydrogenase 1–positive cancer stem cells mediate metastasis and poor clinical outcome in inflammatory breast cancer. Clin. Cancer Res. 16, 45–55.

Leccia, F., Del Vecchio, L., Mariotti, E., Di Noto, R., Morel, A.-P., Puisieux, A., Salvatore, F., Ansieau, S., 2014. ABCG2, a novel antigen to sort luminal progenitors of BRCA1-breast cancer cells. Mol. Cancer 13, 1–13.

Liu, J., Ye, Z., Xiang, M., Chang, B., Cui, J., Ji, T., Zhao, L., Li, Q., Deng, Y., Xu, L., 2019. Functional extracellular vesicles engineered with lipid-grafted hyaluronic acid effectively reverse cancer drug resistance. Biomaterials 223, 119475.

Müller, A., Homey, B., Soto, H., Ge, N., Catron, D., Buchanan, M.E., McClanahan, T., Murphy, E., Yuan, W., Wagner, S.N., 2001. Involvement of chemokine receptors in breast cancer metastasis. Nature 410, 50–56.

Munz, M., Baeuerle, P.A., Gires, O., 2009. The emerging role of EpCAM in cancer and stem cell signaling. Cancer Res. 69, 5627–5629.

Sarkar, A., Chanda, A., Regmi, S.C., Karve, K., Deng, L., Jay, G.D., Jirik, F.R., Schmidt, T.A., Bonni, S., 2019. Recombinant human PRG4 (rhPRG4) suppresses breast cancer cell invasion by inhibiting TGFβ–Hyaluronan–CD44 signalling pathway. PLoS One 14, e0219697.

Schabath, H., Runz, S., Joumaa, S., Altevogt, P., 2006. CD24 affects CXCR4 function in pre-B lymphocytes and breast carcinoma cells. J. Cell Sci. 119, 314–325.

Sena, L.A., Chandel, N.S., 2012. Physiological roles of mitochondrial reactive oxygen species. Mol. Cell 48, 158–167.

Sun, M., Yang, C., Zheng, J., Wang, M., Chen, M., Le, D.Q.S., Kjems, J., Bünger, C.E., 2015. Enhanced efficacy of chemotherapy for breast cancer stem cells by simultaneous suppression of multidrug resistance and antiapoptotic cellular defense. Acta Biomater. 28, 171–182.

CHAPTER 10

Targeting tumor microenvironment for breast cancer treatment

Manzoor Ahmad Mir[a] and Burhan ul Haq[b]
[a]Department of Bioresources, School of Biological Sciences, University of Kashmir, Srinagar, Jammu and Kashmir, India
[b]Department of Biotechnology, Central University of Kashmir, Ganderbal, India

10.1 Introduction

The tumor microenvironment is characterized by a hypoxic and acidic environment that is enriched with immune or inflammatory cells (Mehraj et al., 2021a). And this tumor microenvironment has an important part to play in the development, growth, and progression of the tumor and the resistance to therapy being applied to treat the tumor. It has drawn a lot of attention for targeting solid tumors. To avoid the low penetration and less accessibility that is witnessed in the case of chemotherapy, the small-molecule inhibitors are now being widely used for treating cancers as these possess better accessibility and penetration than the chemotherapeutic agents (Mehraj et al., 2021c). Due to the property of the tumor microenvironment to show better penetration and accessibility for small-molecule inhibitors in comparison to the tumor cells, special drug delivery systems have been introduced that release the cytotoxic drugs in the tumor microenvironment specifically or target its components (Jan et al., 2021). Be it the progression of the tumor or the development of multidrug resistance (MDR), it has already been elucidated that the tumor microenvironment has an active role in these processes, but still, the focus of cancer research has been directed toward tumor cells majorly (Tsai et al., 2014). Compared to traditional cancer therapies, nanochemotherapeutics have precedence over these due to the low drug toxicity with higher efficiency, meticulousness for the site of the tumor, upgraded stability, and solubility of drugs, and imaging methods, the higher half-life of drugs in circulation as well as the regulated release (Mir et al., 2020). We need to focus on the major events that support or assist the primary tumor growth and development within the domain of the tumor microenvironment and try to elucidate the possible ways by which such events control the change within the tumor microenvironment as this will aid in the development of systematic therapy plans (Yuan et al., 2016). There have been tremendous improvements in antitumor therapies, but the effective management of breast cancer faces significant hurdles because of drug resistance. Many studies have disclosed that the two-way communication between the growing tumor cells and the neighboring stromal components has a pivotal role in response to the therapy or

Role of Tumor Microenvironment in Breast Cancer and Targeted Therapies
https://doi.org/10.1016/B978-0-443-18696-7.00008-7

249

treatment (Samadi et al., 2016). The research focused on targeting the tumor microenvironment constituents is maturing at either preclinical or clinical stages. And these studies indicate that if the components of the tumor microenvironment are targeted in combination with other therapies that are tumor-directed, it hugely diminishes the growth of tumors, the metastasis, and the resistance to the therapy being applied (Bahrami et al., 2018; Cassetta and Pollard, 2018; Roma-Rodrigues et al., 2019; Shee et al., 2018).

10.2 Tumor microenvironment—A suitable target for treating breast cancer

Different tumor microenvironment components have different roles to play in promoting the tumor. Fibroblasts (Roche, 2018; Yu et al., 2014) and macrophages (Wyckoff et al., 2004; Su et al., 2014) are known to promote EMT and angiogenesis. Lymphocytes (Marigo et al., 2020) and mesenchymal stem cells (Hill et al., 2020) exhibit immunosuppressive function. The metastasis is enhanced by endothelial cells (Sa-Nguanraksa and O-Charoenrat, 2012; Ghajar et al., 2013), and the cancer motility is enhanced by the extracellular matrix (Pickup et al., 2014).

The cancer cells and the constituents of the tumor microenvironment show frequent adjustments or alterations with respect to their surroundings, affecting the tumor growth and development as well. Both cellular and noncellular elements make up the tumor microenvironment. Endothelial cells, myeloid-derived suppressor cells, tumor-infiltrating lymphocytes, cancer-associated fibroblasts, and tumor-associated macrophages are among the cellular components, and the extracellular matrix, interstitial fluids, cytokines, chemokines, growth factors, and metabolites are among the noncellular components Fig. 10.1. All are very significant for determining the status of the tumor microenvironment.

The specific tumor microenvironment (TME) has been shown to significantly determine the development of the tumor as well as influence the prognosis and efficacy of the chemotherapy being applied (Netea-Maier et al., 2018). Since the constitution of the tumor microenvironment witnesses changes as the tumor develops, elucidating how the changes occur could aid in the progression of better therapeutic plans to better handle the stage-specific tumor. Various prognostic biomarkers are disclosed while studying the tumor microenvironment as the tumor develops, and these could aid in liquid biopsy or imaging analysis, which are significant to choose the best therapy (Abadjian et al., 2017; Willumsen et al., 2018; Wu et al., 2017; Mir et al., 2022a). The tumor microenvironment displays high heterogeneity and complexity toward the later stage of solid tumors. There is a larger impact of tumor cell genomic profiles for controlling the area of the tumor (Hanahan and Coussens, 2012; Hanahan and Weinberg, 2011; Tahmasebi Birgani and Carloni, 2017). There is an onset of multiple events due to the tumor cells'

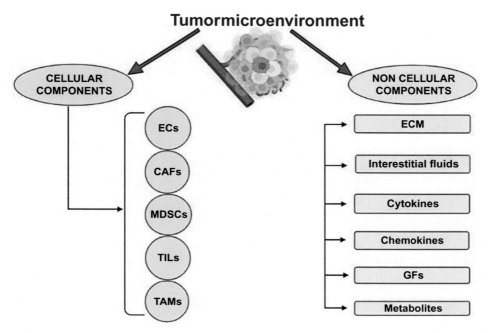

Fig. 10.1 The tumor microenvironment's cellular and noncellular components: (A) Cellular components include: Tumor-associated macrophages, cancer-associated fibroblasts, endothelial cells, tumor-infiltrating lymphocytes, and myeloid-derived suppressor cells. (B) Noncellular components include: Extracellular matrix, cytokines, growth factors, metabolites, interstitial fluids, and chemokines.

swift expansion, like the development of hypoxic conditions, and it may lead to the tumor cells' metabolic reprogramming as well as acclimatization of the tumor microenvironment to the prevailing environment (Sormendi and Wielockx, 2018; Vaupel and Mayer, 2014; Masoud and Li, 2015; Kim, 2018; Kato et al., 2018). Many strategies are employed to specifically target the TME components, including Targeting hypoxia and acidosis, extracellular matrix, cancer-associated fibroblasts, tumor cell-derived exosomes, avoiding neovascularization, aiming at chronic inflammation by inhibiting macrophages recruitment and differentiation, and by activating humoral activity of immune system are some of the ways to target the tumor microenvironment components (Qayoom et al., 2021) Fig. 10.2.

There is a huge change witnessed in the cellular elements of the tumor microenvironment and the reorganization of the extracellular matrix and the development of disordered vascularization apparatus due to the interactions between the tumor and nearby cells like the stromal cells and the immune which may progress toward metastasis Fig. 10.3 (Willumsen et al., 2018; Mir and Mehraj, 2019).

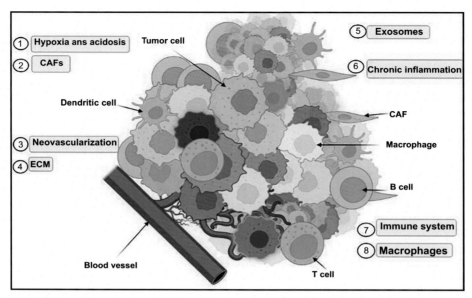

Fig. 10.2 Various ways to target TME components including 1. Hypoxia and acidosis 2. Cancer-associated fibroblasts 3. Neovascularization 4. Extracellular matrix 5. Exosomes 6. Chronic inflammation 7. Immune system and 8. Macrophages.

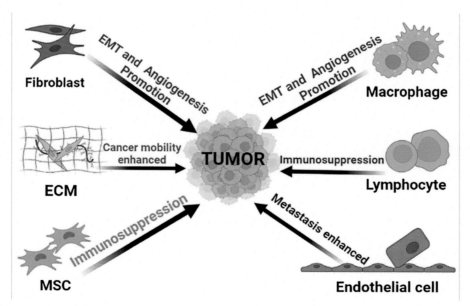

Fig. 10.3 Different tumor microenvironment components have different roles in promoting the tumor: Fibroblasts and Macrophages promote the EMT and angiogenesis. Lymphocytes and Mesenchymal stem cells have immunosuppressive roles. The metastasis is enhanced by Endothelial cells and the cancer motility is increased by ECM.

The tumor microenvironment has drawn a lot of attention for the growth and metastasis of cancer. Treatment strategies, including targeted therapy, chemotherapy, nanoparticle systems, immunotherapy, traditional Chinese medicine, and combined drug therapies Table 10.4, are being employed to alter the tumor microenvironment. Many drugs have successfully been part of clinical trials and are being checked for their efficacies. An example is provided by the clinical study with respect to triple-negative breast cancer [TNBC], namely "Effects of MK-3475 (Pembrolizumab) on the breast tumor microenvironment in triple-negative breast cancer" and the associated therapy is Merck-3475 (Pembrolizumab) [(NCT02977468) as identified by the Clinicaltrials. gov]. It has been witnessed in mouse models with breast and ovarian cancer that the doxorubicin adds to its aim via exosomes and successfully prevents the development of cancer (Uribesalgo et al., 2019). Georgoudaki et al. revealed that in breast cancer, the immunotherapy using MARCO [Macrophage receptor with collagen structure] might hinder the growth and resettling and enhance the tumor microenvironment immunogenicity besides melanoma models and colon cancer. An achievable way for cancer immunotherapy is by employing the *E*-programming of macrophages in the tumor microenvironment using monoclonal antibodies (Georgoudaki et al., 2016).

10.2.1 The traditional cancer therapies and their interactions with the tumor microenvironment

When the chemotherapy is applied, it harms the fast-dividing cancer cells. These damages could ultimately result in programmed cell death, the apoptosis. However, the success of these conventional treatments can be determined by the inflammatory and stromal cells already present in the microenvironment of the tumor, and these therapies could alter the tumor microenvironment constituents. These alterations are numerous and can either promote the tumor or act against it. The following characteristics of the tumor microenvironment make it a suitable target for treating cancer. The primary characteristic is its immunosuppressive nature, which helps tumor cells against inspection from the immune system (Mir et al., 2022b). The secondary characteristic is that the tumor microenvironment is highly adaptive to aid the growing tumor and its progression, coupled with its property to oppose any insults (for example, chemotherapy) and stress (Gilkes et al., 2014; Luo et al., 2007). Thus, the tumor microenvironment serves as the finest target for cancer treatment.

10.3 Chemotherapy and tumor microenvironment

10.3.1 Chronic inflammation in the tumor microenvironment

The cytokines and many other inflammatory impulses lead to the inflammation that is chronic inside the tumor microenvironment, and the former are the secretions of the tumor-associated macrophages (TAMs) (Na et al., 2018; Netea-Maier et al., 2018). This

Table 10.1 The following table presents the therapeutic potential of various microenvironment components along with their clinical evidence.

S.no.	Components	Action	Therapeutic possibilities	Reference of clinical evidence
1.	CAFs	VEGF secretion	VEGF inhibitors (bevacizumab)	Miller et al. (2007), Redondo et al. (2014), Kontopodis et al. (2015), Fang et al. (2015)
2.	DC	Inhibition of T cell proliferation	DC vaccines	Baek et al. (2011), Qi et al. (2012)
3.	TAM	M_2 polarization	TAM inhibitors (trabectedin)	Solinas et al. (2009), Delaloge et al. (2014)
		ECM remodeling via MP[a] secretion	TAM depletion (DOX)	Hannesdóttir et al. (2013)
4.	T regulatory cells	Suppression of immune cells	Anti CD25 antibodies	Rech et al. (2012)
5.	Effector T cells	T-cell exhaustion via PD-1/ PDL-1 signaling	Anti PD-1 antibodies/anti PDL-1 antibodies	Brahmer et al. (2010), Brahmer et al. (2012a), Brahmer et al. (2012b), Topalian et al. (2012), Gibson (2015)
6.	Extracellular matrix	ECM remodeling	ECM degradation inhibitors	Berkenblit et al. (2005)

[a]The MP stands for metalloproteinases.

becomes the rationale for terming tumors "wounds that never heal" (Dvorak, 1986; Hanahan and Coussens, 2012). The progression of early neoplasia toward a fully evolved cancer could be due to inflammation (Denardo et al., 2010; Jiang et al., 2017; Grivennikov et al., 2010; Qian and Pollard, 2010; Tashireva et al., 2017). The FDA (Food and drug administration) approved drug Anakinra (Kineret) is an interleukin-1 receptor antagonist employed in the second-line treatment of rheumatoid arthritis, and its encouraging outcomes have been witnessed for curing breast cancer bone metastasis (Holen et al., 2016; Tulotta and Ottewell, 2018). Cancer-associated fibroblasts (CAFs) are known to produce desmoplasia and are usually connected with the development of tumors and metastasis in breast cancer (Otranto et al., 2012) And being profuse cell type, the CAFs in the tumor microenvironment have also been inspected as a possible target for treating cancer. The therapeutic capabilities of various TME components can be exploited to target tumor Table 10.1 (Sounni and Noel, 2013).

10.3.2 Antiinflammatory drugs and breast cancer

Since the inflammatory state is inclined toward the development of tumors, thus targeting this process may prove to be a good tactic for preventing cancer, following figure represents

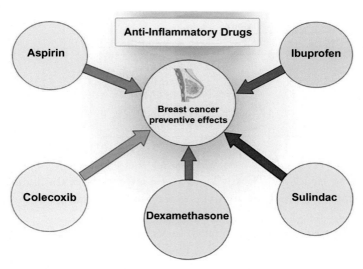

Fig. 10.4 Various antiinflammatory drugs that have been shown to possess preventive effect in case Breast Cancer include Aspirin, Celecoxib, Ibuprofen, Sulindac and Dexamethasone.

the drugs that are antiinflammatory in action Fig. 10.4 and their effects on preventing breast cancer. Aspirin, ibuprofen (Harris et al., 2003), celecoxib (Fabi et al., 2008), sulindac (Yin et al., 2016), and dexamethasone (Wang et al., 2007) all have been shown to display preventive effects on breast cancer.

The *pro-tumorigenic components* of the tumor microenvironment are the CAFs, Lymphatic vessels, Tumor endothelial cells, Tumor-associated macrophages, Tie-2 expressing monocytes, Neutrophils, Myeloid-derived suppressor cells, Extracellular matrix, B cells, Regulatory T cells.

1. *CAFs, the cancer-associated fibroblasts* known to amplify the proliferative signaling, angiogenesis, and metastasis, modulate the process of inflammation, and evade immune destruction (Wang et al., 2017; Wei et al., 2020; Yu et al., 2014).
2. *Lymphatic vessels* are known to induce enlargement of the tumor-associated lymphatic vessels via VEGF-C upregulation and enhance the lymph flow coupled with cancer cells' intravasation into the lymphatics. Also, the HGF overexpression has been shown to induce hyperplasia of the lymphatic vessel as well as lymphatic metastasis (Skobe et al., 2001; Spinella et al., 2009; Kajiya et al., 2005; Duong et al., 2012; Garnier et al., 2019).
3. *The Tumor endothelial cells [TECs]* are known to secrete factors that are angiocrine in nature, such as the vascular endothelial growth factor A, interleukin-6, and bFGF (Butler et al., 2010; Hida et al., 2018; Goncharov et al., 2020).
4. *The tumor-associated macrophages* mostly display an M2 phenotype; their presence in tumors enhances angiogenesis as well as an invasion (Quail and Joyce, 2013; Lin et al., 2019; Grivennikov et al., 2010; Deligne and Midwood, 2021).

Table 10.2 Drug candidates for potential use in combination therapy.

S.no.	Name of the drug
1.	Aspirin
2.	Statin
3.	Metformin
4.	Celecoxib
5.	β-blocker

5. *Tie-2 expressing monocytes [TEMs]*: Tie-2 acts as a receptor for the angiogenic growth factor angiopoietin, thus these monocytes are also Pro-tumorigenic in nature (Akwii et al., 2019; Zhang et al., 2006).

6. *Neutrophils* have the highest percentage in terms of circulating leukocytes in *Homo sapiens* and are plastic phenotypically. These also fall in the category of being Pro tumorigenic (N2) (Uribe-Querol and Rosales, 2015; Vickers, 2017).

7. *Besides extracellular matrix* (Huang, 2018; Giussani et al., 2018), *B cells* (Quail and Joyce, 2013) and T regulatory cells, and myeloid-derived suppressor cells [MDSCs] (Wei et al., 2020) all fall in the category of being Pro-tumorigenic.

8. Thus, aiming at these Pro-tumorigenic elements of the tumor microenvironment, tumors may be targeted, and better therapy outcomes can be witnessed.

The following Table 10.2 lists some of the conventional drugs which act against tumor and display the possibility of their utilization in combination therapy against the tumor microenvironment.

10.3.3 Aspirin

Given the antiplatelet action of *Aspirin* (Riesenberg et al., 2019), researchers have discovered its ability to act against tumors in the immune microenvironment and its possible use in a combination form with the PD-1 blockade was uncovered. Matching outcomes were noticed in the case of breast cancer cells supplemented by reduced secretions of Interleukin 8 (Johnson et al., 2019) The polarization that is induced by Aspirin by enhancing M1 markers expression and simultaneously reducing the M2 marker expression leads toward the M1 phenotype in macrophages and it negates the growth and resettling of cancer cells in case of cell lines of breast cancer (Hsieh and Wang, 2018). The eradication of the tumor cell debris and the suppression of the pro-inflammatory cytokines secreted by the macrophages has been attributed to Aspirin, which leads to the onset of macrophage activity (Gilligan et al., 2019). Aspirin has a controlling effect on immune cells like T-regulatory cells (Zhang et al., 2019), and based on the aforementioned roles of Aspirin over the modulation of the immune microenvironment, it is the best-suited agent for combination therapy.

10.3.4 Celecoxib

Another antiinflammatory and nonsteroidal drug, which is known as *Celecoxib* specifically suppresses the cyclooxygenase-2, which gets over-expressed in breast cancer, gastric cancer, and lung cancer among others (Dannenberg and Subbaramaiah, 2003) Very promising outcomes have been witnessed in the case of celecoxib both preclinical and clinical investigations for the avoidance as well as treatment of cancers, the breast cancer being among the ones showing best results. The induction of ROS-dependent apoptosis and suppression of oxygen utilization in the metabolism microenvironment of metastatic breast cancer and melanoma is a strong suggestive of the possible use of *Celecoxib* drug as an enhancer for radiation therapy or chemotherapy (Pritchard et al., 2018) Table 10.3.

Studies have revealed that to what extent the drug *Celecoxib* affects the breast cancer relies on the Cyclooxygenase (COX-2) [also known as the prostaglandin-endoperoxide synthase 2 (PTGS2)] expression as well as the status of estrogen receptor and it has been proved in the cell lines of breast cancer having COX2 low/high. The studies carried out in vitro reveal that cancer cell survival is enhanced solely in the cell lines with PTGS2-low levels after providing *Celecoxib* in these cell lines (Hamy et al., 2019). The lipophilic statins' rigorous antitumor effects have been witnessed in various cancers like breast cancer (Liu et al., 2016; Larsen et al., 2017; Beckwitt et al., 2018) (Table 10.4).

There can be the induction of ICD leading to the release of DAMPs which further leads to the switching on of antitumor immune reaction. Some of the agents used in neoadjuvant and primary chemotherapy are anthracyclines, taxanes, and anti-HER2 monoclonal antibodies, which can induce the immunostimulatory outcomes of tumor cell killing via activating the DC (Apetoh et al., 2007). Different agents Fig. 10.5 show different effects on the varied immune compartments. *Anthracyclines* have been shown to

Table 10.3 The following list represents approved repurposed anticancer drugs for breast cancer by the food and drug administration [FDA].

S.no.	Target	Drug name	Use	Status	Reference
1.	Tumor-associated macrophages	Sorafenib[a]	For breast cancer	Approved	Edwards and Emens (2010)
2.	T cells: PD-1	Pembrolizumab	Triple-negative breast cancer	Approved	Chuk et al. (2017)
3.	PD-L1	Avelumab	TNBC	Approved	Juliá et al. (2018), D'Angelo et al. (2018)

[a]Sorafenib MOA: Small-molecule, TKI, has been shown to restore secretion of interleukin-12, production & suppression of interleukin-10.

Table 10.4 The combinatorial therapy has been shown to target the tumor microenvironment in the case of BC and approved by FDA.

S.no.	Drugs approved	Indicated for the cancer type	Reference
1.	Capecitabine and Neratinib[a] (NERLYNX)	Metastatic HER2 + BC[b]	Food (2020)
2.	Cyclophosphamide and Myocet[a]	Metastatic BC[b]	Pillai (2014)
3.	Atezolizumab and Abraxane (Nabpaclitaxel)[a]	Triple-negative breast cancer	Schmid et al. (2018), Mir et al. (2020)

[a]Neratinib (NERLYNX) and Capecitabine were approved by FDA in 2020, Myocet and Cyclophosphamide, in the year 2001, and Atezolizumab and Abraxane (Nab-paclitaxel) were approved by FDA in 2018.
[b]BC, Breast Cancer.

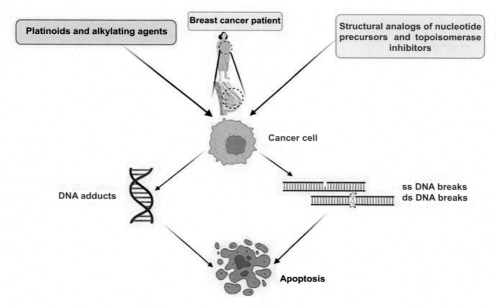

Fig. 10.5 Mode of action of various therapeutic drugs including Platinoids and alkylating agents and structural analogs of nucleotide precursors and topoisomerase inhibitors on the breast cancer cell, ultimately leading to apoptosis.

specifically inhibit the T regulatory cells in the tumor microenvironment to bring out or evoke the ICD (Ladoire et al., 2008; West et al., 2011) Table 10.5.

Research studies done previously have revealed that the outcome in the form of a tumor microenvironment that is immunosuppressive is witnessed due to the activation of platelets and it reprieves cancer cells from the immune watch which results in the migration as well as the growth of cancer cells (Zhang et al., 2019; Riesenberg et al., 2019).

Table 10.5 Lists some of the small-molecule inhibitors employed in breast cancer treatment.

S.no.	Target	Small molecular inhibitor	Reference
1.	Acidic microenvironment	Omeprazole	Luciani et al. (2004)
		Bicarbonate	Robey et al. (2009)
		Sulfonamide-based CAIX inhibitors (CAI17 and U-104)	Lou et al. (2011), Lock et al. (2013), Andreucci et al. (2019)
		Glycosylcoumarins (GC-204 and GC-205)	Lou et al. (2011)
		SLC-0111 (in combined form with doxorubicin, temozolomide, 5-fluorouracil, and dacarbazine)	Andreucci et al. (2019)
		Cariporide	Amith and Fliegel (2013), Di Sario et al. (2007), Harguindey et al. (2013)
2.	TAMs	Bindarit	Zollo et al. (2012)
		AS1517499	Binnemars-Postma et al. (2018)
		BLZ-945	Shen et al., (2017)
		Sorafenib	Edwards and Emens (2010)
3.	CAFs	RKN 5755	Suvarna et al. (2018)
		A C1 MM YR2 (combined with taxol)	Ren et al. (2016)
		WRG-28	Grither and Longmore (2018)
4.	ECs	CX-4945	Siddiqui-Jain et al. (2010)
		TNP-470	Satchi-Fainaro et al. (2005)
5.	Hyaluronan [HA]	4-methylumbelliferone (MU)	Lokeshwar et al. (2010), Yoshihara et al. (2005), Nakazawa et al. (2006)
6.	Matrix metalloproteinases (MMPs)	N-[4-(difluoromethoxy) phenyl]-2-[(4-oxo-6-propyl-1H pyrimidin-2-yl) sulfanyl]-acetamide	Dufour et al., (2011)
7.	Lysophosphatidic acid [LPA]	ONO-8430506	Benesch et al. (2015)

10.4 Therapies that aim at the TME

One of the significant progresses in drugs that act directly on the breast cancer tumor microenvironment involves the *PD-1/PD-L1 inhibitors*. These are known to reinstate the cytotoxic T-cell reaction toward the tumor cells and are authorized for use in metastatic breast cancer treatment (Vaddepally et al., 2020; Mehraj et al., 2022a,b). Even the cytotoxic T-lymphocyte antigen 4 (CTLA-4) has been examined with anti–PD-1/PD-L1 inhibitors (Vonderheide et al., 2010). Moreover, many such immune checkpoint targets are under investigation in trials or active developments. Many novel agents, including those targeting the tumor microenvironment with respect to combating hypoxia, are under clinical investigation (Graham and Unger, 2018). Aside from the effect of hormonal therapy and inhibitors of HER2 on the tumor cells, these have also been shown to affect the microenvironment of the tumor and the hormone receptors do modulate several immune cells within the microenvironment of the tumor (Segovia-Mendoza and Morales-Montor, 2019).

10.5 Radiotherapy and tumor microenvironment

The property of cancer cells to display quicker proliferation in comparison to other normal cells of the patient is exploited in the case of the traditional therapies. It has been witnessed that majorly double-stranded DNA breaks occur when radiation therapy is employed, leading to the death of cells via mitotic damage (Eriksson and Stigbrand, 2010). Radiation therapy also upregulates the secretion of many substances including Interleukin 1β, Interferon type I and III, Tumor necrosis factor α among others Fig. 10.6.

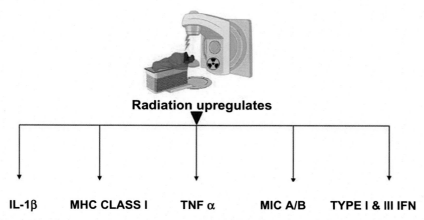

Radiation upregulates

IL-1β   MHC CLASS I   TNF α   MIC A/B   TYPE I & III IFN

Fig. 10.6 Observed effects from radiation treatment: IL-1β, MHC CLASS I, TNF α, MIC A/B and TYPE I and III IFN are upregulated postradiation treatment.

The High mobility group box 1 (HMGB1), ATP calreticulin, and HSP (heat shock protein) are the damage-associated molecular patterns (DAMPs) and are released due to the cancer cell damage or death post radiation therapy and these DAMPs are perceived by the immune cells and are powerful stimulators of inflammatory signals that trigger the dendritic cells. The HMGB1 could trigger the toll-like receptor 4 that is present on these dendritic cells, which results in an increased cross-presentation of tumor antigen and turns on the succeeding cytotoxic T-cell response (Barker et al., 2015; Apetoh et al., 2007). The radiations are also able to produce type 1 interferons (Sun et al., 2013). And interferon conciliates both specific and nonspecific immunities via the CD4 and CD8 T-lymphocyte rise and is known to avert the myeloid-derived suppressor cells assembly, thus driving the immune reaction against tumor instead of being immunosuppressive in nature previously (Ngwa et al., 2018). In the case of breast cancer subjects, elevated levels of T-cell chemoattractant like that of the CXCL9 and CXCL10 indicate an active immune system postradiation treatment (Strom et al., 2017).

10.6 Nanochemotherapeutics and tumor microenvironment

Compared to traditional cancer therapies, nanochemotherapeutics have precedence over these due to the low drug toxicity with higher efficiency, meticulousness for tumor site, upgraded stability and solubility of drugs, imaging methods, and higher half-life of drugs in circulation as well as a regulated release. There has been a significant improvement in the field of nanobiotechnology like the use of nano-based delivery systems for cancer therapy has much more precedence over traditional chemotherapy as these can transfer the drugs favorably to the cancers and this is possible due to their enhanced permeability and retention [EPR] effect, thus sparing the normal tissues from the undesirable secondary effects (Lin et al., 2018; Miao and Huang, 2015; Mei et al., 2021). The complex tumor microenvironment has been shown to hinder the therapy being applied to cancer significantly. Be it the tumor hypoxia which dampens the reaction of the tumor cells toward the drugs or be it the extracellular matrix which is known to impede the penetration of drugs deep into the tumor tissue, novel strategies have been developed to combat these and many such problems like the engineered nanoparticles have been developed to remodel the tumor microenvironment for achieving potential cancer therapy. The high-density lipoprotein, liposomes, micelles, polymeric nanoparticles, dendrimers, and nanoemulsions are all examples of organic nanoparticles, and these have been shown to display more efficient delivery of drugs with minimum toxicity. All the inorganic nanoparticles, including gold nanoparticles, silica nanoparticles, magnetic nanoparticles, carbon nanotubes [CNTs] as well as Quantum dots can get to the discrete sites of action by functionalization (Anchordoquy et al., 2017; Sailor and Park, 2012; Ashfaq et al., 2017). The main targets of nanoparticles are the cells and constitute the cancer stem cells, exosomes, cancer-associated fibroblasts, and extracellular matrix within the tumor microenvironment and these can modify the tumor microenvironment. It has also been revealed that the nanoparticles can modify the complex tumor microenvironment by administering modulators or picking up external physical signals, conquering the physiological hurdles. For responsive delivery of drugs for the tumor microenvironment, small-molecule prodrug nanoassembly is another approach that has recently been matured (Vickers, 2017; Xie et al., 2020).

10.6.1 Targeting the extracellular matrix of TME

The three-dimensional noncellular network which provides support to its cellular components is termed as the extracellular matrix (Walker et al., 2018). Multiple studies have shown that the extracellular matrix acts as the primary barrier to the migration of tumor cells and the further development of the tumor is attributed to the impaired regulation of the extracellular matrix (Harisi and Jeney, 2015). So it becomes important to examine the interaction between the extracellular matrix and the tumor cells to elucidate the possible therapy for treating cancers as well via remodeling the extracellular matrix. The efficacy of the anticancer drugs is reduced due to the higher matrix density of the substances like glycoproteins, collagen and proteoglycans, which are frequently placed in the dense extracellular matrix and it has been witnessed that there occurs obstruction for the nanoparticles to enter the extracellular matrix and diffuse all over the interstitium of the matrix due to its structural complexity (Arneth, 2019; Muntimadugu et al., 2017). Thus, it becomes imperative to decrease the density of the collagen to enhance the entry and accretion of nanoparticles (NPs) in the cancer tissue. One such example is provided by Yao et al., who developed a nanoenzyme capsule by merging the collagenase nanocapsules with that of the heavy chain ferritin nanocages to encase the drug doxorubicin (DOX). These can aid in the relatively easy process of entry of these NPs into the tumor by dissolving the collagen part of the extracellular matrix in the 4T1 breast cancer model. This was possible due to the endopeptidases (the collagenases) capable of digesting the local collagen in the triple helix realm. The collagenase nanocapsules (Col-nc) may aid in safeguarding the enzyme action before reaching the actual site of action, succeeding this, the collagen is dissolved by the released enzyme, thus reducing the extracellular matrix density. The dissolution of collagen by Col-nc/HFn (DOX) and the increased entry of the nanoparticles in solid tumor sites have been witnessed in both in vivo and in vitro studies (Yao et al., 2020). The basic mechanism of action of DOX is depicted Fig. 10.7. The complex formed in both strands of the DNA by Doxorubicin with the bases halts the Topoisomerase II enzyme function and therefore DNA synthesis as well.

Not only the protein-based ways are employed for degrading the extracellular matrix, but other substances which are used exogenously could also help dissolve the components and thus the integrity of the extracellular matrix. One such example is the protein-free method by Dong et al., which dissolves the collagen by activating

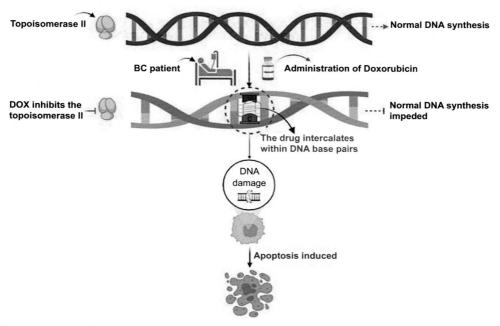

Fig. 10.7 MOA of DOX: The central mechanism of action of doxorubicin embraces the capability of DOX to intercalate within the base pairs of DNA leading to the DNA strands breakage and thwarting synthesis of both DNA and RNA. Doxorubicin retards Topoisomerase II enzyme, generating the damage in DNA and begets apoptosis. The role of the enzyme Topoisomerase II is to relax the supercoiling of DNA to aid in the replication and synthesis of DNA.

endogenous MMPs(matrix metalloproteinases) with NO (Nitric Oxide) (Dong et al., 2019). One more constituent of the extracellular matrix is hyaluronic acid (HA), which has a pivotal role to play in dictating the compressive properties of maximum tissues (Haider et al., 2020). The expression is enhanced in tumors, thus aiding in forming a gel-like matrix, which results in the restriction of entry of external fluid and piling up of drugs, enlarging the interstitial fluid pressures (IFP) (Walker et al., 2018). Thus, HA degradation is the target for better drug penetration for better drug delivery. The drug delivery system that is HAase (hyaluronidase) embedded (NPs-EPI/HAase) which might increase the tumor penetration by modulating the microenvironment of the tumor was constructed by Chen et al. and the property of HAase that can degrade the hydraulic acid to enhance the permeability of the tissues for fluid is exploited. The results were seen in HepG2 tumors, where this drug delivery system was able to dissolve the hyaluronic acid thus enhancing better entry and build-up of nanoparticles thus inhibiting the growth of tumor effectively (Chen et al., 2020; Mir et al., 2020). The Fig. 10.8 lists various nanocarriers that facilitate the cell–nanoparticle interaction with the overall aim of targeting or treating the cancers in a more targeted approach.

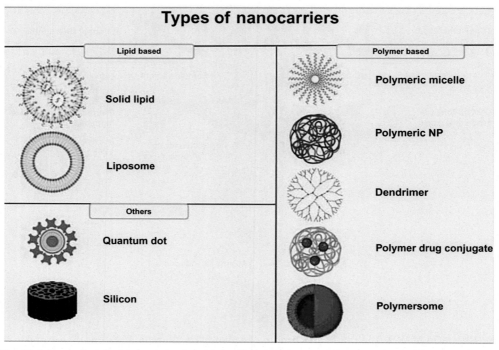

Fig. 10.8 Examples of nanocarrier: (A) Lipid-based: Solid lipid and Liposome type. (B) Polymer-based: polymeric micelle, polymeric nanoparticle, dendrimer, polymer drug conjugate and polymersome types and (C) Other types: quantum dots and silicon based.

10.6.2 Targeting the CAFs of TME

The rich abundance of Cancer-associated fibroblasts is present within the stroma of the tumor (Truffi et al., 2019), and the latter are known to provide multiple growth factors like PDGF, VEGF, TGF-β and in addition yield MMPs (Luo et al., 2015) which are the proteins of extracellular matrix, chemokines and cytokines as well (Mehraj et al., 2021a,b,c, 2022a,b). Thus, a significant role in intensifying the phenotype of tumor is played by cancer-associated fibroblasts, and be it the extracellular matrix remodeling, encouraging the proliferation of tumor cells, creating new blood vessels or inflammation, these cancer-associated fibroblasts have a role to play in all these processes. Studies have revealed that the inefficacious nano therapy delivery and the resistance against drugs in the treatment of cancer are witnessed due to cancer-associated fibroblasts (Vickers, 2017). Therefore, proper regulation of the cancer-associated fibroblasts is a possible approach to enhance the effectiveness of cancer therapies by remodeling the tumor microenvironment. Presently, many nanotechnology-based tactics are available which cancer-associated fibroblast-based therapies are. For instance, the connections between the CAFs and the cancer cells could be interrupted by the disarray of cancer-associated fibroblasts. Thus, their disruption will enhance the drugs' effectiveness in cancers.

10.6.3 Targeting the cancer stem cells of TME

The initiation, progression, metastasis, relapse, and poor prognosis have been associated with the cancer stem cells due to their active participation or involvement in modulating the tumor microenvironment (Das and Law, 2018). The cancer stem cells show increased expression of drug transporters, thus contributing to drug resistance. These have also been reported to uphold a moderate dividing state as well as display swift repair of DNA thus withstanding the radiation therapy also (Bao et al., 2006).

In addition, the cancer stem cells do sustain in circulation too, and these are responsible for developing secondary tumors as well. Therefore, targeting the cancer stem cells will aid in developing anticancer therapies. The role of nanoparticles mediated drug delivery system has been effective for treating cancers. It has been seen that there is an elevated expression of CD44 receptors on the cancer stem cells, and these could act as binding targets (Xin et al., 2006). These CD44 receptors have a strong affinity for chitosan and Rao et al. exploited the same property and formed polymer nanoparticles loaded with the chemotherapy agent, which possessed the conjugated chitosan on their surface (Rao et al., 2015). Thus, the nanoparticles which were delivered to the tumor microenvironment specifically targeted the cancer stem cells overexpressing CD44, thus enhancing the efficiency of treatment in the mammary tumor spheroids model.

10.6.4 Tumor microenvironment targeting by aiming at antiangiogenesis

The vasculature in the tumor is marked by a disarranged network of vessels along with irregular shape and diameter and these vessels are also leaky, dilated, and intermittent, all these together reduce the ability of these vessels to supply nutrients and withdraw the waste materials produced (Siemann, 2011). There is enhanced permeability in these vessels leading to a build-up of vascular substances or materials and an elevated interstitial fluid pressure (IFP). The tumor cells also lead to the development of an acidic tumor microenvironment due to the formation of lactate, H^+ ions, and pyruvate. All these mentioned properties lead to an intricate tumor microenvironment that promotes the development of tumors, drug resistance, and suppression of the immune system due to the hypoxic and acidic as well as increased interstitial fluid pressure development. Due to the dependence of the tumor on blood for growth and metastasis, antiangiogenesis is a possible target for developing better strategies against cancers (Folkman, 1971; Mehraj et al., 2021b). The food and drug administration has approved many compounds that act against angiogenesis like Sorafenib and Aflibercept and Bevacizumab and these have the potential to hinder the process of angiogenesis by combining with the vascular endothelial growth factor or its receptor, i.e., VEGFR (Goel et al., 2011).

10.6.5 Targeting exosomes of TME

The extracellular vesicles (EVS) have a pivotal role in cellular interactions. The cancer cell-derived extracellular vesicles get engaged in cancer propagation and also engage in metastasis of cancer (Tkach and Théry, 2016). Among the extracellular vesicles, exosomes have been reported to reposition the (biological functional) molecules to the receiver cell, aiding the tumor's maturation within the tumor microenvironment. Thus, tumor-derived exosomes (TDEs) act as signaling mediators that modulate the tumor microenvironment, targeting these tumor-derived exosomes will aid in antitumor therapy. Recent studies indicate that the tumor-derived exosomes possess an abundant fount of biomarkers (Meng et al., 2019) which could aid in better therapy. Studies by Lu et al. have revealed that the tumor-derived exosomes can conciliate the cellular communication as well as remodel the tumor microenvironment by miRNA transport (Lu et al., 2018). The nanoparticles-based targeting of exosomes is a favorable approach that could help in the modulation of the tumor microenvironment.

10.6.6 Immediate immune system and tumor microenvironment

Immunotherapy has emerged as a significant option for treating cancers, but there impedes its use like attenuation, varying efficacy, and complications. Thus, nanotechnology comes to the rescue by overcoming the physiological hindrances for better outcomes. It has been seen that the dendritic cells and cytotoxic T lymphocytes are immunostimulatory in nature and applying the nano-drug delivery system (DDS) could aid in the immunostimulation inside the tumor microenvironment. While the myeloid-derived suppressor cells (MDSCs, M2-TAMs, and T-regulatory cells are immunosuppressive in nature. Thus, this needs to be bypassed for effective cancer therapy.

In a recent study, a nanoparticle-based drug delivery system that aims at the BC cells has been formed, and the group has exploited the MNPs, i.e., the mesoporous silica nanoparticles to transport Aspirin to the site of the tumor. It was witnessed through this study that this drug delivery system comprising of various constituents including Mesoporous silica nanoparticles, Aspirin, polydopamine-polyethylene glycol, and folic acid, i.-e., (MNP-Asp-PD-PG-F), displays elevated antiproliferative and cytotoxic outcomes on the breast cancer cells in comparison to the solo drug (Aspirin). This study holds much importance for the possible breast cancer treatment and opens doors for this nanocarrier MNP-PD-PG-F to be utilized for the delivery of other drugs that act against the tumor, thus enhancing their efficacy relatively as has been shown in the case of Aspirin (Kanwal et al., 2021). Still, even after having so much potential, issues like the safety of nanomaterials and other such materials being employed are to be addressed. The availability of nanoparticles also limits their wide-scale application and varying response due to varying tumors is yet another hurdle to be dissolved.

10.6.7 Hypoxia and acidosis in the tumor microenvironment

The neighboring supply of blood is unable to meet the oxygen requirements for the multiplication of tumor cells, and as a consequence, the oxygen accessibility is lowered, leading to increased hypoxia. Compared to normal tissues within the tumor microenvironment, the partial oxygen pressure is generally reduced. The reduced oxygen levels could manifest as acute or chronic hypoxia within the tumor microenvironment (Vaupel and Mayer, 2014). The Hypoxia-induced factor-1 (HIF-1) is a transcriptional factor that has a major role in systematizing the sequence of cellular reactions to prevent the oxygen deficiency, the cell encounters, and these cellular responses are initiated by hypoxia (Vaupel and Mayer, 2007). Various therapies and compounds have previously been made to handle hypoxia-induced factor-1 or its targets to eschew the progression of tumor (Ziello et al., 2007; Paolicchi et al., 2016; Yu et al., 2017; Mir, 2014). In a lately identified operable breast cancer [NCT01763931] in the phase 2 analysis of a clinical trial, Digoxin (DIG-HIF1) effects have also been carried out. Also, to withstand the nutrient and oxygen scarce environment and meet the energy requirements of the multiplicative tumor cells, the latter display the process termed the "Warburg effect" (Kim, 2018).

The metabolic alterations are moderated by the transcriptional modulators of HIF-1, inducing the transporters of glucose (GLUTs) to enhance the import of glucose and modulate metabolism, thus benefitting the process of glycolysis [anaerobic]over the process of oxidative phosphorylation (Kim, 2018; Kato et al., 2018). This leads to the accretion of lactic and carbonic acids (Kim, 2018; Kato et al., 2018).

To circumvent this process of acidification, the researchers have drawn their attention to hindering the proton transporters and exchanges within the tumor microenvironment as well as carbonic anhydrase inhibition main focus (Masoud and Li, 2015; Kato et al., 2018; Singh et al., 2018). Because the change in pH partitioning at the cell membrane induces extracellular accumulation of chemotherapeutic agents that otherwise must passively diffuse into the cells, it seems that this process of acidification inside the microenvironment of the tumor protects the tumor cells from the chemotherapy being applied (Singh et al., 2018).

10.7 Summary

Based on current treatment approaches and research directions, it can be concluded that nanomedicine is a suitable field to achieve the targeted therapy for breast cancer treatment, and nanotechnology is emerging at a higher pace and it may be the future for treating various cancers. The major affairs that assist the tumor growth and development primarily within the domain of tumor microenvironment need to be fully elucidated, and the possible ways by which such events control the change within the tumor microenvironment need to be examined will aid in the development of structured therapy plans. There have been huge improvements in the antitumor therapies, but the constructive management of breast cancer faces weighty hurdles due to drug resistance. It has been witnessed in multiple studies that the two-way communication betwixt the developing tumor cells and the neighboring stromal components has a crucial role to play in response to the treatment being employed. Many studies focused on targeting the tumor micro-environment constituents are advancing at either preclinical or clinical stages. And these studies reveal that if the components of the tumor microenvironment are targeted in combination with other tumor-specific therapies, it significantly decreases the tumor growth, drug resistance, and metastasis. A deeper understanding of the breast cancer tumor microenvironment is important for developing better and targeted therapies that display minimum toxicity and other side effects to different tissues of the body. Chemotherapy, Immunotherapy, and Radiotherapy are also employed in breast cancer treatment, but to minimize their side effects like the nonspecific targeting and toxicity and resistance, more targeted approaches are now being developed for better outcomes. Compared to the above-mentioned traditional cancer therapies, nanochemotherapeutics have precedence over these due to the low drug toxicity with higher efficiency, meticulousness for tumor site, upgraded stability and solubility of drugs, imaging methods, the higher half-life of drugs in circulation as well as a regulated release. Various tumor microenvironment-specific interventions have been made that are producing good outcomes both at preclinical and clinical stages like the use of NPs and other nanocarriers that have been engineered to increase the site-specific delivery of the drugs possessing anti-tumor activity like that of Aspirin, Doxorubicin among others. In the coming years, more such interventions will prove to be a boon for cancer therapies in general and breast cancer in particular. Moreover, various drugs that have been repurposed for breast cancer treatment are approved by FDA and are producing positive results. Combination therapy has also successfully been employed in clinical settings and various drug combinations are used to treat breast cancer patients, it has led to lower drug toxicity and an overall increase in the QOL in the case of BC patients. Similarly, the introduction of small–molecule inhibitors like Omeprazole, Bindarit, and others acts directly on the specific tumor microenvironment components. Although nanoplatforms provide a lot of scopes to improve the already existing therapies available like chemotherapy and even after having so much potential some issues like the safety of nanomaterials and other such materials being employed are to be addressed, and the availability of nanoparticles also limits their wide-scale application, and varying response due to varying tumors is yet another hurdle to be dissolved.

References

Abadjian, M.-C.Z., Edwards, W.B., Anderson, C.J., 2017. Imaging the tumor microenvironment. In: Tumor Immune Microenvironment in Cancer Progression and Cancer Therapy. Springer, pp. 229–257.

Akwii, R., Sajib, M., Zahra, F., Mikelis, C., 2019. Role of Angiopoietin-2 in vascular physiology and pathophysiology. Cell 8, E471.

Amith, S.R., Fliegel, L., 2013. Regulation of the Na+/H+ exchanger (NHE1) in breast cancer metastasis. Cancer Res. 73, 1259–1264.

Anchordoquy, T.J., Barenholz, Y., Boraschi, D., Chorny, M., Decuzzi, P., Dobrovolskaia, M.A., Farhangrazi, Z.S., Farrell, D., Gabizon, A., Ghandehari, H., 2017. Mechanisms and Barriers in Cancer Nanomedicine: Addressing Challenges, Looking for Solutions. ACS Publications.

Andreucci, E., Ruzzolini, J., Peppicelli, S., Bianchini, F., Laurenzana, A., Carta, F., Supuran, C.T., Calorini, L., 2019. The carbonic anhydrase IX inhibitor SLC-0111 sensitises cancer cells to conventional chemotherapy. J. Enzyme Inhib. Med. Chem. 34, 117–123.

Apetoh, L., Ghiringhelli, F., Tesniere, A., Obeid, M., Ortiz, C., Criollo, A., Mignot, G., Maiuri, M.C., Ullrich, E., Saulnier, P., 2007. Toll-like receptor 4–dependent contribution of the immune system to anticancer chemotherapy and radiotherapy. Nat. Med. 13, 1050–1059.

Arneth, B., 2019. Tumor microenvironment. Medicina 56, 15.

Ashfaq, U.A., Riaz, M., Yasmeen, E., Yousaf, M.Z., 2017. Recent advances in nanoparticle-based targeted drug-delivery systems against cancer and role of tumor microenvironment. Crit. Rev. Ther. Drug Carrier Syst. 34.

Baek, S., Kim, C.-S., Kim, S.-B., Kim, Y.-M., Kwon, S.-W., Kim, Y., Kim, H., Lee, H., 2011. Combination therapy of renal cell carcinoma or breast cancer patients with dendritic cell vaccine and IL-2: results from a phase I/II trial. J. Transl. Med. 9, 1–10.

Bahrami, A., Hassanian, S.M., Khazaei, M., Hasanzadeh, M., Shahidsales, S., Maftouh, M., Ferns, G.A., Avan, A., 2018. The therapeutic potential of targeting tumor microenvironment in breast cancer: rational strategies and recent progress. J. Cell. Biochem. 119, 111–122.

Bao, S., Wu, Q., Mclendon, R.E., Hao, Y., Shi, Q., Hjelmeland, A.B., Dewhirst, M.W., Bigner, D.D., Rich, J.N., 2006. Glioma stem cells promote radioresistance by preferential activation of the DNA damage response. Nature 444, 756–760.

Barker, H.E., Paget, J.T., Khan, A.A., Harrington, K.J., 2015. The tumour microenvironment after radiotherapy: mechanisms of resistance and recurrence. Nat. Rev. Cancer 15, 409–425.

Beckwitt, C.H., Brufsky, A., Oltvai, Z.N., Wells, A., 2018. Statin drugs to reduce breast cancer recurrence and mortality. Breast Cancer Res. 20, 1–11.

Benesch, M.G., Tang, X., Dewald, J., Dong, W.F., Mackey, J.R., Hemmings, D.G., McMullen, T.P., Brindley, D.N., 2015. Tumor-induced inflammation in mammary adipose tissue stimulates a vicious cycle of autotaxin expression and breast cancer progression. FASEB J. 29, 3990–4000.

Berkenblit, A., Matulonis, U.A., Kroener, J.F., Dezube, B.J., Lam, G.N., Cuasay, L.C., Brünner, N., Jones, T.R., Silverman, M.H., Gold, M.A., 2005. Å6, a urokinase plasminogen activator (uPA)-derived peptide in patients with advanced gynecologic cancer: a phase I trial. Gynecol. Oncol. 99, 50–57.

Binnemars-Postma, K., Bansal, R., Storm, G., Prakash, J., 2018. Targeting the Stat6 pathway in tumor-associated macrophages reduces tumor growth and metastatic niche formation in breast cancer. FASEB J. 32, 969–978.

Brahmer, J.R., Drake, C.G., Wollner, I., Powderly, J.D., Picus, J., Sharfman, W.H., Stankevich, E., Pons, A., Salay, T.M., Mcmiller, T.L., 2010. Phase I study of single-agent anti–programmed death-1 (MDX-1106) in refractory solid tumors: safety, clinical activity, pharmacodynamics, and immunologic correlates. J. Clin. Oncol. 28, 3167.

Brahmer, J., Tykodi, S., Chow, L., Hwu, W., Topalian, S., Hwu, P., Drake, C., Camacho, L., Kauh, J., Odunsi, K., Wigginton, J.M., 2012a. Safety and activity of anti-PD-L1 antibody in patients with advanced cancer. N. Engl. J. Med. 366, 2455–2465.

Brahmer, J.R., Horn, L., Antonia, S., Spigel, D.R., Gandhi, L., Sequist, L.V., Wigginton, J., McDonald, D., Kollia, G., Gupta, A.K., 2012b. Clinical activity and safety of anti-PD1 (BMS-936558, MDX-1106) in patients with advanced non-small-cell lung cancer (NSCLC). J. Clin. Oncol. 30, 7509.

Butler, J.M., Kobayashi, H., Rafii, S., 2010. Instructive role of the vascular niche in promoting tumour growth and tissue repair by angiocrine factors. Nat. Rev. Cancer 10, 138–146.

Cassetta, L., Pollard, J.W., 2018. Targeting macrophages: therapeutic approaches in cancer. Nat. Rev. Drug Discov. 17, 887–904.

Chen, E., Han, S., Song, B., Xu, L., Yuan, H., Liang, M., Sun, Y., 2020. Mechanism investigation of hyaluronidase-combined multistage nanoparticles for solid tumor penetration and antitumor effect. Int. J. Nanomedicine 15, 6311.

Chuk, M.K., Chang, J.T., Theoret, M.R., Sampene, E., He, K., Weis, S.L., Helms, W.S., Jin, R., Li, H., Yu, J., 2017. FDA approval summary: accelerated approval of pembrolizumab for second-line treatment of metastatic melanoma. Clin. Cancer Res. 23, 5666–5670.

D'angelo, S.P., Russell, J., Lebbé, C., Chmielowski, B., Gambichler, T., Grob, J.-J., Kiecker, F., Rabinowits, G., Terheyden, P., Zwiener, I., 2018. Efficacy and safety of first-line avelumab treatment in patients with stage IV metastatic Merkel cell carcinoma: a preplanned interim analysis of a clinical trial. JAMA Oncol. 4, e180077.

Dannenberg, A.J., Subbaramaiah, K., 2003. Targeting cyclooxygenase-2 in human neoplasia: rationale and promise. Cancer Cell 4, 431–436.

Das, M., Law, S., 2018. Role of tumor microenvironment in cancer stem cell chemoresistance and recurrence. Int. J. Biochem. Cell Biol. 103, 115–124.

Delaloge, S., Wolp-Diniz, R., Byrski, T., Blum, J., Gonçalves, A., Campone, M., Lardelli, P., Kahatt, C., Nieto, A., Cullell-Young, M., 2014. Activity of trabectedin in germline BRCA1/2-mutated metastatic breast cancer: results of an international first-in-class phase II study. Ann. Oncol. 25, 1152–1158.

Deligne, C., Midwood, K.S., 2021. Macrophages and extracellular matrix in breast cancer: partners in crime or protective allies? Front. Oncol. 11, 186.

Denardo, D.G., Andreu, P., Coussens, L.M., 2010. Interactions between lymphocytes and myeloid cells regulate pro-versus anti-tumor immunity. Cancer Metastasis Rev. 29, 309–316.

Di Sario, A., Bendia, E., Omenetti, A., De Minicis, S., Marzioni, M., Kleemann, H., Candelaresi, C., Saccomanno, S., Alpini, G., Benedetti, A., 2007. Selective inhibition of ion transport mechanisms regulating intracellular pH reduces proliferation and induces apoptosis in cholangiocarcinoma cells. Dig. Liver Dis. 39, 60–69.

Dong, X., Liu, H.-J., Feng, H.-Y., Yang, S.-C., Liu, X.-L., Lai, X., Lu, Q., Lovell, J.F., Chen, H.-Z., Fang, C., 2019. Enhanced drug delivery by nanoscale integration of a nitric oxide donor to induce tumor collagen depletion. Nano Lett. 19, 997–1008.

Dufour, A., Sampson, N.S., Li, J., Kuscu, C., Rizzo, R.C., Deleon, J.L., Zhi, J., Jaber, N., Liu, E., Zucker, S., 2011. Small-molecule anticancer compounds selectively target the hemopexin domain of matrix metalloproteinase-9. Cancer Res. 71, 4977–4988.

Duong, T., Koopman, P., Francois, M., 2012. Tumor lymphangiogenesis as a potential therapeutic target. J. Oncol. 2012.

Dvorak, H.F., 1986. Tumors: wounds that do not heal. N. Engl. J. Med. 315, 1650–1659.

Edwards, J.P., Emens, L.A., 2010. The multikinase inhibitor Sorafenib reverses the suppression of IL-12 and enhancement of IL-10 by PGE2 in murine macrophages. Int. Immunopharmacol. 10, 1220–1228.

Eriksson, D., Stigbrand, T., 2010. Radiation-induced cell death mechanisms. Tumor Biol. 31, 363–372.

Fabi, A., Metro, G., Papaldo, P., Mottolese, M., Melucci, E., Carlini, P., Sperduti, I., Russillo, M., Gelibter, A., Ferretti, G., 2008. Impact of celecoxib on capecitabine tolerability and activity in pretreated metastatic breast cancer: results of a phase II study with biomarker evaluation. Cancer Chemother. Pharmacol. 62, 717–725.

Fang, Y., Qu, X., Cheng, B., Chen, Y., Wang, Z., Chen, F., Xiong, B., 2015. The efficacy and safety of bevacizumab combined with chemotherapy in treatment of HER2-negative metastatic breast cancer: a meta-analysis based on published phase III trials. Tumor Biol. 36, 1933–1941.

Folkman, J., 1971. Tumor angiogenesis: therapeutic implications. N. Engl. J. Med. 285, 1182–1186.

Garnier, L., Gkountidi, A.-O., Hugues, S., 2019. Tumor-associated lymphatic vessel features and immunomodulatory functions. Front. Immunol. 10, 720.

Georgoudaki, A.-M., Prokopec, K.E., Boura, V.F., Hellqvist, E., Sohn, S., Östling, J., Dahan, R., Harris, R.A., Rantalainen, M., Klevebring, D., 2016. Reprogramming tumor-associated macrophages by antibody targeting inhibits cancer progression and metastasis. Cell Rep. 15, 2000–2011.

Ghajar, C.M., Peinado, H., Mori, H., Matei, I.R., Evason, K.J., Brazier, H., Almeida, D., Koller, A., Hajjar, K.A., Stainier, D.Y., 2013. The perivascular niche regulates breast tumour dormancy. Nat. Cell Biol. 15, 807–817.

Gibson, J., 2015. Anti-PD-L1 for metastatic triple-negative breast cancer. Lancet Oncol. 16, e264.

Gilkes, D.M., Semenza, G.L., Wirtz, D., 2014. Hypoxia and the extracellular matrix: drivers of tumour metastasis. Nat. Rev. Cancer 14, 430–439.

Gilligan, M.M., Gartung, A., Sulciner, M.L., Norris, P.C., Sukhatme, V.P., Bielenberg, D.R., Huang, S., Kieran, M.W., Serhan, C.N., Panigrahy, D., 2019. Aspirin-triggered proresolving mediators stimulate resolution in cancer. Proc. Natl. Acad. Sci. 116, 6292–6297.

Giussani, M., Landoni, E., Merlino, G., Turdo, F., Veneroni, S., Paolini, B., Cappelletti, V., Miceli, R., Orlandi, R., Triulzi, T., 2018. Extracellular matrix proteins as diagnostic markers of breast carcinoma. J. Cell. Physiol. 233, 6280–6290.

Goel, S., Duda, D.G., Xu, L., Munn, L.L., Boucher, Y., Fukumura, D., Jain, R.K., 2011. Normalization of the vasculature for treatment of cancer and other diseases. Physiol. Rev. 91, 1071–1121.

Goncharov, N., Popova, P., Avdonin, P., Kudryavtsev, I., Serebryakova, M., Korf, E., Avdonin, P., 2020. Markers of endothelial cells in normal and pathological conditions. Biochem. (Mosc.) Suppl. Ser. A Membr. Cell Biol. 14, 167–183.

Graham, K., Unger, E., 2018. Overcoming tumor hypoxia as a barrier to radiotherapy, chemotherapy and immunotherapy in cancer treatment. Int. J. Nanomedicine 13, 6049.

Grither, W.R., Longmore, G.D., 2018. Inhibition of tumor–microenvironment interaction and tumor invasion by small-molecule allosteric inhibitor of DDR2 extracellular domain. Proc. Natl. Acad. Sci. 115, E7786–E7794.

Grivennikov, S.I., Greten, F.R., Karin, M., 2010. Immunity, inflammation, and cancer. Cell 140, 883–899.

Haider, T., Sandha, K.K., Soni, V., Gupta, P.N., 2020. Recent advances in tumor microenvironment associated therapeutic strategies and evaluation models. Mater. Sci. Eng. C 116, 111229.

Hamy, A.-S., Tury, S., Wang, X., Gao, J., Pierga, J.-Y., Giacchetti, S., Brain, E., Pistilli, B., Marty, M., Espié, M., 2019. Celecoxib with neoadjuvant chemotherapy for breast cancer might worsen outcomes differentially by COX-2 expression and ER status: exploratory analysis of the REMAGUS02 trial. J. Clin. Oncol. 37, 624.

Hanahan, D., Coussens, L.M., 2012. Accessories to the crime: functions of cells recruited to the tumor microenvironment. Cancer Cell 21, 309–322.

Hanahan, D., Weinberg, R.A., 2011. Hallmarks of cancer: the next generation. Cell 144, 646–674.

Hannesdóttir, L., Tymoszuk, P., Parajuli, N., Wasmer, M.H., Philipp, S., Daschil, N., Datta, S., Koller, J.B., Tripp, C.H., Stoitzner, P., 2013. Lapatinib and doxorubicin enhance the S tat1-dependent antitumor immune response. Eur. J. Immunol. 43, 2718–2729.

Harguindey, S., Arranz, J.L., Polo Orozco, J.D., Rauch, C., Fais, S., Cardone, R.A., Reshkin, S.J., 2013. Cariporide and other new and powerful NHE1 inhibitors as potentially selective anticancer drugs–an integral molecular/biochemical/metabolic/clinical approach after one hundred years of cancer research. J. Transl. Med. 11, 1–17.

Harisi, R., Jeney, A., 2015. Extracellular matrix as target for antitumor therapy. Onco. Targets. Ther. 8, 1387.

Harris, R.E., Chlebowski, R.T., Jackson, R.D., Frid, D.J., Ascenseo, J.L., Anderson, G., Loar, A., Rodabough, R.J., White, E., Mctiernan, A., 2003. Breast cancer and nonsteroidal anti-inflammatory drugs: prospective results from the Women's Health Initiative. Cancer Res. 63, 6096–6101.

Hida, K., Maishi, N., Annan, D.A., Hida, Y., 2018. Contribution of tumor endothelial cells in cancer progression. Int. J. Mol. Sci. 19, 1272.

Hill, B.S., Sarnella, A., D'avino, G., Zannetti, A., 2020. Recruitment of stromal cells into tumour microenvironment promote the metastatic spread of breast cancer. In: Seminars in Cancer Biology. Elsevier, pp. 202–213.

Holen, I., Lefley, D.V., Francis, S.E., Rennicks, S., Bradbury, S., Coleman, R.E., Ottewell, P., 2016. IL-1 drives breast cancer growth and bone metastasis in vivo. Oncotarget 7, 75571.

Hsieh, C.-C., Wang, C.-H., 2018. Aspirin disrupts the crosstalk of angiogenic and inflammatory cytokines between 4T1 breast cancer cells and macrophages. Mediators Inflamm. 2018.

Huang, H., 2018. Matrix metalloproteinase-9 (MMP-9) as a cancer biomarker and MMP-9 biosensors: recent advances. Sensors 18, 3249.

Jan, S., Qayoom, H., Mehraj, U., Mir, M., 2021. Therapeutic Options for Breast Cancer. Combination Therapies and their Effectiveness in Breast Cancer Treatment. Nova Biomedical Science, New York, USA.

Jiang, H., Hegde, S., Denardo, D.G., 2017. Tumor-associated fibrosis as a regulator of tumor immunity and response to immunotherapy. Cancer Immunol. Immunother. 66, 1037–1048.

Johnson, K.E., Ceglowski, J.R., Roweth, H.G., Forward, J.A., Tippy, M.D., El-Husayni, S., Kulenthirarajan, R., Malloy, M.W., Machlus, K.R., Chen, W.Y., 2019. Aspirin inhibits platelets from reprogramming breast tumor cells and promoting metastasis. Blood Adv. 3, 198–211.

Juliá, E.P., Amante, A., Pampena, M.B., Mordoh, J., Levy, E.M., 2018. Avelumab, an IgG1 anti-PD-L1 immune checkpoint inhibitor, triggers NK cell-mediated cytotoxicity and cytokine production against triple negative breast cancer cells. Front. Immunol., 2140.

Kajiya, K., Hirakawa, S., Ma, B., Drinnenberg, I., Detmar, M., 2005. Hepatocyte growth factor promotes lymphatic vessel formation and function. EMBO J. 24, 2885–2895.

Kanwal, F., Ma, M., Ur Rehman, M.F., Khan, F.-U., Elizur, S.E., Batool, A.I., Wang, C.C., Tabassum, T., Lu, C., Wang, Y., 2021. Aspirin repurposing in folate-decorated nanoparticles: another way to target breast cancer. Front. Mol. Biosci. 8.

Kato, Y., Maeda, T., Suzuki, A., Baba, Y., 2018. Cancer metabolism: new insights into classic characteristics. Jpn. Dent. Sci. Rev. 54, 8–21.

Kim, S.-Y., 2018. Cancer energy metabolism: shutting power off cancer factory. Biomol. Ther. 26, 39.

Kontopodis, E., Kentepozidis, N., Christophyllakis, C., Boukovinas, I., Kalykaki, A., Kalbakis, K., Vamvakas, L., Agelaki, S., Kotsakis, A., Vardakis, N., 2015. Docetaxel, gemcitabine and bevacizumab as salvage chemotherapy for HER-2-negative metastatic breast cancer. Cancer Chemother. Pharmacol. 75, 153–160.

Ladoire, S., Arnould, L., Apetoh, L., Coudert, B., Martin, F., Chauffert, B., Fumoleau, P., Ghiringhelli, F., 2008. Pathologic complete response to neoadjuvant chemotherapy of breast carcinoma is associated with the disappearance of tumor-infiltrating foxp3 + regulatory T cells. Clin. Cancer Res. 14, 2413–2420.

Larsen, S.B., Dehlendorff, C., Skriver, C., Dalton, S.O., Jespersen, C.G., Borre, M., Brasso, K., Nørgaard, M., Johansen, C., Sørensen, H.T., 2017. Postdiagnosis statin use and mortality in Danish patients with prostate cancer. J. Clin. Oncol. 35, 3290–3297.

Lin, G., Chen, S., Mi, P., 2018. Nanoparticles targeting and remodeling tumor microenvironment for cancer theranostics. J. Biomed. Nanotechnol. 14, 1189–1207.

Lin, Y., Xu, J., Lan, H., 2019. Tumor-associated macrophages in tumor metastasis: biological roles and clinical therapeutic applications. J. Hematol. Oncol. 12, 1–16.

Liu, J.-C., Hao, W.-R., Hsu, Y.-P., Sung, L.-C., Kao, P.-F., Lin, C.-F., Wu, A.T., Yuan, K.S.-P., Wu, S.-Y., 2016. Statins dose-dependently exert a significant chemopreventive effect on colon cancer in patients with chronic obstructive pulmonary disease: a population-based cohort study. Oncotarget 7, 65270.

Lock, F., McDonald, P., Lou, Y., Serrano, I., Chafe, S., Ostlund, C., Aparicio, S., Winum, J., Supuran, C., Dedhar, S., 2013. Targeting carbonic anhydrase IX depletes breast cancer stem cells within the hypoxic niche. Oncogene 32, 5210–5219.

Lokeshwar, V.B., Lopez, L.E., Munoz, D., Chi, A., Shirodkar, S.P., Lokeshwar, S.D., Escudero, D.O., Dhir, N., Altman, N., 2010. Antitumor activity of hyaluronic acid synthesis inhibitor 4-methylumbelliferone in prostate cancer cells. Cancer Res. 70, 2613–2623.

Lou, Y., McDonald, P.C., Oloumi, A., Chia, S., Ostlund, C., Ahmadi, A., Kyle, A., Auf Dem Keller, U., Leung, S., Huntsman, D., 2011. Targeting tumor hypoxia: suppression of breast tumor growth and metastasis by novel carbonic anhydrase IX inhibitors. Cancer Res. 71, 3364–3376.

Lu, J., Liu, Q.-H., Wang, F., Tan, J.-J., Deng, Y.-Q., Peng, X.-H., Liu, X., Zhang, B., Xu, X., Li, X.-P., 2018. Exosomal miR-9 inhibits angiogenesis by targeting MDK and regulating PDK/AKT pathway in nasopharyngeal carcinoma. J. Exp. Clin. Cancer Res. 37, 1–12.

Luciani, F., Spada, M., De Milito, A., Molinari, A., Rivoltini, L., Montinaro, A., Marra, M., Lugini, L., Logozzi, M., Lozupone, F., 2004. Effect of proton pump inhibitor pretreatment on resistance of solid tumors to cytotoxic drugs. J. Natl. Cancer Inst. 96, 1702–1713.

Luo, J.-L., Tan, W., Ricono, J.M., Korchynskyi, O., Zhang, M., Gonias, S.L., Cheresh, D.A., Karin, M., 2007. Nuclear cytokine-activated IKKα controls prostate cancer metastasis by repressing Maspin. Nature 446, 690–694.

Luo, H., Tu, G., Liu, Z., Liu, M., 2015. Cancer-associated fibroblasts: a multifaceted driver of breast cancer progression. Cancer Lett. 361, 155–163.

Marigo, I., Trovato, R., Hofer, F., Ingangi, V., Desantis, G., Leone, K., De Sanctis, F., Ugel, S., Canè, S., Simonelli, A., 2020. Disabled homolog 2 controls prometastatic activity of tumor-associated macrophages. Cancer Discov. 10, 1758–1773.

Masoud, G.N., Li, W., 2015. HIF-1α pathway: role, regulation and intervention for cancer therapy. Acta Pharm. Sin. B 5, 378–389.

Mehraj, U., Dar, A.H., Wani, N.A., Mir, M.A., 2021a. Tumor microenvironment promotes breast cancer chemoresistance. Cancer Chemother. Pharmacol., 1–12.

Mehraj, U., Dar, A.H., Wani, N.A., Mir, M.A., 2021b. Tumor microenvironment promotes breast cancer chemoresistance. Cancer Chemother. Pharmacol. 87, 147–158.

Mehraj, U., Ganai, R.A., Macha, M.A., Hamid, A., Zargar, M.A., Bhat, A.A., Nasser, M.W., Haris, M., Batra, S.K., Alshehri, B., 2021c. The tumor microenvironment as driver of stemness and therapeutic resistance in breast cancer: new challenges and therapeutic opportunities. Cell. Oncol., 1–21.

Mehraj, U., Aisha, S., Sofi, S., Mir, M.A., 2022a. Expression pattern and prognostic significance of baculoviral inhibitor of apoptosis repeat-containing 5 (BIRC5) in breast cancer: a comprehensive analysis. Adv. Cancer Biol. Metastasis, 100037.

Mehraj, U., Mushtaq, U., Mir, M.A., Saleem, A., Macha, M.A., Lone, M.N., Hamid, A., Zargar, M.A., Ahmad, S.M., Wani, N.A., 2022b. Chemokines in Triple-Negative Breast cancer Heterogeneity: New Challenges for Clinical Implications. Elsevier.

Mei, Y., Tang, L., Xiao, Q., Zhang, Z., Zhang, Z., Zang, J., Zhou, J., Wang, Y., Wang, W., Ren, M., 2021. Reconstituted high density lipoprotein (rHDL), a versatile drug delivery nanoplatform for tumor targeted therapy. J. Mater. Chem. B 9, 612–633.

Meng, W., Hao, Y., He, C., Li, L., Zhu, G., 2019. Exosome-orchestrated hypoxic tumor microenvironment. Mol. Cancer 18, 1–14.

Miao, L., Huang, L., 2015. Exploring the tumor microenvironment with nanoparticles. In: Nanotechnology-Based Precision Tools for the Detection and Treatment of Cancer. Springer, pp. 193–226.

Miller, K., Wang, M., Gralow, J., Dickler, M., Cobleigh, M., Perez, E.A., Shenkier, T., Cella, D., Davidson, N.E., 2007. Paclitaxel plus bevacizumab versus paclitaxel alone for metastatic breast cancer. N. Engl. J. Med. 357, 2666–2676.

Mir, M.A., 2014. Immunotherapy by reverse signaling inhibits the growth of intracellular pathogens and cancer cells. In: Proceedings of International Research Conference on Engineering, Science and Management (IRCESM-2014).

Mir, M.A., Mehraj, U., 2019. Double-crosser of the immune system: macrophages in tumor progression and metastasis. Curr. Immunol. Rev. 15, 172–184.

Mir, M.A., Qayoom, H., Mehraj, U., Nisar, S., Bhat, B., Wani, N.A., 2020. Targeting different pathways using novel combination therapy in triple negative breast cancer. Curr. Cancer Drug Targets 20, 586–602.

Mir, M., Jan, S., Mehraj, U., 2022a. Novel Biomarkers in Triple-Negative Breast Cancer-Role and Perspective (Chapter-2). Elsevier.

Mir, M., Jan, S., Mehraj, U., Qayoom, H., Nisar, S., 2022b. Immuno-Onco-Metabolism and Therapeutic Resistance. Springer.

Muntimadugu, E., Kommineni, N., Khan, W., 2017. Exploring the potential of nanotherapeutics in targeting tumor microenvironment for cancer therapy. Pharmacol. Res. 126, 109–122.

Na, Y.R., Je, S., Seok, S.H., 2018. Metabolic features of macrophages in inflammatory diseases and cancer. Cancer Lett. 413, 46–58.

Nakazawa, H., Yoshihara, S., Kudo, D., Morohashi, H., Kakizaki, I., Kon, A., Takagaki, K., Sasaki, M., 2006. 4-methylumbelliferone, a hyaluronan synthase suppressor, enhances the anticancer activity of gemcitabine in human pancreatic cancer cells. Cancer Chemother. Pharmacol. 57, 165–170.

Netea-Maier, R.T., Smit, J.W., Netea, M.G., 2018. Metabolic changes in tumor cells and tumor-associated macrophages: a mutual relationship. Cancer Lett. 413, 102–109.

Ngwa, W., Irabor, O.C., Schoenfeld, J.D., Hesser, J., Demaria, S., Formenti, S.C., 2018. Using immunotherapy to boost the abscopal effect. Nat. Rev. Cancer 18, 313–322.

Otranto, M., Sarrazy, V., Bonté, F., Hinz, B., Gabbiani, G., Desmouliere, A., 2012. The role of the myofibroblast in tumor stroma remodeling. Cell Adh. Migr. 6, 203–219.

Paolicchi, E., Gemignani, F., Krstic-Demonacos, M., Dedhar, S., Mutti, L., Landi, S., 2016. Targeting hypoxic response for cancer therapy. Oncotarget 7, 13464.

Pickup, M.W., Mouw, J.K., Weaver, V.M., 2014. The extracellular matrix modulates the hallmarks of cancer. EMBO Rep. 15, 1243–1253.

Pillai, G., 2014. Nanomedicines for cancer therapy: an update of FDA approved and those under various stages of development. SOJ Pharm. Pharm. Sci. 1 (2), 13. Nanomedicines for Cancer therapy: an update of FDA approved and those under various stages of development.

Pritchard, R., Rodríguez-Enríquez, S., Pacheco-Velázquez, S.C., Bortnik, V., Moreno-Sánchez, R., Ralph, S., 2018. Celecoxib inhibits mitochondrial O2 consumption, promoting ROS dependent death of murine and human metastatic cancer cells via the apoptotic signalling pathway. Biochem. Pharmacol. 154, 318–334.

Qayoom, H., Mehraj, U., Aisha, S., Sofi, S., Mir, M.A., 2021. Integrating immunotherapy with chemotherapy: a new approach to drug repurposing. Drug Repurposing, first ed. vol. 1 IntechOpen, pp. 1–37.

Qi, C.-J., Ning, Y.-L., Han, Y.-S., Min, H.-Y., Ye, H., Zhu, Y.-L., Qian, K.-Q., 2012. Autologous dendritic cell vaccine for estrogen receptor (ER)/progestin receptor (PR) double-negative breast cancer. Cancer Immunol. Immunother. 61, 1415–1424.

Qian, B.-Z., Pollard, J.W., 2010. Macrophage diversity enhances tumor progression and metastasis. Cell 141, 39–51.

Quail, D.F., Joyce, J.A., 2013. Microenvironmental regulation of tumor progression and metastasis. Nat. Med. 19, 1423–1437.

Rao, W., Wang, H., Han, J., Zhao, S., Dumbleton, J., Agarwal, P., Zhang, W., Zhao, G., Yu, J., Zynger, D., Nano, A.C.S., 2015. Chitosan-decorated doxorubicin-encapsulated nanoparticle targets and eliminates tumor reinitiating cancer stem-like cells. ACS Nano 9, 5725–5740.

Rech, A.J., Mick, R., Martin, S., Recio, A., Aqui, N.A., Powell Jr., D.J., Colligon, T.A., Trosko, J.A., Leinbach, L.I., Pletcher, C.H., 2012. CD25 blockade depletes and selectively reprograms regulatory T cells in concert with immunotherapy in cancer patients. Sci. Transl. Med. 4, 134ra62.

Redondo, A., Martínez, V., Zamora, P., Castelo, B., Pinto, A., Cruz, P., Higuera, O., Mendiola, M., Hardisson, D., Espinosa, E., 2014. Continuation of bevacizumab and addition of hormone therapy following weekly paclitaxel therapy in HER2-negative metastatic breast cancer. Onco. Targets. Ther. 7, 2175.

Ren, Y., Zhou, X., Liu, X., Jia, H.-H., Zhao, X.-H., Wang, Q.-X., Han, L., Song, X., Zhu, Z.-Y., Sun, T., 2016. Reprogramming carcinoma associated fibroblasts by AC1MMYR2 impedes tumor metastasis and improves chemotherapy efficacy. Cancer Lett. 374, 96–106.

Riesenberg, B.P., Ansa-Addo, E.A., Gutierrez, J., Timmers, C.D., Liu, B., Li, Z., 2019. Cutting edge: targeting thrombocytes to rewire anticancer immunity in the tumor microenvironment and potentiate efficacy of PD-1 blockade. J. Immunol. 203, 1105–1110.

Robey, I.F., Baggett, B.K., Kirkpatrick, N.D., Roe, D.J., Dosescu, J., Sloane, B.F., Hashim, A.I., Morse, D.-L., Raghunand, N., Gatenby, R.A., 2009. Bicarbonate increases tumor pH and inhibits spontaneous metastases. Cancer Res. 69, 2260–2268.

Roche, J., 2018. Erratum: Roche, J. The epithelial-to-mesenchymal transition in cancer. Cancers, 2018, 10, 52. Cancer 10, 79.

Roma-Rodrigues, C., Mendes, R., Baptista, P.V., Fernandes, A.R., 2019. Targeting tumor microenvironment for cancer therapy. Int. J. Mol. Sci. 20, 840.

Sailor, M.J., Park, J.H., 2012. Hybrid nanoparticles for detection and treatment of cancer. Adv. Mater. 24, 3779–3802.

Samadi, N., Barazvan, B., Rad, J.S., 2016. Tumor microenvironment-mediated chemoresistance in breast cancer. Breast 30, 92–100.

Sa-Nguanraksa, D., O-Charoenrat, P., 2012. The role of vascular endothelial growth factor a polymorphisms in breast cancer. Int. J. Mol. Sci. 13, 14845–14864.

Satchi-Fainaro, R., Mamluk, R., Wang, L., Short, S.M., Nagy, J.A., Feng, D., Dvorak, A.M., Dvorak, H.F., Puder, M., Mukhopadhyay, D., 2005. Inhibition of vessel permeability by TNP-470 and its polymer conjugate, caplostatin. Cancer Cell 7, 251–261.

Schmid, P., Adams, S., Rugo, H.S., Schneeweiss, A., Barrios, C.H., Iwata, H., Diéras, V., Hegg, R., Im, S.-A., Shaw Wright, G., 2018. Atezolizumab and nab-paclitaxel in advanced triple-negative breast cancer. N. Engl. J. Med. 379, 2108–2121.

Segovia-Mendoza, M., Morales-Montor, J., 2019. Immune tumor microenvironment in breast cancer and the participation of estrogen and its receptors in cancer physiopathology. Front. Immunol. 10, 348.

Shee, K., Yang, W., Hinds, J.W., Hampsch, R.A., Varn, F.S., Traphagen, N.A., Patel, K., Cheng, C., Jenkins, N.P., Kettenbach, A.N., 2018. Therapeutically targeting tumor microenvironment–mediated drug resistance in estrogen receptor–positive breast cancer. J. Exp. Med. 215, 895–910.

Shen, S., Li, H.-J., Chen, K.-G., Wang, Y.-C., Yang, X.-Z., Lian, Z.-X., Du, J.-Z., Wang, J., 2017. Spatial targeting of tumor-associated macrophages and tumor cells with a pH-sensitive cluster nanocarrier for cancer chemoimmunotherapy. Nano Lett. 17, 3822–3829.

Siddiqui-Jain, A., Drygin, D., Streiner, N., Chua, P., Pierre, F., O'brien, S.E., Bliesath, J., Omori, M., Huser, N., Ho, C., 2010. CX-4945, an orally bioavailable selective inhibitor of protein kinase CK2, inhibits prosurvival and angiogenic signaling and exhibits antitumor efficacy. Cancer Res. 70, 10288–10298.

Siemann, D.W., 2011. The unique characteristics of tumor vasculature and preclinical evidence for its selective disruption by tumor-vascular disrupting agents. Cancer Treat. Rev. 37, 63–74.

Singh, S., Lomelino, C.L., Mboge, M.Y., Frost, S.C., McKenna, R., 2018. Cancer drug development of carbonic anhydrase inhibitors beyond the active site. Molecules 23, 1045.

Skobe, M., Hawighorst, T., Jackson, D.G., Prevo, R., Janes, L., Velasco, P., Riccardi, L., Alitalo, K., Claffey, K., Detmar, M., 2001. Induction of tumor lymphangiogenesis by VEGF-C promotes breast cancer metastasis. Nat. Med. 7, 192–198.

Solinas, G., Germano, G., Mantovani, A., Allavena, P., 2009. Tumor-associated macrophages (TAM) as major players of the cancer-related inflammation. J. Leukoc. Biol. 86, 1065–1073.

Sormendi, S., Wielockx, B., 2018. Hypoxia pathway proteins as central mediators of metabolism in the tumor cells and their microenvironment. Front. Immunol. 9, 40.

Sounni, N.E., Noel, A., 2013. Targeting the tumor microenvironment for cancer therapy. Clin. Chem. 59, 85–93.

Spinella, F., Garrafa, E., Di Castro, V., Rosano, L., Nicotra, M.R., Caruso, A., Natali, P.G., Bagnato, A., 2009. Endothelin-1 stimulates lymphatic endothelial cells and lymphatic vessels to grow and invade. Cancer Res. 69, 2669–2676.

Strom, T., Harrison, L.B., Giuliano, A.R., Schell, M.J., Eschrich, S.A., Berglund, A., Fulp, W., Thapa, R., Coppola, D., Kim, S., 2017. Tumour radiosensitivity is associated with immune activation in solid tumours. Eur. J. Cancer 84, 304–314.

Su, S., Liu, Q., Chen, J., Chen, J., Chen, F., He, C., Huang, D., Wu, W., Lin, L., Huang, W., 2014. A positive feedback loop between mesenchymal-like cancer cells and macrophages is essential to breast cancer metastasis. Cancer Cell 25, 605–620.

Sun, L., Wu, J., Du, F., Chen, X., Chen, Z.J., 2013. Cyclic GMP-AMP synthase is a cytosolic DNA sensor that activates the type I interferon pathway. Science 339, 786–791.

Suvarna, K., Honda, K., Kondoh, Y., Osada, H., Watanabe, N., 2018. Identification of a small-molecule ligand of β-arrestin1 as an inhibitor of stromal fibroblast cell migration accelerated by cancer cells. Cancer Med. 7, 883–893.

Tahmasebi Birgani, M., Carloni, V., 2017. Tumor microenvironment, a paradigm in hepatocellular carcinoma progression and therapy. Int. J. Mol. Sci. 18, 405.

Tashireva, L., Perelmuter, V., Manskikh, V., Denisov, E., Savelieva, O., Kaygorodova, E., Zavyalova, M., 2017. Types of immune-inflammatory responses as a reflection of cell–cell interactions under conditions of tissue regeneration and tumor growth. Biochemistry (Mosc.) 82, 542–555.

Tkach, M., Théry, C., 2016. Communication by extracellular vesicles: where we are and where we need to go. Cell 164, 1226–1232.

Topalian, S.L., Hodi, F.S., Brahmer, J.R., Gettinger, S.N., Smith, D.C., McDermott, D.F., Powderly, J.D., Carvajal, R.D., Sosman, J.A., Atkins, M.B., 2012. Safety, activity, and immune correlates of anti–PD-1 antibody in cancer. N. Engl. J. Med. 366, 2443–2454.

Truffi, M., Mazzucchelli, S., Bonizzi, A., Sorrentino, L., Allevi, R., Vanna, R., Morasso, C., Corsi, F., 2019. Nano-strategies to target breast cancer-associated fibroblasts: rearranging the tumor microenvironment to achieve antitumor efficacy. Int. J. Mol. Sci. 20, 1263.

Tsai, M.-J., Chang, W.-A., Huang, M.-S., Kuo, P.-L., 2014. Tumor microenvironment: a new treatment target for cancer. Int. Sch. Res. Notices 2014.

Tulotta, C., Ottewell, P., 2018. The role of IL-1B in breast cancer bone metastasis. Endocr. Relat. Cancer 25, R421–R434.

Uribe-Querol, E., Rosales, C., 2015. Neutrophils in cancer: two sides of the same coin. J. Immunol. Res. 2015.

Uribesalgo, I., Hoffmann, D., Zhang, Y., Kavirayani, A., Lazovic, J., Berta, J., Novatchkova, M., Pai, T.P., Wimmer, R.A., László, V., 2019. Apelin inhibition prevents resistance and metastasis associated with anti-angiogenic therapy. EMBO Mol. Med. 11, e9266.

US Food and Drug Administration, 2020. FDA Approves Neratinib for Metastatic HER2-Positive Breast Cancer. US Food and Drug Administration.

Vaddepally, R.K., Kharel, P., Pandey, R., Garje, R., Chandra, A.B., 2020. Review of indications of FDA-approved immune checkpoint inhibitors per NCCN guidelines with the level of evidence. Cancer 12, 738.

Vaupel, P., Mayer, A., 2007. Hypoxia in cancer: significance and impact on clinical outcome. Cancer Metastasis Rev. 26, 225–239.

Vaupel, P., Mayer, A., 2014. Hypoxia in tumors: pathogenesis-related classification, characterization of hypoxia subtypes, and associated biological and clinical implications. In: Oxygen Transport to Tissue XXXVI. Springer, pp. 19–24.

Vickers, N.J., 2017. Animal communication: when i'm calling you, will you answer too? Curr. Biol. 27, R713–R715.

Vonderheide, R.H., Lorusso, P.M., Khalil, M., Gartner, E.M., Khaira, D., Soulieres, D., Dorazio, P., Trosko, J.A., Rüter, J., Mariani, G.L., 2010. Tremelimumab in combination with exemestane in patients with advanced breast cancer and treatment-associated modulation of inducible costimulator expression on patient T cells. Clin. Cancer Res. 16, 3485–3494.

Walker, C., Mojares, E., Del Río Hernández, A., 2018. Role of extracellular matrix in development and cancer progression. Int. J. Mol. Sci. 19, 3028.

Wang, H., Wang, Y., Rayburn, E.R., Hill, D.L., Rinehart, J.J., Zhang, R., 2007. Dexamethasone as a chemosensitizer for breast cancer chemotherapy: potentiation of the antitumor activity of adriamycin, modulation of cytokine expression, and pharmacokinetics. Int. J. Oncol. 30, 947–953.

Wang, M., Zhao, J., Zhang, L., Wei, F., Lian, Y., Wu, Y., Gong, Z., Zhang, S., Zhou, J., Cao, K., 2017. Role of tumor microenvironment in tumorigenesis. J. Cancer 8, 761–773.

Wei, R., Liu, S., Zhang, S., Min, L., Zhu, S., 2020. Cellular and extracellular components in tumor microenvironment and their application in early diagnosis of cancers. Anal. Cell. Pathol. 2020.

West, N.R., Milne, K., Truong, P.T., Macpherson, N., Nelson, B.H., Watson, P.H., 2011. Tumor-infiltrating lymphocytes predict response to anthracycline-based chemotherapy in estrogen receptor-negative breast cancer. Breast Cancer Res. 13, 1–13.

Willumsen, N., Thomsen, L.B., Bager, C.L., Jensen, C., Karsdal, M.A., 2018. Quantification of altered tissue turnover in a liquid biopsy: a proposed precision medicine tool to assess chronic inflammation and desmoplasia associated with a pro-cancerous niche and response to immuno-therapeutic anti-tumor modalities. Cancer Immunol. Immunother. 67, 1–12.

Wu, X., Giobbie-Hurder, A., Liao, X., Connelly, C., Connolly, E.M., Li, J., Manos, M.P., Lawrence, D., McDermott, D., Severgnini, M., 2017. Angiopoietin-2 as a biomarker and target for immune checkpoint therapy. Cancer Immunol. Res. 5, 17–28.

Wyckoff, J., Wang, W., Lin, E.Y., Wang, Y., Pixley, F., Stanley, E.R., Graf, T., Pollard, J.W., Segall, J., Condeelis, J., 2004. A paracrine loop between tumor cells and macrophages is required for tumor cell migration in mammary tumors. Cancer Res. 64, 7022–7029.

Xie, H., Zhu, H., Zhou, K., Wan, J., Zhang, L., Yang, Z., Zhou, L., Chen, X., Xu, X., Zheng, S., 2020. Target-oriented delivery of self-assembled immunosuppressant cocktails prolongs allogeneic orthotopic liver transplant survival. J. Control. Release 328, 237–250.

Xin, H.-W., Hari, D.M., Mullinax, J.E., Ambe, C.M., Koizumi, T., Ray, S., Anderson, A.J., Wiegand, G.-W., Garfield, S.H., Thorgeirsson, S.S., 2006. Cancer Stem Cells. Springer Nature.

Yao, H., Guo, X., Zhou, H., Ren, J., Li, Y., Duan, S., Gong, X., Du, B., 2020. Mild acid-responsive "nanoenzyme capsule" remodeling of the tumor microenvironment to increase tumor penetration. ACS Appl. Mater. Interfaces 12, 20214–20227.

Yin, T., Wang, G., Ye, T., Wang, Y., 2016. Sulindac, a non-steroidal anti-inflammatory drug, mediates breast cancer inhibition as an immune modulator. Sci. Rep. 6, 1–8.

Yoshihara, S., Kon, A., Kudo, D., Nakazawa, H., Kakizaki, I., Sasaki, M., Endo, M., Takagaki, K., 2005. A hyaluronan synthase suppressor, 4-methylumbelliferone, inhibits liver metastasis of melanoma cells. FEBS Lett. 579, 2722–2726.

Yu, Y., Xiao, C., Tan, L., Wang, Q., Li, X., Feng, Y., 2014. Cancer-associated fibroblasts induce epithelial–mesenchymal transition of breast cancer cells through paracrine TGF-β signalling. Br. J. Cancer 110, 724–732.

Yu, T., Tang, B., Sun, X., 2017. Development of inhibitors targeting hypoxia-inducible factor 1 and 2 for cancer therapy. Yonsei Med. J. 58, 489–496.

Yuan, Y., Jiang, Y.-C., Sun, C.-K., Chen, Q.-M., 2016. Role of the tumor microenvironment in tumor progression and the clinical applications. Oncol. Rep. 35, 2499–2515.

Zhang, Z.-L., Liu, Z.-S., Sun, Q., 2006. Expression of angiopoietins, Tie2 and vascular endothelial growth factor in angiogenesis and progression of hepatocellular carcinoma. World J Gastroenterol: WJG 12, 4241.

Zhang, X., Feng, Y., Liu, X., Ma, J., Li, Y., Wang, T., Li, X., 2019. Beyond a chemopreventive reagent, aspirin is a master regulator of the hallmarks of cancer. J. Cancer Res. Clin. Oncol. 145, 1387–1403.

Ziello, J.E., Jovin, I.S., Huang, Y., 2007. Hypoxia-Inducible Factor (HIF)-1 regulatory pathway and its potential for therapeutic intervention in malignancy and ischemia. Yale J. Biol. Med. 80, 51.

Zollo, M., Di Dato, V., Spano, D., De Martino, D., Liguori, L., Marino, N., Vastolo, V., Navas, L., Garrone, B., Mangano, G., 2012. Targeting monocyte chemotactic protein-1 synthesis with bindarit induces tumor regression in prostate and breast cancer animal models. Clin. Exp. Metastasis 29, 585–601.

Index

Note: Page numbers followed by *f* indicate figures and *t* indicate tables.

Printed in the United States
by Baker & Taylor Publisher Services